Kotlin Apprentice

Beginning programming with Kotlin

By Irina Galata, Joe Howard & Ellen Shapiro

Kotlin Apprentice

By Irina Galata, Victoria Gonda, Joe Howard & Ellen Shapiro

ISBN: 978-1-950325-37-5

About the Team

Irina Galata is an author of this book. Irina is a software engineer in Linz, Austria, working at Runtastic. She is passionate about programming and learning new things. You can follow her on Twitter @igalata13 .

Ellen Shapiro is an author of this book. She works for Apollo GraphQL, caring for and feeding their iOS SDK. She's been building iOS and Android apps since late 2010, and has written and edited tutorials and books about iOS and Android for raywenderlich.com since 2013. She's also developed several independent applications through her personal company, Designated Nerd Software. When she's not writing code, she's usually tweeting about it at @DesignatedNerd.

Victoria Gonda is the author of this book. She is a software engineer who primarily works with Android. After having studied both dance production and computer science, she focused her career on software because of its potential to help people in a meaningful way. Victoria regularly speaks at conferences, which have been an enjoyable way for her to connect with the technical community and exchange ideas. In her spare time, Victoria enjoys playing board games and curling up with a good book. You can connect with her on Twitter at @TTGonda.

Acknowledgements

We'd also like to acknowledge the efforts of the authors of the *Swift Apprentice* and previous editions of *Kotlin Apprentice* whose work formed the basis for parts of this book:

- **Janie Clayton** is an independent iOS developer. She spent a year apprenticed to a super genius programming robots and learning the forgotten ways of long term software maintenance and development. Janie is the coauthor on several books on iOS and Swift development. Janie lives outside of Madison, Wisconsin with her attempted grumble of pugs and multitude of programming books. Janie writes her various musings on her blog at RedQueenCoder.com.
- **Alexis Gallagher** is a software engineer who is always looking for the conceptual deep dive and always hoping to find pearls down at the bottom. When he's not coding, he's out and about in sunny San Francisco.
- **Matt Galloway** is a software engineer with a passion for excellence. He stumbled into iOS programming when it first was a thing, and has never looked back. When not coding, he likes to brew his own beer.
- **Eli Ganim** is an engineering manager at Facebook. He is passionate about teaching, writing, and sharing his knowledge with others.
- **Joe Howard** is a computational physicist who studied particle physics using parallel Fortran simulations. He gradually shifted into systems engineering and ultimately software engineering around the time of the release of the iOS and Android SDKs. He's been a mobile software developer on iOS and Android since 2009, working primarily at two agencies in Boston, MA since 2011.
- **Erik Kerber** is a software developer in Minneapolis, MN, and the lead iOS developer for the Target app. He does his best to balance a life behind the keyboard with cycling, hiking, scuba diving, and traveling.
- **Ben Morrow** delights in discovering the unspoken nature of the world. He'll tell you the surprising bits while on a walk. He produces beauty by drawing out the raw wisdom that exists within each of us.
- **Cosmin Pupăză** is a software developer and tutorial writer from Romania. He has worked with more than a dozen programming languages over the years, but none of them has made such a great impact on himself as the advent of Swift. When not coding, he either plays the guitar or studies WWII history. Cosmin blogs about Swift at cosminpupaza.wordpress.com.

- **Steven Van Impe** is a computer science lecturer at the University College of Ghent, Belgium. When he's not teaching, Steven can be found on his bike, rattling over cobblestones and sweating up hills, or relaxing around the table, enjoying board games with friends. You can find Steven on Twitter as @svanimpe.
- **Dick Lucas** is a developer by trade but adds value anyway he can. He is also a writer, podcast host, and advisor at nogradient.com. He thinks most things are superfluous.

About the Artist

Vicki Wenderlich is the designer and artist of the cover of this book. She is Ray's wife and business partner. She is a digital artist who creates illustrations, game art and a lot of other art or design work for the tutorials and books on raywenderlich.com. When she's not making art, she loves hiking, a good glass of wine and attempting to create the perfect cheese plate.

Dedications

"To my wife Lilia, for all her support, encouragement, and patience. Love you. 😻"

—Ellen Shapiro

"To my loved ones for their support."

—Irina Galata

"To everyone who has come before me to make this book a reality."

—Victoria Gonda

Table of Contents

Book License

Before You Begin

This section tells you a few things you need to know before you get started, such as what you'll need for hardware and software, where to find the project files for this book, and more.

What You Need

To follow along with this book, you'll need the following:

- **IntelliJ IDEA Community Edition 2020.3.2 or later**, available at https://www.jetbrains.com/idea/. This is the environment in which you'll develop the sample code in this book.
- **Kotlin Plugin for IntelliJ IDEA v1.4.20 or later**, installed (if not included by default) by going to IntelliJ IDEA **Preferences** on macOS (or **Settings** on Windows/Linux) and choosing **Plugins**, then searching on "Kotlin".
- **Java SE Development Kit 8 or later.** Most of the code in this book will be run on the **Java Virtual Machine** or **JVM**, for which you need a **Java Development Kit** or **JDK**. The JDK can be downloaded from Oracle at http://www.oracle.com/technetwork/java/javase/downloads/index.html.
- In Chapters 24 and 25, you'll have the option of using a text editor such as **Visual Studio Code** instead of IntelliJ IDEA.
- In Chapter 26, in place of IntelliJ IDEA, you'll use **Android Studio 4.1** or later and **Xcode 12.4** or later to build a Kotlin Multiplatform app.

If you haven't installed the latest versions of IntelliJ IDEA Community Edition, the Kotlin Plugin, and JDK 8, be sure to do that before continuing with the book. Chapter 1: "Your Kotlin Development Environment" will show you how to get started with IntelliJ IDEA to run Kotlin code on the JVM.

Book Source Code & Forums

Where to download the materials for this book

The materials for this book can be cloned or downloaded from the GitHub book materials repository:

- https://github.com/raywenderlich/ka-materials/tree/editions/3.0

Forums

We've also set up an official forum for the book at https://forums.raywenderlich.com/c/books/kotlin-apprentice/. This is a great place to ask questions about the book or to submit any errors you may find.

About the Cover

Kotlin Apprentice Cover

The parrot has long captured the eye and imagination of humans; from Aesop to Monty Python, from ancient Peruvians to swashbuckling pirates, the beautiful plumage of parrots have made them a recurring theme throughout history.

The expressiveness and mimicry of parrots is very much akin to Kotlin; Kotlin takes the best of many languages and “mimics” those languages in a modern and expressive way. Although Kotlin won’t whistle a tune or ride on your shoulder when you cosplay Long John Silver, Kotlin will still be a great companion to you as you sail the seven seas of programming!

iv Introduction

The Kotlin language has been around since 2011, but its popularity took off in 2017 when Google announced Kotlin's inclusion as a first-class language for Android development. In 2019, Google announced a "Kotlin-first" approach to Android development. With modern and expressive language characteristics such as those found in Apple's Swift, and 100% interoperability with Java, it's no wonder that Kotlin has been named a top 5 most-loved language by Stack Overflow users.

If you're a complete beginner to programming, this is the book for you! There are short exercises and challenges throughout the book to give you some programming practice and test your knowledge along the way.

Through *Kotlin Apprentice*, you'll learn about basic things like constants, values and types, move up to more complicated items such as data structures, classes and enumerators, and finish off with some in-depth knowledge about functional programming, coroutines, and Kotlin Multiplatform.

If you want to get right into Android app development after you work through *Kotlin Apprentice*, we suggest you read the *Android Apprentice*, available on our store:

- https://www.raywenderlich.com/books/android-apprentice

The *Android Apprentice* is your introduction to building great apps in Android, using the Kotlin language, for both novice programmers and those with extensive experience programming for iOS or other platforms.

It will help you master the essential building blocks of Kotlin and Android to start creating apps. As you work on more apps, you'll find the foundations you learn in *Kotlin Apprentice* and *Android Apprentice* will give you the knowledge you need to easily figure out more complicated details on your own.

Section I: Kotlin Basics

The chapters in this section will introduce you to the very basics of programming in Kotlin. From the fundamentals of how computers work, all the way up to language structures, you'll cover enough of the language to be able to work with data and organize your code's behavior.

The section begins with some groundwork to get you started, then you have a chance to *do* things withyour newly learned data types. Finally, you'll move past the variables and constants you've been working with, which have had concrete values, to more tricky data types.

These fundamentals will get you on your way and, before you know it, you'll be ready for the more advanced topics that follow. Let's get started!

Chapter 1: Your Kotlin Development Environment

By Irina Galata

Welcome to *Kotlin Apprentice*! In this first chapter, you're going to set up a development environment to let you program in the Kotlin language and work with the sample projects for each chapter in the book.

Then, you'll write your very first Kotlin code and see how to run the code on your machine.

The primary tool that you'll use in this book to create Kotlin projects is **IntelliJ IDEA** from **JetBrains**. JetBrains is also the company behind the Kotlin language itself, so Kotlin development is very tightly integrated into IntelliJ IDEA.

> **Note**: Learn more about JetBrains at http://www.jetbrains.com.

IntelliJ IDEA is an **Integrated Development Environment**, or **IDE**, and is similar to other IDEs such as **Visual Studio** and **Xcode**. IntelliJ IDEA provides the foundation of many other IDEs from JetBrains, including **Android Studio** for Android app development, **PyCharm** for Python programming and **CLion** for C and C++ programming.

You use an IDE to write code in an editor, **compile** the code into a form that can be run on your computer, see output from your program, fix issues in your code and much more! You'll just scratch the surface of the power of IntelliJ IDEA in this chapter, but you'll be setup to work with the code examples throughout the rest of the book.

Getting started with IntelliJ IDEA

You can download IntelliJ IDEA from the JetBrains website at https://www.jetbrains.com/idea/. There are both **Community** and **Ultimate** editions of the IDE; you'll just need the Community edition to work with the code in this book. The Community edition is a free download.

Go ahead and download IntelliJ IDEA 2020.3 or later on your platform of choice. There are versions for macOS, Windows and Linux. Follow the installation instructions on the JetBrains site to install IntelliJ IDEA on your machine. Most of the screenshots in this book will be from the macOS version, but the Windows and Linux versions are similar.

Before you first run IntelliJ IDEA, you'll also want to install a **Java Development Kit**, or **JDK**, which will easily let you run Kotlin code on your machine.

Java and the JDK

Kotlin allows you to program on a number of different platforms. The two most prominent platforms are the **Java Virtual Machine**, or **JVM**, and **Android**. See Chapter 26: "Kotlin Mulitplatform" for more information on all the different platforms that Kotlin runs on.

In many ways, Kotlin was initially created as a modern replacement for the **Java** programming language. Java was created in the 1990's as an early attempt at a **cross-platform** application language, promising a "Write Once, Run Everywhere" approach to software development.

Instead of compiling to native machine code on each platform, Java programs are compiled into a format called **bytecode**. The bytecode runs inside an application on the Java Virtual Machine. The JVM can be thought of as a layer above your actual machine. By running as bytecode on a virtual machine, you are able to share Java code and applications across many types of computer systems.

One of the goals of the Kotlin programming languages is to be 100% **interoperable** with the Java language. This includes Kotlin code being converted to Java-compatible bytecode by the Kotlin compiler, so that the Kotlin code can be run on the JVM.

Most of the code and projects in this book are meant to be run as Kotlin projects on the JVM. In order to do so, you must install the JDK alongside IntelliJ IDEA. The easiest way to get a JDK for your platform is to visit the Oracle website at:

http://www.oracle.com/technetwork/java/javase/downloads/index.html

You'll want to download and install the latest version of the JDK — at least version 8. The Java software tools go by the name "Java SE," which includes the JDK and also the **Java Runtime Environment**, or **JRE**.

> **Note**: Be sure to download and install the JDK and not just the JRE, since the JRE only lets you run Java applications and does not include the tools to build new ones.

Running IntelliJ IDEA

Once you've installed IntelliJ IDEA and the JDK, follow the normal process of starting the IntelliJ IDEA application on your platform.

If you've installed previous versions of IntelliJ IDEA on the same machine, the installer will likely prompt you to import settings from a previous version. If you've not installed previous versions on the same machine, you'll be prompted to choose a color theme and choose plugins to install into the IDE. You can just choose the default settings and proceed.

You'll then arrive at the **Welcome to IntelliJ IDEA** window.

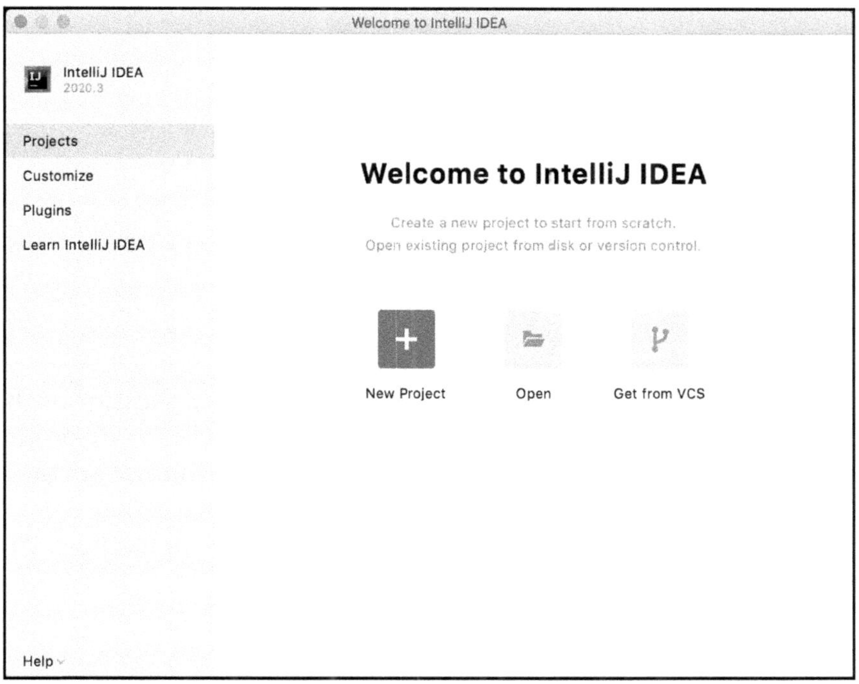

From the welcome window, you can create new projects, import or open existing projects, check out code from a version control system such as **Git**, run configuration tools and get help on the IDE.

Your first project

Go ahead and choose **New Project** on the welcome screen. You'll see the first of two project configuration screens.

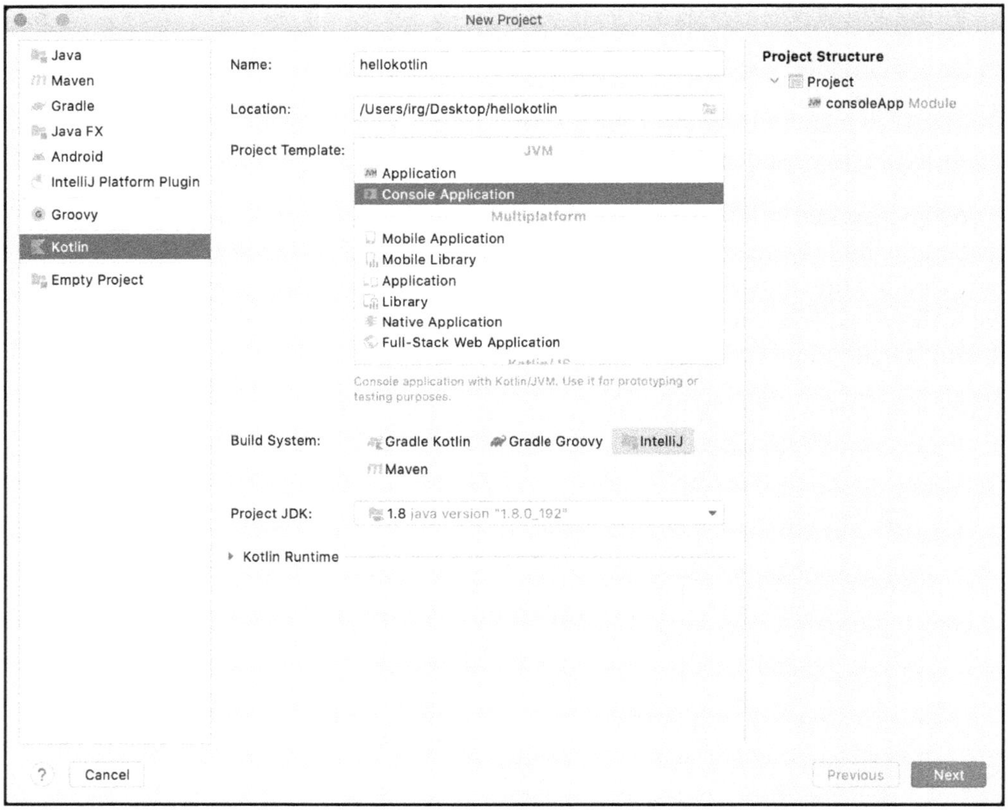

Choose **Kotlin** in the list of options on the left and **Console Application** as the project template. Type in **hellokotlin** as the project name, and choose a project location or accept the default, pick **IntelliJ** as a build system. You also see the **Project JDK**, which should be the JDK version that you installed earlier — or a different JDK version if you have more than one installed on your machine. When you are ready click **Next**.

You'll see the following:

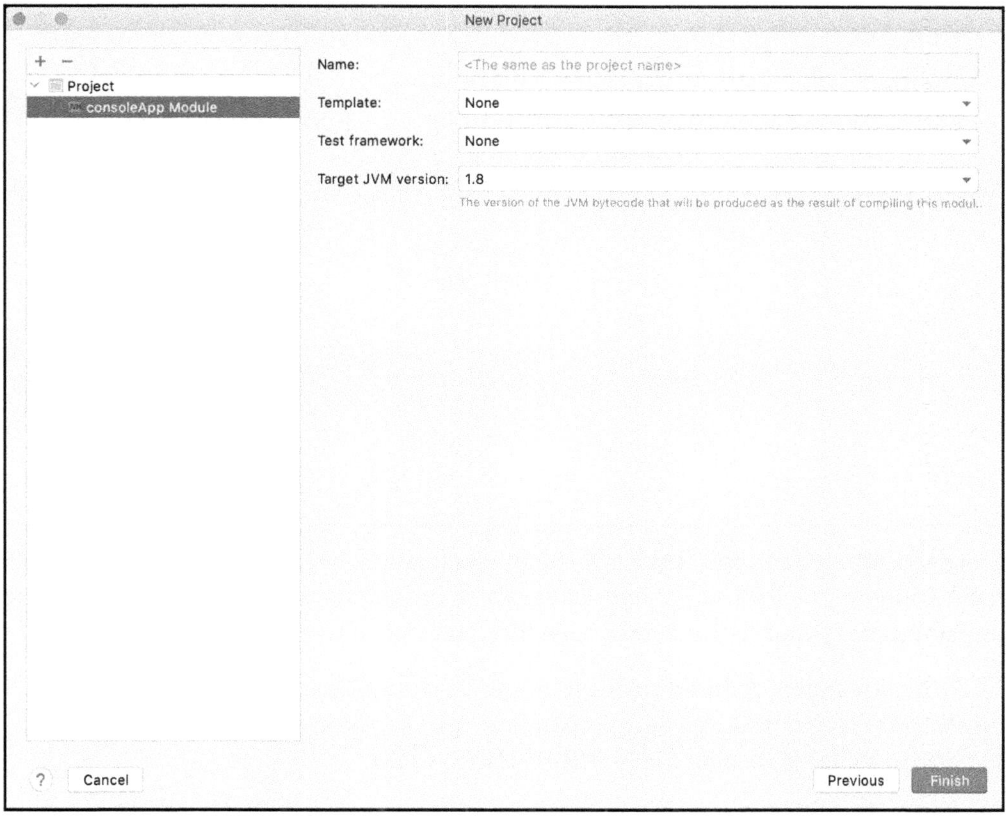

Pick **None** for both template and the test framework, later on, you will use different options for a faster setup of your project. Now click **Finish**.

At this point, IntelliJ IDEA will create and configure the project for you.

When it's finished, you'll arrive at a **Tip of the Day** window, which gives you helpful IntelliJ IDEA tips each time you open the application.

You'll see the following:

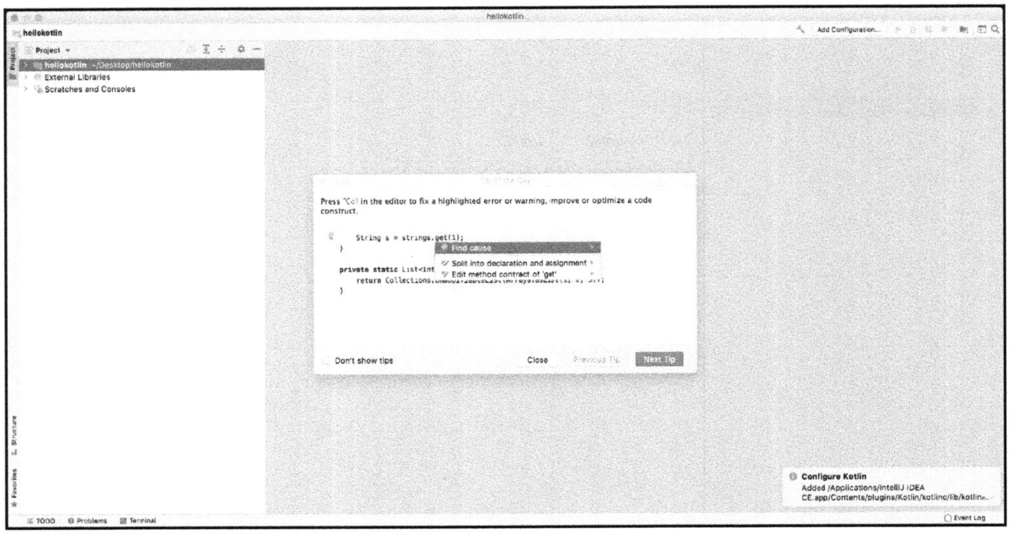

Close the tip window, and check out the **Project** panel on the left of the main IntelliJ IDEA window. The Project panel is where you manage all the files associated with the project, such as your Kotlin source code files, which end with a **.kt** file extension.

Click the arrow next to **hellokotlin** to reveal its contents, and you'll see a **src** folder for the project and its subfolders. Expand the **src** and **main** folders. Right-click on the **kotlin** folder and choose **New ▸ Kotlin File/Class**.

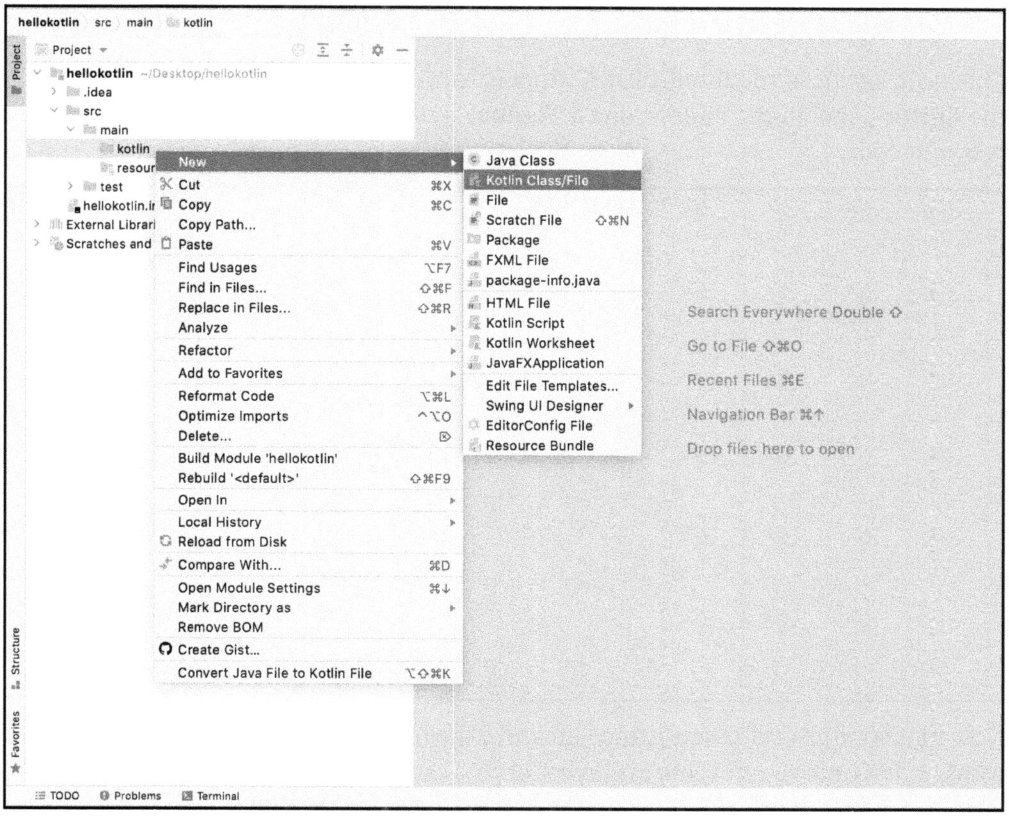

The **New Kotlin File/Class** dialog will open. Enter the name **hello** and double-click **File**.

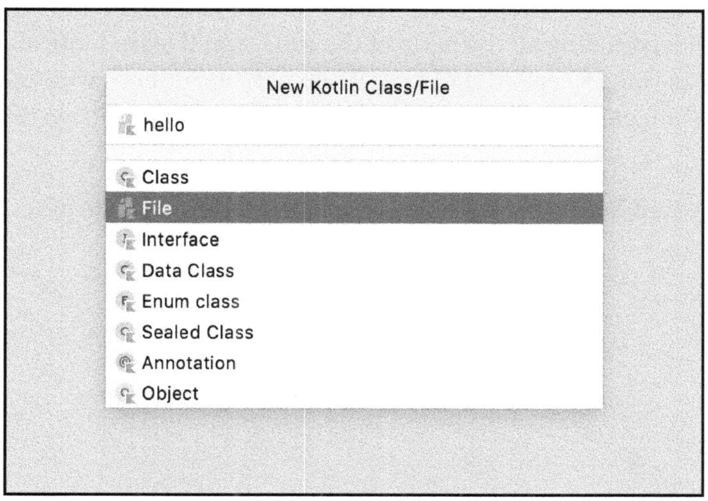

The file **hello.kt** will then open in the IntelliJ IDEA editor.

The basic layout of the IntelliJ IDEA window contains the Project panel on the left, the **Editor** panel in the middle, and a **Toolbar** in the upper right that you can use to run your code.

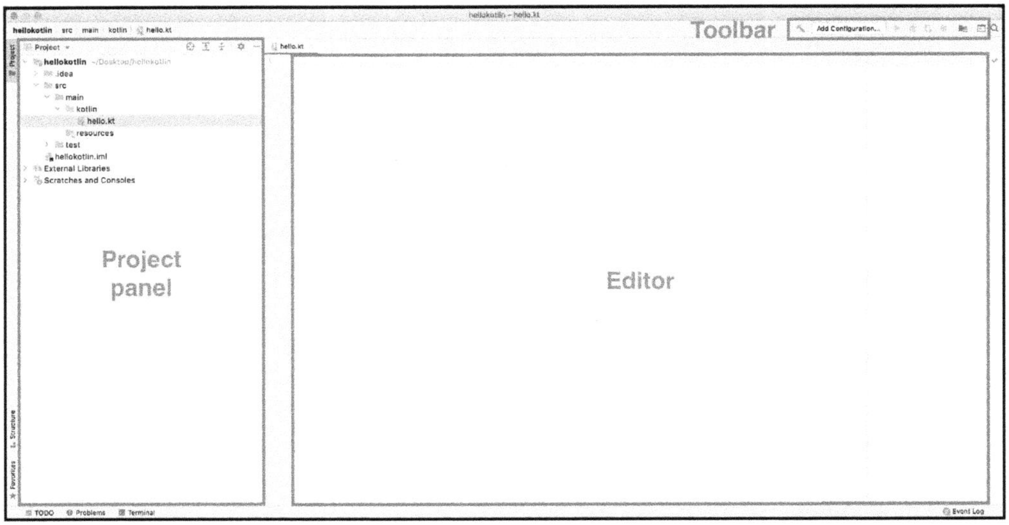

Now that your project is setup and you know the main parts of the IntelliJ IDEA window, it's time to run some Kotlin code!

Hello, Kotlin!

For this first chapter, you'll type some Kotlin code into an editor and run it, without necessarily understanding all the parts of the code. You'll learn more about the code you're typing as you proceed in the book. If you have experience with other programming languages, such as Java, Swift or Python, then the code might look familiar.

In the Editor panel for the file **hello.kt**, type in the following code exactly as written:

```
fun main() {
  println("Hello, Kotlin!")
}
```

You've written a single Kotlin **function** named `main()`, and added a single line of code to the function inside the braces, which then calls another function named `println()`. You're telling Kotlin to print the text "Hello, Kotlin!" to the screen. You'll learn much more about Kotlin functions later in the book.

There are a few different ways you can run this code, including using the IntelliJ IDEA menu, using the toolbar and using certain keystrokes.

The easiest way to run the code is to click the little green Run/Play button to the left of the `main()` function in the Editor panel. It may take a moment to show up after you add the code.

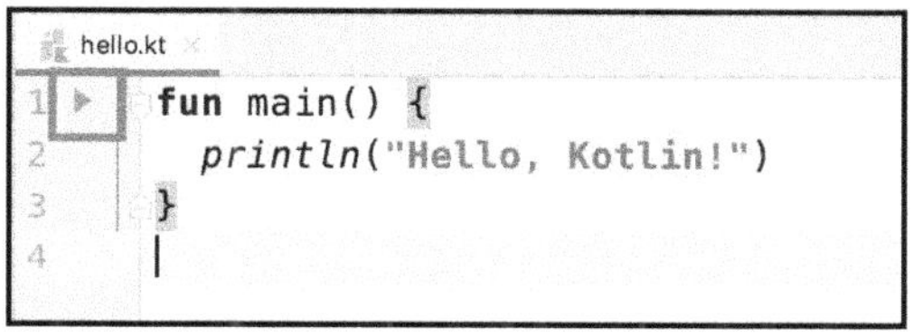

Go ahead and click the green Run button and a menu will open. Choose **Run 'HelloKt'** from the menu.

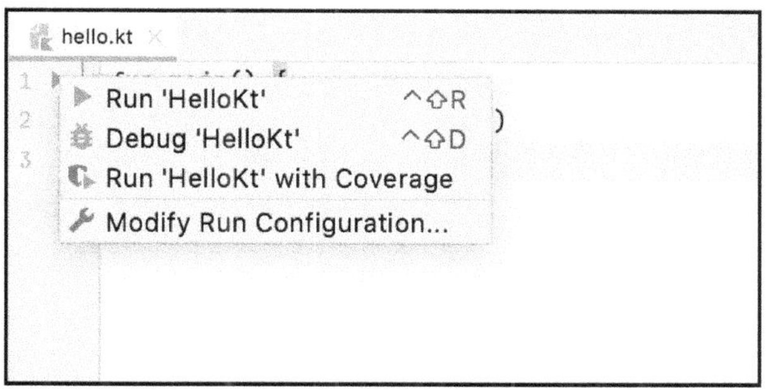

When you do, the Kotlin compiler will parse your code and convert the code to bytecode, and it will run it on your local JVM.

A panel will then open at the bottom of the IntelliJ IDEA window named the **Run** panel, sometimes also called the **console**.

You'll see the program output in the Run panel — in this case, the text that you wanted to show on the screen.

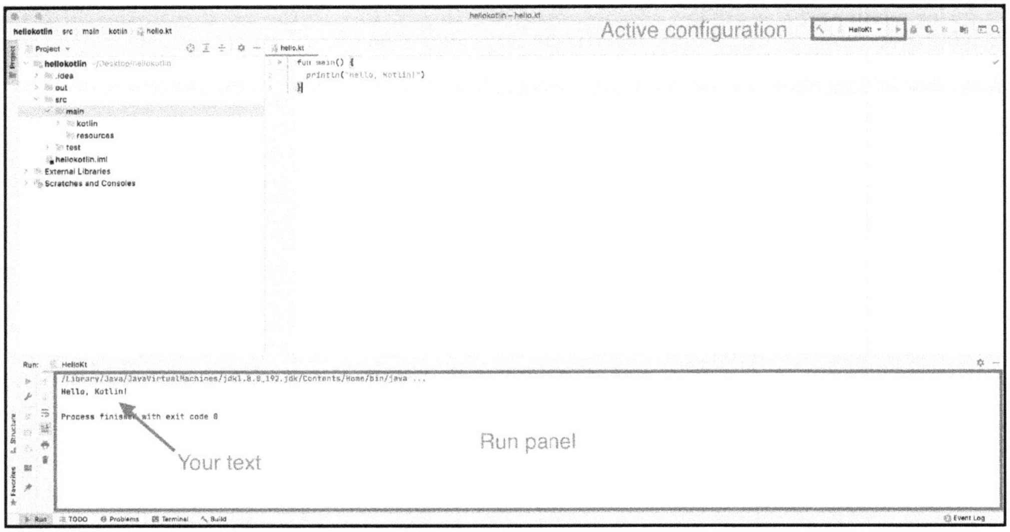

After this first run of the code in your project, you now have an active project **configuration** in the toolbar, and you can run the code by tapping the green Run button in the toolbar.

Nice! You've created your first Kotlin project and run your first Kotlin program!

Book sample projects

The sample code for each chapter of the book, except for the last three chapters, Chapter 24: "Scripting with Kotlin", Chapter 25: "Kotlin/Native", and Chapter 26: "Kotlin Multiplatform", falls into two categories: **Kotlin JVM** projects and **Gradle** projects. The vast majority are the simpler Kotlin JVM projects. The two types of projects are opened in a similar way, as described in this section.

Kotlin JVM projects

Kotlin JVM projects are just like the one you created in the last section of this chapter. For most of the chapters in the book, the projects look just like that project, with a single `main()` function in which you can put the Kotlin code you need to run. In certain cases, you may need to add code outside the `main()` function in the editor, and that will be pointed out when needed.

As you work through these chapters, you can either open the **starter** project for the chapter, which will have an empty `main()` function to which you can add code, or you can create a new project to work with, as you did in the last section.

In either case, you just enter code as you work your way through the chapter. You press the Run button in IntelliJ IDEA to run the code in the project at any point.

If you choose to create your own projects, you can always open the chapter sample code in a text editor if you want to see the code yourself, in order to address any issues you have when entering the code. Just open the files that end with the extension **.kt** in a text editor like **Notepad** on Windows or **TextEdit** on macOS.

Try to avoid copy-and-pasting the code from a text editor into IntelliJ IDEA though, since typing in the code yourself helps to solidify your knowledge.

If you choose to open the starter project instead of making your own, do so by clicking **Open** from the **Welcome to IntelliJ IDEA** window, or selecting **File ▸ Open** from the IntelliJ IDEA menu.

You then just need to choose the root folder for the project, e.g., the folder named **starter** for opening the starter project, and click **Open**.

You'll see the following:

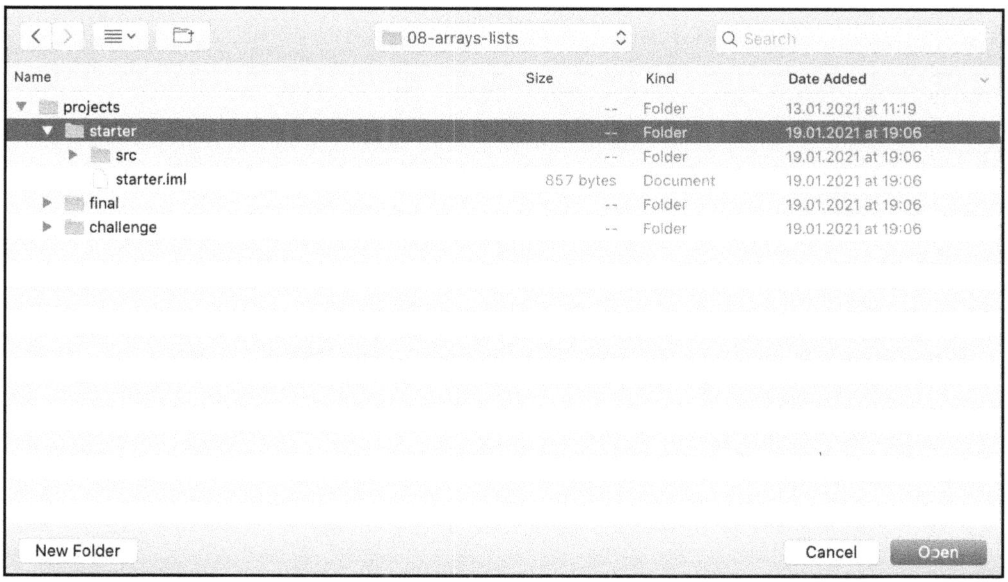

IntelliJ IDEA will then open the project, and you can start entering code as if you had created the project yourself.

When the project opens, you may need to select **View ▸ Tool Windows ▸ Project** to open the Project panel.

You can also click the Project tool button in the upper left of the IntelliJ IDEA window, or press **command-1** on Mac or **Alt-1** on PC to show the Project panel:

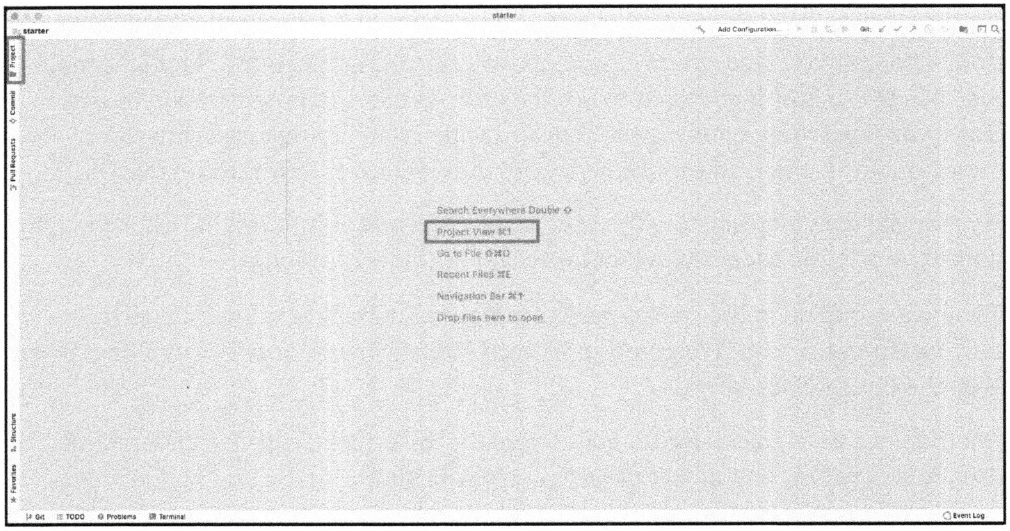

Once the Project panel is open, expand the root project and open up the **kotlin** folder to find the Kotlin source code files for the project:

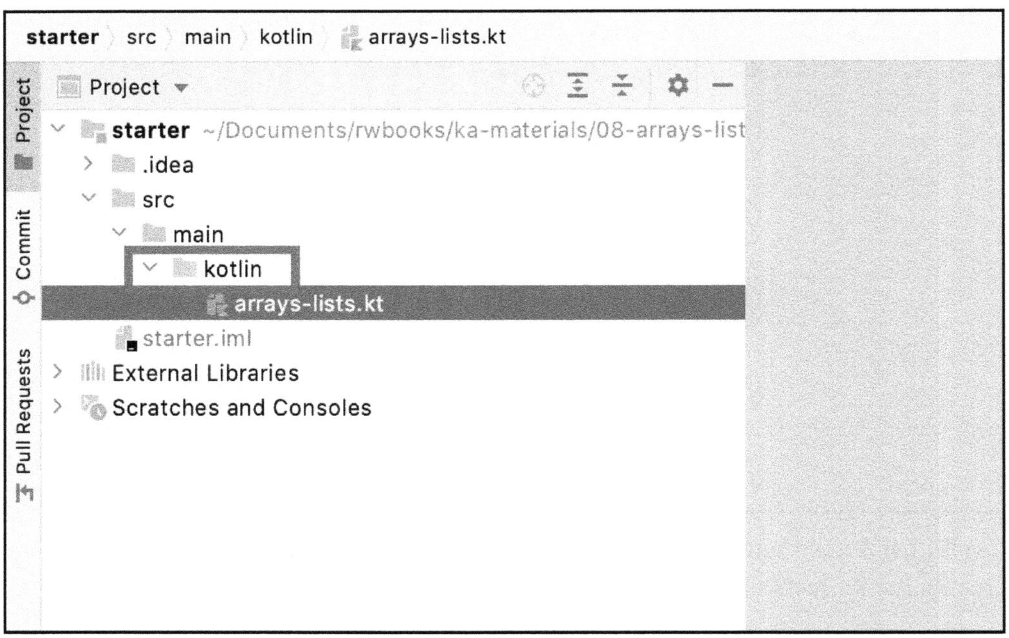

Gradle projects

For a couple of the chapters, the code projects use Gradle, in order to allow pulling an external dependency into the project.

Gradle is a **build system** and **dependency management** tool that is popular within the Java ecosystem. It's an extremely powerful and versatile build tool, and its power goes well beyond our purposes in the book.

Gradle is used as the build system for Android apps built using Android Studio, which, as was mentioned earlier, is based on IntelliJ IDEA.

To open the Gradle projects in Chapter 23, you use the exact same steps as for the Kotlin JVM projects. You choose **File ▸ Open** and then navigate to and select the root folder of the project.

IntelliJ IDEA will detect that the project is Gradle-based and then open and configure the project accordingly.

Final projects and challenges

In addition to a starter project, each chapter also has a folder for the **final** project and a folder with solutions to the **challenges** you find at the end of each chapter. You can open the final and challenge projects in the same manner as described above for the starter projects. The challenge projects also contain solutions to **Mini-Exercises** that you come across in the chapters.

Challenges

Challenges are a key part of working through the *Kotlin Apprentice*. Each chapter contains some challenges at the end of the chapter, and most chapters contain mini-exercises in the text of the chapter. Solving the challenges and mini-exercises will enhance and enforce the knowledge you've learned in each chapter.

As your challenge for this first chapter, make sure you've both run through the process of creating a new Kotlin JVM project, as well as opened an existing project from the final project folder for Chapter 1. Make sure to run the code in both cases. Doing so will ensure that you can run the sample code in the rest of the book.

Key points

- **IntelliJ IDEA** is an **Integrated Development Environment** from JetBrains, the creators of the Kotlin language, in which you can write and run Kotlin code.
- IntelliJ IDEA **Community edition** is a free version to use for the projects in the book.
- Kotlin code runs on many platforms, and one of the most prominent is the **Java Virtual Machine**, which will be used for most of the book.
- To build Kotlin projects with IntelliJ IDEA, you need to install the **Java Development Kit**, version 8 or above.
- The IntelliJ IDEA app window consists of a number of panels, the most relevant of which are the **Project** panel, the **Editor** panel, and the **Run** panel.
- The book starter, final and challenge projects can be opened by choosing **File ▸ Open** from the IntelliJ IDEA menu and selecting the root folder of the corresponding project.

Where to go from here?

There's a lot more to explore in IntelliJ IDEA, including debugging, refactoring, code profiling and version control system integration. You can find out more about these features of IntelliJ IDEA in the official JetBrains documentation.

Now that you're setup with a development environment, in Chapter 2, "Expression, Variables & Constants," you'll first get a primer on how computers work, and then you'll start writing some real Kotlin code!

Chapter 2: Expressions, Variables & Constants

By Irina Galata

In this second chapter, you're going to learn a few basics. You'll learn how code works first. Then, you'll start your adventure into Kotlin by learning some basics such as code comments, arithmetic operations, constants and variables. These are some of the fundamental building blocks of any language, and Kotlin is no different.

First of all, you'll cover the basic workings of computers, because it really pays to have a grounding before you get into more complicated aspects of programming.

How a computer works

You may not believe it when you hear it, but a computer is not very smart on its own. The power of computers is all derived from how they're programmed by people like you and me. If you want to successfully harness the power of a computer — and presumably you do, if you're reading this book — it's important to understand how computers work.

It may also surprise you to learn that computers themselves are rather simple machines. At the heart of a computer is a **Central Processing Unit** (**CPU**). This is essentially a math machine. It performs addition, subtraction, and other arithmetical operations on numbers. Everything you see when you operate your computer is all built upon a CPU crunching numbers many millions of times per second. Isn't it amazing what can come from just numbers?

The CPU stores the numbers it acts upon in small memory units called **registers**. The CPU is able to read numbers into registers from the computer's main memory, known as **Random Access Memory** (**RAM**). It's also able to write the number stored in a register back into RAM. This allows the CPU to work with large amounts of data that wouldn't all fit in the bank of registers.

Here is a diagram of how this works:

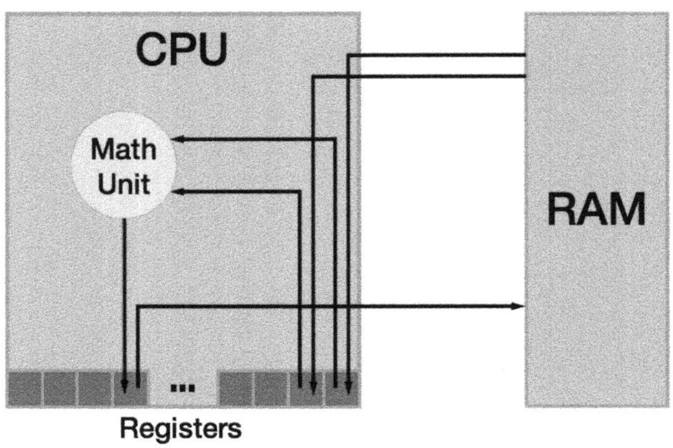

As the CPU pulls values from RAM into its registers, it uses those values in its math unit and stores the results back in another register.

Each time the CPU makes an addition, a subtraction, a read from RAM or a write to RAM, it's executing a single **instruction**. Each computer program is usually made up of thousands to millions of instructions. A complex computer program such as your operating system, be it iOS, Android, macOS, Windows or Linux (yes, they're computer programs too!), may have many millions of instructions in total.

It's entirely possible to write individual instructions to tell a computer what to do, but for all but the simplest programs, it would be immensely time-consuming and tedious. This is because most computer programs aim to do much more than simple math — computer programs let you surf the internet, manipulate images, and allow you to chat with your friends.

Instead of writing individual instructions, you write **code** in a specific **programming language**, which in your case will be Kotlin. This code is put through a computer program called a **compiler**, which converts the code into instructions the CPU knows how to execute. Each line of code you write will turn into many instructions — some lines could end up being tens of instructions!

In the case of Kotlin, with its origins as a language on the **Java Virtual Machine** or **JVM**, there is an extra layer between the compiler and the OS. The Kotlin compiler creates what is known as **bytecode**, which gets run on the JVM and converted to native code along the way. Kotlin began on the JVM but now it is possible to compile Kotlin directly to native code, as you'll see later in the book.

Representing numbers

As you know by now, numbers are a computer's bread and butter, the fundamental basis of everything it does. Whatever information you send to the compiler will eventually become a number. For example, each character within a block of text is represented by a number. You'll learn more about this in Chapter 3, "Types & Operations," which delves into types including **strings**, the computer term for a block of text.

Images are no exception. In a computer, each image is also represented by a series of numbers. An image is split into many thousands, or even millions, of picture elements called **pixels**, where each pixel is a solid color. If you look closely at your computer screen, you may be able to make out these blocks. That is unless you have a particularly high-resolution display where the pixels are incredibly small! Each of these solid color pixels is usually represented by three numbers: one for the amount of red, one for the amount of green and one for the amount of blue. For example, an entirely red pixel would be 100% red, 0% green and 0% blue.

The numbers the CPU works with are notably different from those you are used to. When you deal with numbers in day-to-day life, you work with them in **base 10**, otherwise known as the **decimal** system. Having used this numerical system for so long, you intuitively understand how it works. So that you can you can appreciate the CPU's point of view, consider how base 10 works.

The decimal or base 10 number **423** contains **three units**, **two tens** and **four hundreds**:

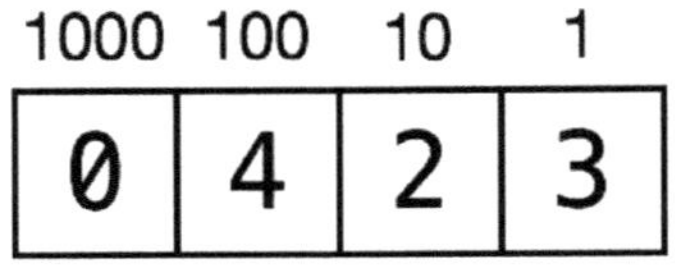

In the base 10 system, each digit of a number can have a value of 0, 1, 2, 3, 4, 5, 6, 7, 8 or 9, giving a total of 10 possible values for each digit. Yep, that's why it's called base 10!

But the true value of each digit depends on its position within the number. Moving from right to left, each digit gets multiplied by an increasing power of 10. So the multiplier for the far-right position is 10 to the power of 0, which is 1. Moving to the left, the next multiplier is 10 to the power of 1, which is 10. Moving again to the left, the next multiplier is 10 to the power of 2, which is 100. And so on.

This means each digit has a value ten times that of the digit to its right. The number **423** is equal to the following:

```
(0 * 1000) + (4 * 100) + (2 * 10) + (3 * 1) = 423
```

Binary numbers

Because you've been trained to operate in base 10, you don't have to think about how to read most numbers — it feels quite natural. But to a computer, base 10 is way too complicated! Computers are simple-minded, remember? They like to work with base 2.

Base 2 is often called **binary**, which you've likely heard of before. It follows that base 2 has only two options for each digit: 0 or 1.

Almost all modern computers use binary because at the physical level, it's easiest to handle only two options for each digit. In digital electronic circuitry, which is mostly what comprises a computer, the presence of an electrical voltage is 1 and the absence is 0 — that's base 2!

> **Note:** There have been computers both real and imagined that use the ternary numeral system, which has three possible values instead of two. Computer scientists, engineers and dedicated hackers continue to explore the possibilities of a base-3 computer. See https://en.wikipedia.org/wiki/Ternary_computer and http://hackaday.com/tag/ternary-computer/.

Here's a representation of the base 2 number 1101:

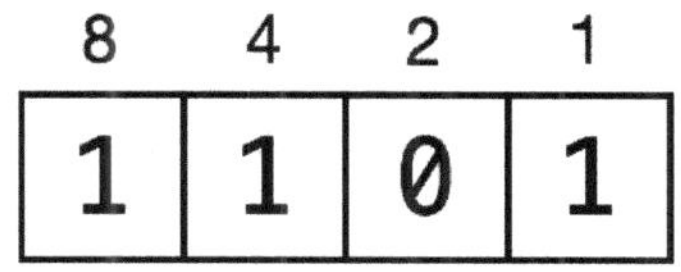

In the base 10 number system, the place values increase by a factor of 10: 1, 10, 100, 1000, etc. In base 2, they increase by a factor of 2: 1, 2, 4, 8, 16, etc. The general rule is to multiply each digit by an increasing power of the base number — in this case, powers of 2 — moving from right to left.

So the far-right digit represents $(1 * 2^0)$, equal to $(1 * 1)$, which is 1. The next digit to the left represents $(0 * 2^1)$, equal to $(0 * 2)$, which is 0. In the illustration above, you can see the powers of 2 on top of the blocks.

Put another way, every power of 2 either is (1) or isn't (0) present as a component of a binary number. The decimal version of a binary number is the sum of all the powers of 2 that make up that number. So the binary number 1101 is equal to:

```
(1 * 8) + (1 * 4) + (0 * 2) + (1 * 1) = 13
```

And if you wanted to convert the base 10 number 423 into binary, you would simply need to break down 423 into its component powers of 2. You would wind up with the following:

```
(1 * 256) + (1 * 128) + (0 * 64) + (1 * 32) + (0 * 16) + (0 * 8)
+ (1 * 4) + (1 * 2) + (1 * 1) = 423
```

As you can see by scanning the binary digits in the above equation, the resulting binary number is 110100111. You can prove to yourself that this is equal to 423 by doing the math! The computer term given to each digit of a binary number is a **bit** (a contraction of "binary digit"). Eight bits make up a **byte**. Four bits is called a **nibble**, a play on words that shows even old-school computer scientists had a sense of humor.

A computer's limited memory means it can normally deal with numbers up to a certain length. Each register, for example, is usually 32 or 64 bits in length, which is why we speak of 32-bit and 64-bit CPUs.

Therefore, a 32-bit CPU can handle a maximum base-number of 4,294,967,295, which is the base 2 number 11111111111111111111111111111111. That is 32 ones—count them!

It's possible for a computer to handle numbers that are larger than the CPU maximum, but the calculations have to be split up and managed in a special and longer way, much like the long multiplication you performed in school.

Hexadecimal numbers

As you can imagine, working with binary numbers can become quite tedious, because it can take a long time to write or type them. For this reason, in computer programming, we often use another number format known as **hexadecimal**, or **hex** for short. This is **base 16**.

Of course, there aren't 16 distinct numbers to use for digits; there are only 10. To supplement these, we use the first six letters, **a** through **f**.

They are equivalent to decimal numbers like so:

- `a = 10`
- `b = 11`
- `c = 12`
- `d = 13`
- `e = 14`
- `f = 15`

Here's a base 16 example using the same format as before:

4096	256	16	1
c	0	d	e

Notice first that you can make hexadecimal numbers look like words. That means you can have a little bit of fun.

Now the values of each digit refer to powers of 16. In the same way as before, you can convert this number to decimal like so:

```
(12 * 4096) + (0 * 256) + (13 * 16) + (14 * 1) = 49374
```

You translate the letters to their decimal equivalents and then perform the usual calculations.

But why bother with this?

Hexadecimal is important because each hexadecimal digit can represent precisely four binary digits. The binary number `1111` is equivalent to hexadecimal `f`. It follows that you can simply concatenate the binary digits representing each hexadecimal digit, creating a hexadecimal number that is shorter than its binary or decimal equivalents.

For example, consider the number `c0de` from above:

```
c = 1100
0 = 0000
d = 1101
e = 1110

c0de = 1100 0000 1101 1110
```

This turns out to be rather helpful, given how computers use long 32-bit or 64-bit binary numbers. Recall that the longest 32-bit number in decimal is 4,294,967,295. In hexadecimal, it is `ffffffff`. That's much more compact and clear.

How code works

Computers have a lot of constraints, and by themselves, they can only do a small number of things. The power that the computer programmer adds, through coding, is putting these small things together, in the right order, to produce something much bigger.

Coding is much like writing a recipe. You assemble ingredients (the data) and give the computer a step-by-step recipe for how to use them.

Here's an example:

```
Step 1. Load photo from hard drive.
Step 2. Resize photo to 400 pixels wide by 300 pixels high.
Step 3. Apply sepia filter to photo.
Step 4. Print photo.
```

This is what's known as **pseudo-code**. It isn't written in a valid computer programming language, but it represents the **algorithm** that you want to use. In this case, the algorithm takes a photo, resizes it, applies a filter and then prints it. It's a relatively straightforward algorithm, but it's an algorithm nonetheless!

Kotlin code is just like this: a step-by-step list of instructions for the computer. These instructions will get more complex as you read through this book, but the principle is the same: You are simply telling the computer what to do, one step at a time.

Each programming language is a high-level, pre-defined way of expressing these steps. The compiler knows how to interpret the code you write and convert it into instructions that the CPU can execute.

There are many different programming languages, each with its own advantages and disadvantages. Kotlin is an extremely modern language. It incorporates the strengths of many other languages while ironing out some of their weaknesses. In years to come, programmers will look back on Kotlin as being old and crusty, too. But for now, it's an extremely exciting language because it is quickly evolving.

This has been a brief tour of computer hardware, number representation and code, and how they all work together to create a modern program. That was a lot to cover in one section! Now it's time to learn about the tools you'll use to write in Kotlin as you follow along with this book.

Getting started with Kotlin

Now that you know how computers work, it's time to start writing some Kotlin!

You may wish to follow along with your own IntelliJ IDEA project. Simply create one using the instructions from the first chapter and type in the code as you go.

First up is something that helps you organize your code. Read on!

Code comments

The Kotlin compiler generates bytecode or executable code from your source code. To accomplish this, it uses a detailed set of rules you will learn about in this book. Sometimes these details can obscure the big picture of *why* you wrote your code a certain way or even what problem you are solving. To prevent this, it's good to document what you wrote so that the next human who passes by will be able to make sense of your work. That next human, after all, may be a future you.

Kotlin, like most other programming languages, allows you to document your code through the use of what are called **comments**. These allow you to write any text directly along side your code which is ignored by the compiler.

The first way to write a comment is like so:

```
// This is a comment. It is not executed.
```

This is a **single line comment**.

You could stack these up like so to allow you to write paragraphs:

```
// This is also a comment.
// Over multiple lines.
```

However, there is a better way to write comments which span multiple lines. Like so:

```
/* This is also a comment.
   Over many..
   many...
   many lines. */
```

This is a **multi-line comment**. The start is denoted by `/*` and the end is denoted by `*/`. Simple!

Kotlin also allows you to nest comments, like so:

```
/* This is a comment.

  /* And inside it
  is
  another comment.
  */

  Back to the first.
  */
```

This might not seem particularly interesting, but it may be if you have seen other programming languages. Many do not allow you to nest comments like this as when it sees the first `*/` it thinks you are closing the first comment. You should use code comments where necessary to document your code, explain your reasoning, or simply to leave jokes for your colleagues.

Printing out

It's also useful to see the results of what your code is doing. In Kotlin, you can achieve this through the use of the `println` command.

`println` will output whatever you want to the **console**.

For example, consider the following code:

```
println("Hello, Kotlin Apprentice reader!")
```

This will output a nice message to the console, like so:

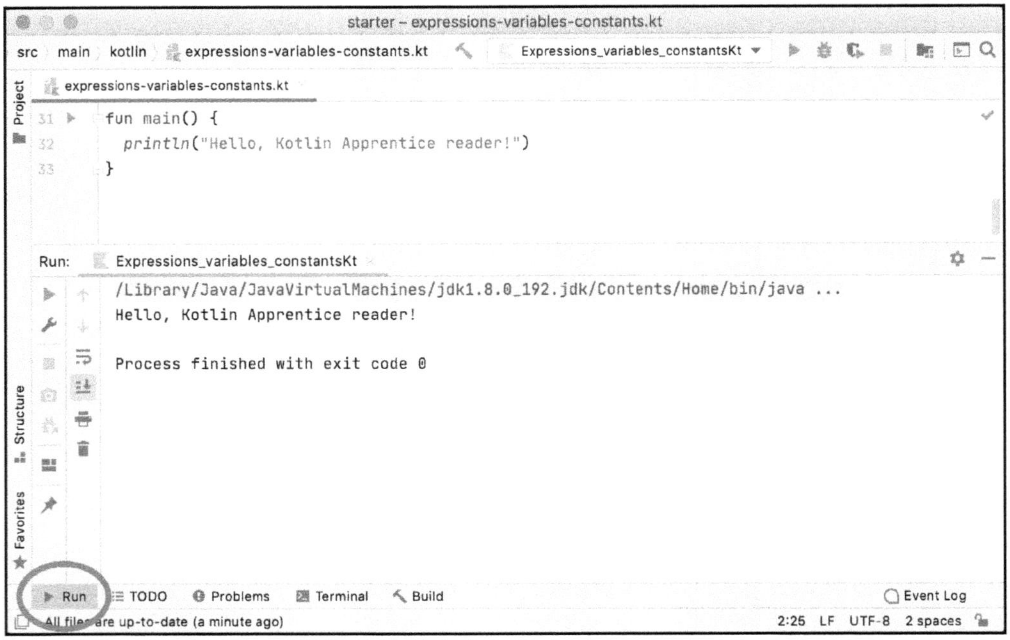

You can hide or show the console using the **Run** button at the bottom highlighted with the red oval in the picture above.

Arithmetic operations

When you take one or more pieces of data and turn them into another piece of data, this is known as an **operation**.

The simplest way to understand operations is to think about arithmetic. The addition operation takes two numbers and converts them into the sum of the two numbers. The subtraction operation takes two numbers and converts them into the difference of the two numbers. You'll find simple arithmetic all over your apps; from tallying the number of "likes" on a post, to calculating the correct size and position of a button or a window, numbers are indeed everywhere!

In this section, you'll learn about the various arithmetic operations that Kotlin has to offer by considering how they apply to numbers. In later chapters, you see operations for types other than numbers.

Simple operations

All operations in Kotlin use a symbol known as the **operator** to denote the type of operation they perform. Consider the four arithmetic operations you learned in your early school days: addition, subtraction, multiplication and division.

For these simple operations, Kotlin uses the following operators:

- Add: +
- Subtract: -
- Multiply: *
- Divide: /

These operators are used like so:

```
2 + 6
10 - 2
2 * 4
24 / 3
```

Each of these lines is what is known as an **expression**. An expression has a value. In these cases, all four expressions have the same value: 8. You write the code to perform these arithmetic operations much as you would write it if you were using pen and paper.

In your IDE, you can see the values of these expressions as output in the console using `println()`:

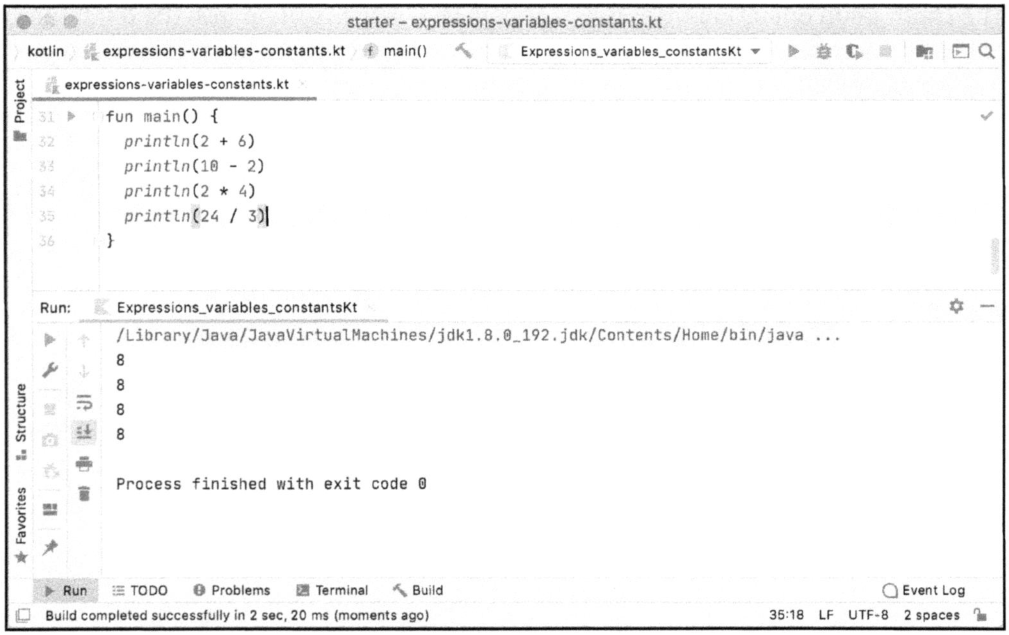

If you want, you can remove the whitespace surrounding the operator:

```
2+6
```

You can even mix where you put the whitespace. For example:

```
2+6   // OK
2 + 6 // OK
2 +6  // OK
2+ 6  // OK
```

It's often easier to read expressions if you have white space on either side of the operator.

Decimal numbers

All of the operations above have used whole numbers, more formally known as **integers**. However, as you know, not every number is whole.

As an example, consider the following:

```
22 / 7
```

This, you may be surprised to know, results in the number 3. This is because if you only use integers in your expression, Kotlin makes the result an integer also. In this case, the result is rounded down to the next integer.

You can tell Kotlin to use decimal numbers by changing it to the following:

```
22.0 / 7.0
```

This time, the result is 3.142857142857143 as expected.

The remainder operation

The four operations you've seen so far are easy to understand because you've been doing them for most of your life. Kotlin also has more complex operations you can use, all of them standard mathematical operations, just less common ones. Let's turn to them now.

The first of these is the **remainder** operation, also called the **modulo** operation. In division, the denominator goes into the numerator a whole number of times, plus a remainder. This remainder is exactly what the remainder operation gives. For example, 10 modulo 3 equals 1, because 3 goes into 10 three times, with a remainder of 1.

In Kotlin, the remainder operator is the `%` symbol, and you use it like so:

```
28 % 10
```

In this case, the result equals `8`, because 10 goes into 28 twice with a remainder of 8. If you want to compute the same thing using decimal numbers you do it like so:

```
28.0 % 10.0
```

The result is identical to `%` when there are no decimals, which you can see by printing it out using a **format specifier**:

```
println("%.0f".format(28.0 % 10.0))
```

Shift operations

The **Shift left** and **Shift right** operations take the binary form of a decimal number and shift the digits left or right, respectively. Then they return the decimal form of the new binary number.

For example, the decimal number 14 in binary, padded to 8 digits, is `00001110`. Shifting this left by two places results in `00111000`, which is 56 in decimal.

Here's an illustration of what happens during this shift operation:

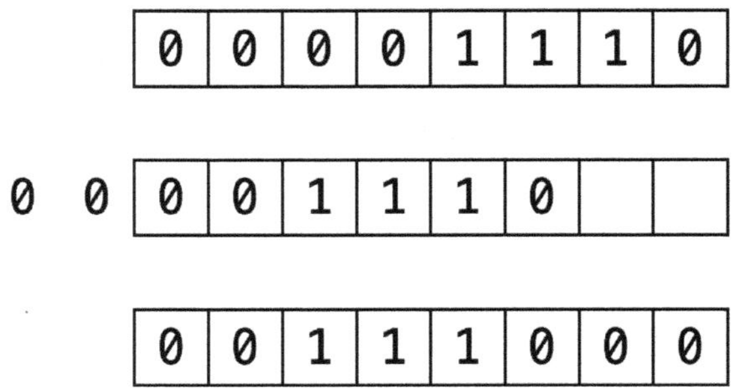

The digits that come in to fill the empty spots on the right become `0`. The digits that fall off the end on the left are lost. Shifting right is the same, but the digits move to the right. The Kotlin functions for these two operations are as follows:

- Shift left: `shl`
- Shift right: `shr`

These are **infix** functions that you place in between the operands so that the function call looks like an operation. You'll learn more about infix functions later.

Here's an example:

```
1 shl 3
32 shr 2
```

Both of these values equal the number 8.

One reason for using shifts is to make multiplying or dividing by powers of two easy. Notice that shifting left by one is the same as multiplying by two, shifting left by two is the same as multiplying by four, and so on. Likewise, shifting right by one is the same as dividing by two, shifting right by two is the same as dividing by four, and so on.

In the old days, code often made use of this trick because shifting bits is much simpler for a CPU to do than complex multiplication and division arithmetic. Therefore the code was quicker if it used shifting. However these days, CPUs are much faster and compilers can even convert multiplication and division by powers of two into shifts for you. So you'll see shifting only for binary twiddling, which you probably won't see unless you become an embedded systems programmer!

Order of operations

Of course, it's likely that when you calculate a value, you'll want to use multiple operators. Here's an example of how to do this in Kotlin:

```
((8000 / (5 * 10)) - 32) shr (29 % 5)
```

Note the use of parentheses, which in Kotlin serve two purposes: to make it clear to anyone reading the code — including yourself — what you meant, and to disambiguate.

For example, consider the following:

```
350 / 5 + 2
```

Does this equal 72 (350 divided by 5, plus 2) or 50 (350 divided by 7)? Those of you who paid attention in school will be screaming "72!" And you would be right!

Kotlin uses the same reasoning and achieves this through what's known as **operator precedence**. The division operator (/) has a higher precedence than the addition operator (+), so in this example, the code executes the division operation first.

If you wanted Kotlin to do the addition first — that is, to return 50 — then you could use parentheses like so:

```
350 / (5 + 2)
```

The precedence rules follow the same that you learned in math at school. Multiply and divide have the same precedence, higher than add and subtract which also have the same precedence.

Math functions

Kotlin also has a vast range of math functions in it's **standard library** for you to use when necessary. You never know when you need to pull out some trigonometry, especially when you're a pro at Kotlin and writing those complex games!

To use the following math functions, make sure you have this **import** near the top of your file. Otherwise, IntelliJ IDEA will tell you it can't find these functions.

```
import kotlin.math.*
```

For example, consider the following:

```
sin(45 * PI / 180)
// 0.7071067811865475

cos(135 * PI / 180)
// -0.7071067811865475
```

These compute the sine and cosine respectively. Notice how both make use of `PI` which is a constant Kotlin provides us, ready-made with π to as much precision as is possible by the computer.

Then there's this:

```
sqrt(2.0)
// 1.414213562373095
```

This computes the square root of 2. Did you know that sin(45°) equals 1 over the square root of 2?

Not to mention these would be a shame:

```
max(5, 10)
// 10

min(-5, -10)
// -10
```

These compute the maximum and minimum of two numbers respectively.

If you're particularly adventurous you can even combine these functions like so:

```
max(sqrt(2.0), PI / 2)
// 1.570796326794897
```

Naming data

At its simplest, computer programming is all about manipulating data. Remember, everything you see on your screen can be reduced to numbers that you send to the CPU. Sometimes you yourself represent and work with this data as various types of numbers, but other times the data comes in more complex forms such as text, images and collections.

In your Kotlin code, you can give each piece of data a name you can use to refer to it later. The name carries with it an associated **type** that denotes what sort of data the name refers to, such as text, numbers, or a date.

You'll learn about some of the basic types in this chapter, and you'll encounter many other types throughout the rest of this book.

Constants

Take a look at this:

```
val number: Int = 10
```

This uses the `val` keyword to declare a constant called `number` which is of type `Int`. Then it sets the value of the constant to the number `10`.

> **Note:** Thinking back to operators, here's another one. The equals sign, =, is known as the **assignment operator**.

The type `Int` can store integers. The way you store decimal numbers is like so:

```
val pi: Double = 3.14159
```

This is similar to the `Int` constant, except the name and the type are different. This time, the constant is a `Double`, a type that can store decimals with high precision.

There's also a type called `Float`, short for floating point, that stores decimals with lower precision than `Double`. In fact, `Double` has about double the precision of `Float`, which is why it's called `Double` in the first place. A `Float` takes up less memory than a `Double` but generally, memory use for numbers isn't a huge issue and you'll see `Double` used in most places.

Even though we call an item created with `val` a "constant," it's more correct to say that the identifier marked with `val` is what is constant.

Once you've declared a constant, you can't change its data. For example, consider the following code:

```
val number: Int = 10
number = 0
```

This code produces an error:

```
Val cannot be reassigned
```

In your IDE, you would see the error represented this way:

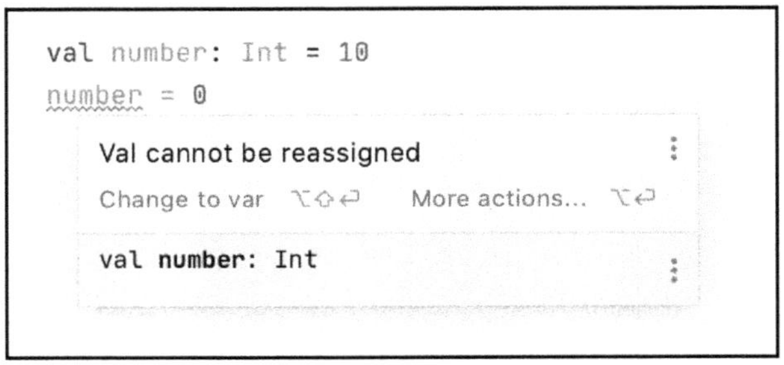

Constants are useful for values that aren't going to change. For example, if you were modeling an airplane and needed to keep track of the total number of seats available, you could use a constant.

You might even use a constant for something like a person's age. Even though their age will change as their birthday comes, you might only be concerned with their age at this particular instant.

In certain situations, for example, at the top level of your code outside of any functions, you can add the `const` keyword to a `val` to mark it as a **compile-time constant**:

```
const val reallyConstant: Int = 42
```

Values marked with `const` must initialized with a `String` or a primitive type such as an `Int` or `Double`. You can also use `const` inside a Kotlin type that you'll learn about in Chapter 12: "Objects."

Variables

Often you want to change the data behind a name. For example, if you were keeping track of your bank account balance with deposits and withdrawals, you might use a variable rather than a constant.

If your program's data never changed, then it would be a rather boring program! But as you've seen, it's not possible to change the data behind a constant.

When you know you'll need to change some data, you should use a variable to represent that data instead of a constant. You declare a variable in a similar way, like so:

```
var variableNumber: Int = 42
```

Only the first part of the statement is different: You declare constants using `val`, whereas you declare variables using `var`.

Once you've declared a variable, you're free to change it to whatever you wish, as long as the type remains the same. For example, to change the variable declared above, you could do this:

```
variableNumber = 0
variableNumber = 1_000_000
```

To change a variable, you simply assign it a new value.

> **Note**: In Kotlin, you can optionally use underscores to make larger numbers more human-readable. The quantity and placement of the underscores is up to you.

Using meaningful names

Always try to choose meaningful names for your variables and constants. Good names can act as documentation and make your code easy to read. A good name *specifically* describes the role of variable or constant. Here are some examples of good names:

- `personAge`
- `numberOfPeople`
- `gradePointAverage`

Often a bad name is simply not descriptive enough. Here are some examples of bad names:

- `a`
- `temp`
- `average`

The key is to ensure that you'll understand what the variable or constant refers to when you read it again later. Don't make the mistake of thinking you have an infallible memory! It's common in computer programming to look back at your own code as early as a day or two later and have forgotten what it does. Make it easier for yourself by giving your variables and constants intuitive, precise names.

Also, note how the names above are written. In Kotlin, it is common to **camel case** names. For variables and constants, follow these rules to properly case your names:

- Start with a lowercase letter.
- If the name is made up of multiple words, join them together and start every word other than the first word with an uppercase letter.
- If one of these words is an abbreviation, follow the same pattern as if it was a word (e.g., `sourceUrl` and `urlDescription`).

Increment and decrement

A common operation that you will need is to be able to increment or decrement a variable. In Kotlin, this is achieved like so:

```
var counter: Int = 0

counter += 1
// counter = 1

counter -= 1
// counter = 0
```

The `counter` variable begins as `0`. The increment sets its value to `1`, and then the decrement sets its value back to `0`.

These operators are similar to the assignment operator (=), except they also perform an addition or subtraction. They take the current value of the variable, add or subtract the given value and assign the result to the variable.

In other words, the code above is shorthand for the following:

```
var counter: Int = 0
counter = counter + 1
counter = counter - 1
```

Similarly, the `*=` and `/=` operators do the equivalent for multiplication and division, respectively:

```
counter = 10

counter *= 3  // same as counter = counter * 3
// counter = 30

counter /= 2  // same as counter = counter / 2
// counter = 15
```

Mini-exercises

If you haven't been following along with the code in IntelliJ IDEA, now's the time to try some exercises to test yourself!

1. Declare a constant of type `Int` called `myAge` and set it to your age.
2. Declare a variable of type `Double` called `averageAge`. Initially, set it to your own age. Then, set it to the average of your age and the age of `30`.
3. Create a constant called `testNumber` and initialize it with whatever integer you'd like. Next, create another constant called `evenOdd` and set it equal to `testNumber` modulo 2. Now change `testNumber` to various numbers. What do you notice about `evenOdd`?
4. Create a variable called `answer` and initialize it with the value `0`. Increment it by `1`. Add `10` to it. Multiply it by `10`. Then, shift it to the right by `3`. After all of these operations, what's the answer?

Challenges

Before moving on, here are some challenges to test your knowledge of variables and constants. You can try the code in IntelliJ IDEA to check your answers. If you get stuck, check out the solutions included in the materials for this chapter.

1. Declare a constant `exercises` with value 9 and a variable `exercisesSolved` with value 0. Increment this variable every time you solve an exercise (including this one).

2. Given the following code:

```
age = 16
print(age)
age = 30
print(age)
```

Declare `age` so that it compiles. Did you use `var` or `val`?

3. Consider the following code:

```
val a: Int = 46
val b: Int = 10
```

Work out what `answer` equals when you add the following lines of code:

```
// 1
val answer1: Int = (a * 100) + b
// 2
val answer2: Int = (a * 100) + (b * 100)
// 3
val answer3: Int = (a * 100) + (b / 10)
```

4. Add parentheses to the following calculation. The parentheses should show the order in which the operations are performed and should not alter the result of the calculation.

```
5 * 3 - 4 / 2 * 2
```

5. Declare two constants `a` and `b` of type `Double` and assign both a value. Calculate the average of `a` and `b` and store the result in a constant named `average`.

6. A temperature expressed in °C can be converted to °F by multiplying by 1.8 then incrementing by 32. In this challenge, do the reverse: convert a temperature from °F to °C. Declare a constant named `fahrenheit` of type `Double` and assign it a value. Calculate the corresponding temperature in °C and store the result in a constant named `celcius`.

7. Suppose the squares on a chessboard are numbered left to right, top to bottom, with 0 being the top-left square and 63 being the bottom-right square. Rows are numbered top to bottom, 0 to 7. Columns are numbered left to right, 0 to 7. Declare a constant `position` and assign it a value between 0 and 63. Calculate the corresponding row and column numbers and store the results in constants named `row` and `column`.

8. A circle is made up of 2π radians, corresponding with 360 degrees. Declare a constant `degrees` of type `Double` and assign it an initial value. Calculate the corresponding angle in radians and store the result in a constant named `radians`.

9. Declare four constants named `x1`, `y1`, `x2` and `y2` of type `Double`. These constants represent the two-dimensional coordinates of two points. Calculate the distance between these two points and store the result in a constant named `distance`.

Key points

- Computers, at their most fundamental level, perform simple mathematics.
- A programming language allows you to write code, which the compiler converts into instructions that the CPU can execute. Kotlin code on the JVM is first converted to bytecode.
- Computers operate on numbers in base 2 form, otherwise known as binary.
- Code comments are denoted by a line starting with // or multiple lines bookended with /* and */.
- Code comments can be used to document your code.
- You can use `println` to write things to the console area.
- The arithmetic operators are:

```
Add: +
Subtract: -
Multiply: *
Divide: /
Remainder: %
```

- Constants and variables give names to data.
- Once you've declared a constant, you can't change its data, but you can change a variable's data at any time.
- Always give variables and constants meaningful names to save yourself and your colleagues headaches later.
- Operators to perform arithmetic and then assign back to the variable:

```
Add and assign: +=
Subtract and assign: -=
Multiply and assign: *=
Divide and assign: /=
```

Where to go from here?

In this chapter, you've dealt with only numbers, both integers and decimals. Of course, there's more to the world of code than that! In the next chapter, you're going to learn about more types such as strings, which allow you to store text.

Chapter 3: Types & Operations

By Irina Galata

Now that you know how to perform basic operations and manipulate data using operations, it's time to learn more about **types**. Formally, a **type** describes a set of values and the operations that can be performed on them.

In this chapter, you'll learn about handling different types, including strings which allow you to represent text. You'll learn about converting between types and you'll also be introduced to type inference which makes your life as a programmer a lot simpler.

You'll also learn about `Pair` and `Triple`, which allow you to make your own types made up of two or three values of any type, respectively.

Finally, you'll learn about the important types `Any`, `Unit`, and `Nothing`.

Type conversion

Sometimes you'll have data in one format and need to convert it to another. The naïve way to attempt this would be like so:

```
var integer: Int = 100
var decimal: Double = 12.5
integer = decimal
```

Kotlin will complain if you try to do this and will spit out the following error:

```
Type mismatch.
Required: Int
Found:    Double
```

Some programming languages aren't as strict and will perform conversions like this automatically. Experience shows this kind of automatic conversion is a source of software bugs and often hurts performance.

Kotlin disallows you from assigning a value of one type to another and avoids these issues.

Remember, computers rely on us programmers to tell them what to do. In Kotlin, that includes being explicit about type conversions. If you want the conversion to happen, you have to say so!

Instead of simply assigning, you need to explicitly say that you want to convert the type. You do it like so:

```
integer = decimal.toInt()
```

The assignment now tells Kotlin unequivocally that you want to convert from the original type, `Double`, to the new type, `Int`.

> **Note**: In this case, assigning the decimal value to the integer results in a loss of precision: The `integer` variable ends up with the value 12 instead of `12.5`. This is why it's important to be explicit. Kotlin wants to make sure you know what you're doing and that you may end up losing data by performing the type conversion.

Operators with mixed types

So far, you've only seen operators acting independently on integers or doubles. But what if you have an integer that you want to multiply by a double?

You might think you have to do something like this:

```
val hourlyRate: Double = 19.5
val hoursWorked: Int = 10
val totalCost: Double = hourlyRate * hoursWorked.toDouble()
```

In this example, `hoursWorked` is explicitly converted to a `Double`, to match the type of `hourlyRate`. But, it turns out, this is unnecessary. Kotlin will allow you to multiply these values without any conversion, like so:

```
val totalCost: Double = hourlyRate * hoursWorked
```

In Kotlin, you can apply the * operator to mixed types. This rule also applies to the other arithmetic operators. Even though `hoursWorked` is an `Int`, this will not remove the precision of `hourlyRate`. The result will still be `195.0`! Kotlin attempts to be as concise as possible as often as possible and will try to infer the expected behavior when it can. This way you spend less time worrying about types and more time building awesome things!

Type inference

Up to this point in this book, each time you've seen a variable or constant declared it's been accompanied by a type declaration. You may be asking yourself why you need to bother writing the `: Int` and `: Double`, since the right hand side of the assignment *is already* an `Int` or a `Double`. It's redundant, to be sure; your clever brain can see this without too much work.

It turns out the Kotlin compiler can deduce this as well. It doesn't need you to tell it the type all the time — it can figure it out on its own. This is done through a process called **type inference**. Not all programming languages have this, but Kotlin does, and it's a key component of Kotlin's power as a language.

So, you can simply drop the type in most places where you see one.

For example, consider the following constant declaration:

```
val typeInferredInt = 42
```

Sometimes it's useful to check the inferred type of a variable or constant. You can do this in IntelliJ by clicking on the variable or constant's name and holding down the **Control** + **Shift** + **P** keys. IntelliJ will display a popover like this:

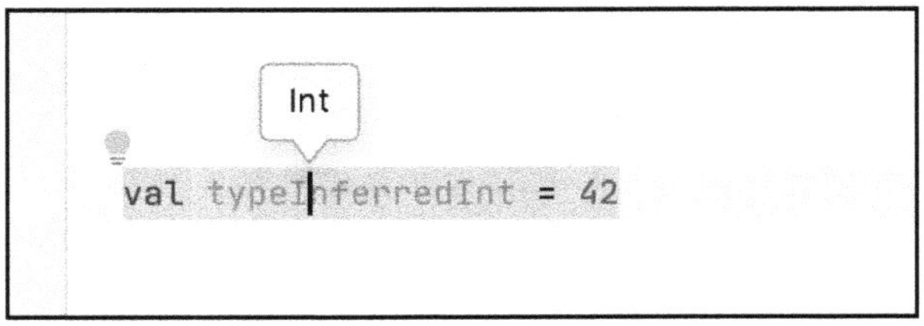

IntelliJ tells you the inferred type by giving you the declaration you would have had to use if there were no type inference. In this case, the type is `Int`.

It works for other types, too:

```
val typeInferredDouble = 3.14159
```

Holding down the **Control** + **Shift** + **P** keys reveals the following:

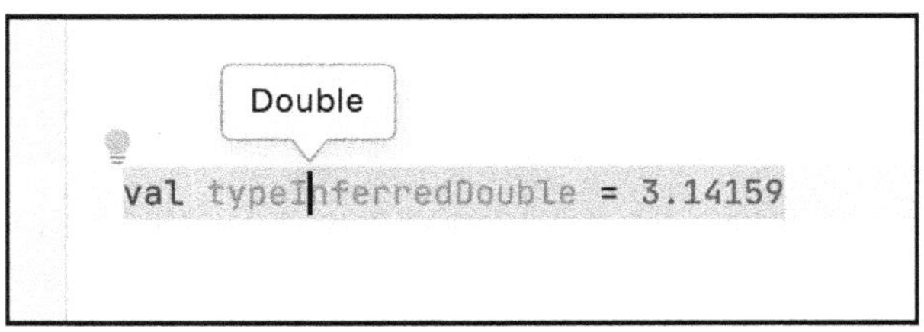

You can see from this that type inference isn't magic. Kotlin is simply doing what your brain does very easily. Programming languages that don't use type inference can often feel verbose, because you need to specify the often obvious type each time you declare a variable or constant.

> **Note**: In later chapters, you'll learn about more complex types where sometimes Kotlin can't infer the type. That's a pretty rare case though, and you'll see type inference used for most of the code examples in this book — except in cases where you want to highlight the type.

Sometimes you want to define a constant or variable and ensure it's a certain type, even though what you're assigning to it is a different type. You saw earlier how you can convert from one type to another. For example, consider the following:

```
val wantADouble = 3
```

Here, Kotlin infers the type of `wantADouble` as `Int`. But what if you wanted `Double` instead? The first thing you could do is the following:

```
val actuallyDouble = 3.toDouble()
```

This is like you saw before with type conversion.

Another option would be to not use type inference at all and do the following:

```
val actuallyDouble: Double = 3.0
```

Something you may be tempted to try is this:

```
val actuallyDouble: Double = 3
```

This is not allowed and results in the compiler giving you the following error: `The integer literal does not conform to the expected type Double.`

> **Note**: In Kotlin literal values like `3` have a specific type, `Int`. If you want to convert them to a different type, you must do so explicitly, by calling `toDouble()` for example. A literal number value that contains a decimal point can only be used as a `Double` and must be explicitly converted if you want to use it as something else. This is why you're not allowed to assign the value `3` to constant `actuallyDouble`.
>
> Likewise, literal number values that *do* contain a decimal point cannot be integers. This means you could have avoided this entire discussion had you started with:
>
> `val wantADouble = 3.0`
>
> Sorry!

Mini-exercises

1. Create a constant called `age1` and set it equal to `42`. Create a constant called `age2` and set it equal to `21`. Check using Control+Shift+P that the type for both has been inferred correctly as `Int`.
2. Create a constant called `avg1` and set it equal to the average of `age1` and `age2` using the naive operation `(age1 + age2) / 2`. Use Control+Shift+P to check the type and check the result of `avg1`. Why is it wrong?
3. Correct the mistake in the above exercise by converting `age1` and `age2` to type `Double` in the formula. Use Control+Shift+P to check the type and check the result of `avg1`. Why is it now correct?

Strings

Numbers are essential in programming, but they aren't the only type of data you need to work with in your apps. Text is also an extremely common data type, such as people's names, their addresses, or even the words of a book. All of these are examples of text that an app might need to handle.

Most computer programming languages store text in a data type called a **string**. This chapter introduces you to strings, first by giving you background on the concept of strings and then by showing you how to use them in Kotlin.

How computers represent strings

Computers think of strings as a collection of individual **characters**. In Chapter 1 of this book, you learned that numbers are the language of CPUs, and all code, in whatever programming language, can be reduced to raw numbers. Strings are no different!

That may sound very strange. How can characters be numbers? At its base, a computer needs to be able to translate a character into the computer's own language, and it does so by assigning each character a different number. This forms a two-way mapping from character to number that is called a **character set**.

When you press a character key on your keyboard, you are actually communicating the number of the character to the computer. Your word processor application converts that number into a picture of the character and finally, presents that picture to you.

Unicode

In isolation, a computer is free to choose whatever character set mapping it likes. If the computer wants the letter **a** to equal the number 10, then so be it. But when computers start talking to each other, they need to use a common character set. If two computers used different character sets, then when one computer transferred a string to the other, they would end up thinking the strings contained different characters.

There have been several standards over the years, but the most modern standard is **Unicode**. It defines the character set mapping that almost all computers use today.

> **Note**: You can read more about Unicode at its official website, http://unicode.org/.

As an example, consider the word **cafe**. The Unicode standard tells us that the letters of this word should be mapped to numbers like so:

c	a	f	e
99	97	102	101

The number associated with each character is called a **code point**. So in the example above, **c** uses code point 99, **a** uses code point 97, and so on.

Of course, Unicode is not just for the simple Latin characters used in English, such as **c**, **a**, **f** and **e**. It also lets you map characters from languages around the world. The word **cafe**, as you're probably aware, is derived from French, in which it's written as **café**. Unicode maps these characters like so:

c	a	f	é
99	97	102	233

And here's an example using Chinese characters (this, according to Google translate, means "Computer Programming"):

电	脑	编	程
30005	33041	32534	31243

You've probably heard of emojis, which are small pictures you can use in your text. These pictures are, in fact, just normal characters and are also mapped by Unicode. For example:

💩	😀
128169	128512

This is only two characters. The code points for these are very large numbers, but each is still only a single code point. The computer considers these as no different than any other two characters.

> **Note**: The word "emoji" comes from Japanese, where "e" means picture and "moji" means character.

Strings in Kotlin

Kotlin, like any good programming language, can work directly with characters and strings. It does so through the data types `Char` and `String`, respectively. In this section, you'll learn about these data types and how to work with them.

Characters and strings

The `Char` data type can store a single character which must be wrapped in single quotes. For example:

```
val characterA: Char = 'a'
```

This data type is designed to hold only single characters. The `String` data type, on the other hand, stores multiple characters, which must be wrapped in double quotes. For example:

```
val stringDog: String = "Dog"
```

It's as simple as that! The right-hand side of this expression is what's known as a **string literal**; it's the Kotlin syntax for representing a string.

Of course, type inference applies here as well. If you remove the type in the above declaration, then Kotlin does the right thing and makes the `stringDog` a `String` constant:

```
val stringDog = "Dog" // Inferred to be of type String
```

Concatenation

You can do much more than create simple strings. Sometimes you need to manipulate a string, and one common way to do so is to combine it with another string.

In Kotlin, you do this in a rather simple way: by using the addition operator. Just as you can add numbers, you can add strings:

```
var message = "Hello" + " my name is "
val name = "Joe"
message += name // "Hello my name is Joe"
```

You need to declare `message` as a variable rather than a constant because you want to modify it. You can add string literals together, as in the first line, and you can add string variables or constants together, as in the last line.

It's also possible to add characters directly to a string. This is similar to how you can easily work with numbers if one is an `Int` and the other is a `Double`.

To add a character to a string, you do this:

```
val exclamationMark: Char = '!'
message += exclamationMark // "Hello my name is Joe!"
```

No need to explicitly convert the `Character` to a `String` before you add it to `message`; Kotlin takes care of that for you!

String templates

You can also build up a string by using **string templates**, which use a special Kotlin syntax that lets you build a string in a way that's easy to read:

```
message = "Hello my name is $name!" // "Hello my name is Joe!"
```

This is much more readable than the example from the previous section. It's an extension of the string literal syntax, whereby you replace certain parts of the string with other values. Simply prepend the value you want to insert with a `$` symbol.

This syntax works in the same way to build a string from other data types, such as numbers:

```
val oneThird = 1.0 / 3.0
val oneThirdLongString = "One third is $oneThird as a decimal."
```

Here, you use a `Double` in the template. At the end of this code, your `oneThirdLongString` constant will contain the following:

```
One third is 0.3333333333333333 as a decimal.
```

Of course, it would actually take infinite characters to represent one third as a decimal, because it's a repeating decimal. Using string templates with a `Double` gives you no way to control the precision of the resulting string.

This is an unfortunate consequence of using string templates: they're simple to use, but offers no ability to customize the output.

You can also put expressions inside a string template, by following the `$` symbol with a pair of braces that contain the expression:

```
val oneThirdLongString = "One third is ${1.0 / 3.0} as a
decimal."
```

The result is just the same as before.

Multi-line strings

Kotlin has a neat way to express strings that contain multiple lines. This can be rather useful when you need to put a very long string in your code.

You do it like so:

```
val bigString = """
   |You can have a string
   |that contains multiple
   |lines
   |by
   |doing this.
  """.trimMargin()
println(bigString)
```

The three double-quotes signify that this is a multi-line string. Handily, the first and final new lines do not become part of the string. This makes it more flexible as you don't have to have the three double-quotes on the same line as the string.

In the case above, it will print the following:

```
You can have a string
that contains multiple
lines
by
doing this.
```

Notice `|`, also known as the "pipe character", at the start of each line as well as the call to `trimMargin()`. This prevents the string from having leading spaces, allowing you to format your code with pretty indentation without affecting the output.

Mini-exercises

1. Create a string constant called `firstName` and initialize it to your first name. Also create a string constant called `lastName` and initialize it to your last name.
2. Create a string constant called `fullName` by adding the `firstName` and `lastName` constants together, separated by a space.
3. Using string templates, create a string constant called `myDetails` that uses the `fullName` constant to create a string introducing yourself. For example, it could read: `"Hello, my name is Joe Howard."`.

Pairs and Triples

Sometimes data comes in groups. An example of this is a pair of (x, y) coordinates on a 2D grid. Similarly, a set of coordinates on a 3D grid is comprised of an x-value, a y-value and a z-value. In Kotlin, you can represent such related data in a very simple way through the use of a `Pair` or `Triple`.

Other languages use a type named "Tuple" to hold similar combinations of values.

`Pair` or `Triple` are types that represent data composed of two or three values of any type. If you want to have more than three values, you use what Kotlin calls a *data class*, which you will cover in a future chapter.

Sticking with `Pair` for now, as an example you can define a pair of 2D coordinates where each axis value is an integer, like so:

```
val coordinates: Pair<Int, Int> = Pair(2, 3)
```

The type of `coordinates` is `Pair<Int, Int>`. The types of the values within the `Pair`, in this case `Int`, are separated by commas and surrounded by <>. The code for creating the `Pair` is much the same, with each value separated by commas and surrounded by parentheses.

Type inference can infer `Pair` types too:

```
val coordinatesInferred = Pair(2, 3)
```

You can make this even more concise, which Kotlin loves to do, by using the `to` operator:

```
val coordinatesWithTo = 2 to 3
```

You could similarly create a `Pair` of `Double` values, like so:

```
val coordinatesDoubles = Pair(2.1, 3.5)
// Inferred to be of type Pair<Double, Double>
```

Or you could mix and match the types comprising the pair, like so:

```
val coordinatesMixed = Pair(2.1, 3)
// Inferred to be of type Pair<Double, Int>
```

And here's how to access the data inside a `Pair`:

```
val x1 = coordinates.first
val y1 = coordinates.second
```

You can reference each item in the `Pair` by its position in the pair, starting with `first`. So in this example, `x1` will equal 2 and `y1` will equal 3.

In the previous example, it may not be immediately obvious that the first value is the x-coordinate and the second value is the y-coordinate. This is another demonstration of why it's important to *always* name your variables in a way that avoids confusion.

Fortunately, Kotlin allows you to use a *destructuring declaration* on individual parts of a `Pair`, and you can be explicit about what each part represents. For example:

```
val (x, y) = coordinates
```

```
// x and y both inferred to be of type Int
```

Here, you extract the values from `coordinates` and assign them to `x` and `y`.

`Triple` works much the same way as `Pair`, just with three values instead of two.

If you want to access multiple parts of a `Triple` at the same time, as in the examples above, you can also use a shorthand syntax to make it easier:

```
val coordinates3D = Triple(2, 3, 1)
val (x3, y3, z3) = coordinates3D
```

This declares three new constants, `x3`, `y3` and `z3`, and assigns each part of the `Triple` to them in turn. The code is equivalent to the following:

```
val coordinates3D = Triple(2, 3, 1)
val x3 = coordinates3D.first
val y3 = coordinates3D.second
val z3 = coordinates3D.third
```

If you want to ignore a certain element of a `Pair` or `Triple`, you can replace the corresponding part of the declaration with an underscore. For example, if you were performing a 2D calculation and wanted to ignore the z-coordinate of `coordinates3D`, then you'd write the following:

```
val (x4, y4, _) = coordinates3D
```

This line of code only declares `x4` and `y4`. The `_` is special and simply means you're ignoring this part for now.

Mini-exercises

1. Declare a constant `Triple` that contains three `Int` values. Use this to represent a date (month, day, year).
2. Extract the values in the triple into three constants named `month`, `day` and `year`.
3. In one line, read the month and year values into two constants. You'll need to employ the underscore to ignore the day.
4. Since the values inside `Pairs` and `Triples` cannot be modified, you will need to extract the values from them, make any modifications you want, and then create a new `Pair` or `Triple`. Using the values you extracted in step three, modify the month value and create a new `Pair` containing the modified month along with the unmodified year.

Number types

Many C-based languages like Java have primitive types that take up a specific number of bytes. For example, in Java, a 32-bit signed primitive number is an `int`. There is also an object version of an `int` known as an `Integer`. You may be wondering why it is necessary to have two types that store the same number type.

Well, primitives require less memory, which means they are better for performance, but they also lack some of the features of `Integer`. The good news is in Kotlin, you don't have to worry about whether you need to use a primitive type or an object type. Kotlin handles that complexity for you, so all you have to do is use an `Int`.

You've been using `Int` to represent whole numbers which are represented using 32 bits. Kotlin provides many more number types that use different amounts of storage. For whole numbers, you can use `Byte`, `Short`, and `Long`. These types consume 1, 2, and 8 bytes of storage respectively. Each of these types use one bit to represent the sign.

Here is a summary of the different integer types and their storage size in bytes. Most of the time you will just want to use an `Int`. These become useful if your code is interacting with another piece of software that uses one of these more exact sizes or if you need to optimize for storage size.

Type	Minimum value	Maximum value	Storage size
Byte	-128	127	1
Short	-32768	32767	2
Int	-2147483648	2147483647	4
Long	-9223372036854775807	9223372036854775806	8

You've been using `Double` to represent fractional numbers. Kotlin offers a `Float` type which has less range and precision than `Double`, but requires half as much storage. Modern hardware has been optimized for `Double` so it is the one that you should reach for unless you have good reason not to.

Type	Minimum value	Maximum value	Precision	Storage size
Float	-3.4028235E+38	3.4028235E+38	6 digits	1
Double	-1.797693E+308	1.797693E+308	15 digits	2

Most of the time you will just use `Int` and `Double` to represent numbers, but every once in a while, you might encounter the other types. Suppose you need to add together a `Short` with a `Byte` and a `Long`. You can do that like so:

```
val a: Short = 12
val b: Byte = 120
val c: Int = -100000

val answer = a + b + c // Answer will be an Int
```

Any, Unit, and Nothing Types

The `Any` type can be thought of as the mother of all other types (except nullable types, which will be covered in Chapter 7). Every type in Kotlin, whether an `Int` or a `String`, is also considered an `Any`. This is similar to the `Object` type in Java, which is the root of all types except primitives.

For example, it is perfectly valid Kotlin to declare an `Int` literal and `String` literal as `Any` like so:

```
val anyNumber: Any = 42
val anyString: Any = "42"
```

`Unit` is a special type which only ever represents one value: the Unit object. It is similar to the `void` type in Java, except it makes working with generics easier (which will be covered in Chapter 18). Every function (you will cover functions in Chapter 6, but for now think of a function as a piece of reusable code) which does not explicitly return a type, e.g., a `String`, returns `Unit`.

For example, here is a function that simply adds `2 + 2` and prints the result but does not actually return anything:

```
fun add() {
  val result = 2 + 2
  println(result)
}
```

The return type `Unit` is implied, so the above function is the same as this:

```
fun add(): Unit {
  val result = 2 + 2
  println(result)
}
```

`Nothing` is a type that is helpful for declaring that a function not only doesn't return anything, but also never completes.

This can occur if a function either causes the program to stop completely by throwing an `Exception` or if it simply goes on forever without ever finishing.

By way of example, the saddest function ever written:

```
fun doNothingForever(): Nothing {
  while(true) {

  }
}
```

You will cover `while` loops more in the next chapter, but for now understand that this function will simply run forever without ever returning anything. Welcome to the land of Nothing!

Challenges

1. Create a constant called `coordinates` and assign a pair containing two and three to it.

2. Extract the values 2 and 3 from `coordinates` into two variables called `row` and `column`.

3. Which of the following are valid statements?

```
val character: Character = "Dog"
val character: Char = 'd'
val string: String = "Dog"
val string: String = 'd'
```

4. Is this valid code?

```
val date = Triple(15, 8, 2015)
val day = date.First
```

5. What is wrong with the following code?

```
val name = "Joe"
name += " Howard"
```

6. What is the type of the constant named `value`?

```
val triple = Triple(100, 1.5, 10)
val value = triple.second
```

7. What is the value of the constant named `month`?

```
val newDate = Triple(15, 8, 2015)
val month = newDate.second
```

8. What is the value of the constant named `summary`?

```
val number = 10
val multiplier = 5
val summary = "$number multiplied by $multiplier equals ${number
* multiplier}"
```

9. What is the sum of `a` and `b`, minus `c`? What is its type?

```
val a = 4
val b: Short = 100
val c: Byte = 12
```

10. What is the numeric difference between `kotlin.math.PI` and `kotlin.math.PI.toFloat()`?

Key points

- Type conversion allows you to convert values of one type into another.
- Kotlin will convert types for you when using an operator, such as the basic arithmetic operators (+, -, *, /), with mixed types.
- Type inference allows you to omit the type when Kotlin already knows it.
- **Unicode** is the standard for mapping characters to numbers.
- A single mapping in Unicode is called a **code point**.
- The `Character` data type stores single characters. The `String` data type stores collections of characters, or strings.
- You can combine strings by using the addition operator.
- You can use **string templates** to build a string in-place.
- You can use `Pairs` and `Triples` to group data into a single data type.
- There are many kinds of numeric types with different storage and precision capabilities.
- `Any` is the mother of all non-nullable types, `Unit` is kind of like `void` in Java, and `Nothing` is well, nothing.

Where to go from here?

You can find all the code from this chapter, along with solutions to the mini-exercises and challenges, in the materials for this chapter.

Types are a fundamental part of programming. They're what allow you to correctly store your data. You've seen a few more here, including strings, pairs, and triples as well as a bunch of numeric types. Later on in the book you'll learn how to define your own types with **classes, enums** and **interfaces**.

In the next chapter, you'll learn about Boolean logic and simple control flow. This is required for any program to be able to make decisions about how the program should proceed based on the data it's manipulating.

Chapter 4: Basic Control Flow

By Irina Galata

When writing a computer program, you need to be able to tell the computer what to do in different scenarios. For example, a calculator app would need to do one thing if the user tapped the addition button and another thing if the user tapped the subtraction button.

In computer-programming terms, this concept is known as **control flow**. It is so named because the flow of the program is controlled by various methods. In this chapter, you'll learn how to make decisions and repeat tasks in your programs by using syntax to control the flow. You'll also learn about **Booleans**, which represent true and false values, and how you can use these to compare data.

Open up a project in IntelliJ to follow along!

Comparison operators

You've seen a few types now, such as `Int`, `Double` and `String`. Here you'll learn about another type, one that will let you compare values through the **comparison operators**.

When you perform a comparison, such as looking for the greater of two numbers, the answer is either *true* or *false*. Kotlin has a data type just for this! It's called a `Boolean`, after a rather clever man named George Boole who invented an entire field of mathematics around the concept of true and false.

This is how you use a Boolean in Kotlin:

```
val yes: Boolean = true
val no: Boolean = false
```

And because of Kotlin's type inference, you can leave off the type annotation:

```
val yes = true
val no = false
```

A Boolean can only be either true or false, denoted by the keywords `true` and `false`. In the code above, you use the keywords to set the state of each constant.

Boolean operators

Booleans are commonly used to compare values. For example, you may have two values and you want to know if they're equal: either they are (true) or they aren't (false).

In Kotlin, you do this using the **equality operator**, which is denoted by ==. Try it out:

```
val doesOneEqualTwo = (1 == 2)
```

Kotlin infers that `doesOneEqualTwo` is a `Boolean`. Clearly, 1 does not equal 2, and therefore `doesOneEqualTwo` will be `false`.

Similarly, you can find out if two values are *not* equal using the `!=` operator:

```
val doesOneNotEqualTwo = (1 != 2)
```

This time, the comparison is true because 1 does not equal 2, so `doesOneNotEqualTwo` will be `true`.

The prefix `!` operator, also called the **not-operator**, toggles true to false and false to true. Another way to write the above is:

```
val alsoTrue = !(1 == 2)
```

Because 1 does not equal 2, `(1 == 2)` is `false`, and then `!` flips it to `true`.

Two more operators let you determine if a value is greater than (>) or less than (<) another value. You'll likely know these from mathematics:

```
val isOneGreaterThanTwo = (1 > 2)
val isOneLessThanTwo = (1 < 2)
```

And it's not rocket science to work out that `isOneGreaterThanTwo` will equal `false` and `isOneLessThanTwo` will equal `true`.

There's also an operator that lets you test if a value is less than *or* equal to another value: <=. It's a combination of < and ==, and will therefore return `true` if the first value is either less than the second value or equal to it.

Similarly, there's an operator that lets you test if a value is greater than or equal to another — you may have guessed that it's >=.

Boolean logic

Each of the examples above tests just one condition. When George Boole invented the Boolean, he had much more planned for it than these humble beginnings. He invented Boolean logic, which lets you combine multiple conditions to form a result.

One way to combine conditions is by using **AND**. When you AND together two Booleans, the result is another Boolean. If both input Booleans are `true`, then the result is `true`. Otherwise, the result is `false`.

George Boole

In Kotlin, the operator for Boolean AND is &&, used like so:

```
val and = true && true
```

In this case, `and` will be `true`. If either of the values on the right was `false`, then `and` would be `false`.

Another way to combine conditions is by using **OR**. When you OR together two Booleans, the result is `true` if *either* of the input Booleans is `true`. Only if *both* input Booleans are `false` will the result be `false`.

In Kotlin, the operator for Boolean OR is ||, used like so:

```
val or = true || false
```

In this case, `or` will be `true`. If both values on the right were `false`, then `or` would be `false`. If both were `true`, then `or` would still be `true`.

In Kotlin, Boolean logic is usually applied to multiple conditions. Maybe you want to determine if two conditions are true; in that case, you'd use AND. If you only care about whether one of two conditions is true, then you'd use OR.

For example, consider the following code:

```
val andTrue = 1 < 2 && 4 > 3
val andFalse = 1 < 2 && 3 > 4

val orTrue = 1 < 2 || 3 > 4
val orFalse = 1 == 2 || 3 == 4
```

Each of these tests two separate conditions, combining them with either AND or OR.

It's also possible to use Boolean logic to combine more than two comparisons. For example, you can form a complex comparison like so:

```
val andOr = (1 < 2 && 3 > 4) || 1 < 4
```

The parentheses disambiguates the expression. First Kotlin evaluates the sub-expression inside the parentheses, and then it evaluates the full expression, following these steps:

```
1. (1 < 2 && 3 > 4) || 1 < 4
2. (true && false) || true
3. false || true
4. true
```

String equality

Sometimes you want to determine if two strings are equal. For example, a children's game of naming an animal in a photo would need to determine if the player answered correctly.

In Kotlin, you can compare strings using the standard equality operator, ==, in exactly the same way as you compare numbers. For example:

```
val guess = "dog"
val dogEqualsCat = guess == "cat"
```

Here, `dogEqualsCat` is a Boolean that in this case equals `false`, because `"dog"` does not equal `"cat"`. Simple!

Just as with numbers, you can compare not just for equality, but also to determine if one value is greater than or less that another value. For example:

```
val order = "cat" < "dog"
```

This syntax checks if one string comes before another alphabetically. In this case, `order` equals `true` because `"cat"` comes before `"dog"`.

Mini-exercises

1. Create a constant called `myAge` and set it to your age. Then, create a constant named `isTeenager` that uses Boolean logic to determine if the age denotes someone in the age range of 13 to 19.

2. Create another constant named `theirAge` and set it to the age 30. Then, create a constant named `bothTeenagers` that uses Boolean logic to determine if both you and them are teenagers.

3. Create a constant named `reader` and set it to your name as a string. Create a constant named `author` and set it to the name Richard Lucas. Create a constant named `authorIsReader` that uses string equality to determine if `reader` and `author` are equal.

4. Create a constant named `readerBeforeAuthor` which uses string comparison to determine if `reader` comes before `author`.

The if expression

The first and most common way of controlling the flow of a program is through the use of an **`if` expression**, which allows the program to do something only *if* a certain condition is true. For example, try typing out and running the following:

```
if (2 > 1) {
  println("Yes, 2 is greater than 1.")
}
```

This is a simple `if` expression. If the condition is true, then the expression will execute the code between the braces. If the condition is false, then the expression won't execute the code between the braces. It's as simple as that!

The term **`if` expression** is used here instead of **`if` statement**, since, unlike many other programming languages, a value is returned from the `if` expression. The value returned is the value of the last expression in the `if` block.

You are not required to use the returned value or assign it to a variable. You'll see more on returning a value below.

The else expression

You can extend an `if` expression to provide code to run in case the condition turns out to be false. This is known as the **else clause**. Here's an example:

```
val animal = "Fox"

if (animal == "Cat" || animal == "Dog") {
  println("Animal is a house pet.")
} else {
  println("Animal is not a house pet.")
}
```

Here, if `animal` equals either `"Cat"` or `"Dog"`, then the expression will run the first block of code. If `animal` does not equal either `"Cat"` or `"Dog"`, then the expression will run the block inside the `else` part of the `if` expression, printing the following to the console:

```
Animal is not a house pet.
```

You can also use an `if-else` expression on one line. Let's take a look at how this can make your code more concise and readable.

If you wanted to determine the minimum and maximum of two variables, you *could* use `if` expressions like so:

```
val a = 5
val b = 10

val min: Int
if (a < b) {
  min = a
} else {
  min = b
}

val max: Int
if (a > b) {
  max = a
} else {
  max = b
}
```

By now you know how this works, but it's a lot of code. Let's take a look at how we can improve this using the fact that the `if-else` expression returns a value.

Simply remove the brackets and put it all on one line, like so:

```
val a = 5
val b = 10

val min = if (a < b) a else b
val max = if (a > b) a else b
```

In the first example, the condition is `a < b`. If this is true, the result assigned back to `min` will be the value of `a`; if it's false, the result will be the value of `b`. So `min` is set to 5. In the second example, `max` is assigned the value of `b`, which is 10.

I'm sure you'll agree that's much simpler! This is an example of **idiomatic** code, which means you are writing code in the expected way for a particular programming language. You want to use idioms whenever they make your code clearer, as it not only makes the code better, but it allows other developers familiar with the language to comprehend your code quickly.

> **Note**: Because finding the greater or smaller of two numbers is such a common operation, the Kotlin standard library provides two functions for this purpose: `max()` and `min()`. If you were paying attention earlier in the book, then you'll recall you've already seen these.

The else-if expression

But you can go even further than that with `if` expressions. Sometimes you want to check one condition, then another. This is where **`else-if`** comes into play, nesting another `if` clause in the `else` clause of a previous `if` clause.

You can use `else-if` like so:

```
val hourOfDay = 12

val timeOfDay = if (hourOfDay < 6) {
  "Early morning"
} else if (hourOfDay < 12) {
  "Morning"
} else if (hourOfDay < 17) {
  "Afternoon"
} else if (hourOfDay < 20) {
  "Evening"
} else if (hourOfDay < 24) {
  "Late evening"
} else {
  "INVALID HOUR!"
}
println(timeOfDay)
```

These nested `if` clauses test multiple conditions one by one until a true condition is found. Only the code associated with that first true condition is executed, regardless of whether subsequent `else-if` conditions are true. In other words, the order of your conditions matters!

You can add an `else` clause at the end to handle the case where none of the conditions are true. This `else` clause is optional if you don't need it; in this example you *do* need it, to ensure that `timeOfDay` has a valid value by the time you print it out.

In this example, the `if` expression takes a number representing an hour of the day and converts it to a string representing the part of the day to which the hour belongs. Working with a 24-hour clock, the conditions are checked in order, one at a time:

- The first check is to see if the hour is less than 6. If so, that means it's early morning.
- If the hour is not less than 6, the expression continues to the first `else-if`, where it checks the hour to see if it's less than 12.

- Then in turn, as conditions prove false, the expression checks the hour to see if it's less than 17, then less than 20, then less than 24.
- Finally, if the hour is out of range, the expression returns that the value is invalid.

In the code above, the hourOfDay constant is 12. Therefore, the code will print the following:

```
Afternoon
```

Notice that even though both the hourOfDay < 20 and hourOfDay < 24 conditions are also true, the expression only executes and returns the first block whose condition is true; in this case, the block with the hourOfDay < 17 condition.

Short circuiting

An important fact about if expressions and the Boolean operators is what happens when there are multiple Boolean conditions separated by ANDs (&&) or ORs (||).

Consider the following code:

```
if (1 > 2 && name == "Matt Galloway") {
  // ...
}
```

The first condition of the if expression, 1 > 2 is false. Therefore the whole expression cannot ever be true. So Kotlin will not even bother to check the second part of the expression, namely the check of name.

Similarly, consider the following code:

```
if (1 < 2 || name == "Matt Galloway") {
  // ...
}
```

Since 1 < 2 is true, the whole expression must be true as well. Therefore once again, the check of name is not executed. This will come in handy later on when you start dealing with more complex data types.

Encapsulating variables

`if` expressions introduce a new concept, **scope**, which is a way to encapsulate variables through the use of braces.

Imagine you want to calculate the fee to charge your client. Here's the deal you've made:

> You earn $25 for every hour up to 40 hours, and $50 for every hour thereafter.

Using Kotlin, you can calculate your fee in this way:

```
var hoursWorked = 45

var price = 0
if (hoursWorked > 40) {
  val hoursOver40 = hoursWorked - 40
  price += hoursOver40 * 50
  hoursWorked -= hoursOver40
}
price += hoursWorked * 25

println(price)
```

This code takes the number of hours and checks if it's over 40. If so, the code calculates the number of hours over 40 and multiplies that by $50, then adds the result to the price. The code then subtracts the number of hours over 40 from the hours worked. It multiplies the remaining hours worked by $25 and adds that to the total price.

In the example above, the result is as follows:

```
1250
```

The interesting thing here is the code inside the `if` expression. There is a declaration of a new constant, `hoursOver40`, to store the number of hours over 40. Clearly, you can use it inside the `if` statement.

But what happens if you try to use it at the end of the above code?

```
println(price)
println(hoursOver40)
```

This would result in the following error:

```
Unresolved reference: 'hoursOver40'
```

This error informs you that you're only allowed to use the `hoursOver40` constant within the scope in which it was created.

In this case, the `if` expression introduced a new scope, so when that scope is finished, you can no longer use the constant.

However, each scope can use variables and constants from its parent scope. In the example above, the scope inside of the `if` expression uses the `price` and `hoursWorked` variables, which you created in the parent scope.

Mini-exercises

1. Create a constant named `myAge` and initialize it with your age. Write an `if` expression to print out `Teenager` if your age is between 13 and 19, and `Not a teenager` if your age is not between 13 and 19.
2. Create a constant called `answer` and use a single line `if-else` expression to set it equal to the result you print out for the same cases in the above exercise. Then print out `answer`.

Loops

Loops are Kotlin's way of executing code multiple times. In this section, you'll learn about one type of loop: the `while` loop.

If you know another programming language, you'll find the concepts and maybe even the syntax to be familiar.

While loops

A **while loop** repeats a block of code while a condition is true. You create a `while` loop this way:

```
while (/* CONDITION */) {
  /* LOOP CODE */
}
```

The loop checks the condition for every iteration. If the condition is `true`, then the loop executes and moves on to another iteration.

If the condition is `false`, then the loop stops. Just like `if` expressions, `while` loops introduce a scope.

The simplest `while` loop takes this form:

```
while (true) {
}
```

This is a `while` loop that never ends because the condition is always `true`. Of course, you would never write such a `while` loop, because your program would spin forever! This situation is known as an **infinite loop**, and while it might not cause your program to crash, it will very likely cause your computer to freeze.

Here's a more useful example of a `while` loop:

```
var sum = 1

while (sum < 1000) {
  sum = sum + (sum + 1)
}
```

This code calculates a mathematical sequence, up to the point where the value is greater than `1000`.

The loop executes as follows:

- **Before iteration 1:** `sum` = 1, loop condition = true
- **After iteration 1:** `sum` = 3, loop condition = true
- **After iteration 2:** `sum` = 7, loop condition = true
- **After iteration 3:** `sum` = 15, loop condition = true
- **After iteration 4:** `sum` = 31, loop condition = true
- **After iteration 5:** `sum` = 63, loop condition = true
- **After iteration 6:** `sum` = 127, loop condition = true
- **After iteration 7:** `sum` = 255, loop condition = true
- **After iteration 8:** `sum` = 511, loop condition = true
- **After iteration 9:** `sum` = 1023, loop condition = false

After the ninth iteration, the `sum` variable is `1023`, and therefore the loop condition of `sum < 1000` becomes false. At this point, the loop stops.

Repeat-while loops

A variant of the `while` loop is called the **do-while loop**. It differs from the `while` loop in that the condition is evaluated *at the end* of the loop rather than at the beginning.

You construct a `do-while` loop like this:

```
do {
  /* LOOP CODE */
} while (/* CONDITION */)
```

Here's the example from the last section, but using a `repeat-while` loop:

```
sum = 1

do {
  sum = sum + (sum + 1)
} while (sum < 1000)
```

In this example, the outcome is the same as before. However, that isn't always the case; you might get a different result with a different condition. Consider the following `while` loop:

```
sum = 1

while (sum < 1) {
  sum = sum + (sum + 1)
}
```

Consider the corresponding `do-while` loop, which uses the same condition:

```
sum = 1

do {
  sum = sum + (sum + 1)
} while (sum < 1)
```

In the case of the regular `while` loop, the condition `sum < 1` is `false` right from the start. That means the body of the loop won't be reached because the condition is checked at the beginning! The value of `sum` will equal `1` because the loop won't execute any iterations.

In the case of the `do-while` loop, `sum` will equal `3` because the loop executes once and then the condition is checked for the first time.

Breaking out of a loop

Sometimes you want to break out of a loop early. You can do this using the `break` statement, which immediately stops the execution of the loop and continues on to the code after the loop.

For example, consider the following code:

```
sum = 1

while (true) {
  sum = sum + (sum + 1)
  if (sum >= 1000) {
    break
  }
}
```

Here, the loop condition is `true`, so the loop would normally iterate forever. However, the `break` means the `while` loop will exit once the sum is greater than or equal to `1000`.

You've seen how to write the same loop in different ways, demonstrating that in computer programming, there are often many ways to achieve the same result.

You should choose the method that's easiest to read and conveys your intent in the best way possible. This is an approach you'll internalize with enough time and practice.

Mini-exercises

1. Create a variable named `counter` and set it equal to `0`. Create a while loop with the condition `counter < 10` which prints out `counter is X` (where `X` is replaced with `counter` value) and then increments `counter` by `1`.

2. Create a variable named `counter` and set it equal to `0`. Create another variable named `roll` and set it equal to `0`. Create a `do-while` loop.

Inside the loop, set `roll` equal to `Random().nextInt(6)` which means to pick a random number between `0` and `5`. Then increment `counter` by `1`.

> **Note**: Add the line `import java.util.*` to the top of your Kotlin file to be able to use `Random`.

Finally, print `After X rolls, roll is Y` where `X` is the value of `counter` and `Y` is the value of `roll`. Set the loop condition such that the loop finishes when the first `0` is rolled.

Challenges

Time to test your knowledge! If you need any help along the way, check out the solutions in the materials for this chapter.

1. What's wrong with the following code?

```
val firstName = "Joe"

if (firstName == "Howard") {
  val lastName = "Lucas"
} else if (firstName == "Ray") {
  val lastName = "Wenderlich"
}

val fullName = firstName + " " + lastName
```

2. In each of the following statements, what is the value of the Boolean `answer` constant?

```
val answer1 = true && true
val answer2 = false || false
val answer3 = (true && 1 != 2) || (4 > 3 && 100 < 1)
val answer4 = ((10 / 2) > 3) && ((10 % 2) == 0)
```

3. Suppose the squares on a chessboard are numbered left to right, top to bottom, with 0 being the top-left square and 63 being the bottom-right square. Rows are numbered top to bottom, 0 to 7. Columns are numbered left to right, 0 to 7. Given a current position on the chessboard, expressed as a row and column number, calculate the next position on the chessboard, again expressed as a row and column number. The ordering is determined by the numbering from 0 to 63. The position after 63 is again 0.

4. Given the coefficients a, b and c, calculate the solutions to a quadratic equation with these coefficients. Take into account the different number of solutions (0, 1 or 2). If you need a math refresher, this Wikipedia article on the quadratic equation will help: https://en.wikipedia.org/wiki/Quadratic_formula.

> **Note**: Add `import kotlin.math.sqrt` to the top of your file to access the `sqrt` operation.

5. Given a month (represented with a string in all lowercase) and the current year (represented with an `Int`), calculate the number of days in the month. Remember that because of leap years, "february" has 29 days when the year is a multiple of 4 but not a multiple of 100. February also has 29 days when the year is a multiple of 400.

6. Given a number as a `Double` value, determine if this number is a power of 2.

> **Hint**: You can use `log2(number)` to find the base 2 logarithm of `number`. `log2(number)` will return a whole number if `number` is a power of two. Add `import kotlin.math.log2` to the top of your file to use `log2`.
>
> You can also solve the problem using a loop and no logarithm.

7. Print a table of the first 10 powers of 2.

8. Given a number n, calculate the n-th Fibonacci number. (Recall Fibonacci is 1, 1, 2, 3, 5, 8, 13, ... Start with 1 and 1 and add these values together to get the next value. The next value is the sum of the previous two. So the next value in this case is 8+13 = 21.)

9. Given a number n, calculate the factorial of n. (Example: 4 factorial is equal to 1 * 2 * 3 * 4.)

10. Given a number between 2 and 12, calculate the odds of rolling this number using two six-sided dice. Compute it by exhaustively looping through all of the combinations and counting the fraction of outcomes that give you that value. Don't use a formula.

Key points

- You use the Boolean data type `Boolean` to represent true and false.
- The comparison operators, all of which return a Boolean, are:

```
Equal: `==`
Not equal: `!=`
Less than: `<`
Greater than: `>`
Less than or equal: `<=`
Greater than or equal: `>=`
```

- You can use Boolean logic with && and || to combine comparison conditions.
- You use `if` expressions to make simple decisions based on a condition, and return a value.
- You use `else` and `else-if` within an `if` expression to extend the decision-making beyond a single condition.
- You can use a single line `if-else` expression to make your code more clear and concise.
- Short circuiting ensures that only the minimal required parts of a Boolean expression are evaluated.
- Variables and constants belong to a certain scope, beyond which you cannot use them. A scope inherits visible variables and constants from its parent.
- `while` loops allow you to perform a certain task a number of times until a condition is met.
- The `break` statement lets you break out of a loop.

Where to go from here?

Apps very rarely run all the way through the same way every time; depending on what data comes in from the internet or from user input, your code will need to make decisions on which path to take. With `if` and `else`, you can have your code make decisions on what to do based on some condition.

In the next chapter, you'll see how to use more advanced control flow statements. This will involve more loops like the `while` loop you saw in this chapter, and a new construct called the `when` expression.

Chapter 5: Advanced Control Flow

By Irina Galata

In the previous chapter, you learned how to control the flow of execution using the decision-making powers of `if` expressions and the `while` loop. In this chapter, you'll continue to learn how to control the flow of execution. You'll learn about another loop known as the `for` loop.

Loops may not sound very interesting, but they're very common in computer programs. For example, you might have code to download an image from the cloud; with a loop, you could run that multiple times to download your entire photo library. Or if you have a game with multiple computer-controlled characters, you might need a loop to go through each one and make sure it knows what to do next.

You'll also learn about `when` expressions, which are particularly powerful in Kotlin. They let you inspect a value and decide what to do based on that value. They're incredibly powerful when used with argument matching.

Open of the starter project for this chapter or create a fresh project to get going.

Ranges

Before you dive into the `for` loop statement, you need to know about the **range** data types, which let you represent a sequence of countable integers. Let's look at two types of ranges.

First, there's a **closed range**, which you represent like so:

```
val closedRange = 0..5
```

The two dots (`..`) indicate that this range is closed, which means the range goes from 0 to 5 inclusive. That's the numbers `(0, 1, 2, 3, 4, 5)`.

Second, there's a **half-open range**, which you represent like so:

```
val halfOpenRange = 0 until 5
```

Here, you replace the two dots with `until`. Half-open means the range goes from 0 up to, but not including, 5. That's the numbers `(0, 1, 2, 3, 4)`.

Open and half-open ranges created with the `..` and `until` operators are always increasing. In other words, the second number must always be greater than or equal to the first. To create a decreasing range, you can use `downTo`, which is inclusive:

```
val decreasingRange = 5 downTo 0
```

That will include the numbers `(5, 4, 3, 2, 1, 0)`.

Ranges are commonly used in both `for` loops and `when` expressions, which means that throughout the rest of the chapter, you'll use ranges as well!

For loops

In the previous chapter you looked at `while` loops. Now that you know about ranges, it's time to look at another type of loop: The **`for` loop**. This is probably the most common loop you'll see, and you'll use it to run code a certain number of times.

You construct a `for` loop like this:

```
for (/* VARIABLE */ in /* RANGE */) {
  /* LOOP CODE */
}
```

The loop begins with the `for` keyword, followed by a name given to the loop variable (more on that shortly), followed by `in`, followed by the range to loop through. Here's an example:

```
val count = 10

var sum = 0
for (i in 1..count) {
  sum += i
}
```

In the code above, the `for` loop iterates through the range 1 to `count`. At the first iteration, `i` will equal the first element in the range: 1. Each time around the loop, `i` will increment until it's equal to `count`; the loop will execute one final time and then finish.

> **Note**: If you'd used a half-open range, the last iteration would see `i` equal to `count - 1`.

Inside the loop, you add `i` to the `sum` variable; it runs 10 times to calculate the sequence `1 + 2 + 3 + 4 + 5 + ...` all the way up to 10.

Here are the values of the constant `i` and variable `sum` for each iteration:

- **Start of iteration 1:** `i` = 1, `sum` = 0
- **Start of iteration 2:** `i` = 2, `sum` = 1
- **Start of iteration 3:** `i` = 3, `sum` = 3
- **Start of iteration 4:** `i` = 4, `sum` = 6
- **Start of iteration 5:** `i` = 5, `sum` = 10
- **Start of iteration 6:** `i` = 6, `sum` = 15
- **Start of iteration 7:** `i` = 7, `sum` = 21
- **Start of iteration 8:** `i` = 8, `sum` = 28
- **Start of iteration 9:** `i` = 9, `sum` = 36
- **Start of iteration 10:** `i` = 10, `sum` = 45
- **After iteration 10:** `sum` = 55

In terms of scope, the `i` constant is only visible inside the scope of the `for` loop, which means it's not available outside of the loop.

Repeat loops

Finally, sometimes you only want to loop a certain number of times, and so you don't need to use the loop constant at all. In that case, you can employ a `repeat` loop, like so:

```
sum = 1
var lastSum = 0
repeat(10) {
  val temp = sum
  sum += lastSum
  lastSum = temp
}
```

Steps in loops

It's also possible to only perform certain iterations in the range. For example, imagine you wanted to compute a sum similar to that of triangle numbers, but only for odd numbers:

```
sum = 0
for (i in 1..count step 2) {
  sum += i
}
```

The previous loop has a `step` operator in the `for` loop statement. The loop will only run through the values that the step falls on. In this case, rather than step through every value in the range, it will step through every other value. As such, `i` will always be odd because the starting value is `1`.

You can even count down in a for loop using `downTo`. In this case if `count` is `10` then the loop will iterate through the following values `(10, 8, 6, 4, 2)`.

```
sum = 0
for (i in count downTo 1 step 2) {
  sum += i
}
```

Labeled statements

Sometimes you'd like to skip a loop iteration for a particular case without breaking out of the loop entirely. You can do this with the `continue` statement, which immediately ends the current iteration of the loop and starts the next iteration. The `continue` statement gives you a higher level of control, letting you decide where and when you want to skip an iteration.

Take the example of an 8 by 8 grid, where each cell holds a value of the row multiplied by the column. It looks much like a multiplication table, doesn't it?

	0	1	2	3	4	5	6	7
0	0	0	0	0	0	0	0	0
1	0	1	2	3	4	5	6	7
2	0	2	4	6	8	10	12	14
3	0	3	6	9	12	15	18	21
4	0	4	8	12	16	20	24	28
5	0	5	10	15	20	25	30	35
6	0	6	12	18	24	30	36	42
7	0	7	14	21	28	35	42	49

Let's say you wanted to calculate the sum of all cells but exclude all even rows, as shown below:

	0	1	2	3	4	5	6	7
0								
1	0	1	2	3	4	5	6	7
2								
3	0	3	6	9	12	15	18	21
4								
5	0	5	10	15	20	25	30	35
6								
7	0	7	14	21	28	35	42	49

Using a `for` loop, you can achieve this as follows:

```
sum = 0
for (row in 0 until 8) {
  if (row % 2 == 0) {
    continue
  }
```

```
    for (column in 0 until 8) {
      sum += row * column
    }
  }
```

When the row modulo 2 equals 0, the row is even. In this case, `continue` makes the `for` loop skip to the next row.

The `break` statement you saw in the last chapter used with `while` loops also works with `for` loops, and takes you to the next statement after the `for` loop. Just like `break`, `continue` works with both `for` loops and `while` loops.

The second code example will calculate the sum of all cells, excluding those where the column is greater than or equal to the row.

To illustrate, it should sum the following cells:

	0	1	2	3	4	5	6	7
0								
1	0							
2	0	2						
3	0	3	6					
4	0	4	8	12				
5	0	5	10	15	20			
6	0	6	12	18	24	30		
7	0	7	14	21	28	35	42	

Using a `for` loop, you can achieve this as follows:

```
sum = 0
rowLoop@ for (row in 0 until 8) {
  columnLoop@ for (column in 0 until 8) {
    if (row == column) {
      continue@rowLoop
    }
    sum += row * column
  }
}
```

The previous code block makes use of a **label**, labeling the two loops as `rowLoop` and `columnLoop`, respectively. When the row equals the column inside the inner `columnLoop`, the outer `rowLoop` will continue.

You can use labeled statements like these with `break` to break out of a certain loop. Normally, `break` and `continue` work on the innermost loop, so you need to use labeled statements if you want to manipulate an outer loop.

Mini-exercises

1. Create a constant named `range` and set it equal to a range starting at 1 and ending with 10 inclusive. Write a `for` loop which iterates over this range and prints the square of each number.
2. Write a `for` loop to iterate over the same range as in the exercise above and print the square root of each number. You'll need to type convert your loop constant.
3. Above, you saw a `for` loop which iterated over only the even rows like so:

```
sum = 0
for (row in 0 until 8) {
  if (row % 2 == 0) {
    continue
  }

  for (column in 0 until 8) {
    sum += row * column
  }
}
```

Change this to use a `step` clause on the first `for` loop to skip even rows instead of using `continue`. Check that the sum is 448 as in the initial example.

When expressions

You can also control flow via the `when` expression. It executes different code depending on the value of a variable or constant. Here's a `when` expression that acts on an integer:

```
val number = 10

when (number) {
  0 -> println("Zero")
  else -> println("Non-zero")
}
```

In this example, the code will print the following:

```
Non-zero
```

The purpose of this `when` expression is to determine whether or not a number is zero. It will get more complex — I promise!

To handle a specific case, you add the value followed by -> which indicates the code that will execute if the condition is met. Then, you use `else` to signify what should happen for all other values. Unlike other languages such as Java, there is no need to include a `break` statement in each branch, as the `when` expression will only use the first matching branch and then return.

Here's another example:

```
when (number) {
  10 -> println("It's ten!")
}
```

This time you check for 10, in which case, you print a message. Nothing should happen for other values.

Of course, `when` expressions also work with data types other than integers. Here's an example using a string:

```
val string = "Dog"
when (string) {
  "Cat", "Dog" -> println("Animal is a house pet.")
  else -> println("Animal is not a house pet.")
}
```

This will print the following:

```
Animal is a house pet.
```

In this example, you provide two values for the first argument, meaning that if the value is equal to either `"Cat"` or `"Dog"`, then the statement will execute that branch of the expression.

Returning values

You can also give your when expressions more than one branch. And, due to the fact that when is an expression, you can use it to return a value, just like you can with if expressions. You can also ignore the value if you want to just use when as a statement. A when expression will return the value from the first branch with a matching argument.

If you want to determine the name of the number, you can assign the value with a when expression as follows

```
val numberName = when (number) {
  2 -> "two"
  4 -> "four"
  6 -> "six"
  8 -> "eight"
  10 -> "ten"
  else -> {
    println("Unknown number")
    "Unknown"
  }
}

println(numberName) // > ten
```

In the else branch, you've used braces to include an entire block of code in the branch. The last value in the block is returned from the branch, so if number were not in (2, 4, 6, 8, 10) then numberName would have the value "Unknown".

Advanced when expressions

In the previous chapter, you saw an if expression that used multiple else clauses to convert an hour of the day to a string describing that part of the day. You could rewrite that with a when expression, like so:

```
val hourOfDay = 12
val timeOfDay: String

timeOfDay = when (hourOfDay) {
  0, 1, 2, 3, 4, 5 -> "Early morning"
  6, 7, 8, 9, 10, 11 -> "Morning"
  12, 13, 14, 15, 16 -> "Afternoon"
  17, 18, 19 -> "Evening"
  20, 21, 22, 23 -> "Late evening"
  else -> "INVALID HOUR!"
}
println(timeOfDay)
```

This code will print the following:

```
Afternoon
```

Using when expressions with ranges

Remember ranges? Well, you can use ranges to simplify this when expression. You can rewrite the above code using ranges:

```
timeOfDay = when (hourOfDay) {
  in 0..5 -> "Early morning"
  in 6..11 -> "Morning"
  in 12..16 -> "Afternoon"
  in 17..19 -> "Evening"
  in 20..23 -> "Late evening"
  else -> "INVALID HOUR!"
}
```

This is more succinct than writing out each value individually for all branches.

When there are multiple branches, the expression will execute the first one that matches. You'll probably agree that this is more succinct and more clear than using an `if` expression for this example.

It's slightly more precise as well, because the `if` expression method didn't address negative numbers, which here are correctly deemed to be invalid.

Using when expressions with conditions

It's also possible to match a branch to a condition based on a property of the value, without any argument being supplied to the when expression. As you learned in Chapter 2, you can use the modulo operator to determine if an integer is even or odd.

Consider this code:

```
when {
  number % 2 == 0 -> println("Even")
  else -> println("Odd")
}
```

This will print the following:

```
Even
```

The first branch of this when expression uses the == operator, meaning the argument will match only when a certain condition is true.

In this example, you've designed the argument to match if the value is even — that is, if the value modulo 2 equals 0.

Another example of using conditions in when expressions to great effect is as follows:

```
val (x, y, z) = Triple(3, 2, 5)

when {
  x == 0 && y == 0 && z == 0 -> println("Origin")
  y == 0 && z == 0 -> println("On the x-axis at x = $x")
  x == 0 && z == 0 -> println("On the y-axis at y = $y")
  x == 0 && y == 0 -> println("On the z-axis at z = $z")
  else -> println("In space at x = $x, y = $y, z = $z")
}
```

Here's what each branch does, in order:

1. Matches precisely the case where the value is `(0, 0, 0)`. This is the origin of 3D space.
2. Matches y=0, z=0 and any value of x. This means the coordinate is on the x-axis.
3. Matches x=0, z=0 and any value of y. This means the coordinate is on the y-axis.
4. Matches x=0, y=0 and any value of z. This means the coordinate is on the z-axis.
5. Matches the remainder of coordinates.

The final branch with the `else` clause is the default; it matches anything, because there are no constraints on any part of the coordinates. Here's an example of a more complex case:

```
when {
  x == y -> println("Along the y = x line.")
  y == x * x -> println("Along the y = x^2 line.")
}
```

Here, you match the "y equals x" and "y equals x squared" lines. Since there is no argument to the when expression, you do not need an `else` branch, and the when expression will not execute a branch if there is no matching condition. And those are the basics of when expressions!

Mini-exercises

1. Write a when expression that takes an age as an integer and prints out the life stage related to that age. You can make up the life stages, or use the categorization as follows: 0-2 years, Infant; 3-12 years, Child; 13-19 years, Teenager; 20-39, Adult; 40-60, Middle aged; 61+, Elderly.
2. Write a `when` expression that destructures a `Pair` containing a string and an integer. The string is a name, and the integer is an age. Use the same cases that you used in the previous exercise to print out the name followed by the life stage. For example, for myself it would print out `"Joe is an adult."`.

Challenges

1. In the following `for` loop, what will be the value of `sum`, and how many iterations will happen?

```
var sum = 0
for(i in 0..5) {
  sum += i
}
```

2. In the `while` loop below, how many instances of "a" will there be in `aLotOfAs`? Hint: `aLotOfAs.count` tells you how many characters are in the string `aLotOfAs`.

```
var aLotOfAs = ""
while (aLotOfAs.length < 10) {
  aLotOfAs += "a"
}
```

3. Consider the following `when` expression:

```
when {
  x == y && y == z -> println("x = y = z")
  z == 0 -> println("On the x/y plane")
  y == 0 -> println("On the x/z plane")
  x == 0 -> println("On the y/z plane")
  else -> println("Nothing special")
}
```

What will this code print when `coordinates` is each of the following?

```
val (x, y, z) = Triple(1, 5, 0)
val (x, y, z) = Triple(2, 2, 2)
val (x, y, z) = Triple(3, 0, 1)
val (x, y, z) = Triple(3, 2, 5)
val (x, y, z) = Triple(0, 2, 4)
```

4. A closed range can never be empty. Why?
5. Print a countdown from 10 to 0 without using `downTo`.
6. Print 0.0, 0.1, 0.2, 0.3, 0.4, 0.5, 0.6, 0.7, 0.8, 0.9, 1.0.

> **Note**: You may find some rounding issues with Challenge #6 where the decimals are slightly off. For example, `0.3` might print out as something like `0.30000000000000004`. This is okay for this solution. The reason for this is because of the way computers handle numbers and is too complex for this chapter.

Key points

- You can use **ranges** to create a sequence of numbers, incrementing to move from one value to another.
- **Closed ranges** include both the start and end values.
- **Half-open ranges** include the start value and stop one before the end value.
- **For loops** allow you to iterate over a range.
- The **continue** statement lets you finish the current iteration of a loop and begin the next iteration.
- **Labeled statements** let you use `break` and `continue` on an outer loop.
- You use **`when`** expressions to decide which code to run depending on the value of a variable or constant.
- The power of a `when` expression comes from leveraging **pattern matching** to compare values using complex rules.

Where to go from here?

You've learned about the core language features for dealing with data over these past few chapters, from data types to variables, then on to decision-making with Booleans and loops with ranges. In the next chapter you'll learn one of the key ways to make your code more reusable and easy to read through the use of functions.

Chapter 6: Functions

By Irina Galata

Functions are a core part of many programming languages. Simply put, a function lets you define a block of code that performs a task. Then, whenever your app needs to execute that task, you can run the function instead of having to copy and paste the same code everywhere.

In this chapter, you'll learn how to write your own functions, and see firsthand how Kotlin makes them easy to use.

Function basics

Imagine you have an app that frequently needs to print your name. You can write a function to do this. Try out this code:

```
fun printMyName() {
  println("My name is Joe Howard.")
}
```

The code above is known as a **function declaration**. You define a function using the `fun` keyword. After that comes the name of the function, followed by parentheses. You'll learn more about the need for these parentheses in the next section.

After the parentheses comes an opening brace, followed by the code you want to run in the function, followed by a closing brace. With your function defined, you can use it like so:

```
printMyName()
```

This prints out the following:

```
My name is Joe Howard.
```

If you suspect that you've already used a function in previous chapters, you're correct! `println`, which prints the text you give it to the console, is indeed a function. This leads nicely into the next section, in which you'll learn how to pass data to a function and get data back in return.

Function parameters

In the previous example, the function simply prints out a message. That's great, but sometimes you want to **parameterize** your function, which lets the function perform differently depending on the data passed into it via its **parameters**.

As an example, consider the following function:

```
fun printMultipleOfFive(value: Int) {
  println("$value * 5 = ${value * 5}")
}
printMultipleOfFive(10)
```

Here, you can see the definition of one parameter inside the parentheses after the function name, named `value` and of type `Int`. In any function, the parentheses contain what's known as the **parameter list**. These parentheses are required both when declaring and when invoking the function, even if the parameter list is empty. This function will print out any given multiple of five. In the example, you call the function with an **argument** of 10, so the function prints the following:

```
10 * 5 = 50
```

> **Note:** Take care not to confuse the terms "parameter" and "argument". A function declares its *parameters* in its parameter list. When you call a function, you provide values as *arguments* for the functions parameters.

You can take this one step further and make the function more general. With two parameters, the function can print out a multiple of any two values.

```
fun printMultipleOf(multiplier: Int, andValue: Int) {
  println("$multiplier * $andValue = ${multiplier * andValue}")
}
printMultipleOf(4, 2)
```

There are now two parameters inside the parentheses after the function name: one named `multiplier` and the other named `andValue`, both of type `Int`.

Parameter named arguments

Sometimes it is helpful to use **named arguments** when calling a function to make it easier to understand the purpose of each argument.

```
printMultipleOf(multiplier = 4, andValue = 2)
```

It is now immediately obvious at the *call site* of the function what purpose the arguments serve. This is especially helpful when a function has several parameters.

Parameter default values

You can also give **default values** to parameters:

```
fun printMultipleOf(multiplier: Int, value: Int = 1) {
  println("$multiplier * $value = ${multiplier * value}")
}

printMultipleOf(4)
```

The difference is the `= 1` after the second parameter, which means that if no value is provided for the second parameter, it defaults to `1`.

Therefore, this code prints the following:

```
4 * 1 = 4
```

It can be useful to have a default value when you expect a parameter to be one particular value the majority of the time, and it will simplify your code when you call the function.

Return values

All of the functions you've seen so far have performed a simple task: Printing something out. Functions can also return a value. The caller of the function can assign the return value to a variable or constant, or use it directly in an expression.

This means you can use a function to manipulate data. You simply take in data through parameters, manipulate it and then return it.

Here's how you define a function that returns a value:

```
fun multiply(number: Int, multiplier: Int): Int {
  return number * multiplier
}
```

To declare that a function returns a value, you add a `:` followed by the type of the return value after the set of parentheses and before the opening brace. In this example, the function returns an `Int`.

Inside the function, you use a `return` statement to return the value. In this example, you return the product of the two parameters.

It's also possible to return multiple values through the use of `Pairs`:

```
fun multiplyAndDivide(number: Int, factor: Int): Pair<Int, Int>
{
  return Pair(number * factor, number / factor)
}
val (product, quotient) = multiplyAndDivide(4, 2)
```

This function returns *both* the product and quotient of the two parameters by returning a `Pair` containing two `Int` values.

If a function consists solely of a single expression, you can assign the expression to the function using = while at the same time not using braces, a return type, or a `return` statement:

```
fun multiplyInferred(number: Int, multiplier: Int) = number *
multiplier
```

In such a case, the type of the function return value is *inferred* to be the type of the expression assigned to the function. In the example, the return type is inferred to be `Int` since both `number` and `multiplier` are `Int`s.

Parameters as values

Function parameters are constants by default, which means they can't be modified.

To illustrate this point, consider the following code:

```
fun incrementAndPrint(value: Int) {
  value += 1
  print(value)
}
```

This results in an error:

```
Val cannot be reassigned
```

The parameter `value` is the equivalent of a constant declared with `val` and hence cannot be reassigned. Therefore, when the function attempts to increment it, the compiler emits an error.

Usually you want this behavior. Ideally, a function doesn't alter its parameters. If it did, then you couldn't be sure of the parameters' values and you might make incorrect assumptions in your code, leading to the wrong data.

If you want a function to alter a parameter and return it, you must do so indirectly by declaring a new variable like so:

```
fun incrementAndPrint(value: Int): Int {
  val newValue = value + 1
  println(newValue)
  return newValue
}
```

> **Note:** As you'll see in a later chapter, when adding parameters to the primary constructor when defining a class, you *do* add `var` or `val` to the parameters. You do this to indicate that the parameters are properties of the class and also that they either can or cannot be reassigned.

Overloading

What if you want more than one function with the same name?

```
fun getValue(value: Int): Int {
  return value + 1
}

fun getValue(value: String): String {
  return "The value is $value"
}
```

This is called **overloading** and lets you define similar functions using a single name.

However, the compiler must still be able to tell the difference between these functions within a given scope. Whenever you call a function, it should always be clear which function you're calling.

This is usually achieved through a difference in the parameter list:

- A different number of parameters.
- Different parameter types.

> **Note**: The return type alone is not enough to distinguish two functions.

For example, defining two methods like so will result in an error:

```
fun getValue(value: String): String {
  return "The value is $value"
}

// Conflicting overloads error
fun getValue(value: String): Int {
    return value.length
}
```

The methods above both have the same name, parameter types and number of parameters. Kotlin will not be able to distinguish them!

It's worth noting that overloading should be used with care. Only use overloading for functions that are related and similar in behavior.

Mini-exercises

1. Write a function named `printFullName` that takes two strings called `firstName` and `lastName`. The function should print out the full name defined as `firstName + " " + lastName`. Use it to print out your own full name.
2. Call `printFullName` using named arguments.
3. Write a function named `calculateFullName` that returns the full name as a string. Use it to store your own full name in a constant.
4. Change `calculateFullName` to return a `Pair` containing both the full name and the length of the name. You can find a string's length by using the `length` property. Use this function to determine the length of your own full name.

Functions as variables

Functions in Kotlin are simply another data type. You can assign them to variables and constants just as you can any other type of value, such as an `Int` or a `String`.

To see how this works, consider the following function:

```
fun add(a: Int, b: Int): Int {
  return a + b
}
```

This function takes two parameters and returns the sum of their values.

You can assign this function to a variable using the **method reference operator**, `::`, like so:

```
var function = ::add
```

Here, the name of the variable is `function` and its type is inferred as `(Int, Int) -> Int` from the `add` function you assigned to it. The `function` variable is of a function type that takes two `Int` parameters and returns an `Int`.

Now you can use the `function` variable in just the same way you'd use `add`, like so:

```
function(4, 2)
```

This returns 6.

Now consider the following code:

```
fun subtract(a: Int, b: Int) : Int {
  return a - b
}
```

Here, you declare another function that takes two `Int` parameters and returns an `Int`. You can set the `function` variable from before to your new `subtract` function, because the parameter list and return type of `subtract` are compatible with the type of the `function` variable.

```
function = ::subtract
function(4, 2)
```

This time, the call to `function` returns 2.

The fact that you can assign functions to variables comes in handy because it means you can pass functions to other functions. Here's an example of this in action:

```
fun printResult(function: (Int, Int) -> Int, a: Int, b: Int) {
  val result = function(a, b)
  print(result)
}
printResult(::add, 4, 2)
```

`printResult` takes three parameters:

1. `function` is of a function type that takes two `Int` parameters and returns an `Int`, declared like so: `(Int, Int) -> Int`.
2. `a` is of type `Int`.
3. `b` is of type `Int`.

`printResult` calls the passed-in function, passing into it the two `Int` parameters. Then it prints the result to the console:

```
6
```

It's extremely useful to be able to pass functions to other functions, and it can help you write reusable code. Not only can you pass data around to manipulate, but passing functions as parameters also means you can be flexible about what code executes.

Assigning functions to variables and passing functions around as arguments is one aspect of **functional programming**, which you'll learn much more about in Chapter 21.

The land of no return

There are some functions which are designed to never, ever, return. This may sound confusing, but consider the example of a function that is designed to crash an application. This may sound strange, but if an application is about to work with corrupt data, it's often best to crash rather than continue in an unknown and potentially dangerous state.

Another example of a non-returning function is one which handles an event loop. An event loop is at the heart of every modern application which takes input from the user and displays things on a screen. The event loop services requests coming from the user, then passes these events to the application code, which in turn causes the information to be displayed on the screen. The loop then cycles back and services the next event.

These event loops are often started in an application by calling a function which is known to never return. If you start developing Android apps, think back to this paragraph when you encounter the **main thread**, also known as the **UI thread**.

Kotlin has a way to tell the compiler that a function is known to never return. You set the return type of the function to the `Nothing` type, indicating that nothing is ever returned from the function.

A crude, but honest, implementation of a function that wouldn't return would be as follows:

```
fun infiniteLoop(): Nothing {
  while (true) {

  }
}
```

You may be wondering why bother with this special return type. It's useful because by the compiler knowing that the function won't ever return, it can make certain optimizations when generating the code to call the function.

Essentially, the code which calls the function doesn't need to bother doing anything after the function call, because it knows that this function will never end before the application is terminated.

Writing good functions

There are many ways to solve problems with functions. The best (easiest to use and understand) functions do *one simple task* rather than trying to do many. This makes them easier to mix and match and assemble into more complex behaviors. Good functions also have a well defined set of inputs that produce the same output every time. This makes them easier to reason about and test in isolation. Keep these rules-of-thumb in mind as you create functions.

Before you move on, check out the challenges ahead as you'll need to fully grasp functions before understanding some of the upcoming topics! If you need help when solving them, use the solutions included in the chapter materials for a hint.

Challenges

Challenge 1: It's prime time

When acquainting yourself with a programming language, a good exercise to do is write a function to determine whether or not a number is prime. That's your first challenge.

First, write the following function:

```
fun isNumberDivisible(number: Int, divisor: Int): Boolean
```

You'll use this to determine if one number is divisible by another. It should return `true` when `number` is divisible by `divisor`.

Hint: You can use the modulo (`%`) operator to help you out here.

Next, write the main function:

```
fun isPrime(number: Int): Boolean
```

This should return `true` if `number` is prime, and `false` otherwise. A number is prime if it's only divisible by 1 and itself. You should loop through the numbers from 1 to the number and find the number's divisors.

If it has any divisors other than 1 and itself, then the number isn't prime. You'll need to use the `isNumberDivisible()` function you wrote earlier.

Use this function to check the following cases:

```
isPrime(6) // false
isPrime(13) // true
isPrime(8893) // true
```

Hint 1: Numbers less than 0 should not be considered prime. Check for this case at the start of the function and return early if the number is less than 0.

Hint 2: Use a `for` loop to find divisors. If you start at 2 and end before the number itself, then as soon as you find a divisor, you can return `false`.

Hint 3: If you want to get *really* clever, you can simply loop from 2 until you reach the square root of `number`, rather than going all the way up to `number` itself. I'll leave it as an exercise for you to figure out why. It may help to think of the number 16, whose square root is 4. The divisors of 16 are 1, 2, 4, 8 and 16.

Challenge 2: Recursive functions

In this challenge, you're going to see what happens when a function calls *itself*, a behavior called **recursion**. This may sound unusual, but it can be quite useful.

You're going to write a function that computes a value from the **Fibonacci sequence**. Any value in the sequence is the sum of the previous two values. The sequence is defined such that the first two values equal 1. That is, `fibonacci(1) = 1` and `fibonacci(2) = 1`.

Write your function using the following declaration:

```
fun fibonacci(number: Int): Int
```

Then, verify you've written the function correctly by executing it with the following numbers:

```
fibonacci(1)  // = 1
fibonacci(2)  // = 1
fibonacci(3)  // = 2
fibonacci(4)  // = 3
fibonacci(5)  // = 5
fibonacci(6)  // = 8
fibonacci(7)  // = 13
fibonacci(10) // = 55
```

Hint 1: For values of `number` less than 0, you should return 0.

Hint 2: To start the sequence, hard-code a return value of 1 when `number` equals 1 or 2.

Hint 3: For any other value, you'll need to return the sum of calling `fibonacci` with `number - 1` and `number - 2`.

> **Note**: This way of calculating the Fibonacci numbers is not terribly efficient. One technique to improve the performance is called **memoization**, which stores the results of previous calculations and reuses them when possible.

Key points

- You use a **function** to define a task, which you can execute as many times as you like without having to write the code multiple times.
- Functions can take zero or more **parameters** and optionally return a value.
- For clarity at the call site you can use named arguments when calling a function.
- Specifying default function values can make those functions easier to work with and reduce the amount of code you have to write.
- Functions can have the same name with different parameters. This is called **overloading**.
- You can assign functions to variables and pass them to other functions.
- Functions can have a special `Nothing` return type to inform Kotlin that this function will never exit.
- Strive to create functions that are clearly named and have one job with repeatable inputs and outputs.

Where to go from here?

Functions are the first step in grouping small pieces of code together into a larger unit. In the next chapter, you'll learn about **nullability**, which is an important part of Kotlin's syntactic arsenal.

Chapter 7: Nullability

By Irina Galata

All the variables and constants you've dealt with so far have had concrete values. When you had a string variable, like `var name`, it had a string value associated with it, like `"Joe Howard"`. It could have been an empty string, like `""`, but nevertheless, there was a value to which you could refer.

That's one of the built-in safety features of Kotlin: If the type says `Int` or `String`, then there's an actual integer or string there — guaranteed.

This chapter will introduce you to **nullable** types, which allow you to represent not just a value, but also the absence of a value. By the end of this chapter, you'll know why you need nullable types and how to use them safely.

Introducing null

Sometimes, it's useful to be able to represent the absence of a value. Imagine a scenario where you need to refer to a person's identifying information; you want to store the person's name, age and occupation. Name and age are both things that must have a value — everyone has them. But not everyone is employed, so the absence of a value for occupation is something you need to be able to handle.

Without knowing about nullables, this is how you might represent the person's name, age and occupation:

```
var name = "Joe Howard"
var age = 24
var occupation = "Software Developer & Author"
```

But what if I become unemployed? Maybe I've reached enlightenment and wish to live out the rest of my days on top of a mountain. This is when it would be useful to be able to refer to the absence of a value.

Why couldn't you just use an empty string? You *could*, but nullable types are a much better solution. Read on to see why.

Sentinel values

A valid value that represents a special condition, such as the absence of a value, is known as a **sentinel value**. That's what your empty string would be in the previous example.

Let's look at another example. Say your code requests something from a server, and you use a variable to store any returned error code:

```
var errorCode = 0
```

In the success case, you represent the lack of an error with a zero. That means `0` is a sentinel value. Just like the empty string for occupation, this works, but it's potentially confusing for the programmer. `0` might actually be a valid error code — or could be in the future, if the server changed how it responded. Either way, you can't be completely confident that the server didn't return an error without consulting the documentation. In these two examples, it would be much better if there were a special type that could represent the absence of a value. It would then be explicit when a value exists and when one doesn't.

Null is the name given to the absence of a value, and you're about to see how Kotlin incorporates this concept directly into the language in a rather elegant way. Some other programming languages simply use sentinel values. Some have the concept of a null value, but it is merely a synonym for zero. It is just another sentinel value.

Kotlin introduces a whole new set of types, **nullable types**, that handles the possibility a value could be `null`. If you're handling a non-null type, then you're guaranteed to have a value and don't need to worry about the existence of a valid value. Similarly, if you are using a nullable type, then you know you must handle the `null` case. It removes the ambiguity introduced by using sentinel values.

Introducing nullable types

Nullables are Kotlin's solution to the problem of representing both a value and the absence of a value. A nullable is allowed to hold either a value *or* `null`.

Think of a nullable as a box: it either contains a value, or it doesn't. When it doesn't contain a value, it's said to contain `null`. The box itself always exists; it's always there for you to open and look inside.

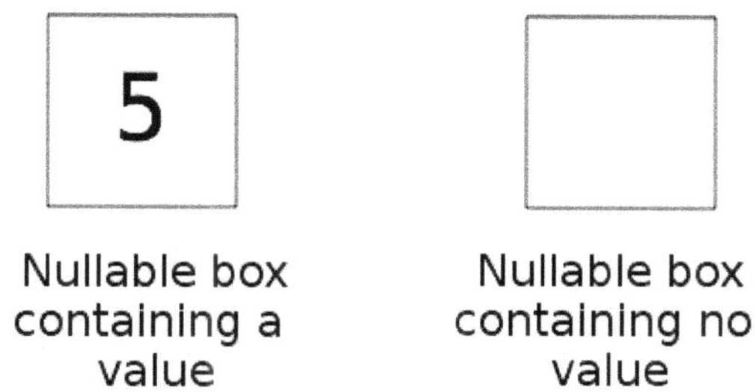

A `String` or an `Int`, on the other hand, doesn't have this box around it. Instead there's always a value, such as `"hello"` or 42. Remember, non-null types are guaranteed to have an actual value.

> **Note:** Those of you who've studied physics may be thinking about Schroedinger's cat right now. Nullables are a little bit like that, except it's not a matter of life and death!

You declare a variable of a nullable type by using the following syntax:

```
var errorCode: Int?
```

The only difference between this and a standard declaration is the question mark at the end of the type. In this case, `errorCode` is a "nullable `Int`". This means the variable itself is like a box containing either an `Int` or `null`.

> **Note:** You can add a question mark after any type to create a nullable type. For example, nullable type `String?` is a nullable `String`. In other words: a nullable box of type `String?` holds either a `String` or `null`.
>
> Also, note how a nullable type must be made explicit using a type declaration (here `: Int?`). Nullable types can never be inferred from initialization values, as those values are of a regular, non-null type.
>
> The exception is if you're assigning the value using the result of a function call. If the return type of the function is nullable, the variable will be inferred to be nullable.

Setting the value is simple. You can either set it to an `Int`, like so:

```
errorCode = 100
```

Or you can set it to `null`, like so:

```
errorCode = null
```

This diagram may help you visualize what's happening:

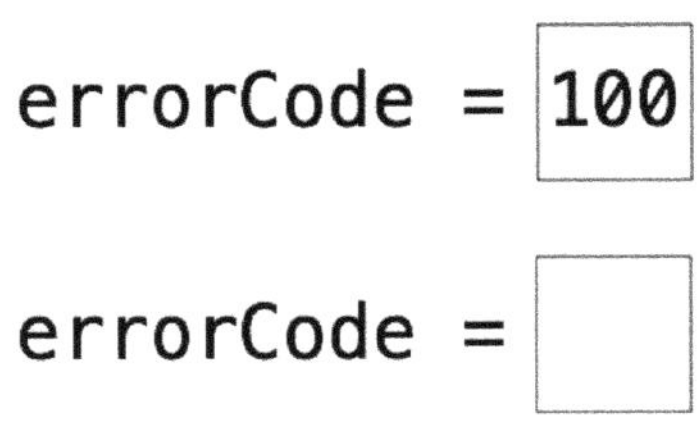

The nullable box always exists. When you assign `100` to the variable, you're filling the box with the value. When you assign `null` to the variable, you're emptying the box.

Take a few minutes to think about this concept. The box analogy will be a big help as you go through the rest of the chapter and begin to use nullables.

Mini-exercises

1. Make a nullable `String` called `myFavoriteSong`. If you have a favorite song, set it to a string representing that song. If you have more than one favorite song or no favorite, set the nullable to `null`.
2. Create a constant called `parsedInt` and set it equal to `"10".toIntOrNull()`; this will try to parse the string `"10"` and convert it to an `Int`. Check the type of `parsedInt` by clicking `toIntOrNull()` and holding `Control` + `Shift` + `P`. Why is it a nullable?
3. Change the string being parsed in the above exercise to a non-integer (try `dog` for example). What does `parsedInt` equal now?

Checking for null

It's all well and good that nullables exist, but you may be wondering how you can look inside the box and manipulate the value it contains.

In some limited cases, you can just use the nullable as if it were a non-null type.

Take a look at what happens when you print out the value of a nullable:

```
var result: Int? = 30
println(result)
```

This just prints out 30.

To see how a nullable type is different from a non-null type, see what happens if you try to use `result` in an expression as if it were a normal integer:

```
println(result + 1)
```

This code triggers an error:

```
Operator call corresponds to a dot-qualified call
'result.plus(1)' which is not allowed on a nullable receiver
'result'.
```

It doesn't work because you're trying to add an integer to a box — not to the value inside the box, but to the box itself. That doesn't make sense!

Not-null assertion operator

The error message gives an indication of the solution: It tells you that the nullable is still inside its box. You need to remove the value from its box. It's like Christmas!

Let's see how that works. Consider the following declarations:

```
var authorName: String? = "Joe Howard"
var authorAge: Int? = 24
```

There are two different methods you can use to remove these nullables from the box. The first is using the **not-null assertion operator** `!!`, which you do like so:

```
val ageAfterBirthday = authorAge!! + 1
println("After their next birthday, author will be
$ageAfterBirthday")
```

This code prints:

```
After their next birthday, author will be 25
```

Great! That's what you'd expect.

The double-exclamation mark after the variable name tells the compiler that you want to look inside the box and take out the value. The result is a value of the non-null type. This means `ageAfterBirthday` is of type `Int`, not `Int?`.

The use of the word "assertion" and the exclamation marks `!!` probably conveys a sense of danger to you, and it should. You should use not-null assertions sparingly. To see why, consider what happens when the nullable doesn't contain a value:

```
authorAge = null
println("After two birthdays, author will be ${authorAge!! +
2}")
```

This code produces the following runtime error:

```
Exception in thread "main" kotlin.KotlinNullPointerException
```

The **null-pointer exception** occurs because the variable contains no value when you try to use it. What's worse is that you get this exception at runtime rather than compile time — which means you'd only notice the exception if you happened to execute this code with some invalid input. Worse yet, if this code were inside an app, the null-pointer exception would cause the app to crash!

How can you play it safe? For that, you'll turn to the second way to get a value out of the nullable.

Smart casts

Under certain conditions, you can check whether a nullable has a value, and if so, you can use the variable as if it were not `null`:

```
var nonNullableAuthor: String
var nullableAuthor: String?

if (authorName != null) {
  nonNullableAuthor = authorName
} else {
  nullableAuthor = authorName
}
```

You'll immediately notice that there are no exclamation marks here when using the nullable `authorName`. Using nullable checks in this way is an example of Kotlin **smart casts**.

If the nullable contains a value, the `if` expression then executes the first block of code, within which Kotlin will smart cast `authorName` to a regular non-null `String`. If the nullable doesn't contain a value, then the `if` expression executes the `else` block.

You can see how using smart casts is much safer than not-null assertions, and you should use them whenever a nullable might be `null`. Not-null assertion is only appropriate when a nullable *is guaranteed* to contain a value.

Using smart casts for nullables is only helpful if the nullable being checked is not or cannot be changed after the null check occurs. For example, if the nullable is assigned to a `var` that is not-changed after the smart cast occurs and before usage or is assigned to a `val`.

Now you know how to safely look inside a nullable and extract its value, if one exists.

Mini-exercises

1. Using your `myFavoriteSong` variable from earlier, use a null check and smart cast to check if it contains a value. If it does, print out the value. If it doesn't, print `"I don't have a favorite song."`

2. Change `myFavoriteSong` to the opposite of what it is now. If it's `null`, set it to a string; if it's a string, set it to `null`. Observe how your printed result changes.

Safe calls

Suppose you want to do something with a nullable string other than print it, such as accessing its length. Using a smart cast inside a null check is overkill for such a simple use of the string. If you try to access the length as if the string were not-nullable and without a smart cast, you'll get a compiler error:

```
Only safe (?.) or non-null asserted (!!) calls are allowed on a
nullable receiver of type String?
```

The error tips you off to the solution, which is to use a **safe call** with the `?.` operator:

```
var nameLength = authorName?.length
println("Author's name has length $nameLength.")
// > Author's name has length 10.
```

By using the safe call operator, you're able to access the `length` property.

Safe calls can be chained:

```
val nameLengthPlus5 = authorName?.length?.plus(5)
println("Author's name length plus 5 is $nameLengthPlus5.")
// > Author's name length plus 5 is 15.
```

If a safe call is made on a value that is null, the expression stops evaluating the chain and returns null.

Since the result of a safe call can be `null`, expressions using safe calls on nullables return nullable types. For example, `nameLength` above is of type `Int?` and not `Int`, even though the `length` property on a string is not-nullable. The type of the entire expression is nullable.

The let() function

The safe call operator provides another way to use smart casts to work with the non-null value inside a nullable, via the `let()` function from the standard library:

```
authorName?.let {
  nonNullableAuthor = authorName
}
```

Within a `let` function call following the safe call operator, the variable becomes non-nullable, so you can access its properties without using the safe call operator:

```
authorName?.let {
  nameLength = authorName.length
}
```

You'll learn more about the syntax used to call the `let` function, called *trailing lambda* syntax, in the next section of the book.

Elvis operator

There's another handy way to get a value from a nullable. You use it when you want to get a value out of the nullable *no matter what* — and in the case of `null`, you'll use a default value.

Here's how it works:

```
var nullableInt: Int? = 10
var mustHaveResult = nullableInt ?: 0
```

The operator used on the second line `?:` is known as the **Elvis operator**, since it resembles a certain rock star when rotated by 90 degrees clockwise.

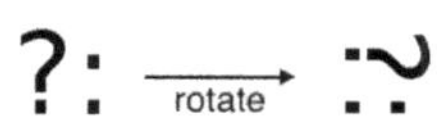

Elvis operator

Using the Elvis operator means `mustHaveResult` will equal either the value inside `nullableInt`, or `0` if `nullableInt` contains `null`. In this example, `mustHaveResult` is inferred to be of type `Int` and contains the concrete `Int` value of `10`. The previous code using the Elvis operator is equivalent to the following use of a null check and smart cast, but is more concise:

```
var nullableInt: Int? = 10
var mustHaveResult = if (nullableInt != null) nullableInt else 0
```

Set the `nullableInt` to `null`, like so:

```
nullableInt = null
mustHaveResult = nullableInt ?: 0
```

Now `mustHaveResult` equals `0`.

Challenges

You've learned the theory behind nullables and seen them in practice. Now it's your turn to play!

Challenge 1: You be the compiler

Which of the following are valid statements?

```
var name: String? = "Ray"
var age: Int = null
val distance: Float = 26.7
var middleName: String? = null
```

Challenge 2: Divide and conquer

First, create a function that returns the number of times an integer can be divided by another integer without a remainder. The function should return `null` if the division doesn't produce a whole number. Name the function `divideIfWhole`.

Then, write code that tries to extract the nullable result of the function. There should be two cases: upon success, print "`Yep, it divides $answer times`", and upon failure, print "`Not divisible :[`".

Finally, test your function:

1. Divide 10 by 2. This should print "`Yep, it divides 5 times`"
2. Divide 10 by 3. This should print "`Not divisible :[`"

Hint 1: Use the following as the start of the function signature:

```
fun divideIfWhole(value: Int, divisor: Int)
```

You'll need to add the return type, which will be a nullable!

Hint 2: You can use the modulo operator (`%`) to determine if a value is divisible by another; recall that this operation returns the remainder from the division of two numbers. For example, `10 % 2 = 0` means that 10 is divisible by 2 with no remainder, whereas `10 % 3 = 1` means that 10 is divisible by 3 with a remainder of 1.

Challenge 3: Refactor and reduce

The code you wrote in the last challenge used `if` statements. In this challenge, refactor that code to use the Elvis operator. This time, make it print `"It divides X times"` in all cases, but if the division doesn't result in a whole number, then `X` should be `0`.

Key points

- `null` represents the absence of a value.
- Non-null variables and constants must always have a non-null value.
- **Nullable** variables and constants are like boxes that can contain a value *or* be empty (`null`).
- To work with the value inside a nullable, you must typically first check that the value is not null.
- The safest ways to work with a nullable's value is by using **safe calls** or the **Elvis operator**. Use **not-null assertions** only when appropriate, as they could produce a runtime error.

Where to go from here?

Nullables are a core Kotlin feature that helps make the language safe and easy to use. They force you to consciously choose when values should and should not be nullable, and you should prefer the latter as the default case. You'll find yourself using them when needed, making your code safe by ensuring that the absence of values is handled explicitly.

That is something that you'll come to admire over the course of your Kotlin experience! In particular, look forward to using nullables in Section II, where you'll learn about **collections** and **lambdas**.

Section II: Collections & Lambdas

So far, you've mostly seen data in the form of single elements. Although pairs and triples can have multiple pieces of data, you're limited to combining only two or three items with them. In this section, you'll learn about **collection types** in Kotlin. Collections are flexible "containers" that let you store any number of values together.

The chapters in this section will give you the foundation that you need to organize your data and code so that you can begin to do more sophisticated programming in Kotlin!

Chapter 8: Arrays & Lists

By Irina Galata

As discussed in the introduction to this section, collections are flexible "containers" that let you store any number of values together. Two of the most common collections types in Kotlin are **arrays** and **lists**.

Arrays

Arrays in Kotlin correspond to the basic array type available in Java. Arrays are typed, just like regular variables and constants, and store multiple values in a contiguous portion of memory.

Before you create your first array, take some time to consider in detail what an array is and why you might want to use one.

What is an array?

An array is an ordered collection of values of the same type. The elements in the array are **zero-indexed**, which means the index of the first element is 0, the index of the second element is 1, and so on. Knowing this, you can work out that the last element's index is the number of values in the array less 1.

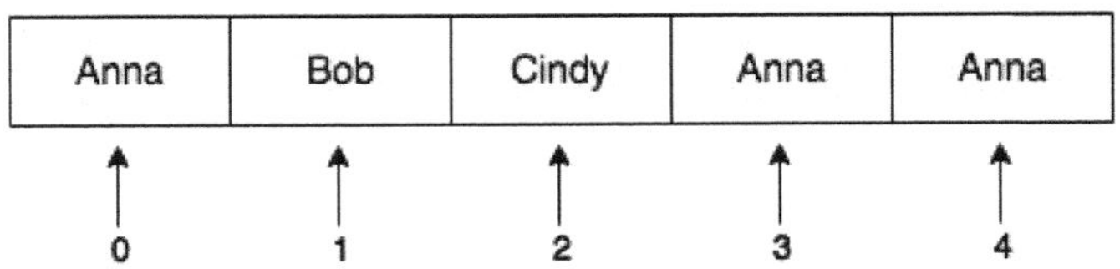

There are five elements in this array, at indices 0–4.

All values are of type `String`, so you can't add non-string types to an array that holds strings. Notice that the same value can appear multiple times.

When are arrays useful?

Arrays are useful when you want to store your items in a particular order. You may want the elements sorted, or you may need to fetch elements by index without iterating through the entire array.

For example, if you were storing high score data, then order would matter. You would want the highest score to come first in the list (i.e. at index 0) with the next-highest score after that, and so on.

Creating arrays

The easiest way to create an array is by using a function from the Kotlin standard library, `arrayOf()`. This is a concise way to provide array values.

```
val evenNumbers = arrayOf(2, 4, 6, 8)
```

Since the array only contains integers, Kotlin infers the type of `evenNumbers` to be an array of `Int` values. This type is written as `Array<Int>`. The type inside the angle brackets defines the type of values the array can store, which the compiler will enforce when you add elements to the array. If you try to add a string, for example, the compiler will return an error and your code won't compile. This syntax for the array type is an example of a **type argument** or **generic**, which you'll learn more about in a later chapter.

It's also possible to create an array with all of its values set to a default value:

```
val fiveFives = Array(5, { 5 }) // 5, 5, 5, 5, 5
```

You'll learn more about the `{ 5 }` syntax in the chapter on **lambdas**.

As with any type, it's good practice to declare arrays that aren't going to change as constants using `val`. For example, consider this array:

```
val vowels = arrayOf("a", "e", "i", "o", "u")
```

`vowels` is an array of strings and its values can't be changed. But that's fine, since the list of vowels doesn't tend to change very often!

Arrays of primitive types

When using `arrayOf()` and creating arrays with types such as `Array<Int>`, the resulting array is a list of object types. In particular, if you're running on the JVM, the integer type will be the boxed `Integer` class and not the primitive `int` type. Using primitive types over their boxed counterparts will consume less memory and result in better performance. Unfortunately you can't use primitives with lists (covered in the next section), so it will be up to you to determine on a case by case basis if the trade off is worth it!

The Kotlin standard library contains functions other than `arrayOf()` that make it possible to create arrays that correspond to arrays of primitive types. For example, you can create an array of odd numbers as follows:

```
val oddNumbers = intArrayOf(1, 3, 5, 7)
```

When running Kotlin on the JVM, the `oddNumbers` array is compiled to a Java array of type `int[]`.

Other standard library functions include `floatArrayOf()`, `doubleArrayOf()`, and `booleanArrayOf()`. These various functions create arrays of type `IntArray`, `FloatArray`, `DoubleArray`, etc. You can also pass a number into the constructor for these types, for example, to create an array of zeros.

```
val zeros = DoubleArray(4) // 0.0, 0.0, 0.0, 0.0
```

You can convert between the boxed and primitive arrays using functions like `toIntArray()`.

```
val otherOddNumbers = arrayOf(1, 3, 5, 7).toIntArray()
```

The type of `otherOddNumbers` is `IntArray` and not `Array<Int>`.

Arguments to main()

The `main()` function is the entry point to Kotlin programs. From Kotlin 1.3 onwards, the `main()` function has an optional parameter named `args` that is an `Array<String>`:

```
fun main(args: Array<String>) {
}
```

When running a Kotlin program from the command-line, you can send arguments to `main()` like you would a typical command-line program.

Since we're using IntelliJ IDEA in the book, you can send arguments to `main()` using the project configuration, accessed via the **Edit Configurations...** menu in the IntelliJ toolbar:

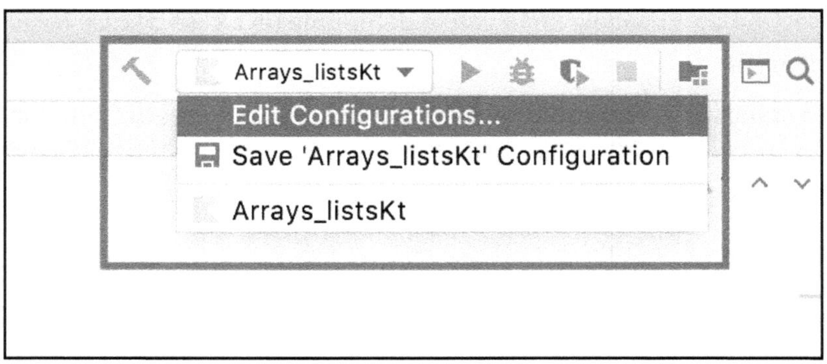

This will pop up the **Run/Debug Configurations** window. Make sure your configuration is selected in the panel on the left, then add arguments to the **Program arguments** field on the right and click **OK**:

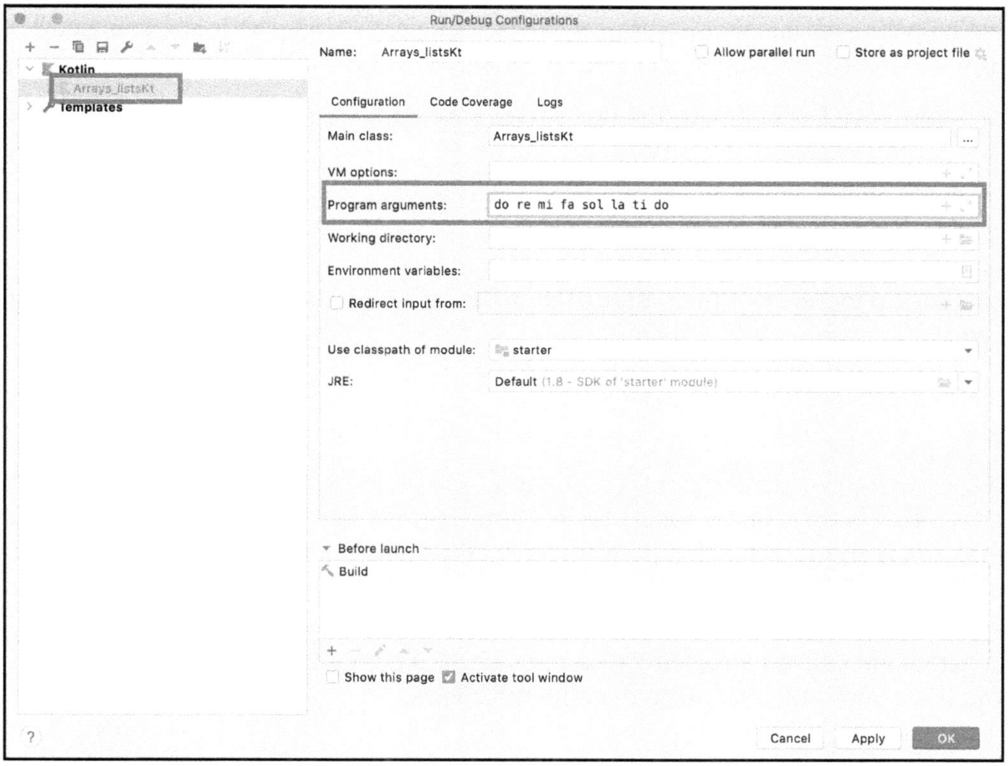

Iterating over an array

To see the arguments passed to `main()`, you can use the `for` loop you read about in Chapter 5, "Advanced Control Flow".

However, for iterating over an array, instead of using a count and a range in the `for` loop, you give a name like `arg` to each element of the array `args`:

```
for (arg in args) {
  println(arg)
}
// do
// re
// mi
// fa
// sol
// la
```

```
// ti
// do
```

The value of `arg` is updated for each iteration of the loop. There is one iteration of the loop for each element in the array `args`. Using `println(arg)` in the loop body prints each of the arguments passed to the `main()` function.

An alternative form of iteration uses `forEach` as a call on the array:

```
args.forEach { arg ->
    println(arg)
}
```

You'll learn more about the syntax used in the call to `forEach`, called *trailing lambda* syntax, in Chapter 10, "Lambdas".

Lists

A type that is very similar conceptually to an array is a **list**. Like in Java, the **List** type in Kotlin is an **interface** that has concrete realizations in types such as `ArrayList`, `LinkedList` and others. Arrays are typically more efficient than lists in terms of raw performance, but lists have the additional feature of being **dynamically-sized**. That is, arrays are of fixed-size, but lists can be setup to grow and shrink as needed, as you'll see later when learning about mutable lists.

Creating lists

Like with arrays, the standard library has a function to create a list.

```
val innerPlanets = listOf("Mercury", "Venus", "Earth", "Mars")
```

The type of `innerPlanets` is inferred to be `List<String>`, with `String` being another example of a type argument. So `innerPlanets` can be passed into any function that needs a `List`. Under the hood, the type used to store `innerPlanets` is an `ArrayList`. If, for some reason, you explicitly want `innerPlanets` to have the type `ArrayList`, there is a different standard library function you can use:

```
val innerPlanetsArrayList =
  arrayListOf("Mercury", "Venus", "Earth", "Mars")
```

An empty list can be created by passing no arguments into `list()`. Because the compiler isn't able to infer a type from this, you need to use a type declaration to make the type explicit:

```
val subscribers: List<String> = listOf()
```

You could also put the the type argument on the function:

```
val subscribers = listOf<String>()
```

Since the list returned from `listOf()` is immutable, you won't be able to do much with this empty list. Empty lists become more useful as a starting point for a list when they're **mutable**.

None of `innerPlanets`, `innerPlanetsArrayList` or `subscribers` can be altered once created. For that, you'll need to instead create a mutable list.

Mutable lists

Once again, the standard library has a function to use here.

```
val outerPlanets =
  mutableListOf("Jupiter", "Saturn", "Uranus", "Neptune")
```

You've made `outerPlanets` a mutable list, just in case Planet X is ever discovered in the outer solar system. You can create an empty mutable list by passing no arguments to the function:

```
val exoPlanets = mutableListOf<String>()
```

You'll see later in the chapter how to add and remove elements from a mutable list.

Accessing elements

Being able to create arrays and lists is useless unless you know how to fetch values from them. In this section, you'll learn several different ways to access the elements. The syntax is similar for both arrays and lists.

Using properties and methods

Imagine you're creating a game of cards, and you want to store the players' names in a list. The list will need to change as players join or leave the game, so you need to declare a mutable list:

```
val players = mutableListOf("Alice", "Bob", "Cindy", "Dan")
```

In this example, `players` is a mutable list because you used the `mutableListOf()` standard library function.

Before the game starts, you need to make sure there are enough players. You can use the `isEmpty()` *method* to check if there's at least one player:

```
print(players.isEmpty())
// > false
```

The list isn't empty, but you need at least two players to start a game. You can get the number of players using the `size` *property*:

```
if (players.size < 2) {
  println("We need at least two players!")
} else {
  println("Let's start!")
}
// > Let's start!
```

> **Note**: You'll learn all about properties and methods in Chapter 11, "Classes," and even more in Chapters 13 and 14. For now, just think of properties as variables that are built into values. To access a property, place a dot after the name of the constant or variable that holds the value and follow it by the name of the property you want to access. Similarly, think of methods as functions that are built in to values.

It's time to start the game! You decide that the order of play is by the order of names in the list. How would you get the first player's name?

Lists provide the `first()` method to fetch the first object of a list:

```
var currentPlayer = players.first()
```

Printing the value of `currentPlayer` reveals an interesting question:

```
println(currentPlayer) // > Alice
```

What would be printed if the `players` list were empty? It turns out trying to do so will throw an exception, so be careful when using some of these properties and methods on lists!

Similarly, lists have a `last()` method that returns the last value in a list, or throws an exception if the list is empty:

```
println(players.last()) // > Dan
```

Another way to get values from a list is by calling `minOrNull()`. This method returns the element with the lowest *value* in the list — not the lowest index!

If the array contained strings, then it would return the string that's the lowest in alphabetical order, which in this case is `"Alice"`:

```
val minPlayer = players.minOrNull()
minPlayer.let {
  println("$minPlayer will start") // > Alice will start
}
```

Instead of throwing an exception if no minimum can be determined, `minOrNull()` returns a nullable type, so you need to check if the value returned is null.

Obviously, `first()` and `minOrNull()` will not always return the same value. For example:

```
println(arrayOf(2, 3, 1).first())
// > 2
println(arrayOf(2, 3, 1).min())
// > 1
```

As you might have guessed, lists also have a `maxOrNull()` method.

```
val maxPlayer = players.maxOrNull()
if (maxPlayer != null) {
  println("$maxPlayer is the MAX") // > Dan is the MAX
}
```

> **Note**: The `size` property and the `first()`, `last()`, `minOrNull()` and `maxOrNull()` methods aren't unique to arrays or lists. Every collection type has such properties and methods, in addition to a plethora of others. You'll learn more about this behavior when you read about interfaces in Chapter 17, "Interfaces."

The methods seen so far are helpful if you want to get the first, last, minimum or maximum elements. But what if the element you want can't be obtained with one of these methods?

Using indexing

The most convenient way to access elements in an array or list is by using the indexing syntax. This syntax lets you access any value directly by using its index inside square brackets:

```
val firstPlayer = players[0]
println("First player is $firstPlayer")
// > First player is Alice
```

Because arrays and lists are zero-indexed, you use index 0 to fetch the first object.

The indexing syntax is equivalent to calling `get()` on the array or list and passing in the index as an argument.

```
val secondPlayer = players.get(1)
```

You can use a greater index to get the next elements in the array or list, but if you try to access an index that's beyond the size of the array or list, you'll get a runtime error.

```
val player = players[4] // > IndexOutOfBoundsException
```

You receive this error because `players` contains only four strings. Index 4 represents the fifth element, but there *is* no fifth element in this list.

Using ranges to slice

You can use the `slice()` method with ranges to fetch more than a single value from an array or list.

For example, if you'd like to get the next two players, you could do this:

```
val upcomingPlayersSlice = players.slice(1..2)
println(upcomingPlayersSlice.joinToString()) // > Bob, Cindy
```

The range you used is `1..2`, which represents the second and third items in the array. You can use an index here as long as the start value is smaller than or equal to the end value and both are within the bounds of the array. If the start value is greater than the end value, the result will be empty.

The object returned from the `slice()` method is a separate array or list from the original, so making modifications to the slice does not affect the original array or list.

Checking for an element

You can check if there's at least one occurrence of a specific element by using the `in` operator, which returns `true` if it finds the element, and `false` otherwise.

You can use this strategy to write a function that checks if a given player is in the game:

```
fun isEliminated(player: String): Boolean {
  return player !in players
}
```

You're using the `!` operator to see if a `player` is *not* in `players`. Now you can use this function any time you need to check if a player has been eliminated:

```
println(isEliminated("Bob")) // > false
```

The `in` operator corresponds to the `contains()` method. You can test for the existence of an element in a specific range using `slice()` and `contains()` together:

```
players.slice(1..3).contains("Alice") // false
```

Now that you can get data *out* of your arrays and lists, it's time to look at mutable lists and how to change their values.

Modifying lists

You can make all kinds of changes to mutable lists, such as adding and removing elements, updating existing values, and moving elements around into a different order. In this section, you'll see how to work with the list to match up with what's going on in your game.

Appending elements

If new players want to join the game, they need to sign up and add their names to the list. Eli is the first player to join the existing four players.

You can add Eli to the end of the array using the `add()` method:

```
players.add("Eli")
```

If you try to add anything other than a string, the compiler will show an error. Remember, lists can only store values of the same type. Also, `add()` only works with mutable lists.

The next player to join the game is Gina. You can add her to the game another way, by using the += operator:

```
players += "Gina"
```

The right-hand side of this expression is a single element: the string `"Gina"`. By using +=, you're adding the element to the end of `players`. Now the list looks like this:

```
println(players.joinToString())
// > "Alice", "Bob", "Cindy", "Dan", "Eli", "Gina"
```

Here, you added a single element to the array, but you can see how easy it would be to add *multiple* items using the += operator by adding more names after Gina's.

While arrays are of fixed-size, you *can* in fact use the += operator with an array that is declared as `var`.

```
var array = arrayOf(1, 2, 3)
array += 4
println(array.joinToString()) // > 1, 2, 3, 4
```

But beware that you are not actually appending the value onto the existing array, but instead creating an entirely new array that has the additional element and assigning the new array to the original variable.

Inserting elements

An unwritten rule of this card game is that the players' names have to be in alphabetical order. This list is missing a player that starts with the letter F. Luckily, Frank has just arrived. You want to add him to the list between Eli and Gina. To do that, you can use a variant of the `add()` method that accepts an index as the first argument:

```
players.add(5, "Frank")
```

The first argument defines where you want to add the element. Remember that the list is zero-indexed, so index 5 is Gina's index, causing her to move up as Frank takes her place.

Removing elements

During the game, the other players caught Cindy and Gina cheating. They should be removed from the game! You can remove them by name using the `remove()` method:

```
val wasPlayerRemoved = players.remove("Gina")
println("It is $wasPlayerRemoved that Gina was removed")
// > It is true that Gina was removed
```

This method does two things: It removes the element and then returns a Boolean indicating whether the removal was successful, so that you can make sure the cheater has been removed!

To remove Cindy from the game, you need to know the exact index where her name is stored. Looking at the list of players, you see that she's third in the list, so her index is 2. You can remove Cindy using `removeAt()`.

```
val removedPlayer = players.removeAt(2)
println("$removedPlayer was removed") // > Cindy was removed
```

Unlike `remove()`, `removeAt()` returns the element that was removed from the list. You could then add that element to a list of cheaters!

But how would you get the index of an element if you didn't already know it? There's a method for that! `indexOf()` returns the *first index* of the element, because the list might contain multiple copies of the same value. If the method doesn't find the element, it returns `-1`.

Mini-exercise

Use `indexOf()` to determine the position of the element `"Dan"` in `players`.

Updating elements

Frank has decided everyone should call him Franklin from now on. You could remove the value `"Frank"` from the list and then add `"Franklin"`, but that's too much work for a simple task. Instead, you should use the indexing syntax to update the name.

```
println(players.joinToString())
// > "Alice", "Bob", "Dan", "Eli", "Frank"
players[4] = "Franklin"
println(players.joinToString())
// > "Alice", "Bob", "Dan", "Eli", "Franklin"
```

Be careful to not use an index beyond the bounds of the list, or your code will crash.

As the game continues, some players are eliminated, and new ones come to replace them. You can use indexing to replace the old players with the new:

```
players[3] = "Anna"
players.sort()
println(players.joinToString()) // > "Alice", "Anna", Bob",
"Dan", "Franklin"
```

This code replaces the player Eli with the player Anna. You then call `sort()` on the list to make sure the list remains sorted in alphabetical order.

When updating an element, the indexing syntax is equivalent to calling `set()` on the list.

```
players.set(3, "Anna")
```

As IntelliJ IDEA will tell you, using the indexing syntax is generally preferred over using `get()` and `set()` on the collection types.

Note that while arrays are of fixed size and can otherwise not be changed, you *can* update the elements of an array using indexing syntax.

```
val arrayOfInts = arrayOf(1, 2, 3)
arrayOfInts[0] = 4
println(arrayOfInts.joinToString()) // > 4, 2, 3
```

Iterating through a list

It's getting late, so the players decide to stop for the night and continue tomorrow. In the meantime, you'll keep their scores in a separate list. You'll investigate a better approach for this when you learn about maps, but for now you can continue to use lists:

```
val scores = listOf(2, 2, 8, 6, 1)
```

Before the players leave, you want to print the names of those still in the game. Like for arrays, you can do this using the `for` loop you read about in Chapter 5, "Advanced Control Flow":

```
for (player in players) {
  println(player)
}
// > Alice
// > Anna
// > Bob
// > Dan
// > Franklin
```

This code goes over all the elements of `players`, from index 0 up to `players.size - 1` and prints their values. In the first iteration, `player` is equal to the first element of the list; in the second iteration, it's equal to the second element of the list; and so on, until the loop has printed all the elements in the list.

If you need the index of each element, you can iterate over the return value of the list's `withIndex()` method, which can be *destructed* to each element's index and value:

```
for ((index, player) in players.withIndex()) {
  println("${index + 1}. $player")
}
// > 1. Alice
// > 2. Anna
// > 3. Bob
```

```
// > 4. Dan
// > 5. Franklin
```

Now you can use the technique you've just learned to write a function that takes a list of integers as its input and returns the sum of its elements:

```
fun sumOfElements(list: List<Int>): Int {
  var sum = 0
  for (number in list) {
    sum += number
  }
  return sum
}
```

You could use this function to calculate the sum of the players' scores:

```
println(sumOfElements(scores))  // > 19
```

Mini-exercise

Write a `for` loop that prints the players' names and scores.

Nullability and collection types

When working with arrays, lists, and other collection types, special consideration should be given to nullability. Are the elements of a collection nullable, for example, or is the collection itself nullable?

A nullable list can be created as follows:

```
var nullableList: List<Int>? = listOf(1, 2, 3, 4)
```

The individual elements are of type `Int` and cannot be null, but the list itself *can* be null.

```
nullableList = null
```

On the other hand, you can create a list with elements that are nullable by shifting nullability to the type argument:

```
var listOfNullables: List<Int?> = listOf(1, 2, null, 4)
```

If you try to set the list itself to null, you'll get a compiler error.

```
listOfNullables = null // Error: Null can not be a value of a
non-null type
```

You can go to the extreme with nullability by letting both the list and its elements be null.

```
var nullableListOfNullables: List<Int?>? = listOf(1, 2, null, 4)
nullableListOfNullables = null
```

As with all nullable types, you should always be conscious of when you should allow the collection or its elements to be null.

Challenges

Check out the following challenges to test your knowledge of Kotlin arrays and lists. As always, you can check out the solutions in the materials for this chapter.

1. Which of the following 1-10 are valid statements?

```
1. val array1 = Array<Int>()
2. val array2 = arrayOf()
3. val array3: Array<String> = arrayOf()
```

For the next three statements, `array4` has been declared as:

```
val array4 = arrayOf(1, 2, 3)
```

```
4. println(array4[0])
5. println(array4[5])
6. array4[0] = 4
```

For the final five statements, `array5` has been declared as:

```
val array5 = arrayOf(1, 2, 3)
```

```
7. array5[0] = array5[1]
8. array5[0] = "Six"
9. array5 += 6
10. for item in array5 { println(item) }
```

2. Write a function that removes the first occurrence of a given integer from a list of integers. This is the signature of the function:

```
fun removeOne(item: Int, list: List<Int>): List<Int>
```

3. Write a function that removes all occurrences of a given integer from a list of integers. This is the signature of the function:

```
fun remove(item: Int, list: List<Int>): List<Int>
```

4. Arrays and lists have a `reverse()` method that reverses all the elements in-place, that is, within the original array or list. Write a function that does a similar thing, without using `reverse()`, and returns a new array with the elements of the original array in reverse order. This is the signature of the function:

```
fun reverse(array: Array<Int>): Array<Int>
```

5. The function below returns a random number between `from` (inclusive) and the `to` (exclusive):

```
import java.util.Random
val random = Random()
fun rand(from: Int, to: Int) : Int {
 return random.nextInt(to - from) + from
}
```

Use it to write a function that shuffles the elements of an array in random order. This is the signature of the function:

```
fun randomized(array: Array<Int>): Array<Int>
```

6. Write a function that calculates the minimum and maximum value in an array of integers. Calculate these values yourself; don't use the methods `min` and `max`. Return `null` if the given array is empty.

This is the signature of the function:

```
fun minMax(numbers: Array<Int>): Pair<Int, Int>?
```

Hint: You can use the `Int.MIN_VALUE` and `Int.MAX_VALUE` constants within the function.

Key points

- **Arrays** are ordered collections of values of the same type.
- There are special classes such as `IntArray` created as arrays of Java primitive types.
- **Lists** are similar to arrays but have the additional feature of being dynamically-sized.
- You can add, remove, update, and insert elements into **mutable lists**.
- Use **indexing** or one of many methods to access and update elements.
- Be wary of accessing an index that's out of bounds.
- You can iterate over the elements of an array or list using a `for` loop or using `forEach`.
- You can check for elements in an array or list using `in`.
- Special consideration should be given when working with nullable lists and lists with nullable elements.

Where to go from here?

Now that you've learned about the array and list collection types in Kotlin, you can now move on to learning about two other common collection types: **maps** and **sets**.

Chapter 9: Maps & Sets

By Irina Galata

A map is an unordered collection of pairs, where each pair is comprised of a **key** and a **value**.

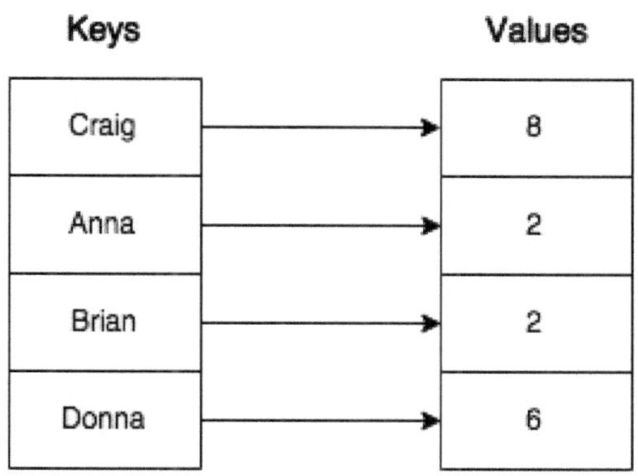

As shown in the diagram above, keys are unique. The same key can't appear twice in a map, but different keys may point to the same value. All keys have to be of the same type, and all values have to be of the same type.

Maps are useful when you want to look up values by means of an identifier. For example, the table of contents of this book maps chapter names to their page numbers, making it easy to skip to the chapter you want to read.

How is this different from an array? With an array, you can only fetch a value by its index, which has to be an integer, and all indexes have to be sequential. In a map, the keys can be of any type and are generally in no particular order.

Creating maps

The easiest way to create a map is by using the standard library `mapOf()` function. This function takes a list of Kotlin `Pair` objects separated by commas:

```
var yearOfBirth = mapOf(
  "Anna" to 1990,
  "Brian" to 1991,
  "Craig" to 1992,
  "Donna" to 1993
)
```

The Kotlin `Pair` objects are created using the infix `to` function. Note that `Map<K, V>` is an *interface*, which you'll learn more about later on. The concrete type that is created depends on which standard library function is called. The `mapOf()` function returns an immutable map of fixed size.

For your card game from an earlier chapter, instead of using the two arrays to map players to their scores, you can use a map:

```
var namesAndScores = mutableMapOf(
  "Anna" to 2,
  "Brian" to 2,
  "Craig" to 8,
  "Donna" to 6
)
println(namesAndScores) // > {Anna=2, Brian=2, Craig=8, Donna=6}
```

In this example, the type of the map is inferred to be `MutableMap<String, Int>`. This means `namesAndScores` is a map with strings as keys and integers as values, that is, a map from strings to integers.

When you print the map, you see there's generally no particular order to the pairs. Remember that, unlike arrays, maps are not guaranteed to be ordered!

You can pass in no arguments to the standard library functions to create an empty map like so:

```
namesAndScores = mutableMapOf()
```

...or create a new empty map by calling a map constructor:

```
var pairs = HashMap<String, Int>()
```

Specifying the type on the variable is not required here, since the compiler can infer the type from the constructor being called.

> **Note**: If you're following along, you'll need to add the import, `import java.util.HashMap`, to the top of the file to use `HashMap`.

When you create a map, you can define its capacity:

```
pairs = HashMap<String, Int>(20)
```

This is an easy way to improve performance when you have an idea of how much data the map needs to store.

Accessing values

As with arrays, there are several ways to access map values.

Using the index operator

Maps support using square brackets to access values. Unlike arrays, you don't access a value by its index but rather by its key. For example, if you want to get Anna's score, you would type:

```
namesAndScores = mutableMapOf(
  "Anna" to 2,
  "Brian" to 2,
  "Craig" to 8,
  "Donna" to 6
)
// Restore the values

println(namesAndScores["Anna"])
// > 2
```

The map will check if there's a pair with the key `Anna`, and if there is, return its value. If the map doesn't find the key, it will return `null`.

```
namesAndScores["Greg"] // null
```

With arrays, out-of-bounds index access causes a runtime error, but not so for maps.

Index access on maps by the key is really powerful. You can find out if a specific player is in the game without having to iterate over all the keys, as you must do when you use an array.

Using properties and methods

In addition to using indexing, you can also use the `get()` function to access a value:

```
println(namesAndScores.get("Craig"))
// > 8
```

In fact, using the index for a map is translated to a call the `get()` operator function.

Maps share many of the same properties and methods of other collection types. For example, both arrays and maps have `isEmpty()` and `size` members:

```
namesAndScores.isEmpty() // false
namesAndScores.size      // 4
```

Modifying mutable maps

It's easy enough to create maps and access their contents — but what about modifying them? You'll need a mutable map to do so.

Adding pairs

Bob wants to join the game. Take a look at his details before you let him join:

```
val bobData = mutableMapOf(
  "name" to "Bob",
  "profession" to "CardPlayer",
  "country" to "USA"
)
```

This map is of type `MutableMap<String, String>`. Imagine you received more information about Bob and you wanted to add it to the map. This is how you'd do it:

```
bobData.put("state", "CA")
```

There's even a shorter way to add pairs, using subscripting:

```
bobData["city"] = "San Francisco"
```

Bob's a professional card player. So far, he sounds like a good addition to your roster.

Mini-exercise

Write a function that prints a given player's city and state.

Updating values

It appears that in the past, Bob was caught cheating when playing cards. He's not just a professional — he's a card shark! He asks you to change his name and profession so no one will recognize him.

Because Bob seems eager to change his ways, you agree. First, you change his name from Bob to Bobby:

```
bobData.put("name", "Bobby") // Bob
```

You saw this method above when you read about adding pairs. Why does it return the string `Bob`? `put(key: K, value: V): V?` replaces the value of the given key with the new value and returns the old value. If the key doesn't exist, this method will add a new pair and return `null`.

As with adding, you can do this with less code by using subscripting:

```
bobData["profession"] = "Mailman"
```

Like `put()`, this code updates the value for this key or, if the key doesn't exist, creates a new pair.

You can also use the += infix operator to add a pair:

```
val pair = "nickname" to "Bobby D"
bobData += pair

println(bobData)
// > {name=Bobby, profession=Mailman, country=USA, state=CA,
city=San Francisco, nickname=Bobby D}
```

Removing pairs

Bob — er, sorry — *Bobby*, still doesn't feel safe, and he wants you to remove all information about his whereabouts:

```
bobData.remove("city")
bobData.remove("state", "CA")
```

This first call to `remove()` will remove the key `city` and its associated value from the map. The second call will remove the key only if the value matches the second argument.

Iterating through maps

The `for-in` loop works when you want to iterate over a map. But since the items in a map are pairs, you need to use a destructuring declaration:

```
for ((player, score) in namesAndScores) {
  println ("$player - $score")
}
// > Anna - 2
// > Brian - 2
// > Craig - 8
// > Donna - 6
```

It's also possible to iterate over just the keys:

```
for (player in namesAndScores.keys) {
  print("$player, ") // no newline
}
println() // print a newline
// > Anna, Brian, Craig, Donna,
```

You can iterate over just the values in the same manner with the `values` property of the map.

Running time for map operations

In order to be able to examine how maps work, you need to understand what **hashing** is and how it works. Hashing is the process of transforming a value — `String`, `Int`, `Double`, `Boolean`, etc — to a numeric value, known as the *hash value*. This value can then be used to quickly look up the values in a *hash table*.

The Kotlin Any type defines a `hashCode()` method that will return a hash value for any object. All basic types already have a hash value. Here's an example:

```
println("some string".hashCode())
// > 1395333309

println(1.hashCode())
// > 1
println(false.hashCode())
// > 1237
```

The hash value has to be deterministic — meaning that a given value must *always* return the same hash value. No matter how many times you calculate the hash value for `some string`, it will always give the same value.

You should never save a hash value, however, as there is no guarantee it will be the same from run-to-run of your program. Here's the performance of various hash map operations. This great performance hinges on having a good hashing function that avoids value collisions. If you have a poor hashing function, all of the operations below degenerate to linear time, or $O(n)$ performance. Fortunately, the built-in types have great, general purpose `hashCode()` implementations.

Accessing elements: Getting the value for a key is a constant time operation, or $O(1)$.

Inserting elements: To insert an element, the map needs to calculate the hash value of the key and then store data based on that hash. These are all $O(1)$ operations.

Deleting elements: Again, the map needs to calculate the hash value to know exactly where to find the element, and then remove it. This is also an $O(1)$ operation.

Searching for an element: As mentioned above, accessing an element has constant running time, so the complexity for searching is also $O(1)$.

While all of these running times compare favorably to arrays, remember that you generally lose order information when using maps.

For performance-critical code, `HashMap<K, V>` should be used via `hashMapOf()`, instead of `mapOf()`.

Sets

A set is an unordered collection of unique values of the same type. This can be extremely useful when you want to ensure that an item doesn't appear more than once in your collection, and when the order of your items isn't important.

Creating sets

You can declare a set explicitly by using the standard library `setOf()` function:

```
val names = setOf("Anna", "Brian", "Craig", "Anna")
println(names)
// > [Anna, Brian, Craig]
```

Notice in the above example that the duplicate `"Anna"` is not included in the set.

You can create an empty set by calling a constructor:

```
val hashSet = HashSet<Int>()
```

Set from arrays

Sets can be created from arrays. Consider this example:

```
val someArray = arrayOf(1, 2, 3, 1)
```

You can create a set from this array by passing the array into a standard library set function and using the **spread operator**:

```
var someSet = mutableSetOf(*someArray)
```

The array is spread into its elements when creating the set. You don't have to explicitly declare the variable as a `MutableSet<Int>`, since the type is inferred from the argument passed into the function.

To see the most important feature of a set in action, print the set you just created:

```
println(someSet) // > [1, 2, 3]
```

Although you created the set with two instances of the value `1`, that value only appears once. Remember, a set's values must be unique.

Accessing elements

You can use `contains()` to check for the existence of a specific element:

```
println(someSet.contains(1))
// > true
```

You can also use the `in` to check for existence:

```
println(4 in someSet)
// > false
```

You can also use the `first()` and `last()` methods, which return one of the elements in the set. However, because sets are unordered, you won't always know exactly which item you'll get.

Finally, you can iterate through a set using a for loop the same way as you do for other collections:

```
for (number in someSet) {
  println(number)
}
```

Adding and removing elements

You can use `add()` to add elements to a set. If the element already exists, the method does nothing.

```
someSet.add(5)
```

You can remove the element from the set like this:

```
val removedOne = someSet.remove(1)
println(removedOne) // > true

println(someSet)
// > [2, 3, 5]
```

`remove()` returns `true` if the element was removed from the set, or `false` otherwise.

Running time for set operations

Sets have a very similar implementations to those of maps, and they also require the elements to have hash values. The `HashSet` running time of all the operations is identical to those of a `HashMap`.

Challenges

Check out the following challenges to test your knowledge of maps and sets.

1. Which of the following are valid statements?

```
1. val map1: Map<Int to Int> = emptyMap()
2. val map2 = emptyMap()
3. val map3: Map<Int, Int> = emptyMap()
```

For the next four statements, use the following map:

```
val map4 = mapOf("One" to 1, "Two" to 2, "Three" to 3)
```

```
4. map4[1]
5. map4["One"]
6. map4["Zero"] = 0
7. map4[0] = "Zero"
```

For the next three statements, use the following map:

```
val map5 = mutableMapOf(
    "NY" to "New York",
    "CA" to "California"
)
```

```
8. map5["NY"]
9. map5["WA"] = "Washington"
10. map5["CA"] = null
```

2. Given a map with two-letter state codes as keys, and the full state names as values, write a function that prints all the states with names longer than eight characters. For example, for the map `mapOf("NY" to "New York", "CA" to "California")`, the output would be `California`.

3. Write a function that combines two maps into one. If a certain key appears in both maps, ignore the pair from the first maps. This is the function's signature:

```
fun mergeMaps(
 map1: Map<String, String>,
 map2: Map<String, String>
): Map<String, String>
```

4. Declare a function `occurrencesOfCharacters` that calculates which characters occur in a string, as well as how often each of these characters occur. Return the result as a map. This is the function signature:

```
fun occurrencesOfCharacters(text: String): Map<Char, Int>
```

Hint: `String` is a collection of characters that you can iterate over with a for statement.

Bonus: To make your code shorter, maps have a special function that lets you add a default value if it is not found in the map. For example, `map.getOrDefault('a', defaultValue = 0)` returns 0 for the character 'a' if it is not found, instead of simply returning `null`.

5. Write a function that returns `true` if all of the values of a map are unique. Use a set to test uniqueness. This is the function signature:

```
fun isInvertible(map: Map<String, Int>): Boolean
```

6. Given the map:

```
val nameTitleLookup: Map<String, String?>   = mutableMapOf(
 "Mary" to "Engineer",
 "Patrick" to "Intern",
 "Ray" to "Hacker"
)
```

Set the value of the key `"Patrick"` to `null` and completely remove the key and value for `"Ray"`.

Key points

- A **map** is an unordered collection of key-value pairs.
- The **keys** of a map are all of the same type, and the **values** are all of the same type.
- Use **indexing** to get values and to add, update or remove pairs.
- If a key is not in a map, lookup returns `null`.
- Built-in Kotlin types such as `String`, `Int`, `Double` have efficient hash values out of the box.
- Use `HashMap<K, V>` for performance critical code.
- **Sets** are unordered collections of unique values of the same type.
- Sets are most useful when you need to know whether something is included in the collection or not.

Where to go from here?

Now that you've learned about collection types in Kotlin, you should have a good idea of what they can do and when you should use them. You'll see them come up as you continue on in the book.

The next chapter of the book covers **lambdas**. One of the many great features of lambdas is that they let you iterate over the collection types you've learned in a less explicit and more readable manner than loops.

Chapter 10: Lambdas

By Irina Galata

A previous chapter taught you about functions. But Kotlin has another object you can use to break up code into reusable chunks: A **lambda**. These have many uses, and become particularly useful when dealing with collections such as an array or map.

A lambda expression is simply a function with no name; you can assign it to a variable and pass it around like any other value. This chapter shows you how convenient and useful lambdas can be.

Lambda basics

Lambdas are also known as **anonymous functions**, and derive their name from the **lambda calculus** of Alonzo Church, in which all functions are anonymous. Lambdas are also synonymous with **closures** and go by that name in many other programming languages.

Closures are so named because they have the ability to "close over" the variables and constants within the closure's own scope. This simply means that a lambda can access, store and manipulate the value of any variable or constant from the surrounding context, acting as a nested function. Variables and constants used within the body of a lambda are said to have been **captured** by the lambda.

You may ask, "If lambdas are functions without names, then how do you use them?" To use a lambda, you first have to assign it to a variable or constant, including as an argument to another function.

Here's a declaration of a variable that can hold a lambda:

```
var multiplyLambda: (Int, Int) -> Int
```

`multiplyLambda` takes two `Int` values and returns an `Int`. Notice that this is exactly the same as a variable declaration for a function. As was said, a lambda is simply a function without a name. The type of a lambda is a function type.

You assign a lambda to a variable like so:

```
multiplyLambda = { a: Int, b: Int -> Int
  a * b
}
```

This looks similar to a function declaration, but there are subtle differences. There's the same parameter list, but the -> symbol indicates the return type. The body of the lambda begins after the return type. The lambda expression returns the value of the last expression in the body.

With your lambda variable defined, you can use it just as if it were a function, like so:

```
val lambdaResult = multiplyLambda(4, 2) // 8
```

As you'd expect, `result` equals 8. Again, though, there's a subtle difference. A lambda does not allow the use of names for arguments; for instance, you can't write `multiplyLambda(a = 4, b = 2)`. Unlike functions, you can't use the parameter names for labeling the arguments.

Shorthand syntax

Compared to functions, lambdas are designed to be lightweight. There are many ways to shorten their syntax. First, you can use Kotlin's type inference to shorten the syntax by removing the type information:

```
multiplyLambda = { a, b ->
  a * b
}
```

Remember, you already declared `multiplyLambda` as a lambda taking two `Int`s and returning an `Int`, so you can let Kotlin infer these types for you.

it keyword

For a lambda that has only one parameter, you can shorten it even further using the `it` keyword. As an example, look at this lambda:

```
var doubleLambda = { a: Int ->
  2 * a
}
```

Since there is only one parameter and the lambda type is now specified, the lambda can be shortened to:

```
doubleLambda = { 2 * it }
```

You can also use `it` in a new declaration:

```
val square: (Int) -> Int = { it * it }
```

Lambdas as arguments

Consider the following code:

```
fun operateOnNumbers(
  a: Int,
  b: Int,
  operation: (Int, Int) -> Int
): Int {
  val result = operation(a, b)
  println(result)
  return result
}
```

This declares a function named `operateOnNumbers`, which takes `Int` values as its first two parameters. The third parameter is named `operation` and is of a function type. `operateOnNumbers` itself returns an `Int`.

You can then use `operateOnNumbers` with a lambda, like so:

```
val addLambda = { a: Int, b: Int ->
  a + b
}
operateOnNumbers(4, 2, operation = addLambda) // 6
```

Remember, lambdas are simply functions without names. So you shouldn't be surprised to learn that you can also pass in a function as the third parameter of `operateOnNumbers`, like so:

```
fun addFunction(a: Int, b:Int) = a + b

operateOnNumbers(4, 2, operation = ::addFunction) // 6
```

`operateOnNumbers` is called the same way, whether the `operation` is a function or a lambda. The `::` operator is the *reference operator*; in this case, it instructs the program to find `addFunction` in the current scope.

The power of the lambda syntax comes in handy again.

You can define the lambda inline with the `operateOnNumbers` function call, like this:

```
operateOnNumbers(4, 2, operation = { a: Int, b: Int ->
  a + b
})
```

There's no need to define the lambda and assign it to a local variable or constant. You can simply declare the lambda right where you pass it into the function as an argument!

But recall that you can simplify the lambda syntax to remove a lot of the boilerplate code. You can therefore reduce the above to the following:

```
operateOnNumbers(4, 2, { a, b ->
  a + b
})
```

In fact, you can even go a step further. The + operator is just an operator function `plus()` in the `Int` class that takes two arguments and returns one result so you can write:

```
operateOnNumbers(4, 2, operation = Int::plus)
```

There's one more way you can simplify the syntax, but it can only be done when the lambda is the final argument passed to a function. In this case, you can move the lambda outside of the function call:

```
operateOnNumbers(4, 2) { a, b ->
  a + b
}
```

This may look strange, but it's just the same as the previous code snippet using the lambda syntax, except you've removed the `operation` label and pulled the braces outside of the function call parameter list. This is called **trailing lambda syntax**.

Lambdas with no meaningful return value

Until now, all the lambdas you've seen have taken one or more parameters and have returned values. But just like functions, lambdas aren't required to do these things. A lambda will always return the value of its last expression, so here is how you define a lambda that takes no parameters and returns only the `Unit` object:

```
var unitLambda: () -> Unit = {
  println("Kotlin Apprentice is awesome!")
}
unitLambda()
```

The lambda's type is `() -> Unit`. The empty parentheses denote there are no parameters. You must declare a return type, so Kotlin knows you're declaring a lambda. This is where `Unit` comes in handy, when the lambda needs to return no meaningful value.

If you literally want the lambda to not return a value, you must use the `Nothing` type, like so:

```
var nothingLambda: () -> Nothing = {
  throw NullPointerException()
}
```

Since an exception is thrown, the lambda does not actually return a value.

Capturing from the enclosing scope

Let's return to an important characteristic of lambdas, as they act as closures: they can access the variables and constants from within their own scope.

> **Note**: Recall that scope defines the range in which an entity (variable, constant, etc) is accessible. You saw a new scope introduced with `if` statements. Lambdas also introduce a new scope and inherit all entities visible to the scope in which they are defined.

For example, take the following lambda:

```
var counter = 0
val incrementCounter = {
  counter += 1
}
```

`incrementCounter` is rather simple: It increments the `counter` variable. The `counter` variable is defined outside of the lambda. The lambda is able to access the variable because the lambda is defined in the same scope as the variable. The lambda is said to **capture** the `counter` variable. Any changes it makes to the variable are visible both inside and outside the lambda.

Let's say you call the lambda five times, like so:

```
incrementCounter()
incrementCounter()
incrementCounter()
incrementCounter()
incrementCounter()
```

After these five calls, `counter` will equal 5.

The fact that lambdas can be used to capture variables from the enclosing scope can be extremely useful. For example, you could write the following function:

```
fun countingLambda(): () -> Int {
  var counter = 0
  val incrementCounter: () -> Int = {
    counter += 1
    counter
  }
  return incrementCounter
}
```

This function takes no parameters and returns a lambda. The lambda it returns takes no parameters and returns an `Int`.

The lambda returned from this function will increment its internal counter each time it is called. Each time you call this function you get a different counter.

For example, this could be used like so:

```
val counter1 = countingLambda()
val counter2 = countingLambda()

println(counter1()) // > 1
println(counter2()) // > 1
println(counter1()) // > 2
println(counter1()) // > 3
println(counter2()) // > 2
```

The two counters created by the function are mutually exclusive and count independently. Neat!

Custom sorting with lambdas

Lambdas come in handy when you start looking deeper at collections. In Chapter 8, you used array's `sort` method to sort an array. By specifying a lambda, you can customize how things are sorted.

You call `sorted()` to get a sorted version of the array like so:

```
val names = arrayOf("ZZZZZZ", "BB", "A", "CCCC", "EEEEE")
names.sorted() // A, BB, CCCC, EEEEE, ZZZZZZ
```

By specifying a custom lambda passed to `compareBy()`, which returns a `Comparator` for `sortedWith()`, you can change the details of how the array is sorted.

Specify a trailing lambda for `compareBy()` like so:

```
val namesByLength = names.sortedWith(compareBy {
  -it.length
})
println(namesByLength) // > [ZZZZZZ, EEEEE, CCCC, BB, A]
```

Now the array is sorted by the length of the string with longer strings coming first. The minus sign causes the sort to be descending by length.

Iterating over collections with lambdas

In Kotlin, collections implement some very handy features often associated with **functional programming**. These features come in the shape of functions that you can apply to a collection to perform an operation on it.

Operations include things like transforming each element or filtering out certain elements. These functions make use of lambdas.

The first of these functions, `forEach`, lets you loop over the elements in a collection and perform an operation like so:

```
val values = listOf(1, 2, 3, 4, 5, 6)
values.forEach {
  println("$it: ${it * it}")
}
// > 1: 1
// > 2: 4
// > 3: 9
// > 4: 16
// > 5: 25
// > 6: 36
```

This loops through each item in the collection printing the value and its square.

Another function allows you to filter out certain elements:

```
var prices = listOf(1.5, 10.0, 4.99, 2.30, 8.19)

val largePrices = prices.filter {
  it > 5.0
}
```

Here, you create a list of `Double` to represent the prices of items in a shop. To filter out the prices which are greater than $5, you use the `filter` function. This function looks like so:

```
public inline fun <T> Iterable<T>.filter(predicate: (T) ->
Boolean): List<T>
```

This means that `filter` takes a single parameter named `predicate`, which is a lambda (or function) that takes a `T` and returns a `Boolean`. The `filter` function then returns a list of `T`. In this context, `T` refers to the type of items in the list. In the example above, `Double`.

Don't worry if you don't understand the purpose of `T` here. You'll learn more about this in Chapter 18, "Generics."

The lambda's job for `filter` is to return `true` or `false` depending on whether or not the value should be kept or not. The list returned from `filter` will contain all elements for which the lambda returned `true`.

In the example, `largePrices` will contain:

```
[10.0, 8.19]
```

> **Note:** The array that is returned from `filter` (and all of these functions) is a new array. The original is not modified at all.

However, there is more!

Imagine you're having a sale and want to discount all items to 90% of their original price. There's a handy function named `map` which can achieve this:

```
val salePrices = prices.map {
  it * 0.9
}
```

The `map` function will take a lambda, execute it on each item in the list and return a new list containing each result with the order maintained. In this case, `salePrices` will contain:

```
[1.35, 9.0, 4.4910000000000005, 2.07, 7.3709999999999996]
```

> **Note**: Be sure not to confuse the `map` function used to transform collections with the various `Map` types such as `HashMap` or functions like `mapOf` that create map objects.

The `map` function can also be used to change the type. You can do that like so:

```
val userInput = listOf("0", "11", "haha", "42")
val numbers = userInput.map {
  it.toIntOrNull()
}
println(numbers) // > [0, 11, null, 42]
```

This takes some strings that the user input and turns them into an array of `Int?`. They need to be nullable because the conversion from `String` to `Int` might fail.

If you want to filter out the invalid, `null`, values, you can use `mapNotNull()` like so:

```
val numbers2 = userInput.mapNotNull {
  it.toIntOrNull()
}
println(numbers2) // > [0, 11, 42]
```

This is almost the same as `map` except it tosses out the `null` values.

Another handy function is `fold`, which takes a starting value and a lambda. The lambda takes two values: the current value and an element from the list. The lambda returns the next value that should be passed into the lambda as the current value parameter.

This could be used with the `prices` list to calculate the total, like so:

```
var sum = prices.fold(0.0) { a, b ->
  a + b
}
```

The initial value is 0.0. Then the lambda calculates the sum of the current value plus the current iteration's value. Thus you calculate the total of all the values in the array. In this case, `sum` will be:

```
println(sum) // > 26.980000000000004
```

A function closely related to `fold` is `reduce`. In Kotlin, `reduce` uses the first element in the collection as the starting value:

```
sum = prices.reduce { a, b ->
  a + b
}
println(sum) // > 26.980000000000004
```

Now that you've seen `filter`, `map`, `fold`, and `reduce`, hopefully it's becoming clear how powerful these functions can be, especially thanks to the syntax of lambdas. In just a few lines of code, you have calculated some rather complex values from the collection.

Many of these functions can also be used with maps. Imagine you represent the stock in your shop by a dictionary mapping the price to number of items at that price. You could use that to calculate the total value of your stock like so:

```
val stock = mapOf(
  1.5 to 5,
  10.0 to 2,
```

```
    4.99 to 20,
    2.30 to 5,
    8.19 to 30
)
var stockSum = 0.0
stock.forEach {
    stockSum += it.key * it.value
}
```

In this case, the parameter to the `forEach` function is a `Map.Entry` containing the `key` and `value` from the map elements.

Here, the result is:

```
println(stockSum) // > 384.5
```

That wraps up collection iteration with lambdas!

Mini-exercises

1. Create a constant list called `nameList` which contains some names as strings. Any names will do — make sure there's more than three. Now use `fold` to create a string which is the concatenation of each name in the list.

2. Using the same `nameList` list, first filter the list to contain only names which have more than four characters in them, and then create the same concatenation of names as in the above exercise.

> **Hint**: you can chain these operations together.

3. Create a constant map called `namesAndAges` which contains some names as strings mapped to ages as integers. Now use `filter` to create a map containing only people under the age of 18.

4. Using the same `namesAndAges` map, filter out the adults (those 18 or older) and then use `map` to convert to a list containing just the names (i.e., drop the ages).

Challenges

Check out the challenges below to test your knowledge of Kotlin lambdas.

Challenge 1: Repeating yourself

Your first challenge is to write a function that will run a given lambda a given number of times.

Declare the function like so:

```
fun repeatTask(times: Int, task: () -> Unit)
```

The function should run the `task` lambda `times` number of times.

Use this function to print `"Kotlin Apprentice is a great book!"` 10 times.

Challenge 2: Lambda sums

In this challenge, you're going to write a function that you can reuse to create different mathematical sums.

Declare the function like so:

```
fun mathSum(length: Int, series: (Int) -> Int) -> Int
```

The first parameter, `length`, defines the number of values to sum. The second parameter, `series`, is a lambda that can be used to generate a series of values. `series` should have a parameter that is the position of the value in the series and return the value at that position.

`mathSum` should calculate `length` number of values, starting at position 1, and return their sum.

Use the function to find the sum of the first 10 square numbers, which equals 385. Then use the function to find the sum of the first 10 Fibonacci numbers, which equals 143.

For the Fibonacci numbers, you can use the function you wrote in the challenges of the functions chapter — or grab it from the solutions if you're unsure what you've done is correct.

Challenge 3: Functional ratings

In this final challenge, you will have a list of app names with associated ratings they've been given. Note — these are all fictional apps!

Create the data map like so:

```
val appRatings = mapOf(
  "Calendar Pro" to arrayOf(1, 5, 5, 4, 2, 1, 5, 4),
  "The Messenger" to arrayOf(5, 4, 2, 5, 4, 1, 1, 2),
  "Socialise" to arrayOf(2, 1, 2, 2, 1, 2, 4, 2)
)
```

First, create a map called `averageRatings` which will contain a mapping of app names to average ratings. Use `forEach` to iterate through the `appRatings` map, then use `reduce` to calculate the average rating and store this rating in the `averageRatings` map.

Finally, use `filter` and `map` chained together to get a list of the app names whose average rating is greater than 3.

Key points

- **Lambdas** are functions without names. They can be assigned to variables and passed as arguments to functions.
- Lambdas have **shorthand syntax** that makes them a lot easier to use than other functions.
- A lambda can **capture** the variables and constants from its surrounding context.
- A lambda can be used to direct how a collection is sorted.
- There exists a handy set of functions on collections which can be used to iterate over the collection and transform the collection. Transforms include mapping each element to a new value, filtering out certain values, and folding or reducing the collection down to a single value.

Where to go from here?

Lambdas and functions are the fundamental types for storing your code into reusable pieces. Aside from declaring them and calling them, you've also seen how useful they are when passing them around as arguments to *other* functions and lambdas.

That finishes this part of the book on "Collections & Lambdas". Next up, it's time to learn about creating your own types.

Section III: Building Your Own Types

You can create your own type by combining variables and functions into a new type definition. For example, integers and doubles might not be enough for your purposes, and you might need to create a type to store complex numbers. Or maybe storing first, middle and last names in three independent variables is getting difficult to manage, so you decide to create a `FullName` type.

When you create a new type, you give it a name; thus, these custom types are known as **named types**. Named types are a powerful tool for modeling real-world concepts. You can encapsulate related concepts, properties and methods into a single, cohesive model.

Custom types make it possible to build large and complex things with the basic building blocks that you've learned so far. It's time to take your Kotlin apprenticeship to the next level!

Chapter 11: Classes

By Victoria Gonda

In this chapter, you'll get acquainted with **classes**, which are **named types**. Classes are one of the cornerstones of **object-oriented programming**, a style of programming where the types have both data and behavior. In classes, data takes the form of **properties** and behavior is implemented using functions called **methods**.

Open the chapter starter project to start learning!

Creating classes

Consider the following class definition in Kotlin and add it to your Kotlin file, outside of any `main()` function:

```
class Person(var firstName: String, var lastName: String) {
  val fullName
    get() = "$firstName $lastName"
}
```

That's simple enough! The keyword `class` is followed by the name of the class, `Person`. Inside the parentheses after the class name is the **primary constructor** for the class, and for `Person` you're indicating that there are two mutable `String` properties, `firstName` and `lastName`. You'll see how to create other constructors in Chapter 15, "Advanced Classes." Everything in the curly braces is a member of the class.

> **Note**: You can place classes in a file alongside other constructs, or in their own file. For this exercise, you'll put everything in the same file.

You create an **instance** of a class by using the class name and passing in arguments to the constructor. Add this to your `main()` function:

```
val john = Person(firstName = "Johnny", lastName = "Appleseed")
```

The class instances are the **objects** of object-oriented programming, not to be confused with the Kotlin `object` keyword.

`Person` has another property named `fullName` with a **custom getter** that uses the other properties in its definition:

```
println(john.fullName) // > Johnny Appleseed
```

It uses both the `firstName` and `lastName` properties to compute the `fullName`, "Johnny Appleseed".

Reference types

In Kotlin, an instance of a class is a mutable object. Classes are **reference types**. This means a variable of a class type does not store an actual instance, but a **reference** to a location in memory that stores the instance.

Create a `SimplePerson` class and instance with only a name like this:

```
class SimplePerson(val name: String)

var var1 = SimplePerson(name = "John")
```

It looks something like this in memory:

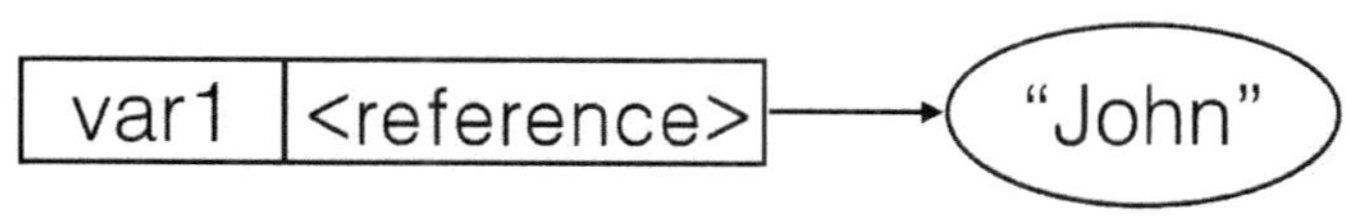

Now, create a new variable `var2` and assign to it the value of `var1`:

```
var var2 = var1
```

The references inside both `var1` and `var2` reference the same place in memory:

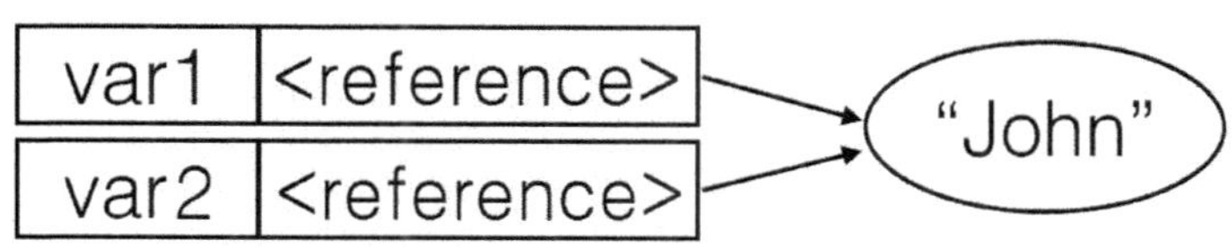

The heap vs. the stack

When you create a reference type such as a class, the system stores the actual instance in a region of memory known as the **heap**. References to the class instances are stored in a region of memory called the **stack**, unless the reference is part of a class instance, in which case the reference is stored on the heap with the rest of the class instance.

Both the heap and the stack have essential roles in the execution of any program:

- The system uses the **stack** to store anything on the immediate thread of execution; it is tightly managed and optimized by the CPU. When a function creates a variable, the stack stores that variable and then destroys it when the function exits. Since the stack is so well organized, it's very efficient, and thus quite fast.
- The system uses the **heap** to store instances of reference types. The heap is generally a large pool of memory from which the system can request and dynamically allocate blocks of memory. The lifetime is flexible and dynamic. The heap doesn't automatically destroy its data like the stack does; additional work is required to do that. This makes creating and removing data on the heap a slower process, compared to on the stack.

When you create an instance of a class, your code requests a block of memory on the heap to store the instance itself. It stores the *address* of that memory in your named variable on the stack.

This has only been a brief introduction to the dynamics of heaps and stacks, but you know enough at this point to understand the reference semantics you'll use to work with classes.

Working with references

Since a class is a reference type, when you assign to a variable of a class type, the system does *not* copy the instance; only a reference is copied.

Add the following code to the bottom of your `main()` function:

```
var homeOwner = john
john.firstName = "John"

println(john.firstName)      // > John
println(homeOwner.firstName) // > John
```

Here, you assign a new variable, `homeOwner`, to the `john` object.

Run the code to see the results. Even though you only changed the first name for `john`, the name was also changed for `homeOwner`, since they both reference the same object. As you can see, `john` and `homeOwner` truly have the same data!

This implied sharing among class instances results in a new way of thinking when passing things around. For instance, if the `john` object changes, then anything holding a reference to `john` will automatically see the update.

Mini-exercise

Change the value of `lastName` on `homeOwner`, then try reading `fullName` on both `john` and `homeOwner`. What do you observe?

Object identity

In the previous code sample, it's easy to see that `john` and `homeOwner` are pointing to the same object. The code is short and both references are named variables. What if you want to see if the value behind a variable *is* John?

You might think to check the value of `firstName`, but how would you know it's the John you're looking for and not an impostor? Or worse, what if John changed his name again?

In Kotlin, the === operator lets you check if the *identity* of one object is equal to the identity of another. Add the following line of code to your example:

```
println(homeOwner === john) // > true
```

Run and observe the results. Similar to how the == operator checks if two *values* are equal, the === identity operator compares the memory address of two *references*. It tells you whether the value of the references are the same; that is, they point to the same block of data on the heap.

Add the following code. You can add print statements if you want to see the results for yourself:

```
val impostorJohn = Person(firstName = "John", lastName =
"Appleseed")

john === homeOwner // true
john === impostorJohn // false
impostorJohn === homeOwner // false

// Assignment of existing variables changes the instances the
variables reference.
homeOwner = impostorJohn
john === homeOwner // false

homeOwner = john
john === homeOwner // true
```

This shows how the === operator can tell the difference between the John you're looking for and an imposter-John.

This can be particularly useful when you cannot rely on regular equality (==) to compare and identify objects you care about. Try the following code:

```
// Create fake, imposter Johns.
var imposters = (0..100).map {
  Person(firstName = "John", lastName = "Appleseed")
}

// Equality (==) is not effective when John cannot be identified
by his name alone
imposters.map {
  it.firstName == "John" && it.lastName == "Appleseed"
}.contains(true) // true
```

In the above code, you can see how the equality operator is not sufficient to identify the original John.

Now, try this code:

```
// Check to ensure the real John is not found among the
imposters.
println(imposters.contains(john)) // > false

// Now hide the "real" John somewhere among the imposters.
val mutableImposters = mutableListOf<Person>()
mutableImposters.addAll(imposters)
mutableImposters.contains(john) // false
mutableImposters.add(Random().nextInt(5), john)

// John can now be found among the imposters.
println(mutableImposters.contains(john)) // > true

// Since `Person` is a reference type, you can use === to grab
the real John out of the list of imposters and modify the value.
// The original `john` variable will print the new last name!
val indexOfJohn = mutableImposters.indexOf(john)
if (indexOfJohn != -1) {
  mutableImposters[indexOfJohn].lastName = "Bananapeel"
}

println(john.fullName) // > John Bananapeel
```

Note: You have to import the `java.util.*` package in order to work with the `Random()` class.

By using the identity operator, you can verify that the *references* themselves are equal, and separate your real John from the crowd.

You may actually find that you won't use the identity operator === very much in your day-to-day Kotlin. What's important is to understand what it does, and what it demonstrates about the properties of reference types.

Mini-exercise

Write a function `memberOf(person: Person, group: List<Person>): Bool` that will return `true` if `person` can be found inside `group`, and `false` if it can not.

Test it by creating two arrays of five `Person` objects for `group` and using `john` as the `person`. Put `john` in one of the arrays, but not in the other.

Methods and mutability

As you've read before, instances of classes are mutable objects. Create the classes `Student` and `Grade` as defined below:

```
class Grade(
  val letter: String,
  val points: Double,
  val credits: Double
)

class Student(
  val firstName: String,
  val lastName: String,
  val grades: MutableList<Grade> = mutableListOf(),
  var credits: Double = 0.0
) {

  fun recordGrade(grade: Grade) {
    grades.add(grade)
    credits += grade.credits
  }
}
```

Now, use these classes in your `main()` function:

```
val jane = Student(firstName = "Jane", lastName = "Appleseed")
val history = Grade(letter = "B", points = 9.0, credits = 3.0)
var math = Grade(letter = "A", points = 16.0, credits = 4.0)

jane.recordGrade(history)
jane.recordGrade(math)
```

Note that `recordGrade()` can mutate the array `grades` by adding more values to the end. Like any mutable list, `grades` can be added to even though the `grades` reference itself is immutable. This is independent of the fact that `jane` is marked as an immutable `val` reference. Similarly, the `credits` `Double` value can be changed in `recordGrade()` because it's defined as a mutable `var` within the `Student` class.

Mutability and constants

The previous example may have had you wondering how you were able to modify `jane` even though it was defined as a constant `val`.

When you define a constant, the value of the constant cannot be changed. It is important to remember that, with reference types, the value is a *reference*.

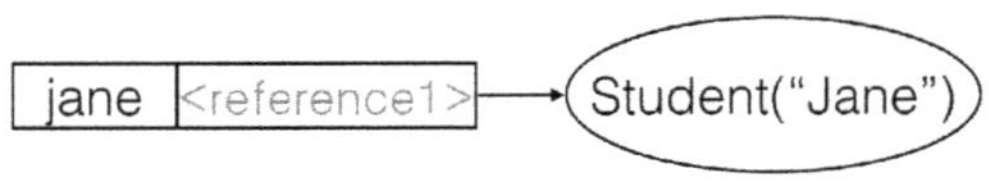

The value of "reference1" in red is the value stored in `jane`. This value is a reference and because `jane` is declared as a constant, this reference is constant. If you were to attempt to assign another student to `jane`, you would get a build error:

```
// Error: jane is a `val` constant
jane = Student(firstName = "John", lastName = "Appleseed")
```

If you declared `jane` as a variable instead, you would be able to assign to it another instance of `Student` on the heap:

```
var jane = Student(firstName = "Jane", lastName = "Appleseed")
jane = Student(firstName = "John", lastName = "Appleseed")
```

After the assignment of another `Student` to `jane`, the reference value behind `jane` would be updated to point to the new `Student` object.

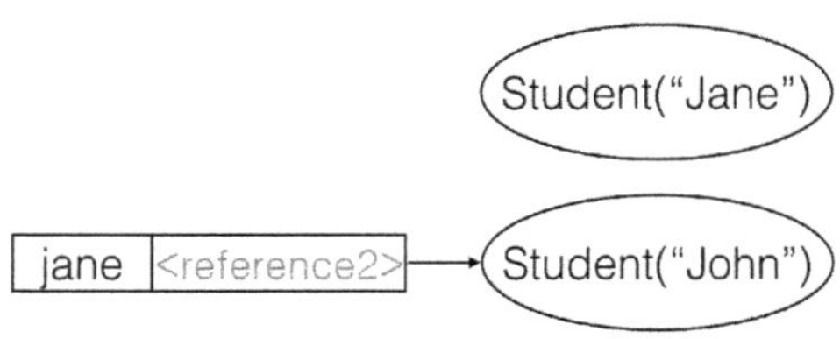

Since nothing would be referencing the original "Jane" object, its memory would be freed to use elsewhere.

Any individual member of a class can be protected from modification through the use of constants, but because reference types are not *themselves* treated as values, they are not protected as a whole from mutation, even when instantiated with `val`.

Mini-exercise

Add a property with a custom getter to `Student` that returns the student's Grade Point Average, or GPA. A GPA is defined as the number of points earned divided by the number of credits taken. For the example above, Jane earned (9 + 16 = **25**) points while taking (3 + 4 = **7**) credits, making her GPA (25 / 7 = **3.57**).

> **Note**: Points in most American universities range from 4 per credit for an A, down to 1 point for a D (with an F being 0 points). For this exercise, you may of course use any scale that you want!

Understanding state and side effects

The referenced and mutable nature of classes leads to numerous programming possibilities, as well as many concerns. If you update a class instance with a new value, then every reference to that instance will also see the new value.

You can use this to your advantage. Perhaps you pass a `Student` instance to a sports team, a report card and a class roster. Imagine all of these entities need to know the student's grades, and because they all point to the same instance, they'll all see new grades as the instance records them.

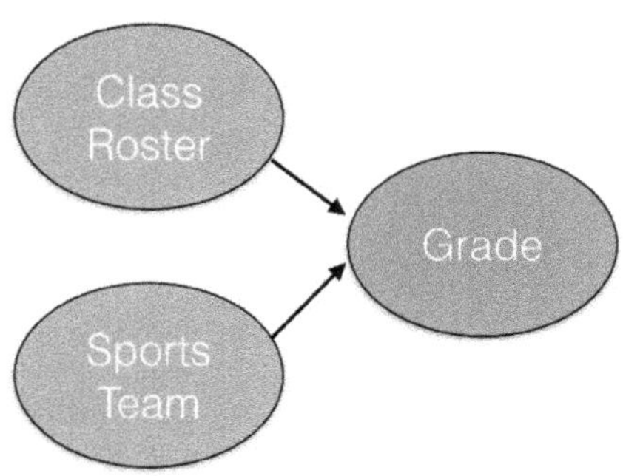

The result of this sharing is that class instances have **state**. Changes in state can sometimes be obvious, but often they're not.

To illustrate this, consider the `credits` property of the `Student` class, which is initialized as:

```
var credits = 0.0
```

The `recordGrade()` member mutates this `credits` property:

```
fun recordGrade(grade: Grade) {
  grades.add(grade)
  credits += grade.credits
}
```

Calling `recordGrade()` has the side effect of updating `credits`.

Now, observe how side effects can result in non-obvious behavior by adding this code:

```
println(jane.credits) // 7

// The teacher made a mistake; math has 5 credits
math = Grade(letter = "A", points = 20.0, credits = 5.0)
jane.recordGrade(math)

println(jane.credits) // 12, not 8!
```

Run your new code. Whoever wrote the `Student` class did so somewhat naïvely by assuming that the same grade won't get recorded twice! But, because `math` was already added in a previous example, it was recorded twice. Because class instances are mutable, you need to be careful about unexpected behavior around shared references.

While confusing in a small example such as this, mutability and state could be extremely jarring as classes grow in size and complexity. Situations like this would be much more common with a `Student` class that scales to 20 properties and has 10 methods.

Data classes

Suppose you want to define a `Student` class and have added functionality, such as the ability to compare whether two students are equal in value or the ability to easily print the student data. You might define the class as follows:

```
class Student(
  var firstName: String,
  var lastName: String,
  var id: Int
) {

  override fun hashCode(): Int {
    val prime = 31
    var result = 1

    result = prime * result + firstName.hashCode()
    result = prime * result + id
    result = prime * result + lastName.hashCode()

    return result
  }

  override fun equals(other: Any?): Boolean {
    if (this === other)
      return true

    if (other == null)
      return false

    if (javaClass != other.javaClass)
      return false

    val obj = other as Student?

    if (firstName != obj?.firstName)
      return false

    if (id != obj.id)
      return false

    if (lastName != obj.lastName)
      return false

    return true
  }

  override fun toString(): String {
    return "Student (firstName=$firstName, lastName=$lastName,
id=$id)"
  }

  fun copy(
    firstName: String = this.firstName,
    lastName: String = this.lastName,
    id: Int = this.id
  ) = Student(firstName, lastName, id)
}
```

You've also added a hash code for each student, and a function to copy one student into another.

Classes with a primary purpose for holding data are very common in programming. They are especially used as **model** objects in many programming patterns that attempt to model real world objects.

When using these model classes, comparing instances, printing them and copying them are all very common actions:

```
val albert = Student(
  firstName = "Albert",
  lastName = "Einstein",
  id = 1
)
val richard = Student(
  firstName = "Richard",
  lastName = "Feynman",
  id = 2
)
val albertCopy = albert.copy()

println(albert)
// > Student (firstName=Albert, lastName=Einstein, id=1)
println(richard)
// > Student (firstName=Richard, lastName=Feynman, id=2)
println(albert == richard) // > false
println(albert == albertCopy) // > true
println(albert === albertCopy) // > false
```

Using the == operator with the instances compares the values in the objects using the `equals()` function, whereas === compares the identity of the references, as was discussed above.

These actions on instances are so common that Kotlin provides a variation on classes named **data classes**. By using data classes, you can avoid having to declare all the boilerplate code that was used in our re-definition of `Student`.

You define a data class just like a regular class except that you prepend the `class` keyword with `data`:

```
data class StudentData(
  var firstName: String,
  var lastName: String,
  var id: Int
)
```

Check out the data class in action. Add the following:

```
val marie = StudentData("Marie", "Curie", id = 1)
val emmy = StudentData("Emmy", "Noether", id = 2)
val marieCopy = marie.copy()

println(marie)
// > StudentData(firstName=Marie, lastName=Curie, id=1)
println(emmy)
// > StudentData(firstName=Emmy, lastName=Noether, id=2)
println(marie == emmy) // > false
println(marie == marieCopy) // > true
println(marie === marieCopy) // > false
```

Now, run it to see the results. The `StudentData` data class has all the same functionality as the new `Student` class, and it's all defined in one statement!

Destructuring declarations

You can extract the data inside of a data class using a **destructuring declaration**. Just assign a variable to each of the properties of the data class in one assignment statement:

```
val (firstName, lastName, id) = marie

println(firstName) // > Marie
println(lastName)  // > Curie
println(id)        // > 1
```

Destructing declarations are particularly useful in returning more than one value from a function. They also work in other contexts, for example, in for loops over map objects.

Be careful, as the variable you're assigning the properties to do not need to have the same name as the property. You could accidentally swap the first and last names! The properties are destructured in the same order as in the constructor.

Challenges

Here are some challenges for you to practice your new knowledge. If you get stuck at any point, check out the solutions in the materials for this chapter.

Challenge 1: Movie lists

Imagine you're writing a movie-viewing application in Kotlin. Users can create lists of movies and share those lists with other users.

Create a `User` class and a `MovieList` class that maintains lists for users.

- `MovieList`: Contains a name and a mutable list of movie titles. The name and titles can all be represented by `String`s. A `print` method will print all the movies in the movie list.
- `User`: Has a method `addList()` which adds the given `MovieList` to a mutable map of `MovieList` objects (using the `name` as a key), and `list(name: String): MovieList?` which will return the `MovieList` for the provided name.
- Create `jane` and `john` users and have them create and share lists. Have both `jane` and `john` modify the same list and call `print` from both users. Are all the changes reflected?

Challenge 2: T-Shirt store — data classes

Your challenge here is to build a set of objects to support a T-shirt store. Decide if each object should be a class or a data class, and go ahead and implement them all.

- `TShirt`: Represents a shirt style you can buy. Each `TShirt` has a size, color, price, and an optional image on the front.
- `User`: A registered user of the t-shirt store app. A user has a name, email, and a `ShoppingCart` (see below).
- `Address`: Represents a shipping address, containing the name, street, city, and zip code.
- `ShoppingCart`: Holds a current order, which is composed of a list of `TShirts` that the `User` wants to buy, as well as a method to calculate the total cost. Additionally, there is an `Address` that represents where the order will be shipped.

Key points

- **Classes** are a named type that can have properties and methods.
- Classes use **references** that are shared on assignment.
- Class instances are called **objects**.
- Objects are **mutable**.
- Mutability introduces **state**, which adds complexity when managing your objects.
- **Data classes** allow you to create simple model objects that avoid a lot of boilerplate for comparing, printing, and copying objects.
- **Destructuring declarations** allow you to easily extract multiple properties of data class objects.

Where to go from here?

You've just scratched the surface of the power and usage of classes!

In the next few chapters, you'll learn more details about class properties and methods as well as advanced usage of classes including inheritance. You'll also take a look at the `object` keyword, which is used when you want to ensure that only one instance of a type is created in your application.

Chapter 12: Objects

By Victoria Gonda

Kotlin introduces a new keyword that is unavailable in other languages Kotlin is often compared to, such as Java and Swift: The `object` keyword.

Like Java and Swift, Kotlin supports **object-oriented programming**. As you saw in Chapter 11, "Classes," you use classes to define custom types, and instances of classes are called **objects**.

Kotlin uses `object` to denote a custom type that can only have a **single instance**. The name choice for the `object` keyword can sometimes lead to confusion with class instances, since they're also called objects. As you'll see in this chapter, you can also use `object` to create **anonymous objects**, for which a new instance is created each time the anonymous object is used, another potential source of confusion.

This chapter will help you make sense of this potential confusion.

In discussing your code, you'll often have to rely on the context to determine whether an "object" is a class instance, the single instance of an entity created using `object` or an anonymous object.

The `object` keyword lets you easily implement a common pattern in software development: The **singleton** pattern.

Singletons

The **singleton** pattern is one of the more straightforward of the software engineering **design patterns**. In most object-oriented languages, the pattern is used when you want to restrict a class to have a single instance during any given run of an application.

There are a few hurdles you must typically jump in order to create a singleton, in terms of setting up the single instance and performing the restriction to one object. Use of singletons is sometimes discouraged because they introduce a **global state** into your application; therefore, you must be careful when accessing a singleton from different application threads. But singletons are useful in certain use cases wherein the scope of use is limited.

Kotlin addresses some of these concerns by giving you a built-in way to create singletons.

Named objects

The `object` keyword in Kotlin lets you define a type that only has a single instance — a **named object**.

A type defined with `object` cannot have constructors: Since there is only one instance of an object, there is no reason to provide constructor functions to create other instances. In a sense, the type *is* the instance.

To see what the Kotlin compiler is doing to follow the singleton pattern, it's instructive to see how the compiled version of Kotlin code created with `object` looks in Java. You can do so by having IntelliJ IDEA **decompile** the Kotlin bytecode into Java.

Getting started

Open the chapter starter project and create a new file by right-clicking on the **src** folder and choosing **New ▸ Kotlin File/Class** and naming the file **X**:

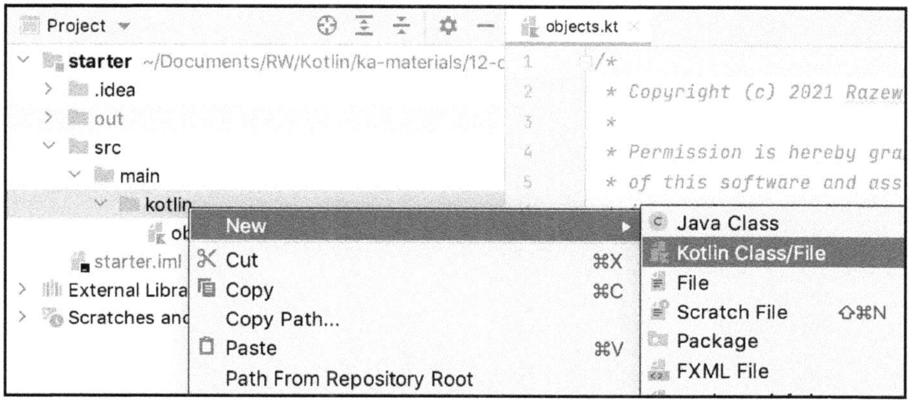

Add the following bare bones object into the new file:

```
object X {
  var x = 0
}
```

Choose **Tools ▸ Kotlin ▸ Show Kotlin Bytecode**, which will open the **Kotlin Bytecode** panel:

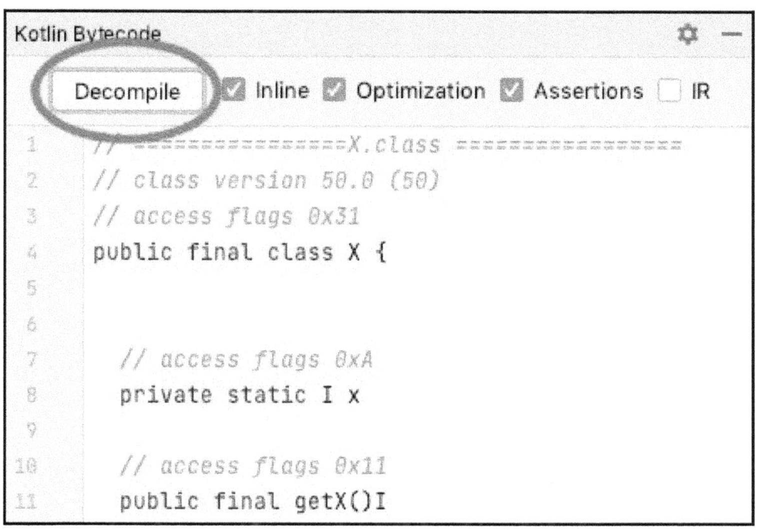

Next, hit the **Decompile** button in the panel. The decompiled Java for the simple object will open in a new editor window:

```
public final class X {
   private static int x;
   public static final X INSTANCE;

   public final int getX() {
      return x;
   }

   public final void setX(int var1) {
      x = var1;
   }

   static {
      X var0 = new X();
      INSTANCE = var0;
   }
}
```

The Java code uses a common approach to create singletons in Java. You have the `static` and `final` `INSTANCE` field that is of the same type as the class.

The `INSTANCE` value is set in a `static` block, and it is set to a new instance of the class. You also have getters and setters for the single-member field `x`.

Comparing the Java and Kotlin versions of the code, you see that the boilerplate singleton setup code has been significantly reduced by using the `object` keyword.

Singleton use cases

An example use case for a singleton is an in-memory repository for a set of data. Consider an app that needs a registry of students who are defined with the following data class. Add this class to **objects.kt**:

```
data class Student(
  val id: Int,
  val firstName:
  String, val
  lastName: String
) {
  var fullName = "$lastName, $firstName"
}
```

And this to the `main()` function:

```
val marie = Student(1, "Marie", "Curie")
val albert = Student(2, "Albert", "Einstein")
val emmy = Student(3, "Emmy", "Noether")
```

This creates your brilliant students, but you still need your registry.

Add the following `StudentRegistry` outside of the `main()` function:

```
object StudentRegistry {
  val allStudents = mutableListOf<Student>()

  fun addStudent(student: Student) {
    allStudents.add(student)
  }

  fun removeStudent(student: Student) {
    allStudents.remove(student)
  }

  fun listAllStudents() {
    allStudents.forEach {
      println(it.fullName)
    }
  }
}
```

Using `object`, you create a registry that:

1. Maintains the list of students in a mutable list.
2. Lets you add and remove students from the registry.
3. Lets you print out the full name of all the students in the registry.

Now, add the following to the bottom of your `main()` function:

```
StudentRegistry.addStudent(marie)
StudentRegistry.addStudent(albert)
StudentRegistry.addStudent(emmy)

StudentRegistry.listAllStudents()
// > Curie, Marie
// > Einstein, Albert
// > Noether, Emmy
```

This adds your students to the registry. You call methods defined on the object using the object name with dot syntax.

Run the code to see your students printed out.

Had you used a class to represent your student registry, your app would allow for mutliple registries to be created, which could lead to inconsistent registries to exist within the software. Using a Kotlin object ensures that only one registry can be created.

Another example use case is to use `object` to provide a **namespace** for constants and methods that need to be referenced from multiple places in your app:

```
object JsonKeys {
  const val JSON_KEY_ID = "id"
  const val JSON_KEY_FIRSTNAME = "first_name"
  const val JSON_KEY_LASTNAME = "last_name"
}
```

This creates a namespace for holding JSON keys that will be used to parse JSON received from a server. By putting constants into an object, you reduce the likelihood of name collisions when your constants are given commonly used names.

Comparison to classes

While constructors are not allowed for objects, they do have many similarities with classes:

- Objects can have properties and member functions.
- Properties of the object must be initialized before use, either at declaration or in an `init` block.
- Objects can inherit from classes and implement interfaces.

Using static members

One of the students you define in this chapter, **Emmy Noether**, was a key contributor to the theory of conservation laws in physics. There appears to be a "law of conservation of keywords" because, while Kotlin has gained the `object` keyword, it's also lost a keyword found in other languages like Java and Swift: There is no `static` keyword in Kotlin.

Portrait of Emmy Noether

The `static` keyword is used in these other languages to denote a class member that is common to all instances of the class and is not specific to each instance. Static members remove the need to duplicate items that are common to all instances.

But removing code duplication is useful, so how does Kotlin allow you to define static members? You do so by creating a **companion object** inside the class.

Creating companion objects

You create the companion object by prepending `companion` to an object defined in the class. Add this class to your file:

```
class Scientist private constructor(
  val id: Int,
  val firstName: String,
  val lastName: String
) {

  companion object {
    var currentId = 0

    fun newScientist(
      firstName: String,
      lastName: String
    ): Scientist {
      currentId += 1
      return Scientist(currentId, firstName, lastName)
    }
  }

  var fullName = "$firstName $lastName"
}
```

In the `Scientist` class, you've included a companion object that holds a `currentId` value that you'll use for generating unique ID numbers for each scientist. The `currentId` value is common to all instances of the class, and it is used by the class to create new ID values when a new scientist instance is created.

A common use case for static members is to implement the **factory** pattern for creating new class instances. You're using the factory pattern in `Scientist` by making the class primary constructor private and adding a factory method `newScientist()` to the companion object, which creates new scientist instances.

By making the constructor private, you enforce that the new scientist instances can only be created using the factory method, ensuring that your `currentId` value is correctly incremented whenever new scientest objects are instantiated.

You can create a repository of scientists as a singleton. Add the following `ScientistRepository`:

```
object ScientistRepository {
  val allScientists = mutableListOf<Scientist>()

  fun addScientist(scientist: Scientist) {
    allScientists.add(scientist)
  }

  fun removeScientist(scientist: Scientist) {
    allScientists.remove(scientist)
  }

  fun listAllScientists() {
    allScientists.forEach {
      println("${it.id}: ${it.fullName}")
    }
  }
}
```

This repository is similar to your `StudentRegistry`, with the exception of the format used to print the names.

Then, create your scientists at the bottom of your `main()` function:

```
val emmy = Scientist.newScientist("Emmy", "Noether")
val isaac = Scientist.newScientist("Isaac", "Newton")
val nick = Scientist.newScientist("Nikola", "Tesla")

ScientistRepository.addScientist(emmy)
ScientistRepository.addScientist(isaac)
ScientistRepository.addScientist(nick)

ScientistRepository.listAllScientists()
```

```
// 1: Emmy Noether
// 2: Isaac Newton
// 3: Nikola Tesla
```

You create new scientist instances using dot syntax to call the companion object method on the class name. Run your additions to see the names printed out with correctly incremented IDs.

Companion naming and accessing from Java

The companion object is given an implicit name of `Companion`. You can use a custom name by adding it after the `companion object` keywords:

```
companion object Factory {
  // companion object members
}
```

You'll see in Chapter 14, "Methods," how the companion object name is used to extend the capabilities of the companion object.

Using the companion object name when accessing companion object members is redundant in Kotlin code. When calling the Kotlin companion object code from Java, however, you must use the companion object name:

```
// java
Scientist isaac =
    Scientist.Factory.newScientist("Isaac", "Newton");
```

If the companion object has not been given a custom name, you'll use the implicit name `Companion` instead.

Mini-exercise

Update the `Student` data class from above to keep track of how many students have been created. Use a companion object method `numberOfStudents()` to get the number of student instances.

> **Hint:** use the `init` block to increment a counter.

If you get stuck, you can look at the challenge project for this chapter.

Using anonymous objects

Anonymous classes are used in Java to override the behavior of existing classes without the need to subclass, and also to implement interfaces without defining a concrete class. In both cases, the compiler creates a single anonymous instance, to which no name need be given. You'll learn more about inheritance in Chapter 15, "Advanced Classes," and interfaces in Chapter 17, "Interfaces."

You use `object` to create the Kotlin version of anonymous classes called **anonymous objects** or **object expressions**.

Suppose you had an interface that let you keep track of how many students and scientists you have in your app. Add this to your file:

```
interface Counts {
  fun studentCount(): Int
  fun scientistCount(): Int
}
```

This interface has two method signatures that an instance needs to implement.

Create an anonymous object using this interface at the bottom of `main()`:

```
val counter = object : Counts {
  override fun studentCount(): Int {
    return StudentRegistry.allStudents.size
  }

  override fun scientistCount(): Int {
    return ScientistRepository.allScientists.size
  }
}

println(counter.studentCount()) // > 3
println(counter.scientistCount()) // > 3
```

You create an instance of the counter using the `object` keyword followed by a colon and the name of the interface. Inside braces, you override each of the interface methods. Run this code so you can see the counts print out.

Unlike named objects, which act as singletons, there will be a different version of an anonymous object in your app each time one is created.

If you were to follow the decompile steps from above to see the Java version of the Kotlin code, you end up with the following Java code for the anonymous object:

```
<undefinedtype> counter = new Counts() {
  public int studentCount() {
    return StudentRegistry.INSTANCE.getAllStudents().size();
  }

  public int scientistCount() {
    return ScientistRepository.INSTANCE
      .getAllScientists().size();
  }
};
```

So the Kotlin compiler is just creating an anonymous Java class for the anonymous object.

Challenges

1. Create a named object that lets you check whether a given `Int` value is above a threshold. Name the object `Threshold` and add a method `isAboveThreshold(value: Int)`.

2. Create a version of the `Student` class that uses a factory method `loadStudent(studentMap: Map<String, String>)` to create a student with a first and last name from a map such as `mapOf("first_name" to "Neils", "last_name" to "Bohr")`. Default to using “First” and “Last” as the names if the map not contain a first name or last name.

3. Create an anonymous object that implements the following interface:

```
interface ThresholdChecker {
  val lower: Int
  val upper: Int

  /**
  * Returns true if value is higher than the upper threshold
  * and false otherwise
  */
  fun isLit(value: Int): Boolean
  /**
  * Returns true if value is less than the lower threshold
  * and false otherwise
  */
  fun tooQuiet(value: Int): Boolean
}
```

Use a lower value of 7 and an upper value of 10 in the anonymous object.

Key points

- The **singleton pattern** is used when you want only one instance of a type to be created in your app.
- The `object` keyword is unique to Kotlin compared with similar languages, and it gives you a built-in way to make **singletons** with **named objects.** It also lets you make **anonymous objects**, the Kotlin version of Java anonymous classes.
- A class **companion object** gives you the Kotlin equivalent of Java static members.
- **Anonymous objects** — or **object expressions** — let you create unnamed instances of interfaces and to override class behavior without subclassing.
- Using **Show Kotlin Bytecode** and decompiling in IntelliJ IDEA is an informative way to understand what the Kotlin compiler is doing.

Where to go from here?

As you've seen in this chapter, just like classes, objects have properties and methods, and there's more to learn about for both. In the next chapter, Chapter 13, "Properties," you'll do a deeper dive into class and object properties.

Chapter 13: Properties

By Victoria Gonda

In Chapter 11, you were introduced to **properties** as the data members of Kotlin classes and objects. They are often used to describe the attributes of the object or hold state.

Open the starter project for this chapter to continue learning.

In the example below, the `Car` class has two properties, both constants that store `String` values:

```
class Car(val make: String, val color: String)
```

The two properties of `Car` are supplied in the primary constructor, and they store different string values for each instance of `Car`.

Properties can also be set up with custom **accessors**, also known as **getters** and **setters**. The properties supplied in the class primary constructor use default implementations of the accessors, storing the data in a **backing field**.

In this chapter, you'll learn much more about properties. You'll learn about property initializers, custom accessors, delegated properties, late initialization of properties and extension properties.

Constructor properties

As you may have guessed from the example in the introduction, you're already familiar with many of the features of properties. To review, imagine you're building an address book. The common unit you'll need is a `Contact`.

Add this class to your Kotlin file:

```
class Contact(var fullName: String, var emailAddress: String)
```

You can use this class over and over again to build an array of contacts, each with a different value. The properties you want to store are an individual's full name and email address.

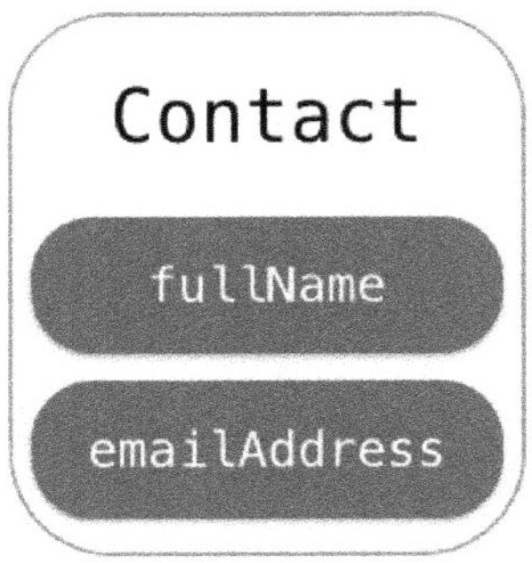

These are the properties of the `Contact` class. You provide a data type for each, but opt not to assign a default value, because you plan to assign the name and email address upon initialization. After all, the values will be different for each instance of `Contact`.

Create a contact in `main()`:

```
val contact = Contact(
  fullName = "Grace Murray",
  emailAddress = "grace@navy.mil"
)
```

You create an object by passing values as arguments into the class primary constructor.

As with any function call not using default values, using named arguments in the primary constructor is optional. Because named arguments are optional, you could also create the class like this:

```
val contact = Contact("Grace Murray", "grace@navy.mil")
```

Now, add the following statements:

```
val name = contact.fullName // Grace Murray
val email = contact.emailAddress // grace@navy.mil
```

Here, you're accessing the properties. You can access the individual properties using dot notation.

Now, assign a new value to the full name. When Grace married, she changed her last name:

```
contact.fullName = "Grace Hopper"
val grace = contact.fullName // Grace Hopper
```

Combining the dot notation with = assignment, you can assign new values. You can assign values to properties as long as they're defined as variables.

If you'd like to prevent a value from changing, you can define a property as a constant instead using `val`.

Consider this contact class:

```
class Contact2(var fullName: String, val emailAddress: String)
```

Notice that the `emailAddress` property uses `val` instead of `var`.

Now, look what happens when you try to change the value:

```
var contact2 = Contact2(
  fullName = "Grace Murray",
  emailAddress = "grace@navy.mil"
)

// Error: Val cannot be reassigned
contact2.emailAddress = "grace@gmail.com"
```

Once you've initialized an instance of the `Contact2` class, you can't change `emailAddress`.

Default values

If you can make a reasonable assumption about what the value of a property should be when the type is initialized, you can give that property a default value.

It doesn't make sense to create a default name or email address for a contact, but imagine there's a new property `type` to indicate what kind of contact it is

Create a contact class that has a default value:

```
class Contact3(
  var fullName: String,
  val emailAddress: String,
  var type: String = "Friend"
)
```

By assigning a value in the definition of type, you give this property a default value. Any contact created will automatically be a friend, unless you change the value of type to something like "Work" or "Family":

```
var contact3 = Contact3(
  fullName = "Grace Murray",
  emailAddress = "grace@navy.mil"
)
```

This contact3 has the type "Friend". You could change that by reassigning the type:

```
contact3.type = "Work"
```

Or supplying the type when you initially create it:

```
var workContact = Contact3(
  fullName = "Grace Murray",
  emailAddress = "grace@navy.mil",
  type = "Work"
)
```

Property initializers

Properties can also be initialized outside of the primary constructor, using literals and values passed into the primary constructor, using a **property initializer**.

Consider the Person class:

```
class Person(val firstName: String, val lastName: String) {
  val fullName = "$firstName $lastName"
}
```

In Person, the fullName property is initialized using the values that are passed into the primary constructor:

```
val person = Person("Grace", "Hopper")
person.fullName // Grace Hopper
```

You can set the value of properties with their declaration, as in `Person`, and also in the **init** block like below:

```
class Address {
  var address1: String
  var address2: String? = null
  var city = ""
  var state: String

  init {
    address1 = ""
    state = ""
  }
}
```

In `Address`, the `address2` and `city` properties are initialized in their declaration. The `address1` and `state` properties are initialized inside of `init`. Since all four properties of `Address` are given values inside the class definition, you can create an `Address` instance using an empty constructor call:

```
val address = Address()
```

Custom accessors

Many properties work just fine with the default accessor implementation, in which dot notation returns the value directly and an assignment statement just sets the value. Properties can also be defined with custom getter and setter methods. If a custom setter is provided, then the property must be declared as a `var`.

Custom getter

The measurement for a TV is the perfect use case for a custom accessor. The industry definition of the screen size of a TV isn't the screen's height or width, but its diagonal measurement.

Add this class:

```
class TV(var height: Double, var width: Double) {
  // 1
  val diagonal: Int
    get() {
      // 2
      val result = Math.sqrt(height * height + width * width)
      // 3
```

```
        return result.roundToInt()
    }
}
```

Going through this code one step at a time:

1. You use an `Int` type for your `diagonal` property. Although `height` and `width` are each a `Double`, TV sizes are usually advertised as nice, round numbers such as 50" rather than 49.52". Instead of the usual assignment operator = to assign a value as you would for a normal property, you use the `get()` function and curly braces to enclose your property's calculation.

2. Once you have the width and height, you can use the Pythagorean theorem to calculate the length of the diagonal. You use the `Math.sqrt()` method to calculate the diagonal.

3. You return the result as a rounded `Int` using `roundToInt()`: if the decimal is 0.5 or above, it rounds up; otherwise it rounds down. Had you converted `result` directly to `Int` without rounding first, the result would have been truncated, so 109.99 would have become 109.

> **Note**: You need to add the import `import kotlin.math.roundToInt` to the top of your file to use `rountToInt()`.

Since you've provided a custom getter, no value is stored for `diagonal`; it is simply returned based on a calculation. From outside of the class, a property with a custom getter can be accessed just like any other property.

Test this with the TV size calculation. Add this code to `main()`:

```
val tv = TV(height = 53.93, width = 95.87)
val size = tv.diagonal // 110
```

You have a 110-inch TV.

Let's say you decide you don't like the standard movie aspect ratio and would instead prefer a square screen.

Add this modification to your TV:

```
tv.width = tv.height
val diagonal = tv.diagonal // 76
```

You cut off some of the screen width to make it equivalent to the height. Now you *only* have a 76-inch square screen. The computed property automatically provides the new value based on the new width.

Mini-exercise

Do you have a television or a computer monitor? Measure the height and width, plug it into a `TV` object, and see if the diagonal measurement matches what you think it is.

Custom setter

The property you wrote in the previous section is a called a **read-only property**. It has a block of code to compute the value of the property: the custom getter. It's also possible to create a **read-write property** with two blocks of code: a custom getter and a **custom setter**. This setter works differently than you might expect. As the property has no place to store a value, the setter usually sets one or more related *other* properties indirectly.

Update your `diagonal` property to look like this:

```
// 1
var diagonal: Int
  // 2
  get() {
    val result = Math.sqrt(height * height + width * width)
    return result.roundToInt()
  }
  set(value) {
    // 3
    val ratioWidth = 16.0
    val ratioHeight = 9.0
    // 4
    val ratioDiagonal = Math.sqrt(
      ratioWidth * ratioWidth + ratioHeight * ratioHeight
    )
    height = value.toDouble() * ratioHeight / ratioDiagonal
    width = height * ratioWidth / ratioHeight
  }
```

Here's what's happening in this code:

1. You've changed `diagonal` to be a `var` instead of a `val`, since you're giving it a setter to change the value.
2. You use the same code as before to compute the value in the getter.
3. For a setter, you usually have to make some kind of assumption. In this case, you provide a reasonable default value for the screen ratio, in this case 16×9.
4. The formulas to calculate a height and width, given a diagonal and a ratio, are a bit deep. You could work them out with a bit of time, but we've done the dirty work for you and provided them here.

The important parts to focus on in the formulas for height and width are:

- The `value` parameter to the custom setter lets you use whatever value was passed in during the assignment.
- Since the `value` is an `Int`, you first convert it to a `Double` using `toDouble()`.
- Once you've done the calculations, you assign the `height` and `width` properties of the `TV` object.

Now, in addition to setting the height and width directly, you can set them *indirectly* by setting the `diagonal` property. When you set this value, your setter will calculate and store the height and width.

Notice that there's no `return` statement in a setter — it only modifies the other stored properties. With the setter in place, you have a nice little screen size calculator. Try it out using the following code:

```
tv.diagonal = 70
println(tv.height) // 34.32...
println(tv.width)  // 61.01...
```

Now you can discover the biggest TV that will fit in your cabinet or on your shelf.

Companion object properties

In the previous section, you learned how to associate properties with instances of a particular class. The properties on your instance of `TV` are separate from the properties on someone else's instance of `TV`.

However, the class *itself* may also need properties that are common across all instances. As you saw in the previous chapter, these properties are put into the **companion object** for the class. Companion object properties are similar to but not exactly like **static** properties that you find in other languages.

Imagine you're building a game with many levels. Each level has a few attributes, passed in the primary constructor

Create this scenario in your code:

```
class Level(
  val id: Int,
  var boss: String,
  var unlocked: Boolean
) {
  companion object {
    var highestLevel = 1
  }
}

val level1 = Level(id = 1, boss = "Chameleon", unlocked = true)
val level2 = Level(id = 2, boss = "Squid", unlocked = false)
val level3 = Level(id = 3, boss = "Chupacabra", unlocked =
false)
val level4 = Level(id = 4, boss = "Yeti", unlocked = false)
```

You can use a companion object property to store the game's progress as the player unlocks each level. Here, `highestLevel` is a property on `Level` itself rather than on the instances.

That means you don't access this property on an instance:

```
// Error: Unresolved reference
// Can't access members of the companion object on an instance
val highestLevel = level3.highestLevel
```

Instead, you access it on the class itself. Add this to your code:

```
val highestLevel = Level.highestLevel // 1
```

Using a companion object property means you can retrieve the same property value from anywhere in the code for your app or algorithm. The game's progress is accessible from any level or any other place in the game, like the main menu.

For Kotlin on the JVM, you can use the `@JvmStatic` annotation to force a property to be a static field in the bytecode, with static getters and setters. This will allow you to avoid having to use the singleton name in your Java code.

Update `Level` to look like this alternative version:

```
class Level(
  val id: Int,
  var boss: String,
  var unlocked: Boolean
) {
  companion object {
    @JvmStatic var highestLevel = 1
  }
}
```

Now, from Java, you can access `highestLevel` as follows:

```
Level.getHighestLevel() // Fine, thanks to @JvmStatic
Level.Companion.getHighestLevel() // Fine too, and necessary if
@JvmStatic were not used
```

`@JvmStatic` gives you nicer code in Java, and doesn't change how you access `highestLevel` in Kotlin.

Delegated properties

Most of the property initialization you've seen so far has been straightforward. You provide an initializer for a property, for example, as a literal value or default value, or you use custom accessors to compute the value.

For more complicated initializations, you may want to pass the initialization off to another object, or delay the initialization from when the instance is created. You may also want to observe when a property changes. For these cases, you can use **delegated properties**, which are indicated with the use of the `by` keyword.

Observable properties

For your `Level` implementation, it would be useful to automatically set the `highestLevel` when the player unlocks a new one. For that, you'll need a way to listen to property changes. Thankfully, you can use a delegated property **observable** to provide a callback for when the property changes.

Creat a new class to practice this:

```
class DelegatedLevel(val id: Int, var boss: String) {
  companion object {
    var highestLevel = 1
```

```
    }
    var unlocked: Boolean by Delegates.observable(false) {
      _, old, new ->
      if (new && id > highestLevel) {
        highestLevel = id
      }
      println("$old -> $new")
    }
}
```

You specify the property observer using `by Delegates.observable()`, whose first parameter is the initial value of the property.

> **Note**: Add the import `import kotlin.properties.Delegates` to use `Delegates`.

In this case, `unlocked` is initially `false`. The second parameter to `observable()` is a lambda with three arguments, the first of which is the property object itself (which you ignore), and the second and third of which are the old and new value of the property respectively.

The lambda is invoked after the value of `unlocked` is changed, so `new` indeed has the new value.

Add the following to try out your delegate:

```
val delegatedlevel1 = DelegatedLevel(id = 1, boss = "Chameleon")
val delegatedlevel2 = DelegatedLevel(id = 2, boss = "Squid")

println(DelegatedLevel.highestLevel) // 1

delegatedlevel2.unlocked = true

println(DelegatedLevel.highestLevel) // 2
```

Now, when the player unlocks a new level, it will update the `highestLevel` of `DelegatedLevel` if the level is a new high.

Limiting a variable

You can also use delegated property observers to limit the value of a variable. Say you had a light bulb that could only support a maximum current flowing through its filament.

Add this class:

```
class LightBulb {
  companion object {
    const val maxCurrent = 40
  }
  var current by Delegates.vetoable(0) {
    _, _, new ->
    if (new > maxCurrent) {
      println(
        "Current too high, falling back to previous setting.")
      false
    } else {
      true
    }
  }
}
```

In this example, you're using `by Delegates.vetoable()` and passing an initial value. The lambda callback passed to `vetoable()` returns a `Boolean` indicating whether the value should be allowed to be changed. If the current flowing into the bulb exceeds the maximum value, it will revert to its last successful value.

Give it a try:

```
val light = LightBulb()
light.current = 50
var current = light.current // 0
light.current = 40
current = light.current // 40
```

You try to set the light bulb to 50 amps, but the bulb rejected that input. Pretty cool!

> **Note:** Do not confuse delegated property observers with getters and setters. Delegated properties cannot have custom accessors. These are completely different concepts!

Lazy properties

If you have a property that might take some time to calculate and you don't want to slow things down until you actually need the property, say hello to **lazy properties**.

These could be useful for such things as downloading a user's profile picture or making a serious calculation.

Add this example of a `Circle` class that uses pi in its circumference calculation:

```
class Circle(var radius: Double = 0.0) {
  val pi: Double by lazy {
    ((4.0 * Math.atan(1.0 / 5.0)) - Math.atan(1.0 / 239.0)) *
4.0
  }
  val circumference: Double
    get() = pi * radius * 2
}
```

Here, you're not trusting the value of pi available to you from the standard library; you want to calculate it yourself.

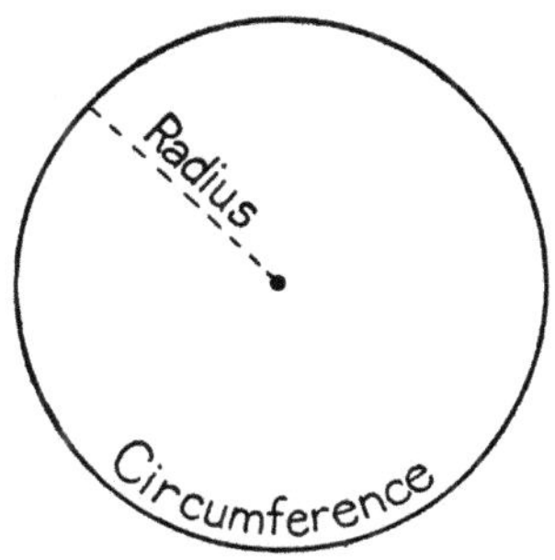

Now, create a new `Circle` instance, and the pi calculation won't run yet:

```
val circle = Circle(5.0) // got a circle, pi has not been run
```

The calculation of `pi` waits patiently until you need it. Only when you ask for the circumference property is `pi` calculated and assigned a value.

Access the value of the `circumference`, and this calculation will happen:

```
val circumference = circle.circumference // 31.42
// also, pi now has a value
```

Since you've got eagle eyes, you've noticed that the delegated property `pi` uses a `by lazy { }` pattern to calculate its value. The trailing parentheses are a lambda that initializes the value for `pi`. But since `pi` is marked as `by lazy`, this calculation is postponed until the first time you access the property.

For comparison, `circumference` is a non-delegated property and therefore is calculated every time it's accessed. You expect the circumference's value to change if the radius changes. `pi`, as a lazy property, is only calculated the first time. That's great, because who wants to calculate the same thing over and over again?

When you first initialize the `Circle` instance, the `pi` property effectively has no value. Then when some part of your code requests the property, its value will be calculated. The value only changes once, so you can use `val` on the property.

Mini-exercises

Of course, you should absolutely trust the value of pi from the standard library. It's a constant in the standard library, and you can access it as `kotlin.math.PI`. Given the `Circle` example above:

1. Remove the lazy property `pi`. Use the value of pi from the standard library instead.
2. Add a lazy property to `Circle` to calculate the area of the circle. Remember, the equation for the area of a circle is **pi*radius*radius**.

lateinit

If you just want to denote that a property will not have a value when the class instance is created, then you can use the **lateinit** keyword.

Create this `Lamp` class that has a `LightBulb` property declared as a `lateinit var`:

```
class Lamp {
  lateinit var bulb: LightBulb
}
```

Since the property has no value when the class instance is initialized, and the property will be changed at some later time, you must use `var` with `lateinit` and not `val`.

So, what if you bought a new lamp and then came home to discover that you had no spare bulbs?

```
val lamp = Lamp()
// ... lamp has no lightbulb, need to buy some!

println(lamp.bulb)
// Error: kotlin.UninitializedPropertyAccessException:
// lateinit property bulb has not been initialized

// ... bought some new ones
lamp.bulb = LightBulb()
```

If you try to access the lateinit `bulb` property before it's been initialized, you'll get an exception. Ouch!

Once you've assigned a value to `bulb`, you can turn the lights on and off as much as you'd like.

Extension properties

A circle has a radius, diameter and circumference that are all related to one another. But the `Circle` class above only includes the radius and circumference. It would be nice if the circle could tell you its diameter too, without you having to perform the calculation every time.

But what if the `Circle` class were provided to you in a library, so you could not modify its definition to add a diameter property? Kotlin uses **extension properties** to allow you to add such functionality without changing the class definition.

To add an extension property, create a new property with the property name appended to the class name, like so:

```
val Circle.diameter: Double
  get() = 2.0 * radius
```

You've created an extension property named `diameter` on the `Circle` class, and are providing a custom getter for `diameter`. Extension properties do not have backing fields, so you can only define them using custom accessors.

You can access the extension property just like any other property defined within the class:

```
val unitCircle = Circle(1.0)
println(unitCircle.diamater) // > 2.0
```

Nice! You no longer have to remember that complicated 2x relationship between radius and diameter yourself.

Challenges

Here are some challenges to test your new knowledge. Take a peek at the challenge solutions in the chapter materials if you need a hint while completing them.

Challenge 1

Rewrite the `IceCream` class below to use default values and lazy initialization:

```
class IceCream {
  val name: String
  val ingredients: ArrayList<String>
}
```

1. Use a default value for the name property.
2. Lazily initialize the `ingredients` list.

Challenge 2

At the beginning of the chapter, you saw a `Car` class. Dive into the inner workings of the car and rewrite the `FuelTank` class below with delegated property observer functionality:

```
class FuelTank {
  var level = 0.0 // decimal percentage between 0 and 1
}
```

1. Add a `lowFuel` property of Boolean type to the class.
2. Flip the `lowFuel` Boolean when the `level` drops below 10%.
3. Ensure that when the tank fills back up, the `lowFuel` warning will turn off.
4. Add a `FuelTank` property to `Car` and fill the tank. Then drive around for awhile.

Key points

- **Properties** are variables and constants that are part of a named type.
- **Default values** can be used to assign a value to a property within the class definition.
- **Property initializers** and the **init block** are used to ensure that the properties of an object are initialized when the object is created.
- **Custom accessors** are used to execute custom code when a property is accessed or set.
- The **companion object** holds properties that are universal to all instances of a particular class.
- **Delegated properties** are used when you want to observe, limit or lazily create a property. You'll want to use **lazy properties** when a property's initial value is computationally intensive or when you won't know the initial value of a property until after you've initialized the object.
- **lateinit** can be used to defer setting the value of a property reference until after the instance is created.
- **Extension properties** allow you to add properties to a class outside of the class definition, for example, if you're using a class from a library.

Where to go from here?

You saw the basics of properties while learning about classes, and now you've seen the more advanced features they have to offer. You've already learned a bit about methods in the previous chapters and will learn even more about them in the next one!

Chapter 14: Methods

By Victoria Gonda

In the previous chapter, you learned about properties, which are constants and variables that are part of classes and objects. **Methods**, as you've already seen, are merely functions that reside inside a class or object.

In this chapter, you'll take a closer look at methods. As with properties, you'll begin to design more complex classes and objects. So, open the starter project and jump right in!

Method refresher

Consider `ArrayList.removeAt()`. It pops the item at a given index off an instance of an array list:

```
val numbers = arrayListOf(1, 2, 3)
numbers.removeAt(numbers.lastIndex)
println(numbers) // > [1, 2]
```

Methods like `removeAt()` help you control the data in the array list.

Comparing methods to getters and setters

With custom accessors, you saw in the last chapter that you could run code from inside a class within a property definition. That sounds a lot like a method. What's the difference? It really comes down to a matter of style, but there are a few helpful thoughts to help you decide.

Properties hold values that you can get and set, while methods perform work. Sometimes this distinction gets fuzzy when a method's sole purpose is to return a single value.

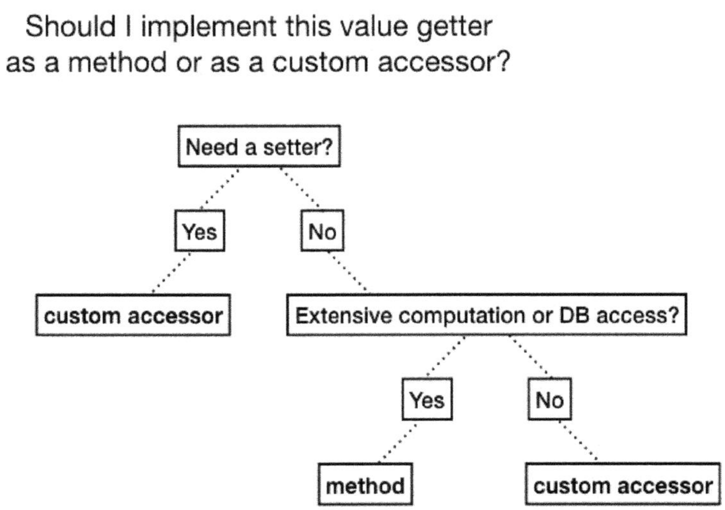

Ask yourself whether you want to be able to set a value as well as get the value. A property can have a custom setter inside to write values. Another question to consider is whether the calculation requires extensive computation or reads from a database.

Even for a simple value, a method helps you indicate to future developers that the call is expensive in time and computational resources. If the call is cheap (as in constant time *O*(1)), stick with custom accessors.

Turning a function into a method

To explore methods, you will create a simple model for dates called `SimpleDate`. Be aware that the various Kotlin platforms, such as the JVM and JS, contain production-ready `Date` classes that correctly handle many of the subtle intricacies of dealing with dates and times.

Add this code so you have something to work with:

```
// 1
val months = arrayOf(
    "January", "February", "March",
    "April", "May", "June",
    "July", "August", "September",
    "October", "November", "December"
)

// 2
class SimpleDate1(var month: String)

// 3
fun monthsUntilWinterBreak(from: SimpleDate1): Int {
  return months.indexOf("December") - months.indexOf(from.month)
}
```

This creates:

1. Ann array of months.
2. A `SimpleDate1` class.
3. A method to calculate the months until winter break.

> **Note**: If you live in the southern hemisphere, you can adjust the month for your winter break.

In the code above, how could you convert `monthsUntilWinterBreak()` into a method?

Create a new class, `SimpleDate2`, with `monthsUntilWinterBreak()` in the body of the class:

```
class SimpleDate2(var month: String) {
  fun monthsUntilWinterBreak(from: SimpleDate2): Int {
    return months.indexOf("December") -
months.indexOf(from.month)
  }
}
```

Making a method is as easy as moving the function inside the class definition.

There's no identifying keyword for a method; it really is just a function inside a class or object. You call methods on an instance using dot syntax just as you do for properties.

And just like properties, as soon as you start typing a method name, IntelliJ IDEA will provide suggestions. You can select one with the Up and Down arrow keys on your keyboard, and you can autocomplete the call by pressing Tab:

Try typing this into your file:

```
val date2 = SimpleDate2("October")
println(date2.monthsUntilWinterBreak(date2)) // > 2
```

If you think about this code for a minute, you'll realize that the method's definition is awkward. There must be a way to access the content stored by the instance instead of passing the instance itself as a parameter to the method. It would be so much nicer to call this:

```
date.monthsUntilWinterBreak() // Error!
```

Introducing this

A class definition is like a blueprint, whereas an instance is a real object. To access the value of an instance, you use the keyword **this** inside the class.

The keyword `this` acts as a reference to the current instance. Make a `SimpleDate3` with this transformed method:

```
// 1
fun monthsUntilWinterBreak(): Int {
  // 2
  return months.indexOf("December") - months.indexOf(this.month)
}
```

Here's what changed:

1. Now there's no parameter in the method definition.
2. In the implementation, `this` replaces the old parameter name.

You can now call the method without passing a parameter. Try it out:

```
val date3 = SimpleDate3("September")
date3.monthsUntilWinterBreak() // 3
```

That's looking a lot cleaner! One more thing you can do to simplify the code is to remove `this`. That might be confusing because you just added it!

`this` is your reference to the instance, but most of the time you don't need to use it because Kotlin understands your intent if you just use a variable name.

While you can always use `this` to access the properties and methods of the current instance, most of the time you won't need to. In `monthsUntilWinterBreak()`, you can just say `month` instead of `this.month`:

```
return months.indexOf("December") - months.indexOf(month)
```

Most programmers use `this` only when it is required, for example, to disambiguate between a local variable and a property with the same name. You'll get more practice using `this` a little later.

Mini-exercise

Since `monthsUntilWinterBreak()` returns a single value and there's not much calculation involved, transform the method into a property with a customer getter.

Object methods

Like classes, Kotlin objects defined with the `object` keyword can have member functions that refer to the object itself.

For class companion objects, like companion object properties, you can use **companion object methods** to access data across all instances. You call companion object methods on the class itself, instead of on an instance. To define a companion object method, you put its definition inside the `companion object` block.

Object methods are useful for things that are *about* a type in general, rather than something about specific instances.

For an example, create this class:

```
class MyMath {
  // 1
  companion object {
    fun factorial(number: Int): Int {
      // 2
      return (1..number).fold(1) { a, b -> a * b }
    }
  }
}

// 3
MyMath.factorial(6) // 720
```

Here, you use object methods to group similar methods into a class. In this case, math operations.

You might have custom calculations for things such as factorial. Instead of having a bunch of free-standing functions, you can group related functions together as methods in a class companion object. The class with its companion object is said to act as a **namespace**. If the class `MyMath` did not need any instances, you could instead just define `MyMath` as a Kotlin `object` to create the namespace.

Here's what's happening in `MyMath`:

1. You use the `companion object` block to declare the method on the class, which accepts an integer and returns an integer.
2. The implementation uses a higher-order function called `fold()`. It effectively follows the formula for calculating a factorial: "The product of all the whole numbers from 1 to *n*". You could write this using a `for` loop, but the higher-order function expresses your intent in a cleaner way.
3. You call the method on `MyMath`, rather than on an instance of the class.

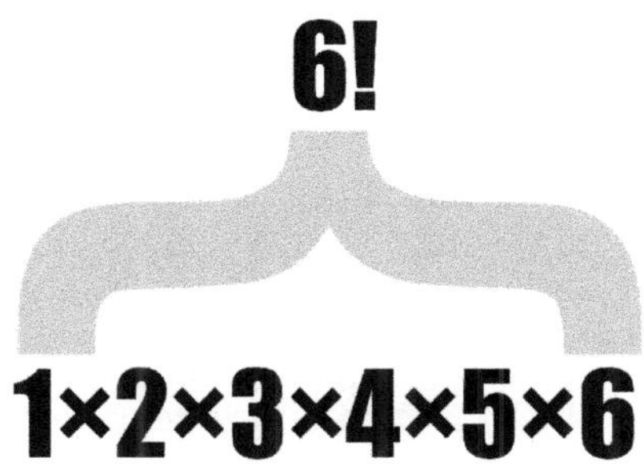

Methods gathered into an object or companion object will advantageously code complete in IntelliJ IDEA.

In this example, you can see all the math utility methods available to you by typing `MyMath.`:

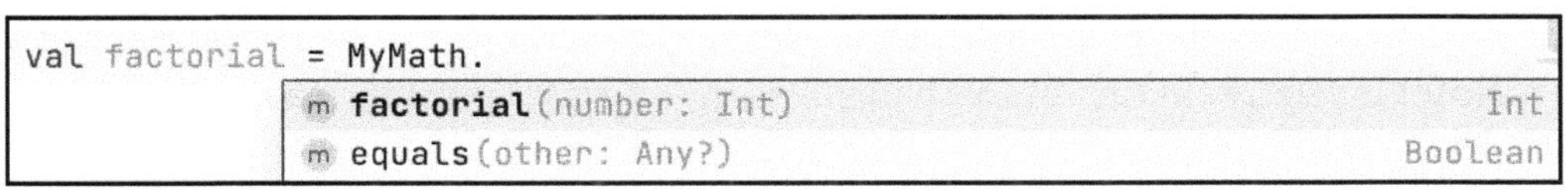

Mini-exercise

Add a method to the `MyMath` class that calculates the *n*-th triangle number. It will be similar to the factorial formula, except instead of multiplying the numbers, you add them.

For an example the triangle number for 3 is 1+2+3=6. If you need a hint, you can look at the challenge solutions for this chapter.

Extension methods

Sometimes you want to add functionality to a class but don't want to muddy up the original definition. And sometimes you can't add the functionality because you don't have access to the source code. Just as for properties, it is possible to augment an existing class or object (even one you do not have the source code for) by adding methods to it.

Suppose you are using a `SimpleDate` class provided by a library that you don't have the source code for. The class provides a method to calculate months until winter break, but you'd like to have the ability to know the number of months until summer break.

To add an extension method onto a class, define a new function with the function name appended to the class name, like so:

```
fun SimpleDate.monthsUntilSummerBreak(): Int {
  val monthIndex = months.indexOf(month)
  return if (monthIndex in 0..months.indexOf("June")) {
    months.indexOf("June") - months.indexOf(month)
  } else if (monthIndex in
      months.indexOf("June")..months.indexOf("August")) {
    0
  } else {
    months.indexOf("June") + (12 - months.indexOf(month))
  }
}
```

Note: If you live in the southern hemisphere, you can adjust the month for your summer break.

This creates an extension method `monthsUntilSummerBreak()` on the `SimpleDate` class.

You can use the extension method just like any other method call on an instance of the class:

```
val date = SimpleDate()
date.month = "December"
println(date.monthsUntilSummerBreak()) // > 6
```

You can add extension methods onto built-in types as well:

```
fun Int.abs(): Int {
  return if (this < 0) -this else this
}

println(4.abs())    // > 4
println((-4).abs()) // > 4
```

You're calling the extension method directly on a number, a literal value of the `Int` class.

> **Note**: The Kotlin standard library has an `abs()` function that you would normally use.

Companion object extensions

If your class has a companion object, you can add extension methods to it by using the implicit companion object name `Companion`, or by using the custom name if the companion object has one.

As an example, you can add a method named `primeFactors()` to `MyMath` using a companion object extension:

```
fun MyMath.Companion.primeFactors(value: Int): List<Int> {
  // 1
  var remainingValue = value
  // 2
  var testFactor = 2
  val primes = mutableListOf<Int>()
  // 3
  while (testFactor * testFactor <= remainingValue) {
    if (remainingValue % testFactor == 0) {
      primes.add(testFactor)
      remainingValue /= testFactor
    } else {
      testFactor += 1
    }
  }

  if (remainingValue > 1) {
    primes.add(remainingValue)
  }

  return primes
}
```

This method finds the prime factors for a given number. For example, 81 returns `[3, 3, 3, 3]`. Here's what's happening in the code:

1. The `value` passed in as a parameter is assigned to the mutable variable, `remainingValue`, so that it can be changed as the calculation runs.
2. The `testFactor` starts with a value of 2 and will be divided into `remainingValue`.
3. The logic runs a loop until the `remainingValue` is exhausted. If it divides evenly, meaning there's no remainder, that value of the `testFactor` is set aside as a prime factor. If it doesn't divide evenly, `testFactor` is incremented for the next loop.

This algorithm takes a brute-force approach, but does contain one optimization: the square of the `testFactor` should never be larger than the `remainingValue`. If it is, the `remainingValue` itself must be prime and is added to the `primes` list.

You've now added a method to `MyMath` without changing its original definition. Verify that the extension works with this code:

```
MyMath.primeFactors(81) // [3, 3, 3, 3]
```

Challenges

As you work through these challenges, remember you can look at the solutions for this chapter at any time for a hint or to check your work.

1. Given the `Circle` class below:

```
import kotlin.math.PI

class Circle(var radius: Double = 0.0) {
 val area: Double
   get() {
     return PI * radius * radius
   }
}
```

Write a method that can change an instance's area by a growth factor. For example if you call `circle.grow(factor = 3)`, the area of the instance will triple.

Hint: Make `area` a `var` and add a setter to it.

2. Here is a naïve way of writing `advance()` for the `SimpleDate` class you saw earlier in the chapter:

```
val months = arrayOf(
   "January", "February", "March",
   "April", "May", "June",
   "July", "August", "September",
   "October", "November", "December"
)

class SimpleDate(var month: String, var day: Int = 0) {
 fun advance() {
   day += 1
 }
}

var date = SimpleDate(month = "December", day = 31)
date.advance()
date.month // December; should be January!
date.day // 32; should be 1!
```

What happens when the function should go from the end of one month to the start of the next? Rewrite `advance()` to account for advancing from December 31st to January 1st.

3. Create a Kotlin object named `MyMath` with `isEven()` and `isOdd()` methods that return `true` if a number is even or odd respectively.

4. Add extension methods `isEven()` and `isOdd()` to `Int`.

Note: Generally, you want to be careful about what functionality you add to standard library types as it can cause confusion for readers.

5. Add the extension method `primeFactors()` to `Int`. Since this is an expensive operation, this is best left as an actual method.

Key points

- **Methods** are behaviors that extend the functionality of a class.
- A typical method is a function defined inside of a class or object.
- A method can access the value of an instance by using the keyword `this`.
- **Companion object methods** add behavior to a class instead of the instances of that class. To define a companion object method, you add a function in the class `companion object` block.
- You can augment an existing class definition and add methods to it using **extension methods**.

Where to go from here?

Methods and properties are the things that make up your classes, instances, and objects. Learning about them as you have these last two chapters is important since you'll use them all the time in Kotlin.

You've tackled the basics of classes. In the next chapter, you'll learn about some advanced ways to use classes such as inheritance and limiting member visibility.

Chapter 15: Advanced Classes

By Victoria Gonda

An earlier chapter introduced you to the basics of defining and using classes in Kotlin. Classes are used to support traditional object-oriented programming.

Class concepts include inheritance, overriding, polymorphism and composition which makes them suited for this purpose. These extra features require special consideration for construction, class hierarchies, and understanding the class lifecycle in memory.

This chapter will introduce you to the finer points of classes in Kotlin, and help you understand how you can create more complex classes. Open up the starter project or a new Kotlin project to get started.

Introducing inheritance

In an earlier chapter, you saw a `Grade` class and a pair of class examples: `Person` and `Student`.

```
data class Grade(
  val letter: Char,
  val points: Double,
  val credits: Double
)

class Person(var firstName: String, var lastName: String) {
  fun fullName() = "$firstName $lastName"
}

class Student(var firstName: String, var lastName: String,
  var grades: MutableList<Grade> = mutableListOf<Grade>()) {

  fun recordGrade(grade: Grade) {
    grades.add(grade)
  }
}
```

There's an incredible amount of redundancy between `Person` and `Student`. They share many of the same properties. Maybe you've also noticed that a `Student` *is* a `Person`!

This simple case demonstrates the idea behind **class inheritance**. Much like in the real world, where you can think of a student as a person, you can represent the same relationship in code by replacing the original `Person` and `Student` class implementations with the following. Add these classes to your code:

```
// 1
open class Person(var firstName: String, var lastName: String) {
  fun fullName() = "$firstName $lastName"
}

// 2
class Student(
  firstName: String,
  lastName: String,
  var grades: MutableList<Grade> = mutableListOf<Grade>()
) : Person(firstName, lastName) {

  open fun recordGrade(grade: Grade) {
    grades.add(grade)
  }
}
```

In this modified example:

1. The `Person` class now includes the `open` keyword.
2. The `Student` class now **inherits** from `Person`, indicated by a colon after the naming of `Student`, followed by the class from which `Student` inherits, which in this case is `Person`.

The `open` keyword means that the `Person` class is *open* to be inherited from; the need for `open` is part of the Kotlin philosophy of requiring choices such as inheritance to be explicitly defined by the programmer.

You must still add parameters such as `firstName` to the `Student` constructor, and they are then passed along as arguments to the `Person` constructor. Notice in the modified example that the `var` keyword is no longer needed on the parameters, since they are already defined as properties in the `Person` class.

Through inheritance, `Student` automatically gets the properties and methods declared in the `Person` class. In code, it would be accurate to say that a `Student` *is-a* `Person`.

With much less duplication of code, you can now create `Student` objects that have all the properties and methods of a `Person`. Add this to `main()`:

```
val john = Person(firstName = "Johnny", lastName = "Appleseed")
val jane = Student(firstName = "Jane", lastName = "Appleseed")

john.fullName() // Johnny Appleseed
jane.fullName() // Jane Appleseed
```

Both `john` and `jane` have all the properties of a `Person` because `Student` inherits from `Person`.

Additionally, only the `Student` object will have all of the properties and methods defined in `Student`. Try this out:

```
val history = Grade(letter = 'B', points = 9.0, credits = 3.0)
jane.recordGrade(history)
// john.recordGrade(history) // john is not a student!
```

You can't record a grade for `john` because he's not a student. The shared properties only go one direction.

A class that inherits from another class is known as a **subclass** or a **derived class**, and the class from which it inherits is known as a **superclass** or **base class**.

The rules for subclassing are fairly simple:

- A Kotlin class can inherit from only one other class, a concept known as **single inheritance**.
- A Kotlin class can only inherit from a class that is **open**.
- There's no limit to the depth of subclassing, meaning you can subclass from a class that is *also* a subclass, like below (and first redefining `Student` with `open`):

```
open class Student(
  firstName: String,
  lastName: String,
  var grades: MutableList<Grade> = mutableListOf<Grade>()
) : Person(firstName, lastName) {

  open fun recordGrade(grade: Grade) {
    grades.add(grade)
  }
}

open class BandMember(
  firstName: String,
  lastName: String
) : Student(firstName, lastName) {
  open val minimumPracticeTime: Int
    get() { return  2 }
}

class OboePlayer(
  firstName: String,
  lastName: String
): BandMember(firstName, lastName) {
  // This is an example of an override, will be covered soon.
  override val minimumPracticeTime: Int =
    super.minimumPracticeTime * 2
}
```

A chain of subclasses is called a **class hierarchy**. In this example, the hierarchy would be `OboePlayer` → `BandMember` → `Student` → `Person`. A class hierarchy is analogous to a family tree. Because of this analogy, a superclass is also called the **parent class** of its **child class**.

Polymorphism

The Student–Person relationship demonstrates a computer science concept known as **polymorphism**. In brief, polymorphism is a programming language's ability to treat an object differently based on context.

An OboePlayer is of course an OboePlayer, but it is also a Person. Because it derives from Person, you could use an OboePlayer object anywhere you'd use a Person object.

This example demonstrates how you can treat an OboePlayer as a Person. Add this to your example:

```
fun phonebookName(person: Person): String {
  return "${person.lastName}, ${person.firstName}"
}

val person = Person(
  firstName = "Johnny",
  lastName = "Appleseed"
)
val oboePlayer = OboePlayer(
  firstName = "Jane",
  lastName = "Appleseed"
)

phonebookName(person)     // Appleseed, Johnny
phonebookName(oboePlayer) // Appleseed, Jane
```

Because OboePlayer derives from Person, it is a valid input into the function phonebookName(). More importantly, the function has no idea that the object passed in is anything *other* than a regular Person. It can only observe the elements of OboePlayer that are defined in the Person base class.

With the polymorphism characteristics provided by class inheritance, Kotlin is treating the object pointed to by oboePlayer differently based on the context. This can be particularly useful to you when you have diverging class hierarchies, but want to have code that operates on a common type or base class.

For example, if you also have a hierarchy SoccerPlayer → StudentAthlete → Student → Person, and you want code that operates on all Students, you can do this regardless of if a student is an OboePlayer or a SoccerPlayer.

Runtime hierarchy checks

Now that you are coding with polymorphism, you will likely find situations where the specific type behind a variable can be different. For instance, you could define a variable `hallMonitor` as a `Student`. Add a `hallMonitor` to `main()`:

```
var hallMonitor =
  Student(firstName = "Jill", lastName = "Bananapeel")
```

But what if `hallMonitor` were a more derived type, such as an `OboePlayer`? Change `hallMonitor` to be an `oboePlayer`.

```
hallMonitor = oboePlayer
```

Because `hallMonitor` is originally defined as a `Student`, the compiler won't allow you to attempt calling properties or methods for a more derived type. You'll get an error if you try to do something like this:

```
hallMonitor.minimumPracticeTime // Error!
```

You get an error here because the compiler only knows that `hallMonitor` is a `Student`. It does not know `hallMonitor` is a `BandMember` or `OboePlayer`.

Fortunately, Kotlin gives you the `is` operator to check whether an instance is part of a given inheritance hierarchy, and `!is` (not-is) for the opposite. Add these checks:

```
println(hallMonitor is OboePlayer) // true, since assigned it to
oboePlayer
println(hallMonitor !is OboePlayer) // also have !is for "not-
is"
println(hallMonitor is Person) // true, because Person is
ancestor of OboePlayer
```

Run your code to see the result.

Kotlin also provides the `as` infix operator to treat a property or a variable as another type:

- `as`: An **unsafe** cast to a specific type that is known at compile time to succeed, such as casting to a supertype.
- `as?`: A **safe** cast (to a subtype). If the cast fails, the result of the expression will be `null`.

These can be used in various contexts to treat the `hallMonitor` as a `BandMember`, or the `oboePlayer` as a less-derived `Student`:

```
(oboePlayer as Student).minimumPracticeTime // Error: No longer
a band member!

(hallMonitor as? BandMember)?.minimumPracticeTime
// 4 if hallMonitor = oboePlayer, else null
```

You may be wondering under what contexts you would use the as operator by itself. Any object contains all the properties and methods of its parent class, so what use is casting it to something it already is?

Kotlin has a strong type system, and the interpretation of a specific type can have an effect on **static dispatch**, or the decision of which specific operation is selected at compile time. Sound confusing? How about an example?

Assume you have two functions with identical names and parameter names for two different parameter types:

```
fun afterClassActivity(student: Student): String {
  return "Goes home!"
}

fun afterClassActivity(student: BandMember): String {
  return "Goes to practice!"
}
```

If you were to pass `oboePlayer` into `afterClassActivity()`, which one of these implementations would get called? The answer lies in Kotlin's dispatch rules, which in this case will select the more specific version that takes in an `OboePlayer`.

If you were to cast `oboePlayer` to a `Student`, the `Student` version would be called:

```
afterClassActivity(oboePlayer) // Goes to practice!
afterClassActivity(oboePlayer as Student) // Goes home!
```

Inheritance, methods and overrides

Subclasses' properties and methods are defined in their superclass, plus any additional properties and methods the subclass defines for itself. In that sense, subclasses are *additive*; for example, you've already seen that the `Student` class can add additional properties and methods for handling a student's grades. These properties and methods wouldn't be available to any `Person` class instances, but they *would* be available to `Student` subclasses.

Besides creating their own methods, subclasses can **override** methods defined in their superclass. Assume that student athletes become ineligible for the athletics program if they're failing three or more classes. That means you need to keep track of failing grades somehow. Add this class to your file:

```
class StudentAthlete(
  firstName: String,
  lastName: String
): Student(firstName, lastName) {
  val failedClasses = mutableListOf<Grade>()

  override fun recordGrade(grade: Grade) {
    super.recordGrade(grade)

    if (grade.letter == 'F') {
      failedClasses.add(grade)
    }
  }

  val isEligible: Boolean
    get() = failedClasses.size < 3
}
```

Take a close look at `recordGrade()`. In this example, the `StudentAthlete` class overrides `recordGrade()` so it can keep track of any courses the student has failed.

The `StudentAthlete` class then has its own computed property, `isEligible`, that uses this information to determine the athlete's eligibility.

When overriding a method, use the `override` keyword before the method declaration.

If your subclass were to have an identical method declaration as its superclass, but you omitted the `override` keyword, Kotlin would indicate a build error.

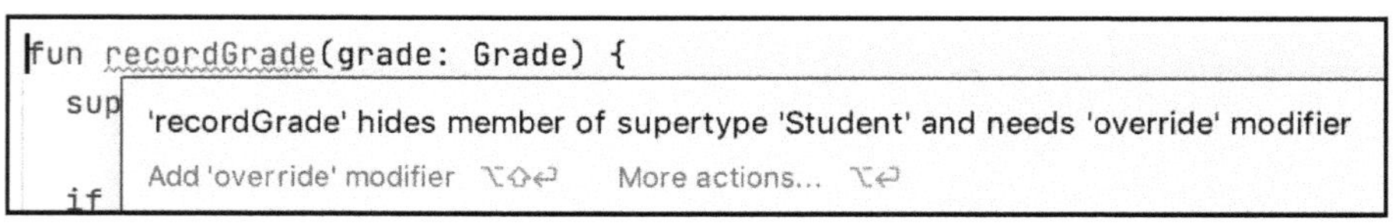

recordGrade hides member of supertype Student and needs override modifier

This makes it very clear whether a method is an override of an existing one or not.

Create an instance of the subclass and make calls to both the overridden and new methods:

```
val math = Grade(letter = 'B', points = 9.0, credits = 3.0)
val science = Grade(letter = 'F', points = 9.0, credits = 3.0)
```

```
val physics = Grade(letter = 'F', points = 9.0, credits = 3.0)
val chemistry = Grade(letter = 'F', points = 9.0, credits = 3.0)

val dom = StudentAthlete(firstName = "Dom", lastName = "Grady")
dom.recordGrade(math)
dom.recordGrade(science)
dom.recordGrade(physics)
println(dom.isEligible) // > true
dom.recordGrade(chemistry)
println(dom.isEligible) // > false
```

Run this code so you can see your changes in action.

Introducing super

You may have also noticed the line `super.recordGrade(grade)` in the overridden method. The `super` keyword is similar to `this`, except it will invoke the method in the nearest implementing superclass. In the example of `recordGrade()` in `StudentAthlete`, calling `super.recordGrade(grade)` will execute the method as defined in the `Student` class.

Remember how inheritance let you define `Person` with first name and last name properties and avoid repeating those properties (using `val` or `var`) in subclasses? Similarly, being able to call the superclass methods means you can write the code to record the grade once in `Student` and then call "up" to it as needed in subclasses.

Although it isn't always required, it's often important to call `super` when overriding a method in Kotlin. The `super` call is what will record the grade itself in the `grades` array, because that behavior isn't duplicated in `StudentAthlete`. Calling `super` is also a way of avoiding the need for duplicate code in `StudentAthlete` and `Student`.

When to call super

As you may notice, exactly *when* you call super can have an important effect on your overridden method.

Suppose you replace the overridden `recordGrade()` method in the `StudentAthlete` class with the following version that recalculates the `failedClasses` each time a grade is recorded:

```
override fun recordGrade(grade: Grade) {
  var newFailedClasses = mutableListOf<Grade>()
  for (grade in grades) {
    if (grade.letter == 'F') {
      newFailedClasses.add(grade)
```

```
    }
  }
  failedClasses = newFailedClasses

  super.recordGrade(grade)
}
```

This version of `recordGrade()` uses the `grades` array to find the current list of failed classes. If you've spotted a bug in the code above, good job! Since you call `super` last, if the new `grade.letter` is an `F`, the code won't update `failedClasses` properly.

While it's not a hard rule, it's generally best practice to call the `super` version of a method first when overriding. That way, the superclass won't experience any side effects introduced by its subclass, and the subclass won't need to know the superclass's implementation details.

Preventing inheritance

Often you'll want to disallow subclasses of a particular class. Kotlin makes this easy since the default for `class` definitions is that classes are **not** open to subclassing; you **must** use the `open` keyword to allow inheritance.

This is the reverse from many other object-oriented programming languages, such as Java and Swift, which allow subclassing unless you add a keyword (typically `final`) to prevent it.

Here's an example in Kotlin:

```
class FinalStudent(firstName: String, lastName: String)
    : Person(firstName, lastName)

class FinalStudentAthlete(firstName: String, lastName: String)
    : FinalStudent(firstName, lastName) // Build error!
```

This causes an error when trying to define `FinalStudentAthlete` because `FinalStudent` is not marked as `open`.

By not marking the `FinalStudent` class `open`, you tell the compiler to prevent any classes from inheriting from `FinalStudent`. Kotlin is designed to improve your use of inheritance by only allowing you to inherit when you specifically want to.

The Kotlin approach is similar with respect to overriding functions in classes. If you only want specific methods to be overridden, you can mark those methods as `open`:

```
open class AnotherStudent(firstName: String, lastName: String)
    : Person(firstName, lastName) {

  open fun recordGrade(grade: Grade) {}
  fun recordTardy() {}
}

class AnotherStudentAthlete(firstName: String, lastName: String)
    : AnotherStudent(firstName, lastName) {

  override fun recordGrade(grade: Grade) {} // OK
  override fun recordTardy() {} // Build error! recordTardy is
final
}
```

Here, you get an error when trying to override `recordTardy()` because it's not `open` in the superclass.

Kotlin's approach of defaulting to classes and methods being final tells the compiler it doesn't need to look for any more subclasses, which can shorten compile time, and it also requires you to be very explicit when deciding to allow a class to be inherited from.

Abstract classes

In certain situations, you may want to prevent a class from being instantiated, but still be able to be inherited from. This will let you define properties and behavior common to all subclasses. You can only create instances of the subclasses and not the base, parent class. Such parent classes are called **abstract**.

Classes declared with the `abstract` keyword are **open** by default and can be inherited from. In abstract classes, you can also declare abstract methods marked with `abstract` that have no body. The abstract methods must be overridden in subclasses.

Add these classes:

```
abstract class Mammal(val birthDate: String) {
  abstract fun consumeFood()
}

class Human(birthDate: String): Mammal(birthDate) {
  override fun consumeFood() {
    // ...
  }
  fun createBirthCertificate() {
    // ...
  }
}
```

Here, you define a `Mammal` class, which is abstract, and a `Human` class, which inherits from `Mammal`.

Now, see what happens when you try to create an instance of each of these:

```
val human = Human("1/1/2000")
val mammal = Mammal("1/1/2000") // Error: Cannot create an
instance of an abstract class
```

You can create an instance of the `Mammal` subclass `Human`, but not of the `Mammal` class itself.

Abstract classes are closely related to **interfaces**, which you'll learn about in Chapter 17: "Interfaces."

Sealed classes

Sealed classes are useful when you want to make sure that the values of a given type can only come from a particular limited set of subtypes. They allow you to define a strict hierarchy of types. The sealed classes themselves are abstract and cannot be instantiated.

Sealed classes act very much like **enum classes**, which you'll learn about in the next chapter, but also allow subtypes which can have multiple instances and have state.

Add a sealed class `Shape` that has subtypes `Circle` and `Square`:

```
sealed class Shape {
  class Circle(val radius: Int): Shape()
  class Square(val sideLength: Int): Shape()
}
```

You've used the keyword sealed to mark Shape as a sealed class. Both circles and squares are shapes, but a circle has a radius and a square has a side length.

Unlike enum classes, you can create multiple instances of each type within the sealed class. Create these instances:

```
val circle1 = Shape.Circle(4)
val circle2 = Shape.Circle(2)
val square1 = Shape.Square(4)
val square2 = Shape.Square(2)
```

You're able to make as many Circles and Squares as you like, but no Shapes.

Functions defined on Shape can distinguish between the different subtypes using a when expression. Add this function:

```
fun size(shape: Shape): Int {
  return when (shape) {
    is Shape.Circle -> shape.radius
    is Shape.Square -> shape.sideLength
  }
}

size(circle1) // radius of 4
size(square2) // sideLength of 2
```

You'll learn more about sealed classes in Chapter 16, "Enum & Sealed Classes."

Secondary constructors

You've seen how to define the primary constructors of classes, by appending a list of property parameters and their types to the class name.

The keyword constructor was implicit in the primary constructor:

```
class Person(var firstName: String, var lastName: String) {
  fun fullName() = "$firstName $lastName"
}

// is the same as

class Person constructor(var firstName: String, var lastName:
String) {
  fun fullName() = "$firstName $lastName"
}
```

Both of the above definitions work the same, even though one uses the `constructor` keyword.

You can also use the `constructor` keyword to define secondary constructors for a class, within the class body. You can call between the various constructors using the `this` keyword:

```
open class Shape {
  constructor(size: Int) {
    // ...
  }

  constructor(size: Int, color: String) : this(size) {
    // ...
  }
}
```

In this case, one secondary constructor is calling another with a single `Int` argument representing the `size`.

When subclassing, you can call from constructors in the subclass to constructors in the superclass using `super`:

```
class Circle : Shape {
  constructor(size: Int) : super(size) {
    // ...
  }

  constructor(size: Int, color: String) : super(size, color) {
    // ...
  }
}
```

Nested and inner classes

When two classes are closely related to each other, sometimes it's useful to define one class within the scope of another class. By doing so, you've namespaced one class within the other.

Add `Car` and `Engine` to your project:

```
class Car(val carName: String) {
  class Engine(val engineName: String)
}
```

Other classes that want to use the `Engine` class must refer to it as `Car.Engine`. In this case, `Engine` is a **nested class** of `Car`.

When a class is nested inside another, it does not by default have access to the other members of the class:

```
class Car(val carName: String) {
  class Engine(val engineName: String) {
    override fun toString(): String {
      return "$engineName in a $carName" // Error: cannot see
carName in outer scope!
    }
  }
}
```

Since `carName` is a property of `Car`, it is not accessible from the nested class `Engine`.

If you want the nested class to have access to the other members, you need to define it with the `inner` keyword.

Update your `Engine` to look like this:

```
inner class Engine(val engineName: String) {
  override fun toString(): String {
    return "$engineName engine in a $carName"
  }
}
```

Since `Engine` is now an inner class of `Car`, it can access the other members of `Car`

Add and run this code:

```
val mazda = Car("mazda")
val mazdaEngine = mazda.Engine("rotary")
println(mazdaEngine) // > rotary engine in a mazda
```

The engine can now get the car type just fine!

Visibility modifiers

While the `open` keyword determines what you can and cannot override in class hierarchies, **visibility modifiers** determine what can and cannot be seen both inside and outside of classes.

The four visibility modifiers available in Kotlin are:

- `public`: Visible from everywhere, within subclasses, other files, and other project modules; if no visibility modifier is specified, it defaults to `public`.
- `private`: Visible only within the same `class` for classes, and only within the same file for top-level functions and other non-class definitions. This means hidden from subclasses, too.
- `protected`: Visible only within subclasses for class hierarchies.
- `internal`: Visible only within the same **module**, for example, an IntelliJ IDEA module.

Generally you want to limit the visibility or **scope** of your classes and variables as much as possible. This will keep the responsibility of your classes clear and prevent you from changing the state of a class when you really shouldn't be.

Add a class hierarchy consisting of a `User` and a `PrivilegedUser` with a list of privileges:

```
data class Privilege(val id: Int, val name: String)

open class User(
  val username: String,
  private val id: String,
  protected var age: Int
)

class PrivilegedUser(username: String, id: String, age: Int)
    : User(username, id, age) {
  private val privileges = mutableListOf<Privilege>()

  fun addPrivilege(privilege: Privilege) {
    privileges.add(privilege)
  }

  fun hasPrivilege(id: Int): Boolean {
    return privileges.map { it.id }.contains(id)
  }

  fun about(): String {
    //return "$username, $id" // Error: id is private
    return "$username, $age" // OK: age is protected
  }
}
```

In the super class, `User`, the `id` property is marked `private`, so can only be referenced inside the `User` class. The `age` property is `protected`, so the subclass `PrivilegedUser` can see it.

Try it out:

```
val privilegedUser =
  PrivilegedUser(username = "sashinka", id = "1234", age = 21)
val privilege = Privilege(1, "invisibility")
privilegedUser.addPrivilege(privilege)
println(privilegedUser.about()) // > sashinka, 21
```

`PrivilegedUser` can access both the `username` property, which is public, and the `age` property.

When and why to subclass

This chapter has introduced you to class inheritance, along with the numerous programming techniques that subclassing enables. But you might be asking, "When should I subclass?"

Rarely is there a right or wrong answer to that important question. Understanding the trade-offs can help you make the best decision for any particular case.

Using the `Student` and `StudentAthlete` classes as an example, you might decide you can simply put all of the characteristics of `StudentAthlete` into `Student`:

```
data class Sport(val name: String)

class Student2(firstName: String, lastName: String)
    : Person(firstName, lastName) {
  var grades = mutableListOf<Grade>()
  var sports = mutableListOf<Sport>()
  // original code
}
```

In reality, this *could* solve all of the use cases for your needs. A `Student2` that doesn't play sports would simply have an empty `sports` array, and you would avoid some of the added complexities of subclassing.

Single responsibility

In software development, however, the guideline known as the **single responsibility principle** states that any class should have a single concern. In Student–StudentAthlete, you might argue that it shouldn't be the Student class's job to encapsulate responsibilities that only make sense to student athletes, and it makes sense to create the StudentAthlete subclass rather than keep a list of sports within Student.

Strong types

Subclassing creates an additional type. With Kotlin's type system, you can declare properties or behavior based on objects that are student athletes, not regular students:

```
class Team {
  var players = mutableListOf<StudentAthlete>()

  val isEligible: Boolean
    get() {
      for (player in players) {
        if (!player.isEligible) {
          return false
        }
      }
      return true
    }
}
```

A team has players who are student athletes. If you tried to add a regular Student object to the array of players, the type system wouldn't allow it. This can be useful as the compiler can help you enforce the logic and requirement of your system.

Shared base classes

You can subclass a shared base class multiple times by classes that have mutually exclusive behavior:

```
// A button that can be pressed.
open class Button {
  fun press() {
  }
}

// An image that can be rendered on a button.
```

```
class Image

// A button that is composed entirely of an image.
class ImageButton(var image: Image): Button()

// A button that renders as text.
class TextButton(val text: String): Button()
```

In this example, you can imagine numerous `Button` subclasses that share only the fact that they can be pressed. The `ImageButton` and `TextButton` classes likely have entirely different mechanisms to render the appearance of a button, so they might have to implement their own behavior when the button is pressed.

You can see here how storing `image` and `text` in the `Button` class — not to mention any other kind of button there might be — would quickly become impractical. It makes sense for `Button` to be concerned with the press behavior, and the subclasses to handle the actual look and feel of the button.

Extensibility

Sometimes you simply must subclass if you're extending the behavior of code you don't own. In the example above, it's possible `Button` is part of a framework you're using, and there's no way you can modify or extend the source code to fit your needs.

In that case, subclass `Button` so you can add your custom subclass and use it with code that's expecting an object of type `Button`. As you've seen earlier in this chapter, the author of a class can designate if any of the members of a class can be overridden or not using the `open` keyword.

> **Note**: When should you subclass versus use an extension function? This will vary depending on use case and team practices. Explore both options and see which is best for your needs.

Identity

Finally, it's important to understand that classes and class hierarchies model what objects *are*. If your goal is to share behavior (what objects *can do*) between types, more often than not you should prefer **interfaces** over subclassing. You'll learn about interfaces in Chapter 17: "Interfaces".

Challenges

1. Create three simple classes called `A`, `B`, and `C` where `C` inherits from `B` and `B` inherits from `A`. In each class initializer, call `println("I'm <X>!")` where X is the name of the class. Create an instance of `C` called `c`. What order do you see each `println()` called in?

2. Cast the instance of type `C` to an instance of type `A`. Which casting operation do you use and why? Create an instance of `A` called `a`. What happens if you try to cast `a` to `C`?

3. Create a subclass of `StudentAthlete` called `StudentBaseballPlayer` and include properties for `position`, `number`, and `battingAverage`. What are the benefits and drawbacks of subclassing `StudentAthlete` in this scenario?

4. Create a sealed class `Resource` with subtypes `Success`, `Loading`, and `Error`. Give the `Success` type a string `data` property and the `Error` type a string `error` property. Can you imagine a use for this `Resource` type?

Key points

- **Class inheritance** is one of the most important features of classes and enables **polymorphism**.
- **Subclassing** is a powerful tool, but it's good to know when to subclass. Subclass when you want to extend an object and could benefit from an "is-a" relationship between subclass and superclass, but be mindful of the inherited state and deep class hierarchies.
- The **open** keyword is used to allow inheritance from classes and also to allow methods to be overridden in subclasses.
- **Sealed classes** allow you to create a strictly defined class hierarchy that is similar to an enum class but that allow multiple instances of each subtype to be created and hold state.
- **Secondary constructors** allow you to define additional constructors that take additional parameters than the primary constructor and take different actions with those parameters.
- **Nested classes** allow you to namespace one class within another.
- **Inner classes** are nested classes that also have access to the other members of the outer class.
- **Visibility modifiers** allow you to control where class members and top-level declarations can be seen within your code and projects.

Where to go from here?

Classes are the programming construct you will most often use to model things in your Kotlin apps, from students to grades to people and much more. Classes allow for the definition of hierarchies of items and also for one type of item to be **composed** within another.

In the next chapter, you'll learn about another special type of class called an **enum class**.

Chapter 16: Enum & Sealed Classes

By Ellen Shapiro

Sometimes you'll have a piece of information that could (or at least, should) have only one of a limited number of potential values. Using what you already know, you could make a `List` of all the acceptable values for that piece of information, and walk (or *enumerate*) through each value, one-by-one, to see if your new piece of information matches one of the expected values.

If you think that sounds boring and repetitive, you're not alone. This is why the concept of the **enum** was invented.

> **Note**: There is some debate over how to pronounce the word **enum**. Since it derives from "enumeration," some people pronounce it *ee-noom*. Some people pronounce it *ee-numb*, since in its shortened form, it looks a lot more like the prefix to the word "number."
>
> This book takes no position on which of these is the preferred pronunciation, but you should note that both pronunciations are used commonly, and people tend to feel quite strongly about which pronunciation is the "correct" one. Caveat coder.

In Kotlin, as in many other programming languages, an enum is its own specialized type, indicating that something has a number of possible values.

One big difference in Kotlin is that enums are made by creating an **enum class**. You get a number of interesting pieces of functionality that enums in other languages don't necessarily have. As you work through this chapter, you'll learn about some of the most commonly-used bits of functionality and how to take advantage of them as you work in Kotlin.

To get started, open the starter project for this chapter and dig in.

Creating your first enum class

Open up **main.kt**. Above the `main()` function, define a new enum class:

```
enum class DayOfTheWeek {
  // more code goes here
}
```

Next, replace the comment by adding a comma-separated list of **cases**, or individual values, for the day of the week:

```
Sunday,
Monday,
Tuesday,
Wednesday,
Thursday,
Friday,
Saturday
```

In the `main()` function, replace the existing `println()` statement with one which goes through and prints out some information you get for free with any enum class:

```
for (day in DayOfTheWeek.values()) {
  println("Day ${day.ordinal}: ${day.name}")
}
```

Run the updated `main()` function, and it should print out the following:

```
Day 0: Sunday
Day 1: Monday
Day 2: Tuesday
Day 3: Wednesday
Day 4: Thursday
Day 5: Friday
```

```
Day 6: Saturday
```

Neat! So what did you just get for free from Kotlin by declaring `DaysOfTheWeek` to be an enum class?

- The `values()` companion function on the enum class gives you a `List` of all the declared cases in the class, making it easy to go through all possibilities, and also to find out how many possibilities exist.
- The `ordinal` property of each case gives that case's index in the list of declared cases. You'll note from what's printed out that the order is zero-indexed.
- The `name` property of each case takes the name of the case in code and gives back the String value of that name.

A lot of this behavior is possible because enum classes are, well, classes. Each case is an instance of the class, so things like compiler-generated companion object functions for the class itself and individual properties for each instance are possible. Additionally, because these properties return objects of their own, you can use other functionality like getting the day based on a passed-in integer index.

For example, let's say your colleagues working somewhere else in the code tell you that they'll hand you an integer representing the day of the week. You could use the functionality of `List`, with which you're already familiar, to get the value at the appropriate index.

Add the following to the `main()` function to see this in action:

```
val dayIndex = 0
val dayAtIndex = DayOfTheWeek.values()[dayIndex]
println("Day at $dayIndex is $dayAtIndex")
```

Run the `main()` function again, and at the end, you'll see:

```
Day at 0 is Sunday
```

If you want, you can even change the index of the day to update the value returned. Make sure not to go beyond the length of `values()`, as that will throw an `ArrayIndexOutOfBoundsException`, just like it will with any other list in Kotlin.

Another nice piece of functionality you get for free is the `valueOf()` method, which takes a `String` and returns the enum instance matching that string.

Add the following to the bottom of the `main()` function:

```
val tuesday = DayOfTheWeek.valueOf("Tuesday")
println("Tuesday is day ${tuesday.ordinal}")
```

Run the `main()` function, and at the end of the output you'll see:

```
Tuesday is day 2
```

Neat! Now, the eagle-eyed among you may have noticed that the `valueOf()` function doesn't return a nullable. So what happens when you try to get the value of an enum case that doesn't exist? Let's find out.

Add the following lines to the `main()` function:

```
val notADay = DayOfTheWeek.valueOf("Blernsday")
println("Not a day: $notADay")
```

Run `main()` again, and:

```
Exception in thread "main" java.lang.IllegalArgumentException:
No enum constant DayOfTheWeek.Blernsday
    at java.lang.Enum.valueOf(Enum.java:238)
    at DayOfTheWeek.valueOf(main.kt)
    at MainKt.main(main.kt:23)
```

Nooooo! Weren't Kotlin's nullables supposed to save us from these "thing doesn't exist" exceptions!?

The designers of Kotlin decided that trying to access an enum case which doesn't exist, akin to accessing an index outside the bounds of an array, was enough of an error that an exception should be thrown. So that stopped your process dead in its tracks.

Delete the last two lines you added looking for "Blernsday" so the rest of your code runs.

Updating case order

Another nice thing about enum classes is that if you find out something needs to be in a different order from a zero-indexed perspective, it's easy to make that change.

For instance, a week is defined from Sunday until Saturday in the United States, as the `DaysOfTheWeek` enum does currently. However, in Europe, weeks generally go from Monday until Sunday. Standards — they're great, eh?

Imagine again that you'll be receiving information about the day of the week from somewhere as an integer value. But this time, instead of receiving it from American colleagues, you'll be receiving it from some European colleagues based on their own understanding of day of the week indexing.

The nice thing about using an enum class is that making this adjustment is super-easy and only requires you to change the order of the list of cases.

In the list of cases for **DaysOfTheWeek**, move `Sunday` down to the bottom of the list:

```
Monday,
Tuesday,
Wednesday,
Thursday,
Friday,
Saturday,
Sunday;
```

Make sure to add a comma after `Saturday`, and replace the comma after `Sunday` with a semicolon. Lists of enum cases are comma-separated, so anything that isn't the very last case has to have a comma. However, you don't leave a comma on the very last case, or the compiler won't understand that you've reached the end of the list.

If you're just making a simple list of cases, the semicolon at the end isn't necessary. However, since you're planning to add more functionality to this enum class, you need to add the semicolon to ensure that the compiler sees the list of cases has ended, and that other functionality declarations have begun.

Now, run the `main()` function again, and the output will update:

```
Day 0: Monday
Day 1: Tuesday
Day 2: Wednesday
Day 3: Thursday
Day 4: Friday
Day 5: Saturday
Day 6: Sunday
Day at 0 is Monday
Tuesday is day 1
```

Without changing any of the code in `main()`, the underlying values for each day's `ordinal` property have been updated to reflect the new order of the cases. Sweet!

Enum class properties and functions

Like other classes, enum classes can have properties and functions. You can even set them up to be passed in as part of the constructor for each case.

As an example, let's make it simple and easy to tell if a given day is on the weekend. Add a Boolean property to the constructor:

```
enum class DayOfTheWeek(val isWeekend: Boolean)
```

Since you've added this property to the constructor without assigning it a default value, you'll need to pass in a value for the `isWeekend` property for each case you're creating. Update your list of cases to use the constructor to set the `isWeekend` value for each case:

```
Monday(false),
Tuesday(false),
Wednesday(false),
Thursday(false),
Friday(false),
Saturday(true),
Sunday(true);
```

Next, update the first print statement in the `main()` function so it also prints out whether the day being logged is a weekend day or not:

```
println(
  "Day ${day.ordinal}: ${day.name}, is weekend: $
{day.isWeekend}"
)
```

Run the `main()` function again, and you'll see the results based on the values you passed in with the constructor:

```
Day 0: Monday, is weekend: false
Day 1: Tuesday, is weekend: false
Day 2: Wednesday, is weekend: false
Day 3: Thursday, is weekend: false
Day 4: Friday, is weekend: false
Day 5: Saturday, is weekend: true
Day 6: Sunday, is weekend: true
```

You can also use default values in constructors the same way you can with other classes. Update the constructor so that the default value of `isWeekend` is `false`:

```
enum class DayOfTheWeek(val isWeekend: Boolean = false)
```

Now, you can delete the `(false)` off of all the non-weekend days, since that's the default value of the `isWeekend` parameter:

```
Monday,
Tuesday,
Wednesday,
Thursday,
Friday,
Saturday(true),
Sunday(true);
```

Run the `main()` function again, and you'll get exactly the same output as before, but now your list of cases in code is slightly easier to read.

Like other classes in Kotlin, enum classes can have companion objects to do things that don't depend on a specific instance of the class. For example, let's say you want to find out which day today is in your `DayOfTheWeek` enum.

You can add a companion object with a function which calculates that, just as you can do with any other class.

In the `DayOfTheWeek` enum class, add a companion object and a skeleton of the function you're about to add:

```
companion object {
  fun today(): DayOfTheWeek {
    // Code goes here
  }
}
```

Here, you'll want to take advantage of Kotlin's interoperability with Java to use the battle-tested Java `Calendar` class to access information about the current day, then calculate how that translates to your `enum class`:

```
// 1
val calendarDayOfWeek =
Calendar.getInstance().get(Calendar.DAY_OF_WEEK)
// 2
var adjustedDay = calendarDayOfWeek - 2
// 3
val days = DayOfTheWeek.values()
if (adjustedDay < 0) {
  adjustedDay += days.count()
}
// 4
val today = days.first { it.ordinal == adjustedDay }
return today
```

> **Note**: You need to add the import, `import java.util.*`, to the top of your file to use `Calendar`.

What's happening in this code?

1. You're using the Java `Calendar`'s shared instance, you get the current day of the week, according to the Calendar class.
2. Because the Java `Calendar` class thinks (a) weeks start on Sunday and (b) weeks are 1-indexed instead of 0-indexed, you adjust the index returned by subtracting 2: 1 to account for the indexing change, and 1 to account for the difference of the first day of the week.
3. Now that you've made this adjustment, you need to make sure you don't accidentally get a value which can't exist. If the adjusted day is less than zero, you add the count of `DayOfTheWeek` values to get it to wrap back around to a value which does exist.
4. Finally, you use the version of `first` which takes a `predicate` lambda to look at the list of all days, and return the first one where the ordinal matches the adjusted day.

Now, it's time to use your new function. At the bottom of the `main()` function, add the following:

```
val today = DayOfTheWeek.today()
val isWeekend =
  "It is${if (today.isWeekend) "" else " not"} the weekend"
println("It is $today. $isWeekend.")
```

Run again, and at the bottom of your output, you should see the following — or whatever values are appropriate values for the day of the week it is for you:

```
It is Monday. It is not the weekend.
```

> **Note**: When you include an enum case directly in string interpolation, like you did here with `$today`, the `name` property of the enum case is automatically used when the string is created. If there's another property you'd prefer to have added to the string other than the name, you'll have to specify that with something like `${today.ordinal}`.

You can also add functions directly to the enum class which depend on a particular instance.

In `DayOfTheWeek`, below the end of the list of cases but above where you've added `companion object`, add a new function to help calculate how many days, including today, it is from the current instance until a given day of the week:

```
fun daysUntil(other: DayOfTheWeek): Int {
  // 1
  return if (this.ordinal < other.ordinal) {
    // 2
    other.ordinal - this.ordinal
  } else {
    //3
    other.ordinal - this.ordinal + DayOfTheWeek.values().count()
  }
}
```

What's happening in this code?

1. First, you're checking whether the ordinal value of the current instance is less than the ordinal of the passed-in index.
2. In the case where the current ordinal is less than the passed-in ordinal, you simply subtract the current ordinal from the passed-in ordinal to get the number of days between them.
3. If the current ordinal is greater than or equal to the passed-in ordinal, you perform the same subtraction, but add the count of the days of the week so that the number is not zero or negative.

Now, add the following lines to the `main()` function, between the declaration of `isWeekend` and your last `println()` statement, to calculate how long it is until Friday:

```
val secondDay = DayOfTheWeek.Friday
val daysUntil = today.daysUntil(secondDay)
```

Next, update the `println()` statement so it also prints out the new information you've given it:

```
println("It is $today. $isWeekend. There are $daysUntil days
until $secondDay.")
```

Run `main()` again, and it will output something similar to this, based on what day it is in your world:

```
It is Monday. It is not the weekend. There are 4 days until
Friday.
```

Note that if today is Friday, you'll see seven days instead of zero days until Friday, since you wrapped the count around if it was equal to today's day.

Using when with enum classes

One of the most powerful features of enum classes is how they combine with the `when` expression. You've already seen how this can be used on basic types like `Int` and `String`.

But having a bit of context as to what the options are in the `when` expression makes it far easier to read and reason about. What does this look like in practice?

Add a `when` expression to the bottom of the `main()` function which prints out some classic '90s song lyrics based on the value of `today`:

```
when (today) {
  DayOfTheWeek.Monday -> println("I don't care if $today's
blue")
  DayOfTheWeek.Tuesday -> println("$today's gray")
  DayOfTheWeek.Wednesday -> println("And $today, too")
  DayOfTheWeek.Thursday -> println("$today, I don't care 'bout
you")
  DayOfTheWeek.Friday -> println("It's $today, I'm in love")
  DayOfTheWeek.Saturday -> println("$today, Wait...")
  DayOfTheWeek.Sunday -> println("$today always comes too late")
}
```

Run the `main()` function, and the appropriate line of the song will print at the end of your log based on the current day:

```
I don't care if Monday's blue
```

But what if you only want to print the lyric in certain circumstances? Well normally, you'd just add an `else` case. Try to do so at the end of your `where` expression:

```
else -> println("I don't feel like singing")
```

You'll get a warning from the compiler about this:

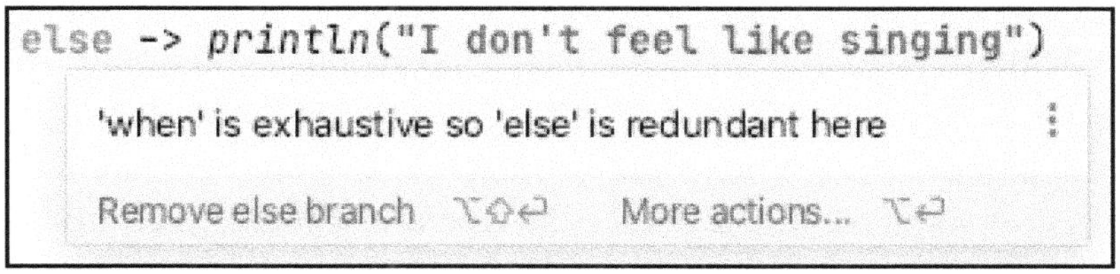

'when' is exhaustive so 'else' is redundant here

This is because you've already defined behavior for every case which exists. Delete or comment out all the cases except for `Friday` and the `else` case. The warning from the compiler will now go away, since the else case can cover at least one case.

Run the `main()` function. If it's not Friday, you should see:

```
I don't feel like singing
```

If it *is* Friday, it'll print out:

```
It's Friday, I'm in love
```

You'll also get a warning if there are unhandled cases. Delete the `else` case, and you'll see the `when` get highlighted by the compiler. Hover over that highlight, and you'll see this warning:

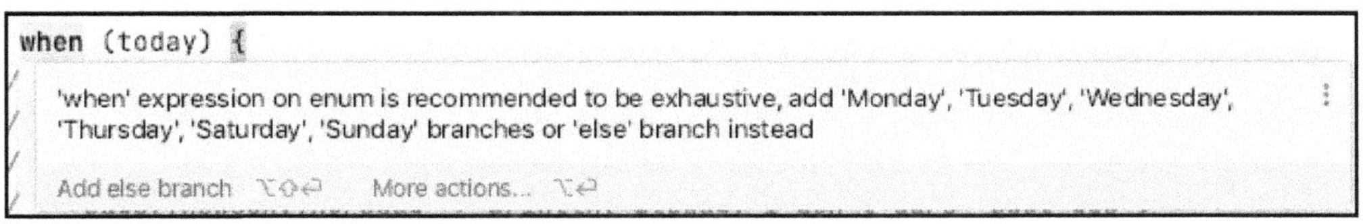

'when' expression on enum is recommended to be exhaustive, add 'Monday', 'Tuesday', 'Wednesday', 'Thursday', 'Saturday', 'Sunday' branches or 'else' branch instead

The code will still run, though! If it is Friday, you'll still see:

```
It's Friday, I'm in love
```

However, if it's not Friday, nothing will print. You'll still have the warning, but if you're not paying attention to it, you can easily miss it. Keep an eye out for this warning especially when adding new cases to an enum class, and make sure you've added appropriate handling for the new cases to your existing `where` expressions. What if you need to have something which defines more behavior than you can do easily in a single type, but still want to take advantage of the functionality that enum classes give you? A great way to do that is to use **sealed classes**.

Sealed classes vs. enum classes

As you saw briefly in the previous chapter, a **sealed class** has a limited number of direct subclasses, all defined in the same file as the sealed class itself. It's known as `sealed` as opposed to `final`, since although some subclassing is permitted (and in fact, required, as you'll see in a moment), the subclassing is extremely limited in scope.

The hope is that this technique allows programmers to take advantage of some of the flexibility of subclassing without permitting them to create massive inheritance trees which lead to terrible, incomprehensible code.

There are a few key points to know about sealed classes:

- They are **abstract**. This means that you can't instantiate an instance of the sealed class directly, only one of the declared subclasses.
- Related to that requirement, sealed classes can have `abstract` members, which must be implemented by all subclasses of the sealed class.
- Unlike enum classes, where each case is a single instance of the class, you can have multiple instances of a subclass of a sealed class.
- You can't make direct subclasses of a sealed class outside of the file where it's declared, and the constructors of sealed classes are always private.
- You *can* create indirect subclasses (such as inheriting from one of the subclasses of your sealed class) outside the file where they're declared, but because of the restrictions above, this usually doesn't end up working very well.

Creating a sealed class

Imagine you're working for a company that mostly works in U.S. dollars, but also accepts payments in Euros and some form of cryptocurrency.

Above the `main()` function, and below the end of your `DayOfTheWeek` enum class, add a new sealed class representing these accepted currencies:

```
sealed class AcceptedCurrency {
  class Dollar: AcceptedCurrency()
  class Euro: AcceptedCurrency()
  class Crypto: AcceptedCurrency()
}
```

In the `main()` function, add the following lines to the bottom:

```
val currency = AcceptedCurrency.Crypto()
println("You've got some $currency!")
```

Run the `main()` function, and you'll now see something like the following print out at the bottom:

```
You've got some AcceptedCurrency$Crypto@76ed5528!
```

Switching from an enum class to a sealed class means you lose all the nice convenience functions for things like name and order. You can see that as the name prints out as a bunch of gibberish.

Fortunately, sealed classes can have non-abstract properties with custom getters, and can also take advantage of `when` expressions.

Below the spot where `Crypto` is declared in the `AcceptedCurrency` sealed class, add the following property with a custom getter:

```
val name: String
  get() = when (this) {
    is Euro -> "Euro"
    is Dollar -> "Dollars"
    is Crypto -> "NerdCoin"
  }
```

Update the `println()` statement at the bottom of the `main()` function to take advantage of this new property:

```
println("You've got some ${currency.name}!")
```

Run the `main()` function again, and you'll see something a little more readable:

```
You've got some NerdCoin!
```

Since your company is U.S.-based, they'll want to know how much each of these currencies is worth in USD.

You can define a requirement for this by adding an `abstract` property on the sealed class, then overriding it in each of the subclasses.

Update the AcceptedCurrency sealed class to add an abstract val, and then override it in the three declared subclasses:

```
sealed class AcceptedCurrency {
  abstract val valueInDollars: Float
  class Dollar: AcceptedCurrency() {
    override val valueInDollars = 1.0f
  }
  class Euro: AcceptedCurrency() {
    override val valueInDollars = 1.25f
  }
  class Crypto: AcceptedCurrency() {
    override val valueInDollars = 2534.92f
  }
  // leave the existing name property alone
}
```

It would probably also help to know how much of a currency is being passed around with a single instance. You *can* add non-abstract vals and vars to a sealed class, as long as you provide them with an initial value.

Right below your abstract declaration of valueInDollars, add a new variable:

```
var amount: Float = 0.0f
```

Now that you have a place to store the value of a particular currency, you can calculate the total value of the accepted currency. You'll do that by adding a non-abstract function to your sealed class. Since every AcceptedCurrency subclass must provide a valueInDollars property, and all subclasses have access to the amount property you just added, you can use those at the AcceptedCurrency level to provide the same functionality across all classes.

Below the name property, add a new function to calculate the total value in dollars of a given currency:

```
fun totalValueInDollars(): Float {
  return amount * valueInDollars
}
```

Now, go back down to the main() function and add the following two lines to set an amount on the currency and print out the total value in dollars:

```
currency.amount = .27541f
println("${currency.amount} of ${currency.name} is "
  + "${currency.totalValueInDollars()} in Dollars")
```

Run the `main()` function, and at the bottom you should see:

```
0.27541 of NerdCoin is 698.1423 in Dollars
```

You're able to have as many instances as you want of any of the various subclasses of `AcceptedCurrency`, and those instances can store properties where enum class instances can't. Now that you know about sealed classes and some of the benefits and drawbacks of using them, you'll go back to dealing with enum classes for the remainder of this chapter. You'll start by looking at another important use of enum classes: **State machines**.

Enumeration as state machine

A **state machine** is essentially an exclusive list of possible states for a given system. Using an enum can make it more clear to the caller what state the system is in at any point.

Open up the provided **Downloader.kt** file, and you'll see a really simple example of this at the top with the `DownloadState` enum.

```
enum class DownloadState {
  Idle,
  Starting,
  InProgress,
  Error,
  Success
}
```

This has five exclusive states:

- `Idle`: Nothing has happened yet.
- `Starting`: The download is being started.
- `InProgress`: Data is actively being downloaded.
- `Error`: An error has occurred and caused the download to terminate.
- `Success`: The data download has completed successfully.

You'll also see a `Downloader` class. This has been provided to give an example of how enums can be used to glean information on the state of a system. This class does the hard work of figuring out how to adjust the state machine based on what's happening under the hood.

For now, the only thing you need to care about is the state your download is in. Fortunately, that's returned to callers of the main method on this class as part of a block indicating progress.

Go back to **main.kt**, and at the bottom of the `main()` method, add some new code:

```
Downloader().downloadData("foo.com/bar",
  progress = { downloadState ->
    //TODO
  },
  completion = { error, list ->
    // TODO
})
```

This code pretends to download some data from the given URL, gives an update about the current state as it goes, and then tells you when the process is done either by displaying an error or a list of items.

First, replace the `TODO` in the `completion` handler with some code that handles completion:

```
error?.let { println("Got error: ${error.message}") }
list?.let { println("Got list with ${list.size} items") }
```

Next, you'll peer into the workings of the state machine in the `progress` handler. Replace the `TODO` there with a `when` statement, printing information about what's going on:

```
when (downloadState) {
  DownloadState.Idle -> println("Download has not yet started.")
  DownloadState.Starting -> println("Starting download...")
  DownloadState.InProgress -> println("Downloading data...")
  DownloadState.Error -> println("An error occurred. Download
terminated.")
  DownloadState.Success -> println("Download completed
successfully.")
}
```

Run your `main()` function, and at the bottom, you'll see output as the download progresses through each of the states:

```
"Downloading" from URL: foo.com/bar
Download has not yet started.
Starting download...
Starting download...
Downloading data...
[etc...]
Downloading data...
```

```
Got list with 100 items
Download completed successfully.
```

The `Download` class is designed to randomly throw an error about 10% of the time. When that happens, you can validate that your error handling code is working, since you'll see something like the following:

```
"Downloading" from URL: foo.com/bar
Download has not yet started.
Starting download...
Starting download...
Downloading data...
Downloading data...
[etc...]
Got error: Your download was eaten by a shark.
An error occurred. Download terminated.
```

Now, with the power of a simple `when` expression, you can easily handle all the various states which your download could be in.

Nullables and enums

Enums can also be dealt with at both the `when` level and as part of an API with nullability. In the `Downloader` class, instead of having an `Idle` option in `DownloadState`, you could express that nothing was happening by allowing the download state to be optional.

Give it a shot! In **Downloader.kt**, delete the `Idle` state from the `DownloadState` enum class.

Next, in the `Downloader` class, update the `downloadState` var to be optional, and null by default:

```
var downloadState: DownloadState? = null
```

Next, within the `Downloader` class, update the method signatures for `downloadData` and `postProgress` to use an optional `DownloadState` instead of a required one:

```
fun downloadData(
  fromUrl: String,
  progress: (state: DownloadState?) -> Unit,
  completion: (error: Error?, data: List<Int>?) -> Unit
) {
  // rest of method unchanged
}
```

```
...
private fun postProgress(
  progress: (state: DownloadState?) -> Unit
) {
   // rest of method unchanged
}
```

Now go back to **main.kt**. In the `main()` function, you'll now see an error in the `when` expression for downloading data:

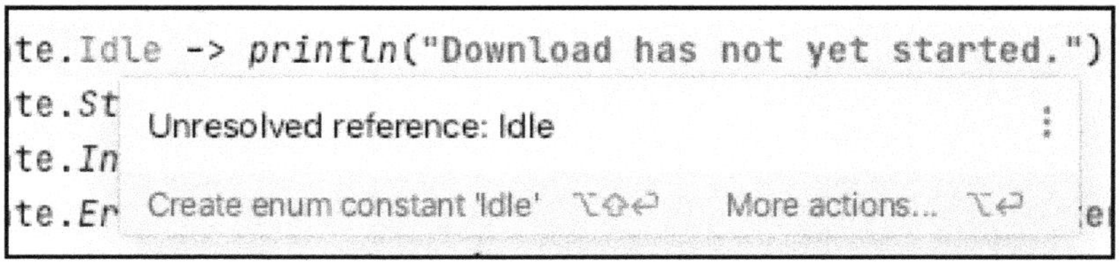

Delete the line for handling the `Idle` state you removed, and replace it with handling for `null`:

```
when (downloadState) {
  null -> println("No download state yet")
  /// rest of when unchanged
}
```

Run the `main()` function one last time, and now, that same `when` expression is handling both null and non-null values coming into it:

```
"Downloading" from URL: foo.com/bar
No download state yet
Starting download...
```

Taking advantage of nullability with enum classes lets you represent state where you haven't received information, or have received unexpected information without having to explicitly create an "Idle" or "Unknown" state.

Challenges

1. Add a companion function to `DayOfTheWeek` which returns a nullable `DayOfTheWeek` based on a passed-in index. Do the same for a passed-in string.

2. Add a function to `DayOfTheWeek` to calculate how many days until the next weekend begins. Then, update your code so that the weekend is Wednesday and Thursday instead of Saturday and Sunday. Does it still work?

3. Create a way to add together the value of two `AcceptedCurrency` objects. Think about the following scenarios:
   - What should happen if both currencies are the same type?
   - What should happen if the currencies are of different types?
4. Create a function that can take a `List` of `AcceptedCurrency` objects and the cost of an item in Dollars, and return whether the user has sufficient funds in the list of currency objects to pay for what they're trying to buy.

Key points

- **Enum classes** are a powerful tool for handling situations where a piece of data will (or at least should) be one of a defined set of pre-existing values. Enum classes come with a number of tools for free, such as getting a list of all the declared cases, and the ability to access the order and names of the cases.
- **Sealed classes** are a powerful tool for handling situations where a piece of data will (or at least should) be one of a defined set of pre existing types.
- Both enum classes and sealed classes let you take advantage of Kotlin's powerful `when` expression to clearly outline how you want to handle various situations.
- Enum classes are particularly useful for creating, updating, and cleaning information about the current state in a **state machine**.

Where to go from here?

There are a few more places where you can learn more about enum classes and sealed classes:

- The official Kotlin documentation for **enum classes**: https://kotlinlang.org/docs/reference/enum-classes.html
- The official Kotlin documentation for **sealed classes**: https://kotlinlang.org/docs/reference/sealed-classes.html

You've spent the last few chapters learning about defining customs types with objects, classes and variants such as data classes, enum classes, and sealed classes. In the next chapter, you'll learn about defining custom types that focus on behavior using **interfaces**.

Chapter 17: Interfaces

By Victoria Gonda

You've learned about two Kotlin custom types: Classes and objects. There's another custom type that's quite useful: **Interfaces**.

Unlike the other custom types, interfaces aren't anything you instantiate directly. Instead, they define a blueprint of behavior that concrete types **conform** to. With an interface, you define a common set of properties and behaviors that concrete types go and implement. The primary difference between interfaces and other custom types is that interfaces themselves cannot contain state.

In this chapter, you'll learn about interfaces and see why they're central to programming in Kotlin. Open up a Kotlin file to get going.

Introducing interfaces

You define an interface much as you do any other custom type. Add this interface to your Kotlin file, outside the `main()` function:

```
interface Vehicle {
  fun accelerate()
  fun stop()
}
```

This creates a `Vehicle` interface with blueprint instructions for two methods: `accelerate()` and `stop()`.

The keyword `interface` is followed by the name of the interface, followed by curly braces with the members of the interface inside. The big difference you'll notice is that the interface *doesn't have to contain any implementation.*

That means you can't instantiate a `Vehicle` directly:

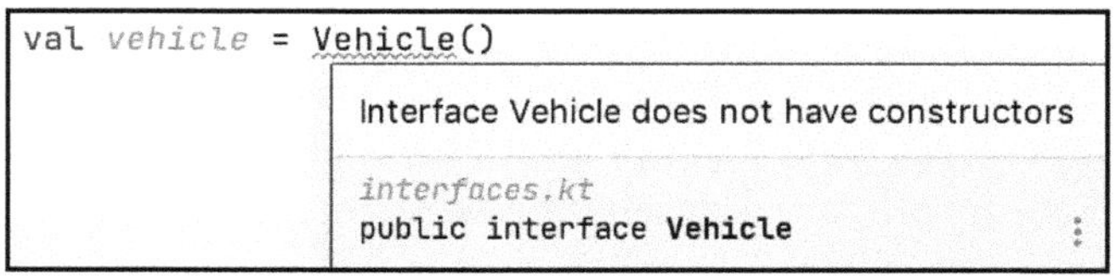

Interface Vehicle does not have constructors

Instead, you use interfaces to enforce methods and properties on *other* types. What you've defined here is something like the *idea* of a vehicle — it's something that can accelerate and stop.

Interface syntax

An interface can be **implemented** by a class or object, and when another type implements an interface, it's required to define the methods and properties defined in the interface. Once a type implements all members of an interface, the type is said to **conform** to the interface.

Here's how you declare interface conformance for your type. Define a new class that will conform to `Vehicle`:

```
class Unicycle: Vehicle {
  var peddling = false

  override fun accelerate() {
    peddling = true
```

```
  }

  override fun stop() {
    peddling = false
  }
}
```

Here, you create a `Unicycle` that inherits from and conforms to `Vehicle`.

You follow the name of the custom type, `Unicycle`, with a colon and the name of the interface you want to conform to, `Vehicle`. This syntax might look familiar, since it's the same syntax you use to make a class inherit from another class.

Note that it *looks* like class inheritance but it isn't; objects and other custom types can also conform to interfaces with this syntax.

If you were to remove the definition of `stop()` from the class `Unicycle` above, Kotlin would display an error since `Unicycle` wouldn't have fully conformed to the `Vehicle` interfaces.

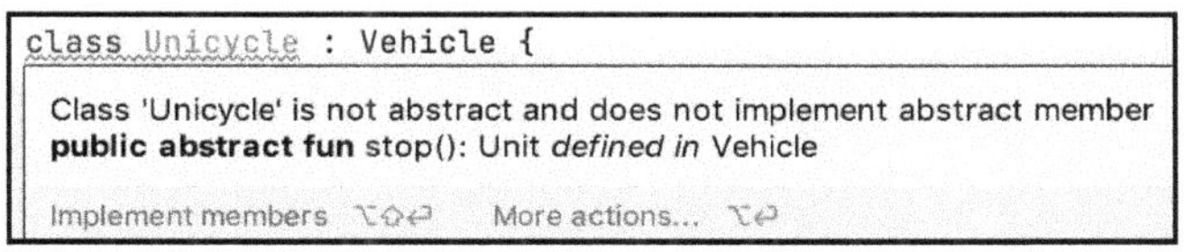

Class Unicycle is not abstract and does not implement abstract member stop defined in Vehicle

You'll come back to the details of implementing interfaces in a bit, but first you'll see what's possible when defining interfaces.

Methods in interfaces

In the `Vehicle` interface above, you define a pair of methods, `accelerate()` and `stop()`, that all types conforming to `Vehicle` must implement.

You declare methods on interfaces much like you would on any class or object with parameters and return values. Add `Direction` and `DirectionalVehicle`:

```
enum class Direction {
  LEFT, RIGHT
}

interface DirectionalVehicle {
  fun accelerate()
  fun stop()
  fun turn(direction: Direction)
```

```
  fun description(): String
}
```

The signature of these methods look the same as methods on a class, but without a body.

Methods declared in interfaces can contain default parameters, just like methods declared in classes and top-level functions. Add this class as an example:

```
interface OptionalDirectionalVehicle {
  fun turn(direction: Direction = Direction.LEFT)
}
```

Here, you specify a default value of `Direction.LEFT`.

When implementing such an interface, the default value of the parameter will fall through to calls on types that implement the interface. Add this class to implement your `OptionalDirectionalVehicle`:

```
class OptionalDirection: OptionalDirectionalVehicle {
  override fun turn(direction: Direction) {
    println(direction)
  }
}
```

Notice that when you implement `turn()` you don't need to repeat the default value of the `direction` parameter.

Now, try it out in your `main()` method:

```
val car = OptionalDirection()
car.turn() // > LEFT
car.turn(Direction.RIGHT) // > RIGHT
```

Run your code to see how the default value specified in the interface is used.

Default method implementations

Just as you can in Java 8, you can define *default implementations* for the methods in an interface.

Add some space travel to your code:

```
interface SpaceVehicle {
  fun accelerate()
  // 1
```

```
    fun stop() {
      println("Whoa, slow down!")
    }
  }

  class LightFreighter: SpaceVehicle {
    // 2
    override fun accelerate() {
      println("Proceed to hyperspace!")
    }
  }
```

Note that here you:

1. Have a default implementation for `stop()` on the `SpaceVehicle` interface.

2. Don't override `stop()` in `LightFreighter`.

See what this means when you run it. Add this example to `main()`:

```
val falcon = LightFreighter()
falcon.accelerate() // > Proceed to hyperspace!
falcon.stop() // > "Whoa, slow down!
```

Run your code. You've defined an implementation for `stop()` inside the interface, but left `accelerate()` undefined. Any types implementing `SpaceVehicle`, such as `LightFreighter` must include an implementation of `accelerate()`.

When an interface defines a default implementation, you can still override the implementation in a type that conforms to the interface. Create a `Starship` that does this:

```
class Starship: SpaceVehicle {
  override fun accelerate() {
    println("Warp factor 9 please!")
  }

  override fun stop() {
    super.stop()
    println("That kind of hurt!")
  }
}
```

Here, `Starship` overrides both of the methods declared in the `SpaceVehicle` interface, and it also uses `super` in `stop()` to call the default implementation.

Try it out:

```
val enterprise = Starship()
enterprise.accelerate()
// > Warp factor 9 please!
enterprise.stop()
// > Whoa, slow down!
// > That kind of hurt!"
```

Just as with subclasses, the `super` call is not required. Because you did call it, both the default implementation and your addition executes.

Properties in interfaces

You can also define properties in an interface. Add this interface:

```
interface VehicleProperties {
  val weight: Int // abstract
  val name: String
    get() = "Vehicle"
}
```

Here, you have a `VehicleProperties` with `weight` and `name`.

Interfaces cannot themselves hold state, as there are no backing fields to hold the data stored in an interface property. You must either let the property be *abstract* with no value, or give the property a default getter, like for `name` in `VehicleProperties`.

Types that implement an interface with properties can either give abstract properties a value, or provide an implementation. Add these examples:

```
class Car: VehicleProperties {
  override val weight: Int = 1000
}

class Tank: VehicleProperties {
  override val weight: Int
    get() = 10000

  override val name: String
    get() = "Tank"
}
```

Note the use of the `override` keyword on the property implementations. The `Car` class gives a value to `weight` and uses the default implementation of `name`, while the `Tank` class gives `weight` a custom getter and overrides `name`.

Interface inheritance

The `Vehicle` interface contains a set of methods that could apply to any type of vehicle, such as a bike, a car, a snowmobile or even an airplane!

You may wish to define an interface that contains all the qualities of a `Vehicle`, but that is also specific to vehicles with wheels. For this, you can have interfaces that inherit from other interfaces, similar to how you can have classes that inherit from other classes

Define a `WheeledVehicle`:

```
interface WheeledVehicle: Vehicle {
  val numberOfWheels: Int
  var wheelSize: Double
}
```

Now any type you mark as conforming to the `WheeledVehicle` interface will have all of the members defined within the braces, in addition to all of the members of `Vehicle`.

Add a `Bike` that conforms to this interface:

```
class Bike: WheeledVehicle {
  var peddling = false
  var brakesApplied = false

  override val numberOfWheels = 2
  override var wheelSize = 622.0

  override fun accelerate() {
    peddling = true
    brakesApplied = false
  }

  override fun stop() {
    peddling = false
    brakesApplied = true
  }
}
```

As with subclassing, any type you mark as a `WheeledVehicle` will have an **is-a** relationship with the interface `Vehicle`. The class `Bike` implements all the methods and properties defined in both `Vehicle` and `WheeledVehicle`. If any of them weren't defined, you'd receive a build error.

Defining an interface guarantees any type that conforms to the interface will have *all* the members you've defined in the interface and its parent interfaces, if any.

Mini-exercises

1. Create an interface `Area` that defines a read-only property `area` of type `Double`.
2. Implement `Area` with classes representing `Square`, `Triangle`, and `Circle`.
3. Add a circle, a square, and a triangle to an array. Convert the array of shapes to an array of areas using `map`.

Look at the challenge solutions for this chapter to check your work.

Implementing multiple interfaces

One class can only inherit from another single class. This is the property of **single inheritance**. In contrast, a class can adopt as many interfaces as you'd like!

Suppose that instead of creating a `WheeledVehicle` interface that inherits from `Vehicle`, you made `Wheeled` its own interface. Add this example:

```
interface Wheeled {
  val numberOfWheels: Int
  val wheelSize: Double
}

class Tricycle: Wheeled, Vehicle {
  // Implement both Vehicle and Wheeled
}
```

Interfaces support **multiple conformance**, so you can apply any number of interfaces to types you define. In the example above, the `Tricycle` class now has to implement all members defined in the `Vehicle` and `Wheeled` interfaces.

Interfaces in the standard library

The Kotlin standard library uses interfaces extensively in ways that may surprise you. Understanding the roles interfaces play in Kotlin can help you write clean, decoupled "Kotliny" code.

This section gives two examples of common interfaces in the standard library.

Iterator

Kotlin lists, maps, and other collection types all provide access to `Iterator` instances. `Iterator` is an interface defined in the Kotlin standard library, and declares methods `next()`, which should give the next element of the collection, and `hasNext()`, which returns a boolean indicating whether the collection has more elements.

Providing iterators that conform to `Iterator` lets you loop over both collections in a standard way using the `in` infix function:

```
val cars = listOf("Lamborghini", "Ferrari", "Rolls-Royce")
val numbers = mapOf("Brady" to 12, "Manning" to 18, "Brees" to
9)

for (car in cars) {
    println(car)
}
for (qb in numbers) {
  println("${qb.key} wears ${qb.value}")
}
```

Even though `cars` is a list and `numbers` is a map, you use the same approach to iterate through them, thanks to `Iterator`.

There is a subtle distinction for the iterators of the list and map types. The `List` type provides an iterator by conforming to `Collection`, which then conforms to another interface named `Iterable`. In comparison, the `Map` type has an iterator due to a `Map` extension function.

Comparable

`Comparable` declares an operator function used to compare an instance to other instances.

```
public interface Comparable<in T> {
  public operator fun compareTo(other: T): Int
}
```

Suppose you want to create a `Boat` class and compare boat sizes, with each boat conforming to a `SizedVehicle` interface:

```
interface SizedVehicle {
  var length: Int
}
```

You can make Boat implement SizedVehicle and also conform to Comparable:

```
class Boat: SizedVehicle, Comparable<Boat> {
  override var length: Int = 0
  override fun compareTo(other: Boat): Int {
    return when {
      length > other.length -> 1
      length == other.length -> 0
      else -> -1
    }
  }
}
```

The implementation of compareTo returns an Int indicating the relative size of two boats based on their lengths.

> **Note**: The meaning of each returned Int might not feel intuitive. For some help, here is the documentation for this interface method. compareTo:
>
> "Returns zero if this object is equal to the specified other object, a negative number if it's less than other, or a positive number if it's greater than other."

You can then compare the sizes of two boats using operators such as >:

```
val titanic = Boat()
titanic.length = 883

val qe2 = Boat()
qe2.length = 963

println(titanic > qe2) // > false
```

Challenges

Create a collection of interfaces for tasks at a pet shop that has dogs, cats, fish and birds.

The pet shop duties can be broken down into these tasks:

- All pets need to be fed.
- Pets that can fly need to be caged.
- Pets that can swim need to be put in a tank.

- Pets that walk need exercise.
- Tanks and cages need to occasionally be cleaned.

1. Create classes for each animal and adopt the appropriate interfaces. Feel free to simply use a `println()` statement for the method implementations.
2. Create homogeneous arrays for animals that need to be fed, caged, cleaned, walked, and tanked. Add the appropriate animals to these arrays. The arrays should be declared using the interface as the element type, for example `var caged: Array<Cageable>`.
3. Write loops that will perform the proper tasks (such as feed, cage, walk) on each element of each array.

Remember, at any time you can look at the challenge solutions for this chapter for help.

Key points

- Interfaces define a contract that classes, objects, and other custom types can **implement**.
- By implementing an interface, a type is required to **conform** to the interface by implementing all methods and properties of the interface.
- A type can implement any number of interfaces, which allows for a quasi-multiple inheritance not permitted through subclassing.
- The Kotlin standard library uses interfaces extensively. You can use many of them, such as `Comparable`, on your own types.

Where to go from here?

Interfaces help you decouple behavior from implementation. Since interfaces are types themselves, you can still declare an array of `Vehicle` instances. The array could then contain bicycles, trucks, or cars. In addition, bicycles could be enumerations and trucks could be classes! But every `Vehicle` has a particular set of properties and methods you know you must implement.

In the next chapter, you'll learn more about a topic that's been briefly mentioned in earlier chapters: The use of **generics** in defining Kotlin types.

Chapter 18: Generics

By Ellen Shapiro

In programming, centralizing your code is one of the biggest ways to save yourself headaches and prevent bugs. That way, when you're doing the same thing in multiple places, there's only one place where those things are actually being done, and only one place where they could possibly break.

A really helpful feature of Kotlin for this is called **generics**. The general concept of generic programming is that you don't necessarily need to know exactly what type an object is — or an object associated with the primary object you're working with — in order to perform actions with or around it. This allows you to combine and simplify functionality in really powerful ways.

Anatomy of standard library generic types

When getting started with generics, it helps to look at the major generic types that are included in Kotlin's standard library. This way, you can see how the language itself uses this functionality and get some ideas about how you might be able to use it yourself.

Lists

You've probably noticed working with **List** objects that you sometimes need to declare them with the type of item you expect in the list in angle brackets, such as `List<String>`, or `List<Int>`.

The primary declaration of `List` looks like this, as of Kotlin 1.2:

```
interface List<out E> : Collection<E>
```

Take this apart a bit:

- This is a declaration of an `interface`, where anything conforming to this interface must be a `Collection`.
- Both `Collection` and `List` have an `E` in angle brackets — this is called the **generic type**. Since it's the same in both places, this indicates that the underlying type of the list and the collection must be the same. You'll delve a bit more into passing generics through to interfaces later in the chapter.
- You'll get to what the `out` bit means much later in the chapter but, for now, you can ignore it.

A lot of the time, you'll see `T` rather than `E` used as the single letter to represent a single generic type. You'll even sometimes see something more elaborate like `Element`. The letter or word representing the generic type is meant more as a hint of what that the type should be, rather than an explicit declaration.

As long as the name of a generic type doesn't collide with the names of any of your classes, you can name a generic type whatever you want. You can think of `T` or `E` or `Element` as a blank, waiting to be filled in with a real, concrete type.

> **Note:** The angle brackets indicating a type is generic were brought over most directly from Java, but this same style is also used in many other programming languages, such as Apple's Swift language.

Now, it's time to play around a bit with `Lists` in code. In **main.kt**, replace the contents of the `main()` function with:

```
val names: List<String> = listOf("Bob", "Carol", "Ted", "Alice")
println("Names: $names")
val firstName = names.first()
```

So what is `first()` doing under the hood? Take a look at its function declaration:

```
fun <T> List<T>.first(): T
```

There are three uses of `T` as a generic type here:

1. The first <T> indicates that this is going to be a function that does something with generic type `T`.
2. The second <T> indicates that the `List` you're calling this function on must be a list containing only objects of that generic type.
3. The third `T` indicates that the return value will be of the same type `T`, which is contained in the list. It doesn't have angle brackets because it's just the simple underlying type of `T` being returned.

The under-the-hood implementation of this function doesn't need to know or care what type `T` is; it just needs to know it's the **same** type in all three places.

You can see this at work by starting to add the following line to **main.kt**:

```
println(firstName)
```

As you type `firstName`, you'll notice that the compiler has already inferred what type it is, without you explicitly declaring the type of `firstName`:

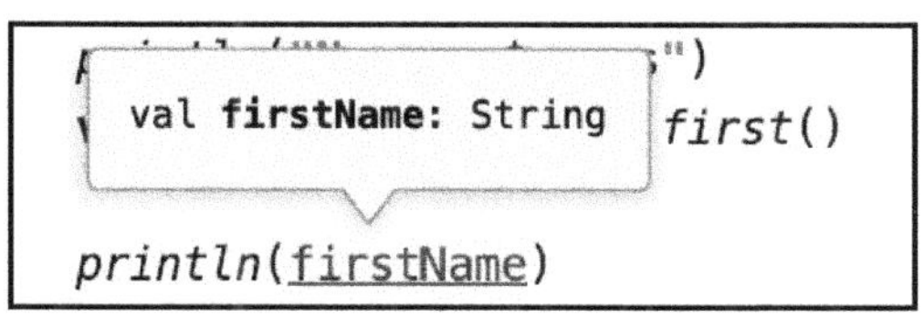

val firstName: String

Next, run the program by pressing the Play button in the left sidebar next to the start of the `main()` function, and you'll see the following print out:

```
Names: [Bob, Carol, Ted, Alice]
Bob
```

The first line prints out the entire list and the second line is the first name in the list you created, which you accessed using `first()` — neat! Even neater is the way that type inference can still work even with generics. Delete the `: List<String>` from the first line so that it reads:

```
val names = listOf("Bob", "Carol", "Ted", "Alice")
```

Run the program again, and you'll see the exact same output!

Under the hood, the compiler has realized that, since the items you passed into `listOf()` were all strings, it's creating a `List<String>` without you having to do anything else.

Even without the explicit declaration of the generic type, you can still use its protections. Add the following line to the bottom of **main.kt**:

```
val firstInt: Int = names.first()
```

Try to run again, and you'll see an error:

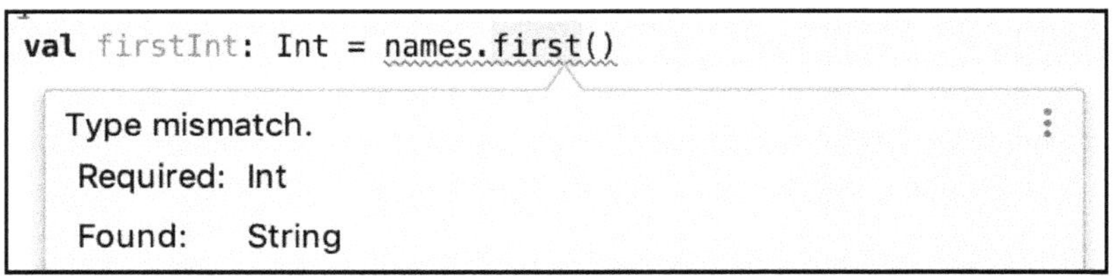

Type mismatch. Required: Int, Found: String

Even though you haven't explicitly told the compiler that `names` contains nothing but `String` objects, it's still used type inference to say hey, you can't get an `Int` out of a list that only contains `String` objects.

> **Note**: Make sure to comment out or delete the `firstInt` line before proceeding to the next step so that the app continues to compile properly.

Now, as you might remember from Chapter 8, "Arrays & Lists," a `List` is read-only. In order to add stuff to the list, it must be a `MutableList`.

In **main.kt**, add the following lines to the bottom of the `main()` function:

```
val things = mutableListOf(1, 2)
things.add("Steve")
println("Things: $things")
```

As you might expect due to type inference, you'll see an error when you try to add "Steve":

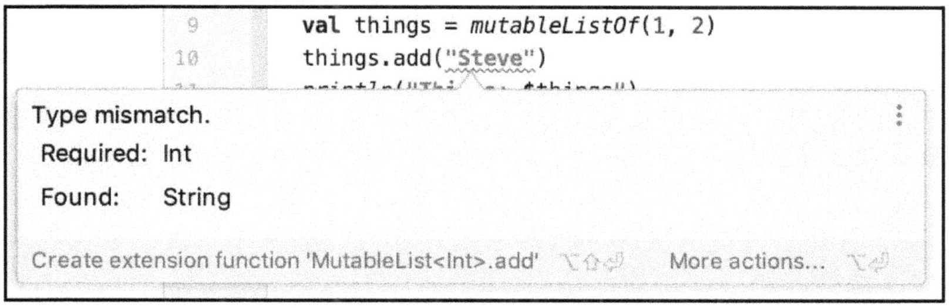

Type mismatch. Required: Int, Found: String

Since Kotlin's type inference system only sees the two `Int` objects passed into `mutableListOf`, it assumes the generic type for the `MutableList` being created is `<Int>`.

This is great if you want to prevent someone from accidentally adding an object of the wrong type to your list. But what if you **want** to be able to add an object of any type to that mutable list?

Fortunately, there's a type for that: `Any`. This is the superclass of every single class in Kotlin, which means that anything can be stuck into an array whose generic type is `Any`.

To do this, you'll have to tell the compiler explicitly that you want to use this type. You can do that one of two ways. You can either specify the type of the variable at the point where it's declared like this:

```
val things: MutableList<Any> = mutableListOf(1, 2)
```

Alternately, you can save yourself a couple of keystrokes and the explicit type declaration, and pass `Any` into the generic type on `mutableListOf` like so:

```
val things = mutableListOf<Any>(1, 2)
```

Either of these will work but, for now, replace the declaration of `things` in **main.kt** with the `mutableListOf<Any>` version, so that the list knows it is of `Any` type. Now, the program should compile again. Build and run, and you'll see at the bottom of the printout:

```
Things: [1, 2, Steve]
```

We'll come back to playing around with lists in a bit, but first take a look at another major use of generic types in the standard library: Maps.

Maps

Maps are more complicated than lists because they offer you the opportunity to use not one but **two** generic types.

As you saw in Chapter 9, "Maps & Sets," a map is an object that contains **keys** and **values**. So you probably won't be too surprised to see the declaration for its interface:

```
interface Map<K, out V>
```

Again, we'll come back to the `out` notation later in the chapter, but you've probably guessed that `K` is the generic type of the keys, and `V` is the generic type of the values.

This allows you to do some fun things like assigning all keys as a specific type, but that values can be of any type.

For instance, at the bottom of **main.kt**'s `main()` function, create a map with several `pair` objects, the first item of which is always a string:

```
val map = mapOf(
  Pair("one", 1),
  Pair("two", "II"),
  Pair("three", 3.0f)
)
```

Type inference allows the compiler to figure out that this is a `Map<String, Any>`. Once it's done that, you'll get more type safety benefits. For instance, if you try to access something with string keys using an integer, it won't work. Add the following to the bottom of the `main()` function:

```
val one = map.get(1)
```

You'll immediately see this warning:

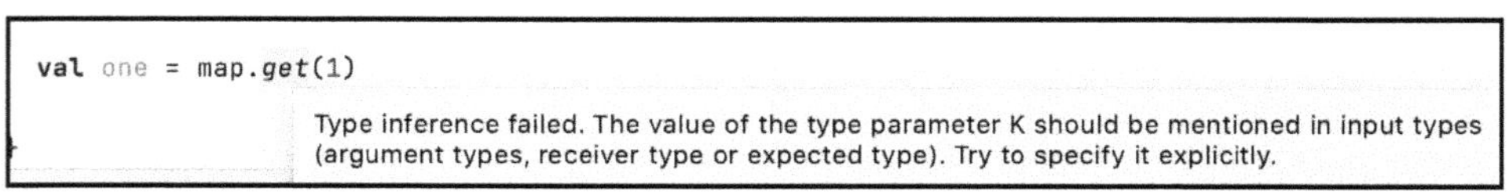

Type inference failed. The value of the type parameter K should be mentioned in input types. Try to specify it explicitly.

This also applies when using subscripting to try to access the values of the array. Replace the previous line with:

```
val one = map[1]
```

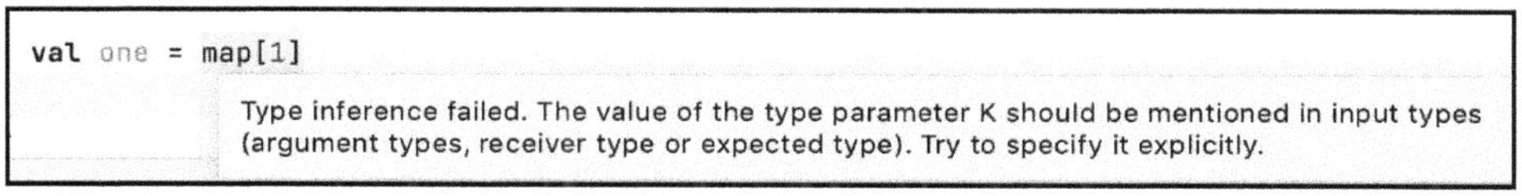

Type inference failed. The value of the type parameter K should be mentioned in input types. Try to specify it explicitly.

This is extra helpful with subscripting, in the event that you forget whether the value you're attempting to subscript is a `Map` or a `List`. If you use the wrong type (and the type of `K` is not `Int`), the compiler will let you know right away!

> **Note**: Comment out or delete the line with the warning before you proceed.

Another nice feature of maps you can take advantage of with generics is that you can do things based on the type of the keys or the values, since each can be accessed separately.

Since all keys must be unique, you can access them as a `Set<K>`. Since values don't need to be unique, they are returned as a `Collection<V>`.

In the case of this `Map`, `keys` will be a `Set<String>` and `values` will be a `Collection<Any>`. You can then do interesting things based on the fact that you know everything in `map.keys` is a `String`.

Add the following lines to the bottom of the `main()` function:

```
val valuesForKeysWithE = map.keys
    .filter { it.contains("e") }
    .map { "Value for $it: ${map[it]}" }
println("Values for keys with E: $valuesForKeysWithE")
```

Build and run the `main()` function, and you'll see:

```
Values for keys with E: [Value for one: 1, Value for three: 3.0]
```

Now, you're printing only the items in `Map`, which have a letter `e` in their key.

While types other than `String` can be used for keys and types other than `Any` can be used for values, the real power of generics lies in what you can do with them when you start to use them in your own types and functions. A good place to start with that is adding an extension function on something that already has a generic constraint.

Extension functions on types with generic constraints

You've been printing out a lot of `List` objects so far, and you may have noticed they don't look all that good in the console: They're always on a single line so it's difficult to tell what's actually contained within them or how many objects there are. Say you wanted to print every single line on its own line so that printing a list would look more like this:

```
- First Item
- Second item
- Third Item
```

The best way to write generic functions is to start simple: Write a function for a case you know you definitely have, using the actual types you need.

At the top of **main.kt**, above the `main()` function declaration, add the following lines:

```
fun List<String>.toBulletedList(): String {
  val separator = "\n - "
  return this.map { "$it" }.joinToString(separator, prefix =
separator, postfix = "\n")
}
```

This is an extension function on a `List` of `String` objects, which will add the bullets to the list as indicated above.

Next, update the first `println` statement in `main()` that prints out `names` to use this new function:

```
println("Names: ${names.toBulletedList()}")
```

Since the `println` statement for `valuesForKeyWithE` is printing a list of `Strings`, that also can be updated:

```
println("Values for keys with E: $
{valuesForKeysWithE.toBulletedList()}")
```

Build and run again, and you'll see the updated printouts:

```
Names:
 - Bob
 - Carol
```

```
  - Ted
  - Alice

Bob
Things: [1, 2, Steve]
Values for keys with E:
 - Value for one: 1
 - Value for three: 3.0
```

It's working for the two lists of `String` objects, but what about the `things` list, which has objects of type `Any`? Go to where that line is printed, and update it to:

```
println("Things: ${things.toBulletedList()}")
```

Immediately, you'll see an error:

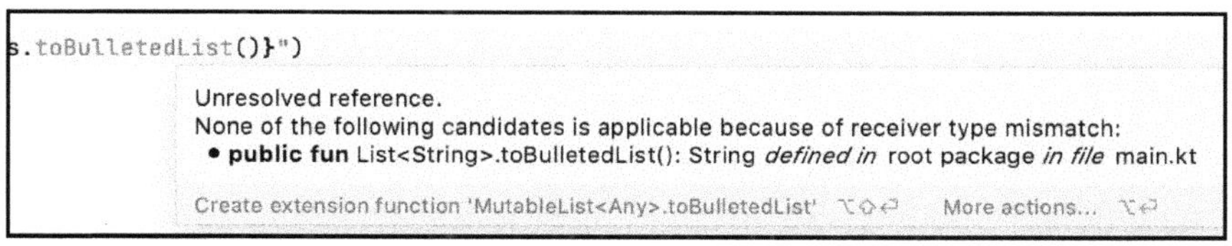

Unresolved reference.

Since `things` is of type `Any`, rather than `String`, it can't use the existing extension method. Time to make it more generic! Start by adding the same functionality for lists with items of type `Any`! Underneath the initial extension function, start trying to add a new function:

```
fun List<Any>.toBulletedList(): String {
}
```

However, before you even add the function body, there's a major error happening:

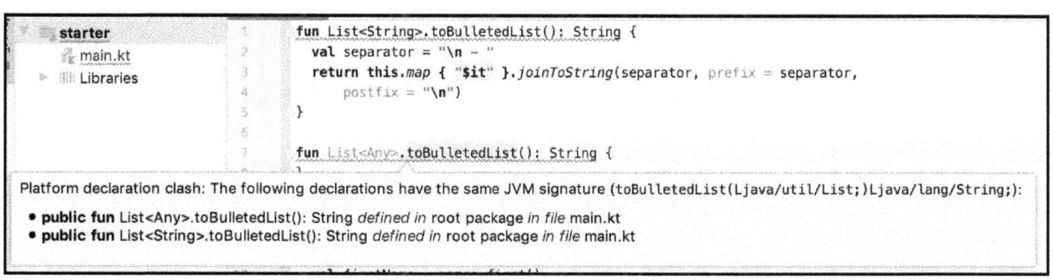

Platform declaration clash: The following declarations have the same JVM signature

The two declarations have the same signature, even though they are using different types for the placeholder type — so the Kotlin compiler can't easily tell which one you're going to use.

Fortunately, since there's nothing in `toBulletedList()` that actually requires anything to be a `String`, you can quickly turn it into a generic function that can be used on a list of whatever type you want!

First, delete or comment out the `Any` function you just added. Next, update the type of the `List` on `toBulletedList()` from `String` to a generic `T`:

```
fun List<T>.toBulletedList(): String
```

Now, at this point, the compiler freaks out a bit because it has no idea what `T` is:

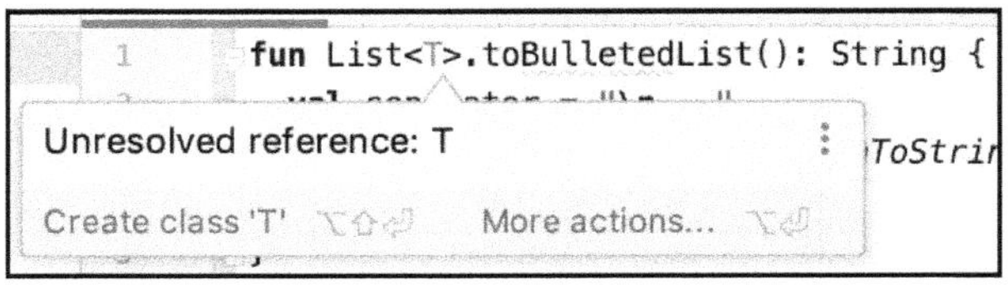

Unresolved reference: T

Fortunately, this is easy to solve: You just need to let the compiler know that this is a generic parameter by adding <T> directly after the `fun` keyword:

```
fun <T> List<T>.toBulletedList(): String
```

Once you do that, all of your errors should be resolved. Build and run the program again. This time where `things` is printed out, you'll also see a nice, pretty bulleted list:

```
Things:
 - 1
 - 2
 - Steve
```

Creating your own generic constraints

Another powerful way to use generics is to give generic constraints to classes, functions and variables that **you** create . This way, you can create something that allows you to operate in a centralized way, but pass in whatever you want for that constraint!

A good place to think about a class with a generic constraint is someplace wherein the fundamental operations happening don't necessarily need to know what kinds of things are happening under the hood.

Moving between an old house or apartment and a new one is a good example. This can be really expensive. Even if you're moving within the same city, you generally have a lot of stuff that you need to move out of your old place and into a truck, and then from that truck into your new place.

However, different moving companies have different specialties, and hiring one that gives you way more protection than you need (or not enough protection) for a particular item can make your move much more expensive than it needs to be.

Fundamentally, however, the same thing happens with everything you move in a situation like this: Things from your old place are moved out and into a truck, the truck goes to your new place and then those things are moved out of the truck and into the new place.

Generally, when you can boil down the description of what's affected under the hood to "things," you've got a good chance that generics could be useful.

Below the `toBulletedList()` extension function and above the `main()` function, add a new generic `Mover` class, which allows you to move a passed-in type of item:

```
// 1
class Mover<T>(
    // 2
    thingsToMove: List<T>,
    val truckHeightInInches: Int = (12 * 12)
) {

  // 3
  private var thingsLeftInOldPlace = mutableListOf<T>()
  private var thingsInTruck = mutableListOf<T>()
  private var thingsInNewPlace = mutableListOf<T>()

  // 4
  init {
    thingsLeftInOldPlace.addAll(thingsToMove)
  }

  // 5
  fun moveEverythingToTruck() {
    while (thingsLeftInOldPlace.count() > 0) {
      val item = thingsLeftInOldPlace.removeAt(0)
      thingsInTruck.add(item)
      println("Moved your $item to the truck!")
    }
  }

  // 6
  fun moveEverythingIntoNewPlace() {
    while (thingsInTruck.count() > 0) {
```

```
      val item = thingsInTruck.removeAt(0)
      thingsInNewPlace.add(item)
      println("Moved your $item into your new place!")
    }
  }

  // 7
  fun finishMove() {
    println("OK, we finished! We were able to move your:$
{thingsInNewPlace.toBulletedList()}")
  }
}
```

What's happening in this code?

1. By giving the `Mover` class a generic constraint of `<T>`, you're saying that anything that creates an instance of this class must fill in the blank for what type `T` actually is.
2. The constructor receives a `List` of the same `T` type that your mover class's generic constraint is, along with the height of the truck in inches, with a default value of 12-feet tall.
3. Some `MutableLists` are declared in order to handle what items are where: in your old place, in your new place or in the `Mover`'s truck.
4. The `init` function takes the passed-in list of items to move from the constructor and adds all of them to the list of things in the old place.
5. A function is added with a loop to move all items from the old place into the truck.
6. A function is added with a loop to move all items from the truck into the new place.
7. A list of what was moved is printed out using `finishMove()`.

One thing you'll notice that is **not** in the `Mover<T>` class: any kind of information about what underlying type `T` could possibly be.

In the moving analogy, if you have some stuff that's big but cheap, you can usually wind up hiring some cheaper movers to move them. You'll do that next.

To start, define a simple class below `Mover<T>` to represent a cheap thing you want moved:

```
class CheapThing(val name: String) {
  override fun toString(): String {
```

```
        return name
    }
}
```

This class doesn't do much besides hang on to the name of the item you're moving and use that name instead of the object's address in memory when the object is printed.

Next, go to the `main()` function and add the following lines at the bottom of the file:

```
val cheapThings = listOf(
    CheapThing("Cinder Block table"),
    CheapThing("Box of old books"),
    CheapThing("Ugly old couch")
)
val cheapMover = Mover(cheapThings)
```

These lines create a list of things and use that list to create a `Mover` object. Note that, because of type inference with your list is of type `List<CheapThing>`, Kotlin knows that your mover is of type `Mover<CheapThing>`.

Underneath that declaration, call the three functions that will actually move all your stuff, and complete the move:

```
cheapMover.moveEverythingToTruck()
cheapMover.moveEverythingIntoNewPlace()
cheapMover.finishMove()
```

Build and run the program. In the console, you should see:

```
Moved your Cinder Block table to the truck!
Moved your Box of old books to the truck!
Moved your Ugly old couch to the truck!
Moved your Cinder Block table into your new place!
Moved your Box of old books into your new place!
Moved your Ugly old couch into your new place!
OK, we finished! We were able to move your:
 - Cinder Block table
 - Box of old books
 - Ugly old couch
```

Without the `Mover` class knowing anything about what type of object is being moved, you were able to create a `Mover` object and have it move all your cheap things!

Unlike big cheap objects, you'll almost always want to hire professional movers to move your breakable things. These sorts of movers might be expensive, but they'll usually keep things from breaking (or they will replace them if they do break).

Below your `CheapThing` class, define a simple class to represent something that's breakable, along with a way to "break" it:

```
class BreakableThing(
    val name: String,
    var isBroken: Boolean = false
) {
  fun smash() {
    isBroken = true
  }

  override fun toString(): String {
    return name
  }
}
```

Next, back at the bottom of the `main()` function, add some breakable things and an expensive mover to move them:

```
val television = BreakableThing("Flat-Screen Television")
val breakableThings = listOf(
      television,
      BreakableThing("Mirror"),
      BreakableThing("Guitar")
  )
val expensiveMover = Mover(breakableThings)
```

Then, call the same functions you called on `cheapMover` to tell the expensive mover to move your breakable things:

```
expensiveMover.moveEverythingToTruck()
expensiveMover.moveEverythingIntoNewPlace()
expensiveMover.finishMove()
```

Build and run again, and the following will print on the console:

```
Moved your Flat-Screen Television to the truck!
Moved your Mirror to the truck!
Moved your Guitar to the truck!
Moved your Flat-Screen Television into your new place!
Moved your Mirror into your new place!
Moved your Guitar into your new place!
OK, we finished! We were able to move your:
 - Flat-Screen Television
 - Mirror
 - Guitar
```

Well, that looks about the same as the output for moving cheap things! But what happens when something breaks?

Between the line moving everything into the truck and the line moving everything into the new place, add the following line:

```
television.smash()
```

Build and run… and it prints out exactly the same lines as above. Uh oh— that expensive mover isn't actually doing anything to find out if something is broken!

That's because there's nothing in the `Mover` class that allows the mover to check if something is broken. How can we make the `Mover` class do that? One way to do it is with smart casts.

Update `moveEverythingToTruck()` to read as follows:

```
fun moveEverythingToTruck() {
  while (thingsLeftInOldPlace.count() > 0) {
    val item = thingsLeftInOldPlace.removeAt(0)

    if (item is BreakableThing) {
      if (!item.isBroken) {
        thingsInTruck.add(item)
        println("Moved your $item to the truck!")
      } else {
        println("Could not move your $item to the truck")
      }
    } else {
      thingsInTruck.add(item)
      println("Moved your $item to the truck!")
    }
  }
}
```

This works! The `(item is BreakableThing)` check makes everything within that if expression aware that the item is of that specific type.

But there are a couple of things that are highly problematic from both a conceptual and practical standpoint about this code:

- A class with a generic constraint shouldn't need to know what specific type `T` is in order to be able to do things with it — but, here, it does. If it has to know what subtype it's holding, the point of generics is somewhat defeated.
- A bunch of logic gets exactly repeated — often a sign that copy-pasting of code was employed. This is dangerous, because it means that whatever bugs were in the code which was copy-pasted also got copy-pasted!

So how can we further constrain the <T> generic type on the `Mover` class so that we know that it can always be checked, without having to make everything descend from the same superclass?

The answer: Interfaces!

Interfaces

Interfaces allow you to declare information about what something **does**, rather than what it **is**, as a class hierarchy would.

Above the declaration of the `Mover<T>` class, add a new interface.

```
interface Checkable {
  fun checkIsOK(): Boolean
}
```

Next, update the generic constraint (i.e., the bit in the angle brackets) of the `Mover` class so it only accepts types that conform to the `Checkable` interface:

```
class Mover<T: Checkable>
```

This updated constraint means that attempting to create a `Mover` with a class that does not conform to `Checkable` will fail at compile time. Before continuing, add one more `private var` to the `Mover` class below the other three to hold things that fail the check:

```
private var thingsWhichFailedCheck = mutableListOf<T>()
```

Next, update the `moveEverythingToTruck()` function to take advantage of the `Mover` class's new knowledge that anything it's receiving has to be of the type `Checkable`:

```
fun moveEverythingToTruck() {
  while (thingsLeftInOldPlace.count() > 0) {
    val item = thingsLeftInOldPlace.removeAt(0)

    if (item.checkIsOK()) {
      thingsInTruck.add(item)
      println("Moved your $item to the truck!")
    } else {
      thingsWhichFailedCheck.add(item)
      println("Could not move your $item to the truck :[")
    }
  }
}
```

Next, update `moveEverythingIntoNewPlace` to also take advantage of this new ability to check if something is okay:

```
fun moveEverythingIntoNewPlace() {
  while (thingsInTruck.count() > 0) {
    val item = thingsInTruck.removeAt(0)
    if (item.checkIsOK()) {
      thingsInNewPlace.add(item)
      println("Moved your $item into your new place!")
    } else {
      thingsWhichFailedCheck.add(item)
      println("Could not move your $item into your new place :
[")
    }
  }
}
```

Next, update the `finishMove` function so that your `Mover` lets their customer know what items were not moved successfully, if there were any that weren't moved:

```
fun finishMove() {
  println("OK, we finished! We were able to move your:$
{thingsInNewPlace.toBulletedList()}")
  if (thingsWhichFailedCheck.isNotEmpty()) {
    println("But we need to talk about your:$
{thingsWhichFailedCheck.toBulletedList()}")
  }
}
```

You've now updated the `Mover` class to handle only this type. You'll still see two errors in your `main()` function, both of which look something like this:

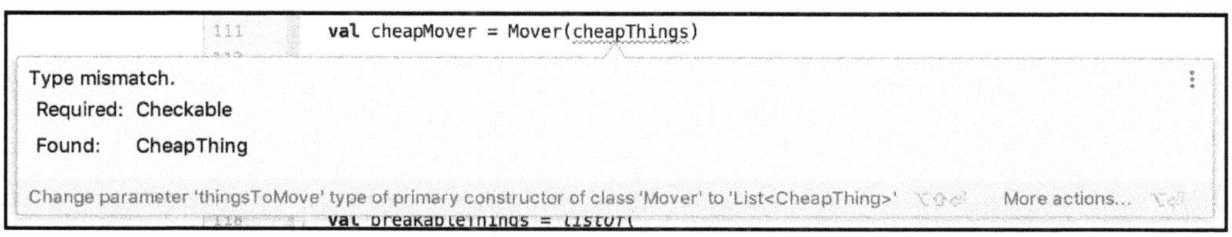

Type mismatch. Required: Checkable, Found: CheapThing

This is because now that `Mover` only accepts types conforming to `Checkable`, it can't accept either `CheapThing` or `BreakableThing` if they don't conform to `Checkable`.

To fix this, first, you need to update `CheapThing` to conform to `Checkable`. Update the declaration:

```
class CheapThing(val name: String): Checkable
```

This will immediately throw up an error that you need to add the function that `Checkable` declares will be there if something conforms:

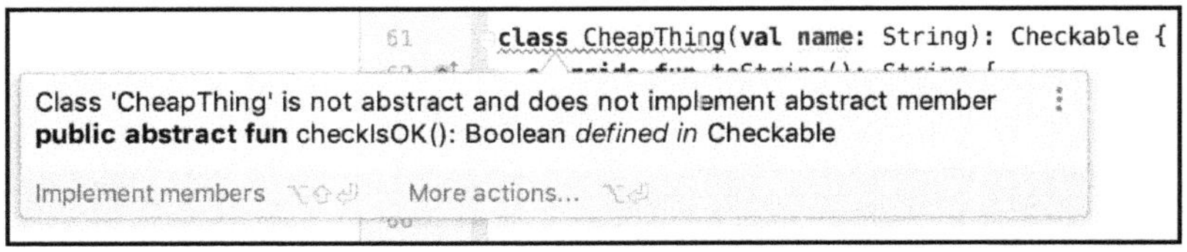

Class 'CheapThing' is not abstract and does not implement abstract member checkIsOK

To fix this error, at the bottom of the `CheapThing` class, add the following line:

```
override fun checkIsOK(): Boolean = true
```

Here, you're overriding the `checkIsOK()` function defined in the `Checkable` interface. However, since you don't really want your movers worrying about whether a cheap thing is OK, your implementation says, "You know what? It's always OK."

Next, go to your `BreakableThing` class and also add conformance to `Checkable` in the declaration:

```
class BreakableThing(
    val name: String,
    var isBroken: Boolean = false
): Checkable
```

Now, at the bottom of the `BreakableThing` class, add an override of the `checkIsOK()` function which actually does a bit of checking to make sure something is OK:

```
override fun checkIsOK(): Boolean {
  return !isBroken
}
```

Build and run, and while you'll still see the same output from the `cheapMover`, the `expensiveMover` will now actually be performing the check you want — and show that your TV got smashed after it got put onto the truck:

```
Moved your Flat-Screen Television to the truck!
Moved your Mirror to the truck!
Moved your Guitar to the truck!
Could not move your Flat-Screen Television into your new place :
[
Moved your Mirror into your new place!
Moved your Guitar into your new place!
OK, we finished! We were able to move your:
 - Mirror
```

```
 - Guitar

But we need to talk about your:
 - Flat-Screen Television
```

You've used an interface to give your generic types more power. But can you go one level deeper: What about making a generic interface?

Generic interfaces

A generic interface is an interface that is constrained to a generic type. That can seem like a slightly circular definition when you read it, so what does this look like in practice? Keep going with the moving metaphor.

Often, when you're moving, you will put one or more things into a box or a plastic tub or some other sort of container to make it easier or safer to move your stuff.

If you want to say that a particular type of thing can only be moved in a particular type of container, you can easily represent this with a generic interface.

Above the `main()` function, add a new interface for a typed container:

```
// 1
interface Container<T> {
  // 2
  fun canAddAnotherItem(): Boolean
  fun addItem(item: T)
  // 3
  fun canRemoveAnotherItem(): Boolean
  fun removeItem(): T
  // 4
  fun getAnother(): Container<T>
  // 5
  fun contents(): List<T>
}
```

You've created a generic interface with several methods — some of which accept generic values and some of which return generic values. What's happening here?

1. You've declared that your interface needs a generic type passed into it whenever a class implementing this interface is created.
2. You've created functions to check whether another item can be added to the container, and then pass an item of the generic type of the container in to be added.

3. You've added functions to do the opposite: checking if there are any more items to remove from the container and then to return an item of the generic type as it's removed from the container.

4. You've added a generic factory method to get a new, empty container. This will help if your container fails the `canAddAnotherItem()` check.

5. You've added a way access a typed list of what items are in the container.

In the `Mover` class, add a new method below `moveEverythingIntoTruck` to move a generic container into the truck:

```
private fun moveContainerToTruck(container: Container<T>) {
  thingsInTruck.add(container)
  println("Moved a container with your $
{container.contents().toBulletedList()} to the truck!")
}
```

You'll see an error show up on the line where you're trying to move the container to the truck:

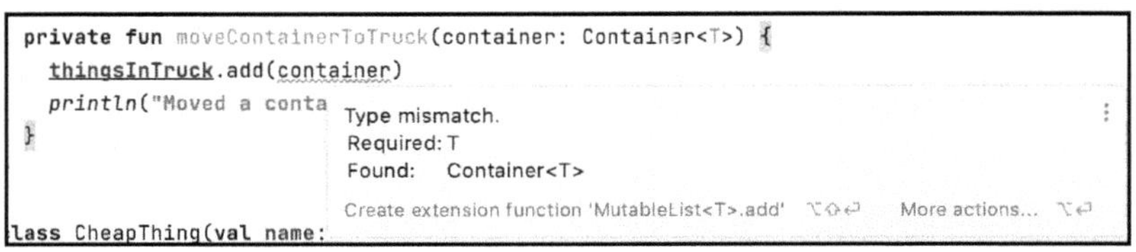

Type mismatch. Required: T, Found: Container<T>

While a generic container takes the same <T> that is being used for the mover class as its type, it's not actually of that type, so trying to add it to the truck will fail.

To fix this, update the type of `thingsInTruck` so that it can accept an object of `Any` type:

```
private var thingsInTruck = mutableListOf<Any>()
```

This will cause a few errors in `moveEverythingIntoNewPlace()`, which we'll return to shortly. What this does do is resolve the error in adding a container to the truck, allowing you to proceed with updating `moveEverythingToTruck()` so that it can add items to a container if one is provided.

First, update the method signature to take a nullable container, typed to the same generic type as is being passed in to the `Mover<T>` class:

```
fun moveEverythingToTruck(startingContainer: Container<T>?)
```

Next, within the method, at the very top above the while loop, add a variable to hang on to whatever the current container is, if it exists:

```
var currentContainer = startingContainer
```

And at the very bottom below the while loop, add a line moving the current container to the truck, if it exists:

```
currentContainer?.let { moveContainerToTruck(it) }
```

Within the `if (item.checkIsOK()) {...}` block where you were previously moving an item to the truck directly, add the following code, so that if a container is provided, you provide logic to pack the item into a container (moving a full container and getting a new one if necessary):

```
// 1
if (currentContainer != null) {
  // 2
  if (!currentContainer.canAddAnotherItem()) {
    moveContainerToTruck(currentContainer)
    currentContainer = currentContainer.getAnother()
  }
  // 3
  currentContainer.addItem(item)
  println("Packed your $item!")
} else {
  // 4
  thingsInTruck.add(item)
  println("Moved your $item to the truck!")
}
```

What's happening in this code?

1. You're checking whether the current container is null. If it isn't, then everything in the `if` block will be smart cast so that `currentContainer` can be accessed without a null check. If it is null, you go to the `else` block (#4).
2. You're checking if the current container is full. If it's full, you move it to the truck and get another container. If it's not, you just keep going.
3. You're adding the item to the `currentContainer`, which may or may not have been replaced.
4. If you're in this block, `currentContainer` was null and you just keep putting items directly in the truck as you were before.

Now, it's time to move on to getting everything back out of the truck and/or whatever container it was packed in. And this is where things start to get pretty complicated because of something Kotlin brought over from Java: type erasure.

Type erasure

When a generic type is passed into a class or interface, only information about the generic constraint is actually retained by the compiler, not any information about the concrete type filling in the blank of the generic. This is known as **type erasure**.

When your generic constraint has an interface that it must adhere to, any functions defined in the interface are available in the interface or class using the generic type. But what if you want to do more than that?

In this case, you've updated the generic constraint of `thingsInTruck` to be `<Any>`, but the things that can go in the apartment still must be of the type being passed in to `Mover<T>`.

Go to `moveEverythingIntoNewPlace()`. You'll see the errors that you ignored earlier:

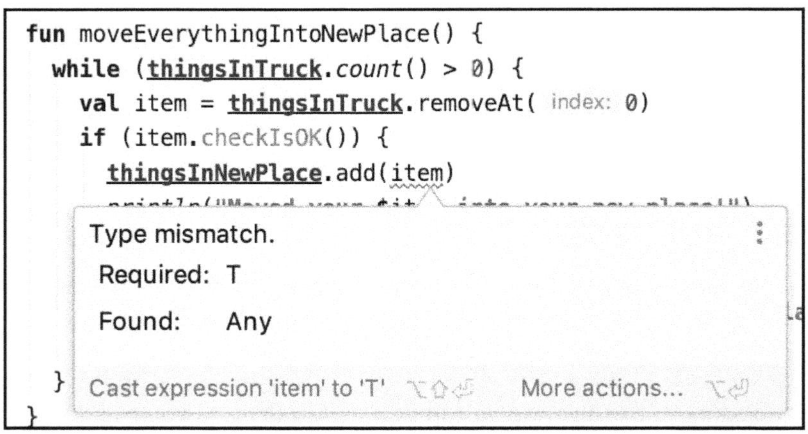

Type mismatch: Required: T, Founds: Any

First, clear up these errors by extracting the bit checking the item into its own private function, passing the item as a generically typed parameter:

```
private fun tryToMoveItemIntoNewPlace(item: T) {
  if (item.checkIsOK()) {
    thingsInNewPlace.add(item)
    println("Moved your $item into your new place!")
```

```
    } else {
      thingsWhichFailedCheck.add(item)
      println("Could not move your $item into your new place :[")
    }
  }
```

Now that the compiler has some assurance that something passed into that function is of the correct type, those errors will go away. So, from there, how do you actually figure out how to get items either out of containers or directly out of the truck, so that they can be passed into that function?

Back in `moveEverythingToNewPlace()`, right below where you remove the item from the truck, try to determine whether the item is of the correct generic type by checking whether it's an instance of that type:

```
if (item is T) {}
```

As the compiler will tell you, type erasure means that this is not possible:

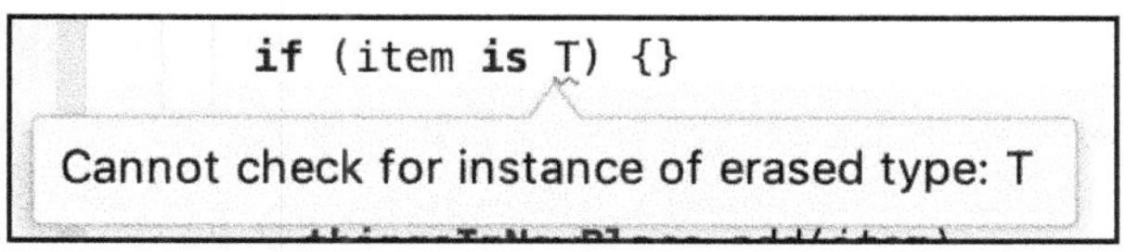

Cannot check for instance of erased type: T

Because the compiler doesn't actually know what type `T` is, you can't use `is` to check its type.

Instead, try the opposite approach: Instead of checking what things in the truck are type `T`, see which ones are of type `Container<T>` by replacing the erroring line with:

```
if (item is Container<T>) {}
```

This will give you another error about erased types:

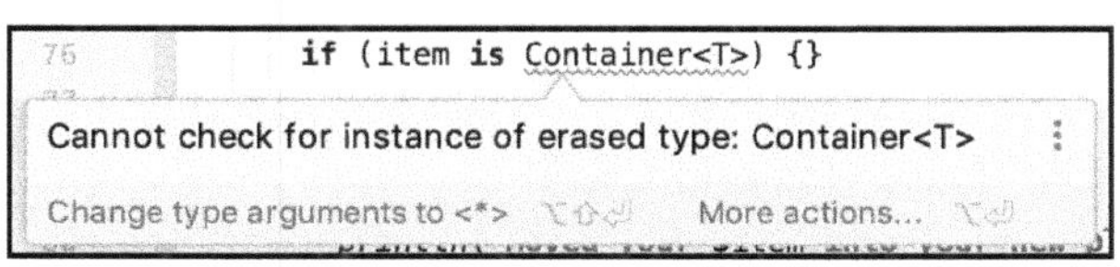

Cannot check for instance of erased type: Container<T>

This error might seem weird, because the compiler definitely knows what a `Container` is — it just doesn't know what type `T` is. This is where a new tool comes in handy: star projection.

Star projection

Replace the T in Container<T> with an asterisk:

```
if (item is Container<*>) {}
```

Now, the error will go away. This is some dark magic known as **star projection**. The "star" part is named after the asterisk.

The "projection" part means that while you know that Container accepts a generic type, you have no idea what that generic type will be. This is a way to tell the compiler, "This could be a Container of anything, but I can tell you that it's definitely a Container."

Now that you can actually access the container, try to remove an item from it:

```
if (item is Container<*>) {
  val itemInContainer = item.removeItem()
}
```

You'll notice a couple things, here. First, smart casting gives you access to the functions defined in Container. Second, when you try to use the function, the type isn't quite what you want it to be:

Instead of T, it's a nullable Any?. This is the essence of star projection's workaround for type erasure: Instead of actually getting information about the generic type, it assumes it must be... some type, which could be nullable.

So this isn't ideal for what you want to do here either, because you still don't know what type is in the container you've been able to extract.

What you really need is even darker magic: **reified** type parameters.

Reified type parameters

Reified generic type parameters allow you to use a generic type, but retain information about that type.

You're going to use a function from the Kotlin standard library, which uses a reified generic type. This is the declaration of that function:

```
inline fun <reified R> Iterable<*>.filterIsInstance(): List<R>
```

There are several things going on in this declaration:

- The `inline` declaration tells the complier that any calls to this method must be compiled inline, so that it's still possible to access the type information of the generic type.
- The `reified` declaration tells the compiler, ok, *actually* hang on to the type information of the generic type being passed in here. This can cause a performance hit, so you must explicitly opt-in to make this happen.
- The `Iterable<*>` in this function is being called on is a star-projected `Iterable` type. Essentially, anything which can be iterated through, with any kind of generic type, can theoretically use this function (you'll see an exception to this shortly).
- Finally, the return type is a `List` of items in the `Iterable`, which are of the `reified` generic type parameter that was passed in.

What does this look like in code? Go back to `moveEverythingIntoNewPlace()` and, at the very top of the method, add a new line:

```
val breakableThings =
thingsInTruck.filterIsInstance<BreakableThing>()
```

Below that, start to type `break` to access the instance you just created. You'll see that because of the `reified` type parameter, the blank of `filterIsInstance`'s `List<R>` return type has been filled in by `BreakableThing`:

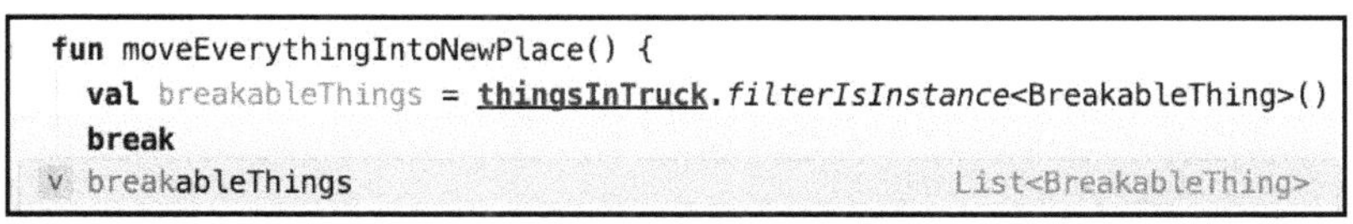

That's how a reified type works when you pass in a concrete type. What happens if you try to pass in a generic type? Comment out or delete the lines you've just added and replace them with a line attempting to filter for items of `Mover<T>`'s generic type:

```
val items = thingsInTruck.filterIsInstance<T>()
```

Unfortunately, this still doesn't work because of type erasure:

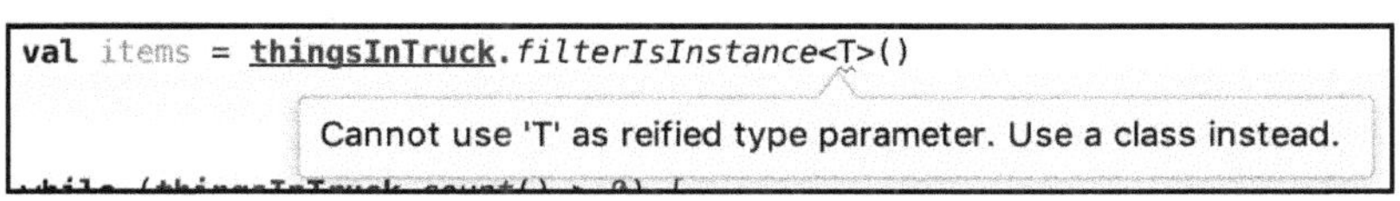

Cannot use 'T' as reified type parameter. Use a class instead.

The type of T was already erased by the time the compiler gets to this point in the code, so there's no way for it to get that information back, even if it wants to. The compiler doesn't know what T is, so it can't check for instances of T.

Comment out or delete the line you just added, and see if you can get it to filter out only star-projected containers:

```
val containers = thingsInTruck.filterIsInstance<Container<*>>()
```

Hey, that works! The problem is that you're back where you were with star projection before: The type of `containers` is `List<Any?>`, and you'd still have to do type casting to ensure that you have the correct type.

Just for laughs, try replacing the * with T — going from star projection to passing the generic type that has been passed into `Mover` into the `Container` you're trying to access:

```
val containers = thingsInTruck.filterIsInstance<Container<T>>()
```

What the... that works?!

While everything else you've tried hasn't worked due to type erasure, here the compiler has just enough information to understand that it needs to get a container of a particular type – but it doesn't actually matter under the hood what type it is.

Now, you're cooking with gas! Because the return type is `List<Container<T>>`, you can once again have type safety when getting items out of the container.

Right below where you got the `containers` list, add the following code to remove all the items from all your containers:

```
for (container in containers) {
  thingsInTruck.remove(container)
  while (container.canRemoveAnotherItem()) {
    val itemInContainer = container.removeItem()
    println("Unpacked your $itemInContainer!")
    tryToMoveItemIntoNewPlace(itemInContainer)
  }
}
```

Again, you'll notice that when you call `container.removeItem()`, because it's a `Container<T>`, the type of `itemInContainer` becomes `T`, and you can pass it to `tryToMoveItemIntoNewPlace` without issue.

But what happens if your items weren't in containers? Anything remaining in the truck should be an item of type `T`, so you can make some assumptions about what it should be.

Below the `for` loop emptying the containers, update the `while` loop to read as follows:

```
while (thingsInTruck.count() > 0) {
  val item = thingsInTruck.removeAt(0) as? T
  if (item != null) {
    tryToMoveItemIntoNewPlace(item)
  } else {
    println("Something in the truck was not of the expected
generic type: $item")
  }
}
```

At this point, there really isn't a great way to avoid using the `as` unchecked cast operator to ensure type safety with `T`. However, you can suppress any exception that would come up by using the nullable version of this operator, `as?`, which will return `null` instead of throwing an exception if the cast fails.

If the `as?` cast fails, it's now printed out for diagnostic purposes, but it doesn't crash your app.

> **Note**: If the unchecked cast warning that you get here bothers you because you're actually returning null if the item is not of the proper type, you can add a `@Suppress("UNCHECKED_CAST")` annotation to the line above the `as?` cast.

Now, it's *finally* time to add a class, which implements the type `Container<T>` for a given type.

You probably wouldn't want to bother with a container for your `CheapThing` objects, but you probably would want to at least put your `BreakableThings` into a box.

Below the definition of your `Container<T>` interface, create a `CardboardBox` implementation of the `Container` interface which holds `BreakableThings`:

```
// 1
class CardboardBox: Container<BreakableThing> {
  //2
  private var items = mutableListOf<BreakableThing>()

  override fun contents(): List<BreakableThing> {
    // 3
```

```
    return items.toList()
  }

  // 4
  override fun canAddAnotherItem(): Boolean {
    return items.count() < 2
  }

  override fun addItem(item: BreakableThing) {
    // 5
    items.add(item)
  }

  override fun canRemoveAnotherItem(): Boolean {
    // 6
    return items.count() > 0
  }

  override fun removeItem(): BreakableThing {
    // 7
    val lastItem = items.last()
    items.remove(lastItem)
    return lastItem
  }

  override fun getAnother(): Container<BreakableThing> {
    // 8
    return CardboardBox()
  }
}
```

What's happening in this code?

1. First, you're declaring a class called `CardboardBox`, which conforms to `Container` and provides `BreakableThing` as the generic type.
2. You're adding a private mutable list to store the items within the `CardboardBox` so that only the `CardboardBox` itself knows about this mutable list.
3. Since `T` has been replaced with `BreakableThing`, you're returning an immutable copy of your mutable list of `BreakableThings` when asked for a list of the contents of the `CardboardBox`.
4. Here, you're assuming that each `CardboardBox` can only fit two things into it. If it's already got two things in it, another item can't be added.
5. You add the passed-in `BreakableThing` to the private mutable list when the `addItem` function is called.

6. You check if there are any more items to remove from the `CardboardBox` — in this case, validating that there are more items in the underlying `items` array.
7. You remove the last item from the underlying `items` array and return it when asked to remove an item from the `CardboardBox`.
8. When asked to create another `Container<BreakableThing>`, you create another `CardboardBox`, since it already conforms to this generic requirement.

Now that you've created a type that implements the `Container` interface, it's time to make it possible to move it!

In the `main()` function, update the `moveEverythingToTruck` call for the cheap mover to explicitly provide a null container (hey, you wanted cheap!):

```
cheapMover.moveEverythingToTruck(null)
```

Next, update the `moveEverythingToTruck` call for the expensive mover to provide a `CardboardBox`:

```
expensiveMover.moveEverythingToTruck(CardboardBox())
```

Build and run your code, and you'll be able to see in the printed logs that your `cheapMover` still moves everything directly into and out of their truck:

```
Moved your Cinder Block table to the truck!
Moved your Box of old books to the truck!
Moved your Ugly old couch to the truck!
Moved your Cinder Block table into your new place!
Moved your Box of old books into your new place!
Moved your Ugly old couch into your new place!
OK, we finished! We were able to move your:
 - Cinder Block table
 - Box of old books
 - Ugly old couch
```

...while your `expensiveMover` packs all your items into containers before moving them:

```
Packed your Flat-Screen Television!
Packed your Mirror!
Moved a container with your
 - Flat-Screen Television
 - Mirror
 to the truck!
Packed your Guitar!
Moved a container with your
 - Guitar
```

```
 to the truck!
Unpacked your Mirror!
Moved your Mirror into your new place!
Unpacked your Flat-Screen Television!
Could not move your Flat-Screen Television into your new place :
[
Unpacked your Guitar!
Moved your Guitar into your new place!
OK, we finished! We were able to move your:
 - Mirror
 - Guitar

But we need to talk about your:
 - Flat-Screen Television
```

So to recap, you've now got a ton of generic tools in this one example with movers:

- A `Checkable` interface.
- A `Mover` with a `<T: Checkable>` constraint, which can move any item that conforms to `Checkable`.
- A `Container<T>` class that can move any items of a specific type.
- The ability to have the mover move your items in a `Container<T>` that uses the same `<T: Checkable>` that was passed into your `Mover`.
- Use of a standard library method using `reified` types.
- A nullable unchecked cast that helps determine if something is of the correct type.

Whew! That is a whole lot of stuff. But there's one more thing to discuss before moving on from generics: variance.

Generic type variance (a.k.a., in and out declarations)

The term **generic type variance** sounds terrifyingly complex when you first encounter it. This concept is nowhere near as complicated as it sounds.

There are two types of variance you can declare with a class or an interface that use a generic type:

- **`in`** variance means that the generic type will only ever be used in parameters or other things being handed *into* your type.

- **`out`** variance means that the generic type will only ever be used in return values or other things coming *out of* your type.

A really quick and easy way to see how this can affect a type you've declared is modifying the **Container** class you declared earlier. Go to the class declaration and add `out` variance to the generic type by updating the declaration as follows:

```
interface Container<out T>
```

Immediately, the compiler will be unhappy:

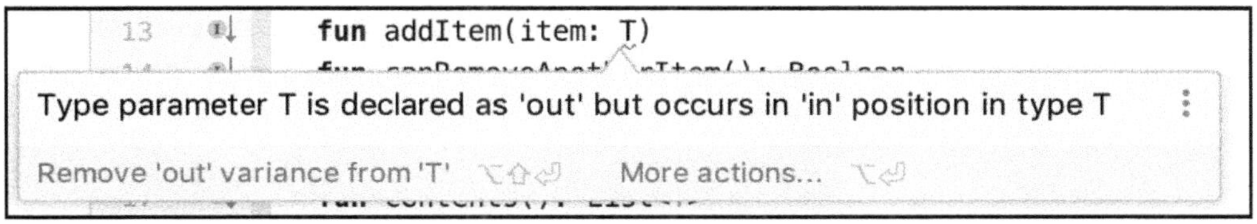

Type parameter T is declared as 'out' but occurs in 'in' position in type T

You've told the compiler that `T` would only be used in an `out` position, but this error is telling you that one of the functions you've already declared is being used as something that is passed in.

Now, try doing the opposite: Declaring that `T` uses `in` variance. Update the declaration to the following:

```
interface Container<in T>
```

The warning will go away on the function with the generic parameter, but it'll pop right back up in two other places:

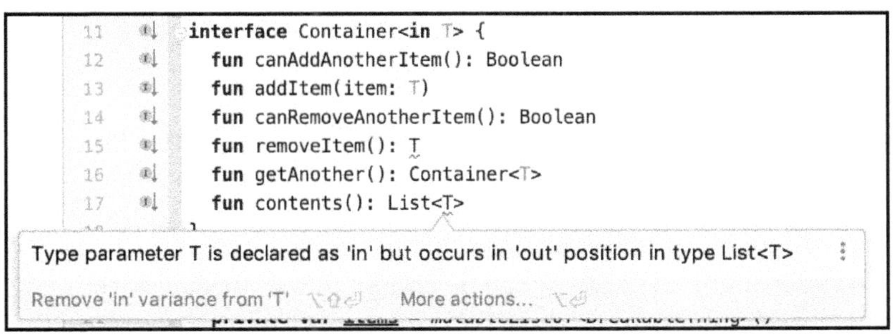

Type parameter T is declared as 'in' but occurs in 'out' position in type T

Now, you're seeing that, while the compiler thinks it's OK for a generically typed parameter to be passed into your class or interface, it's not OK to have a return value of that same generic type or to have a return value of another thing referencing that generic type.

You might be tempted to explicitly state that a class or interface has both `in` and `out` type variance for its generic type, but, if you give it a try, you'll see that the compiler would prefer that you don't do that:

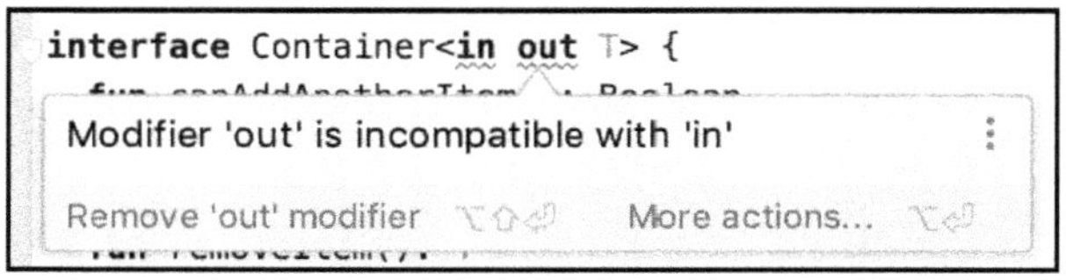

Modifier 'out' is incompatible with 'in'

If a generic type has both `in` and `out` variance, you must leave out both declarations for it to compile. Change `Container`'s interface declaration back to:

```
interface Container<T>
```

Once you do, everything will compile again.

So now that you know **what** this does, there comes a thornier question: **Why** would you want to make this kind of restriction?

You want to make it clear to the caller of your class with a generic constraint, and to the compiler, whether the class is restricted in terms of what it can do with the generic type.

If your type has `out` variance, you can infer some things automatically, while comparing instances with related types.

For instance, recall that `List<T>` is actually declared as `List<out T>`. Add the following lines to the bottom of the `main()` function:

```
val ints = listOf(1, 2, 3)
val numbers: List<Number> = ints
```

This compiles even though the inferred type of `ints` is `List<Int>`. Since `Int` is a subtype of `Number`, anything that's an `Int` will definitely also be a `Number`.

Since anything being returned from `List<Number>` would also be able to return an `Int`, you can infer that a `List<Int>` can be assigned to a variable with the type `List<Number>` without any problems.

However, this restricts you from doing the opposite. Add a line trying to assign `numbers` to a `List<Int>` variable:

```
val moreInts: List<Int> = numbers
```

This causes a type-checking error:

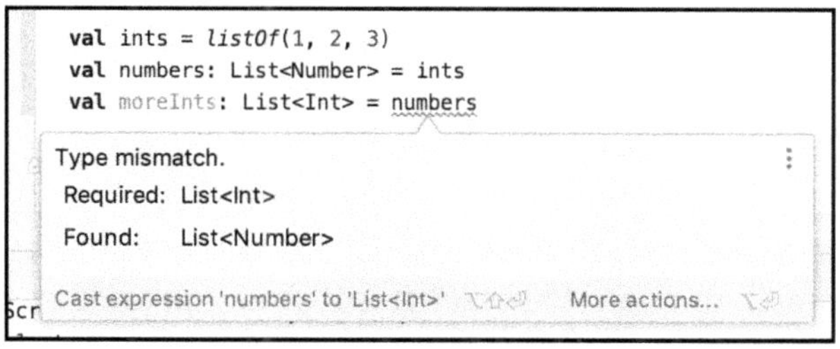

Type mismatch. Required: List<Int>, Found: List<Number>

If `List<Int>` has something with a return value `Int`, you cannot simply return a `Number` since `Number` is also the supertype of several other types in Kotlin, such as `Float`.

It **could** be an `Int` — but it also could be some other subtype of `Number`. This is why the compiler errors out when you try to assign a `List<Number>` to a variable of type `List<Int>`.

> **Note**: Comment out or delete the line you just added to get rid of the error before continuing.

Contrast `List`'s behavior with that of `MutableList<T>`, which has neither an `in` nor an `out` modifier for its generic type.

Add the following lines to the bottom of your `main()` function:

```
val mutableInts = mutableListOf(1, 2, 3)
val mutableNumbers: MutableList<Number> = mutableInts
```

This errors immediately:

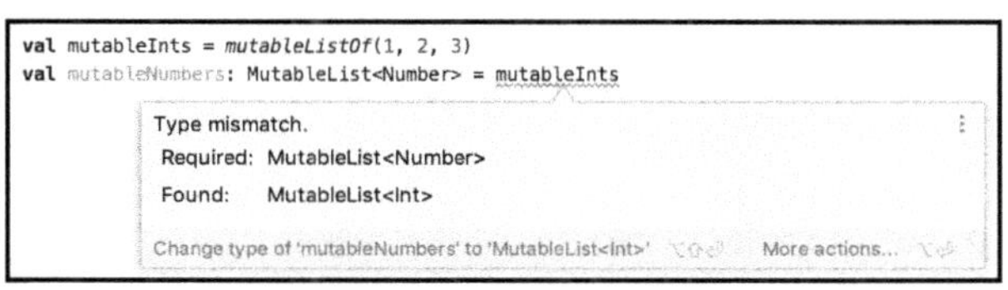

Type mismatch. Required: MutableList<Number>, Found: MutableList<Int>

Because `MutableList` both accepts and returns parameters of type `T`, they always have to be the same type, and you can't make the assumption that you'll be able to use subtypes interchangeably. Therefore `T` must always simply be its own type — not a subtype or a supertype.

There aren't a lot of types that have `in` variance to give an example with, but one is `Comparator`. Its interface looks like this:

```
interface Comparable<in T> {
  operator fun compareTo(other: T): Int
}
```

Since you can't instantiate an interface without a concrete implementation, you're going to create a small function that takes this type as a parameter to examine how this works within your `main()` function.

At the bottom of your `main()` function, add an example function which takes a `Comparable<Number>` and compares it to an `Int` and a `Float`:

```
fun compare(comparator: Comparable<Number>) {
  val int: Int = 1
  comparator.compareTo(int)
  val float: Float = 1.0f
  comparator.compareTo(float)
}
```

Something conforming to `Comparable<Number>` can compare itself to both `Int` and `Float` values, since both are subtypes of `Number`.

This also allows something that initially seems pretty weird to be possible. Add the following line to your `compare` function:

```
val intComparable: Comparable<Int> = comparator
```

This compiles, which is somewhat counterintuitive — `Int` is a subtype of `Number`, not the other way around. But since the `Comparable<Number>` can definitely compare itself to `Int` values, it can also be used as a `Comparable<Int>`.

Being able to make this assignment means that, in exchange, `intComparable` will lose the ability to compare subtypes of `Number` other than `Int`.

Add the following lines to your `compare` function:

```
intComparable.compareTo(int)
intComparable.compareTo(float)
```

You'll see that the first call works fine, but the second one rejects the type:

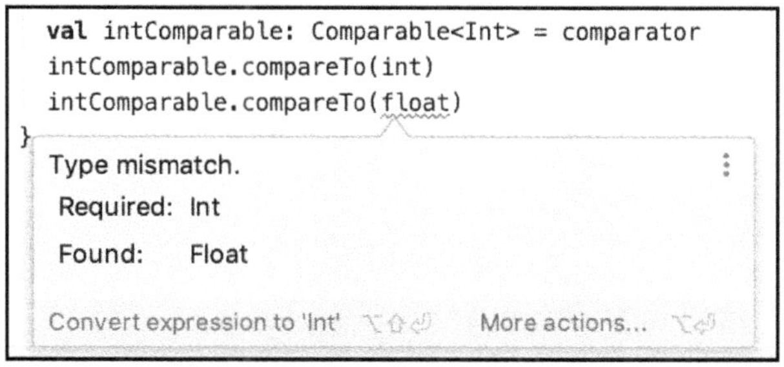

Type mismatch. Required: Int, Found: Float

Because you've made the generic type of `Comparable` more specific, you lose the ability to make comparisons to other subtypes.

Finally, now that you know how and why all these things work, it's useful to know the fancy-sounding technical names for all these different types of variance:

- **Covariant** types are the ones you've seen marked as `<out T>`. Because `T` can only be part of a return value, the relation of objects that take the same generic type is similar to that of supertypes and subtypes. You can assign something typed as `List<Int>` to a variable of type `List<Number>`, since `Int` is a subtype of `Number`.
- **Contravariant** types are the ones you've seen marked as `<in T>`. Since `T` can only be taken in as a parameter, you can assume the inverse relation to a subtype and supertype. You can assign something typed as `Comparable<Number>` to a variable of type `Comparable<Int>`, since `Number` is a supertype of `Int`.
- **Invariant** types are types that are simply marked as `<T>`. You cannot make inferences about relationships with other objects that take the same generic type, since they both take in and return objects of type `T`.

Challenges

1. Use generics to create a function that can print full names of a list of people as long as the objects representing them conform to a certain interface. The interface should allow you to access `String` values for `firstName` and `lastName`. Start with members of your family and your peers (or use fictional family members or peers if you'd prefer).

2. Create a `Vehicle` class that conforms to `Checkable` class and a `ShippingContainer` class that conforms to `Container<Vehicle>`, but that which only takes one vehicle at a time. Each vehicle should:

- Know its own height in inches.
- Know its model and brand names.
- Display a combination of its model and brand names instead of its instance address when printed out using `println`.
- Have a variable for a lambda, which allows callers to verify if the vehicle's height, in inches, is too big for a `Mover`'s truck by passing in the height of the vehicle to the lambda, then returning a `Boolean` value from the lambda of whether or not it will fit. (Hint: You can't do this as part of a constructor, since you won't have a reference to the `Mover` yet.)
- Use that function as part of `checkIsOK()`.

3. Use the default constructor of `Mover<Vehicle>` and the functions you've already used to try to move three vehicles in `ShippingContainers`: A Yamaha Vino, which is 40 inches tall; a Toyota Corolla, which is 58 inches tall; and a Freightliner Cascadia, which is 150 inches tall.After doing that, answer the following questions:

- How many of your vehicles does a mover — who is created using the default values — move?
- Do you need to adjust the height of the moving vehicle in order to get all of the vehicles to be moved? If so, what is the height it needs to be adjusted to?

4. Create a `Mover` object that can move all the `Vehicle`, `BreakableThing` and `CheapThing` objects you've already created.

- What is the type you need to pass to create a mover who can move all of these types of things?
- Is there a kind of `Container` you can pass to this mover? If there is, what kind is it?

Key points

Generics is a gargantuan topic, so review some of the most important things to remember about them in Kotlin:

- **Generics** allow you to create classes or interfaces that operate on a type that is not known when your code for that class or interface is written.
- Generic programming can allow you to centralize pieces of functionality in a highly reusable and easily debuggable fashion.
- **Type erasure** means that, within a class or interface that takes a generic type, you won't have any information about that type at compile time unless you annotate the type with `reified` and inline the function.
- Allowing only `in` or `out` variance of a generic type allows you to restrict whether a generic type can be passed in to extensions or be returned from subclasses or other functions on a particular generic interface or class. This, in turn, allows both you and the compiler to make assumptions about how generic types relate to each other.

Where to go from here?

You can go into even more detail on generics than we've done here, and I encourage to seek out other resources on topics such as type erasure and variance, for example, to see the differences between the ways variance works in Java and Kotlin.

In the next chapter, Chapter 19, "Kotlin/Java Interoperability," we'll take a look at how Kotlin and Java work together, calling Kotlin code from Java and vice-versa.

Section IV: Intermediate Topics

You've made it to the final section of this book! In this section, you'll delve into some important but more intermediate topics to round out your Kotlin apprenticeship.

Chapter 19: Kotlin/Java Interoperability

By Ellen Shapiro

Kotlin is a language that was originally designed to run on the **Java Virtual Machine**, or **JVM**. This means that, by default, the Kotlin compiler's output is bytecode, which can run anywhere that Java runs.

Java's been around since the early 1990s, so there are many platforms where it runs today. Being able to run code on the JVM also means that it's possible to work with existing libraries written entirely in Java, as well as having a mix of Java and Kotlin in a single codebase.

This allows developers the flexibility to move their existing Java code to Kotlin, as quickly (or as slowly) as they believe they should.

Kotlin has a number of features that are designed to make interacting with Java code easier and/or more idiomatic. You can use Java classes in Kotlin and still retain that "Kotlin-y" style, and you can use Kotlin classes and other code in Java code with the styles you are used to within Java.

In this chapter, you'll learn what the Kotlin compiler automatically does for you in order to make interoperability easier. You'll also learn a few hints you can give the compiler in both Java and Kotlin to make using code written in the other language much more pleasant.

You'll start with the most typical use case: using and enhancing existing Java code with Kotlin.

Mixing Java and Kotlin code

There are several things that the Kotlin compiler will automatically do for you in order to make using code written in Java feel more at home when called from Kotlin, as well as interacting with code written in Kotlin from Java. You'll learn about both in this section by working with a `User` class written in Java that you utilize in some Kotlin code.

Getters and setters

To start, open up the starter project for this chapter and go to the **User.java** file. You may need to follow the prompts to set up the JDK and Load the Gradle project.

You'll see a typical Java class, which uses `private` backing variables and only exposes access to them through `get` and `set` methods for anything outside the current class. Next, go to **main.kt**, and delete the `println` statement. Create a new user instead:

```
val user = User()
```

Notice that, even though this is a Java class, the syntax to create a new object is the same as it is for pure Kotlin objects. You do not include the `new` keyword since it's not needed in Kotlin to create a new instance.

Next, go to a new line, and start typing `user.set`. Instead of the explicit `set...` calls that you saw in the **User.java** file, you'll see property names which are generated by the Kotlin compiler:

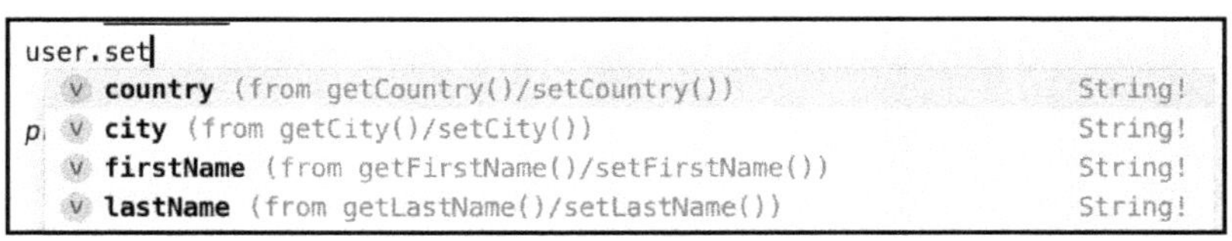

Notice that the IDE also displays the names of the methods, from where it's synthesizing these property names.

It also indicates that the type is `String!` — a `String` that is assumed to be non-null. You'll see how to add proper support for nullability later in this chapter.

In `main()` within **main.kt**, add some details for the user:

```
user.firstName = "Bob"
user.lastName = "Barker"
user.city = "Los Angeles"
user.country = "United States"

println("User info:\n$user")
```

Run **main.kt** using the Play button in the upper-left of the Editor panel by the `main()` declaration, and it will print the following:

```
User info:
Bob Barker
Los Angeles, United States
```

Wow, that's nicely formatted! Why is that? If you open **User.java**, you'll notice that `toString()` is overridden at the bottom of the file.

Whenever `toString()` is overridden in Java, Kotlin's string interpolation syntax will call through to that method when using the `$variableName` syntax.

Right now, the `User` class only knows about the user's city and country. What if you wanted to be able to support a full address?

In theory, you could keep adding more properties to `User`, but for the sake of separation of concerns, you probably want to create a new class. And the fun part is, you can use Kotlin to create your new class, and then use it directly from your Java `User` class!

Adding a Kotlin class as a Java property

In IntelliJ IDEA's menu, select **File ▸ New ▸ Kotlin File/Class**. Name the file you're creating **Address**:

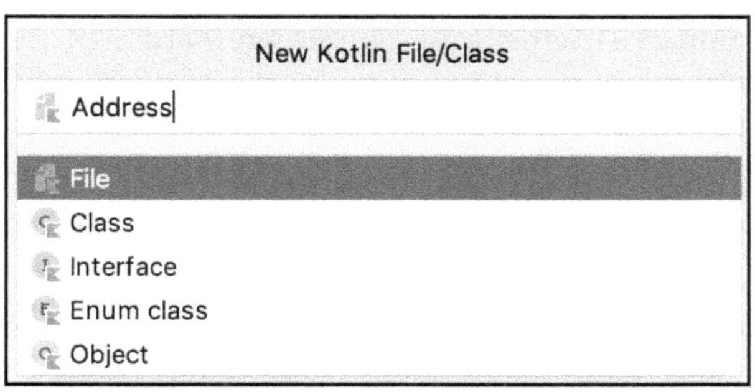

Open the resulting **Address.kt** file, which will be empty. Since there are several possible types of addresses, start by adding an `enum class` to handle those different types:

```
enum class AddressType {
  Billing,
  Shipping,
  Gift
}
```

Next, add a `data classwith` a constructor to handle creating a new `Address` with the appropriate properties:

```
data class Address(
    val streetLine1: String,
    val streetLine2: String?,
    val city: String,
    val stateOrProvince: String,
    val postalCode: String,
    var addressType: AddressType,
    val country: String = "United States"
) {
  // TODO
}
```

You'll also want to be able to have a nicely formatted address for when you need to send this user mail or ship them something. Replace the `TODO` with a function to do that:

```
fun forPostalLabel(): String {
  var printedAddress = streetLine1
  streetLine2?.let { printedAddress += "\n$it" }
  printedAddress += "\n$city, $stateOrProvince $postalCode"
  printedAddress += "\n${country.toUpperCase()}"
  return printedAddress
}
```

Next, go back to **main.kt**. Delete the two lines where you assign the user's city and country.

Underneath where you printed the user information, add code to create and then print out an address:

```
val billingAddress = Address("123 Fake Street",
    "4th floor",
    "Los Angeles",
    "CA",
    "90291",
    AddressType.Billing)

println("Billing Address:\n$billingAddress\n")
```

Run **main.kt** and you'll see the automatically generated details for the address class at the bottom of the console:

```
Billing Address:
Address(streetLine1=123 Fake Street, streetLine2=4th floor,
city=Los Angeles, stateOrProvince=CA, postalCode=90291,
addressType=Billing, country=United States)
```

While this is helpful, it can be a bit difficult to parse visually. In **Address.kt**, override the `toString` function in order to make the printing look a little better:

```
override fun toString(): String {
    return forPostalLabel()
}
```

Run **main.kt** again, and it'll look a little nicer:

```
Billing Address:
123 Fake Street
4th floor
Los Angeles, CA 90291
UNITED STATES
```

Now that you've moved the information for city and country over to the `Address` class, the properties on the `User` class are no longer necessary. In **User.java**, delete city and country member variables, along with their getters and setters. Update the `toString()` function to:

```
@Override
public String toString() {
  return firstName + " " + lastName;
}
```

Combining the first and last names like this seems like a useful thing for which to add a `get()`-only property — and, instead of doing it in the existing Java class, you can create a Kotlin extension to let you centralize this code to Kotlin.

Adding extension functions to a Java class

Go to **File ▸ New ▸ Kotlin File/Class**. Name your new file **UserExtensions**:

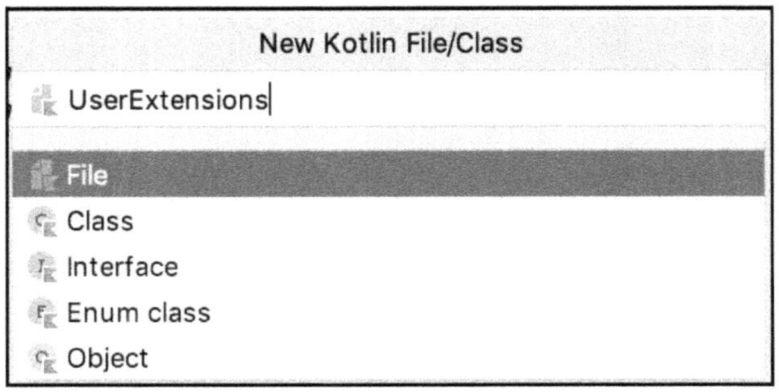

Once the **UserExtensions.kt** file is created, open it and add an extension on the `User` class with your `get()`-only property:

```
val User.fullName: String
  get() = "$firstName $lastName"
```

Now that you have this simplified property, you can go back to **User.java** and update the `toString()` method to call into the extension you just wrote:

```
@Override
public String toString() {
  return UserExtensionsKt.getFullName(this);
}
```

Note that the current user is passed as a parameter, since extensions don't exist in Java. This allows Java functions with potentially clashing names to continue to work correctly since the methods are not being called directly on the object.

By default, unless you provide another name, Kotlin exposes the full file name of a file with extensions or free functions as a wrapper class named `FileNameKt`, and each of those extension methods or free functions as static methods on that wrapper.

That default file naming leaks the fact that you're working with Kotlin in a particular place. If you **want** to know at the call site that you're calling into Kotlin code, then that's fine.

However, if you'd rather have a cleaner name when your Kotlin code comes into Java, you can take advantage of **annotations** to be able to make your file name a bit clearer.

At the top of **UserExtensions.kt**, add the following line:

```
@file:JvmName("UserExtensions")
```

This annotation tells the Kotlin compiler that when creating the Java interop definitions for this file, it should name the wrapper class `UserExtensions` rather than `UserExtensionsKt`.

Now, go back to **User.java** and you can update the `toString()` method to use the name you've set up as the `JvmName`:

```
return UserExtensions.getFullName(this);
```

Neat! There is one pretty significant limitation to what you can do with Kotlin extensions that you may remember from Chapter 13: "Properties": You can't add additional properties with backing fields to them - only properties with custom accessors.

For our next trick, you'll want to scroll back up in **User.java** and add a new property to hold the list of addresses belonging to a user below the other properites:

```
private List<Address> addresses = new ArrayList<>();
```

And then add the corresponding getter and setter below the other getters and setters:

```
public List<Address> getAddresses() {
  return addresses;
}

public void setAddresses(List<Address> addresses) {
  this.addresses = addresses;
}
```

Finally, update `toString()` so you can see how many addresses a user has at a glance in the console:

```
return UserExtensions.getFullName(this) +
    " - Addresses: " + addresses.size();
```

Run **main.kt**, and at the top of the console you'll now see:

```
User info:
Bob Barker - Addresses: 0
```

Now that the backing property `addresses` is set up, you can go back to using Kotlin to work with this backing variable. In **UserExtensions.kt**, add an extension function to get the address of a given type or to return `null` if it doesn't exist:

```
fun User.addressOfType(type: AddressType): Address? {
  return addresses.firstOrNull { it.addressType == type }
}
```

This extension function can be called from either Java or Kotlin but, under the hood, it takes advantage of Kotlin's functional programming and nullability handling. Cool!

You can also add functions that handle validation for adding and removing items from the list of addresses.

In this case, you really only would want one address of a given type — Shipping, Billing or Gift. Add an extension function which adds or updates an address:

```
fun User.addOrUpdateAddress(address: Address) {
  val existingOfType = addressOfType(address.addressType)

  if (existingOfType != null) {
    addresses.remove(existingOfType)
  }

  addresses.add(address)
}
```

Now that all this functionality has been added to the `User` class, it's time to use it in Kotlin! Go to **main.kt**, and below the `println` statement printing out the address, add:

```
user.addOrUpdateAddress(billingAddress)
println("User info after adding address:\n$user")
```

Run **main.kt**, and at the end of the console you'll see:

```
User info after adding address:
Bob Barker - Addresses: 1
```

Now, try to add another address. In **main.kt**, delete the last `println` statement and replace it with:

```
val shippingAddress = Address("987 Unreal Drive",
    null,
    "Burbank",
    "CA",
    "91523",
    AddressType.Shipping)

user.addOrUpdateAddress(shippingAddress)

println("User info after adding addresses:\n$user")
```

Run **main.kt**, and you'll now see at the bottom of the console:

```
User info after adding addresses:
Bob Barker - Addresses: 2
```

Great! Since you have billing and shipping addresses, both are being added. Now, check if the validation you added is working. Update the `AddressType` of `shippingAddress` in the constructor to `AddressType.Billing`.

Run **main.kt** again, and voila!:

```
User info after adding addresses:
Bob Barker - Addresses: 1
```

Since both addresses are showing up as billing address, when the second one is added, it replaces the first one. You've now added a new address to a Java `User`, but done so using validation completely in Kotlin. Congratulations!

> **Note**: Remember to change the `AddressType` of `shippingAddress` back to `AddressType.Shipping` for the next few steps.

Now that you've been able to use extension functions from Java, it's time to see how free functions in Kotlin work with Java code.

Free functions

Free functions in Kotlin are functions that don't extend any existing class and are not tied to a class themselves. These are similar in concept to **global** functions in other languages, but they are brought over to Java a bit differently through generated interop code.

To demonstrate this, you're going to make a file with free functions to allow you to print a full mailing label for a given address.

Go to **File ▸ New Kotlin File/Class**, and name your file **LabelPrinter**:

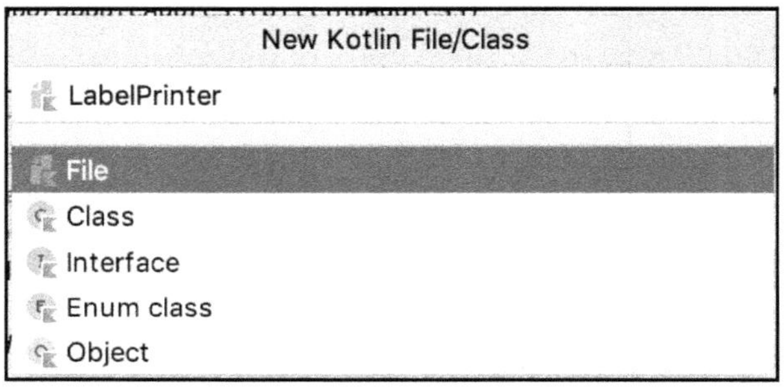

Open the resulting **LabelPrinter.kt** file, and add the following code:

```
// 1
fun labelFor(user: User, type: AddressType): String {
  // 2
  val address = user.addressOfType(type)
  if (address != null) {
    // 3
    var label = "-----\n"
    label += "${user.fullName}\n${address.forPostalLabel()}\n"
    label += "-----\n"
    return label
  } else {
    return "\n!! ${user.fullName} does not have a $type address
set up !!\n"
  }
}

// 4
fun printLabelFor(user: User, type: AddressType) {
    println(labelFor(user, type))
}
```

What's happening in this code:

1. You built a free function to create a label string based on a user and a given type of address.
2. Since you're in Kotlin, you can use the `addressOfType` extension method directly on your `User` object to see if an address of the given type exists.
3. You built up a `String` across multiple lines. In Kotlin, this is as simple as making a `var`, then using the += operator to concatenate strings. This is in sharp contrast to the more painful method in Java, which you'll see shortly.
4. A convenience free function to simply print the label generated by the other free function in this file has been added.

To see how this works in Kotlin, go to **main.kt** and add the following lines:

```
println("Shipping Label:")
printLabelFor(user, AddressType.Shipping)
```

Note that you didn't have to do anything involving the `LabelPrinter` here, since the functions you added to that file are available globally to all your Kotlin code in the project. Run **main.kt** again, and you'll see at the bottom of the console:

```
Shipping Label:
-----
Bob Barker
987 Unreal Drive
Burbank, CA 91523
UNITED STATES
-----
```

OK, that was the easy part. Now for the more cumbersome part.

In **User.java**, add a new method to build up a `String` with all the various types of address label:

```
public String allAddresses() {
  StringBuilder builder = new StringBuilder();
  for (Address address : addresses) {
    builder.append(
      address.getAddressType().name() + " address:\n");
    builder.append(
      LabelPrinterKt.labelFor(this, address.getAddressType()));
  }

  return builder.toString();
}
```

You'll notice two major similarities of the free functions files to the way an extension file works in interop here.

Firstly, a wrapper class called `LabelPrinterKt` is generated with the free functions added as static methods, rather than the functions simply being made global. Note that since you are not extending anything, no additional parameters are generated which need to be passed in.

Secondly, the automatically generated name for the wrapper class in a file with only free functions is of the format `FileNameKt`.

Using the same annotation as you did for `UserExtensions`, update the display name of **LabelPrinter.kt** by adding the following at the top of the file:

```
@file:JvmName("LabelPrinter")
```

Now, when you go back to **User.java**, you can update the `allAddresses()` method to use the updated file name:

```
builder.append(
  LabelPrinter.labelFor(this, address.getAddressType()));
```

Now, update the `toString()` method on `User` to take advantage of this functionality:

```
return UserExtensions.getFullName(this) +
    " - Addresses: " + addresses.size() + "\n" +
    allAddresses();
```

Finally, go back and re-run **main.kt**. The output in the console where you were previously just getting how many addresses the user had (and above the "shipping label" output) will be:

```
User info after adding addresses:
Bob Barker - Addresses: 2
Billing address:
-----
Bob Barker
123 Fake Street
4th floor
Los Angeles, CA 90291
UNITED STATES
-----
Shipping address:
-----
Bob Barker
987 Unreal Drive
```

```
Burbank, CA 91523
UNITED STATES
-----
```

Now that you've got all this information about mixing Java and Kotlin code, it's time to look into another piece of the puzzle when bringing Java code into Kotlin: nullability.

Java nullability annotations

Though Java 8 introduced `Optional` to make null values safer to work with, annotations are the way to go when handling nullability between Kotlin and Java.

JetBrains, the makers of the IntelliJ IDEA IDE you've been using throughout this book, have created annotations that you can add to classes, parameters and methods.

These annotations allow you to indicate to JVM languages that have first-class support for nullability (like Kotlin) whether a given object is supposed to be nullable or not.

At the bottom of **main.kt**, add new code to access how many addresses a second user has:

```
val anotherUser = User()
println("Another User has ${anotherUser.addresses.count()}
addresses")
```

Run **main.kt**, and at the end of the console will be:

```
Another User has 0 addresses
```

If you recall, in **User.java**, you initialized the `addresses` variable with an empty `ArrayList` — so this should theoretically never be null. But what happens if you explicitly make `addresses` null?

Update **main.kt** to add a new line between the `anotherUser` creation and the `println` statement immediately after it:

```
anotherUser.addresses = null
```

Run **main.kt**, and you'll get a runtime error:

```
Exception in thread "main" java.lang.IllegalStateException: anotherUser.addresses must not be null
    at MainKt.main(main.kt:36)
```

anotherUser.addresses must not be null

This is because the `anotherUser.addresses.count()` is expecting `addresses` to never be `null`, because nobody's ever told it that it could be `null`.

By default, Kotlin code that is generated from Java uses the `!` type for all variables unless otherwise annotated. This means that, unless you specifically tell the compiler something could be `null`, it'll assume it's supposed to be there and either error out or crash if it's not there.

You can avoid this behavior using annotations. Go back to **User.java** and add an explicit annotation to the getter to indicate this property could be `null`:

```
@Nullable
public List<Address> getAddresses() { ... }
```

Note: If offered an option of which version of `@Nullable` to use, select the `org.jetbrains.annotations` one rather than any created by other vendors.

Now, when you go back to **main.kt**, the compiler will give an error, which forces you to validate nullability:

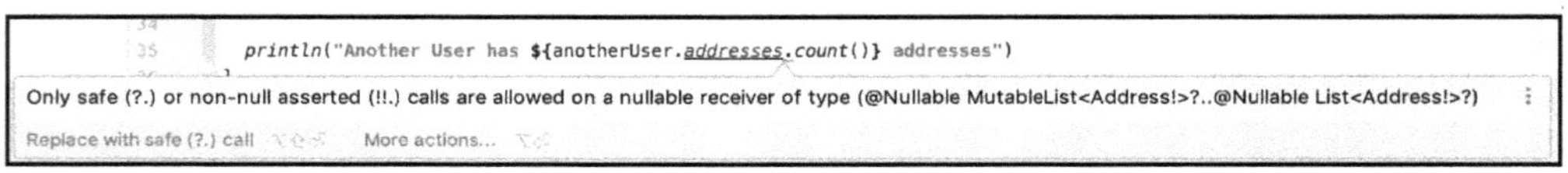

Only safe (?.) or non-null asserted (!!.) calls are allowed on a nullable receiver

Update the line with the error squiggle to add the safe call operator `?.` — indicating that, if something in the chain is `null`, the whole thing should return `null` instead of throwing an exception:

```
println("Another User has ${anotherUser.addresses?.count()}
addresses")
```

Try to run **main.kt** again, and you'll see a few errors in **UserExtensions.kt**:

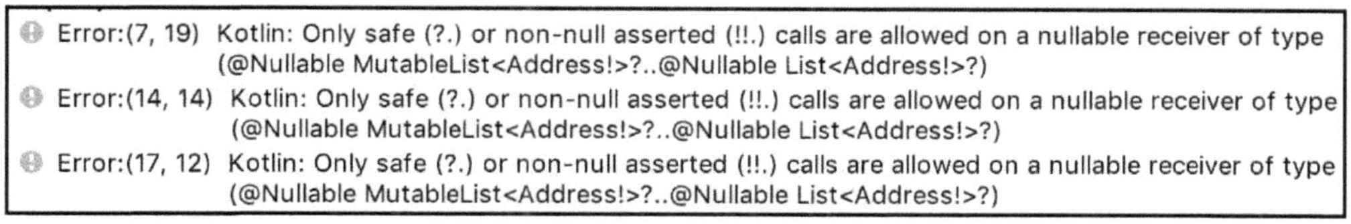

Only safe (?.) or non-null asserted (!!.) calls are allowed on a nullable receiver

Update these three calls to use the same safe call operator style `addresses?.function()`. When the errors are gone, run **main.kt** again and, this time, the bottom of the console will print:

```
Another User has null addresses
```

No crashes! Hooray! But what if you want to take a step beyond not crashing: What if you want to actively prevent a caller from actually setting the `addresses` property, which is set up when the class is set up, to `null`?

Because Kotlin takes the getter and the setter and synthesizes them into properties, you only need to annotate the getter to acheive this!

Go back to **User.java** and update the annotation on the `getAddresses` method:

```
@NotNull
public List<Address> getAddresses() { ... }
```

Now, go back to **main.kt** and you'll notice that, even though you didn't annotate the setter, you're now getting an error about trying to set `addresses` to `null`:

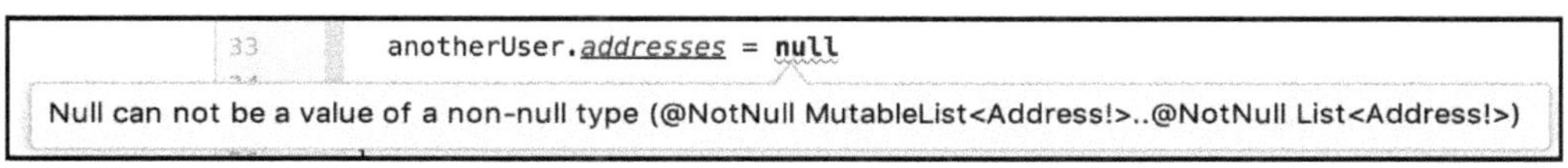

Null can not be a value of a non-null type

Comment out the line setting addresses to `null` and that error will go away. You'll now have four warnings about having an unnecessary safe call on a non-null receiver at the four places you added safe call chaining:

Unnecessary safe call on a non-null receiver

While the project will still build if you have these warnings, it's definitely better to go back and remove them since they're no longer necessary.

Since you really never want any of these properties to be `null`, go to **User.java** and add `@NotNull` annotations above all the other two getters:

```
@NotNull
public String getFirstName() { ... }
...
@NotNull
public String getLastName() { ... }
```

In **main.kt**, add a final line printing out the user's first name:

```
println("Another User first name: ${anotherUser.firstName}")
```

Run **main.kt**, and it'll print out:

```
Another User has 0 addresses
Another User first name: null
```

Wait, what? That's supposed to never be `null`! What's happened here?

Because you haven't actually set a default value for the user's first name the way that you have with the empty addresses `ArrayList`, and you haven't assigned a value for `firstName`, that backing variable is still `null`.

In older versions of IntelliJ and Kotlin, this would actually cause a crash at runtime, since you'd made a promise by using the `NotNull` annotation that the value would never be null.

The good news is that Kotlin no longer blindly assumes that whoever's adding nullabilty annotations to Java code knows what they're doing, so it no longer crashes if that person was wrong.

This is particularly something to watch out for when working with other people's code that has Java nullability annotations.

If you find that the code you wrote made incorrect assumptions about nullability, that's easy to fix. However, you won't be able to fix code you've brought in from other sources, like Android OS code or other framework code.

When working with your own Java code, you need to remember that if you don't provide an initial value for a variable, the variable is nullable and should be annotated as such.

Go back to **User.java** and update the nullability annotations on the `firstName` and `lastName` getters to reflect this:

```
@Nullable
public String getFirstName() { ... }
...
@Nullable
public String getLastName() { ... }
```

Run **main.kt** again and you'll see the same printout:

```
Another User first name: null
```

If you think this looks a little silly, now that you've annotated `getFirstName` as nullable, you can use the Elvis operator to print a more reasonable message. Update the last line of **main.kt** to do this:

```
println("Another User first name: ${anotherUser.firstName ?:
"(not set)"}")
```

Run **main.kt** one last time, and you'll see Elvis in action:

```
Another User first name: (not set)
```

Whew! You've done a lot of interesting stuff calling Java from Kotlin code and a tiny bit of calling Kotlin from Java. But there are a few more things you can do to make your code in Kotlin a bit easier to use in Java.

Making your Kotlin Code Java-friendly

In the starter project, there's also a **main.java** file with a `JavaApplication` class. Open this file and replace the `System.out.println()` command with some new code:

```
// 1
User user = new User();
// 2
user.setFirstName("Testy");
user.setLastName("McTesterson");

// 3
Address address = new Address(
  "345 Nonexistent Avenue NW",
  null,
  "Washington",
```

```
    "DC",
    "20016",
    AddressType.Shipping
  );

  // 4
  UserExtensions.addOrUpdateAddress(user, address);
  LabelPrinter.printLabelFor(user, AddressType.Shipping);
```

What's happening in the code you've added, here?

1. You create a new user using traditional Java syntax. Don't forget the `new` keyword and the semicolon at the end when creating new objects in Java!
2. While Kotlin is able to use synthesized property access, Java isn't without some specific helpers you'll see later, so to set up the user's first and last names, you must add them using the explicit setters.
3. Here, you're calling into the Kotlin constructor, which is created by default for `Address` (you'll take a look at the error in a second).
4. You're using an extension method and a free function (both defined in Kotlin) to add the address to the user and then print a label for them.

The error in the `Address` constructor is a little verbose:

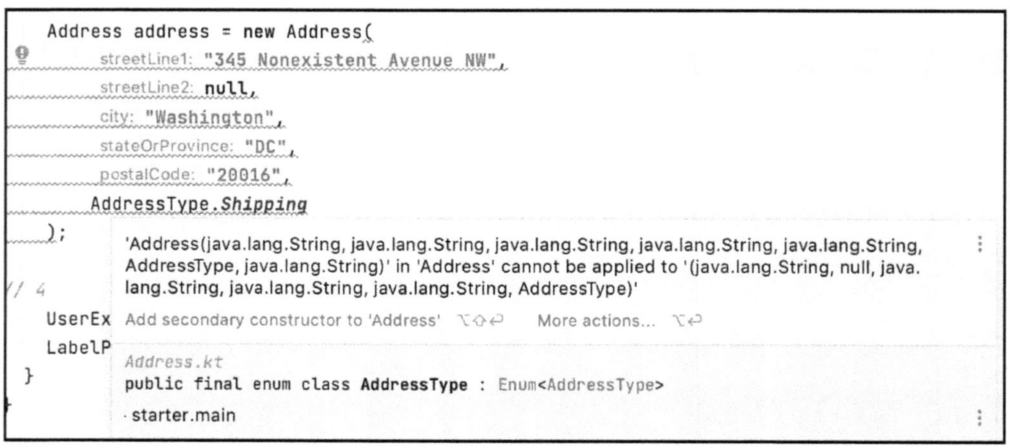

Address constructor cannot be applied to types

But if you look at the hints on the error, you can get a better idea of what's gone wrong here:

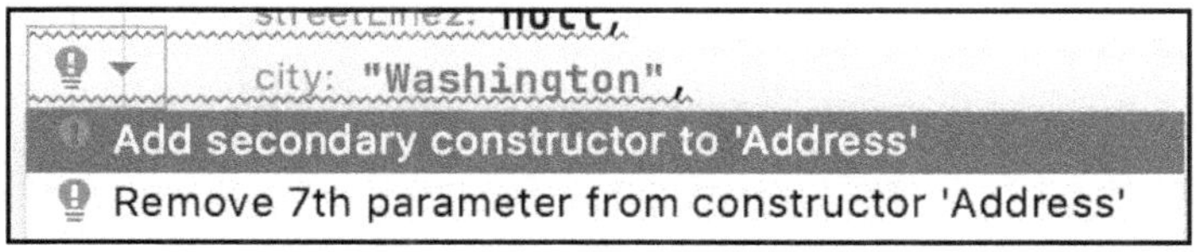

Remove 7th parameter from constructor 'Address'

The hint is asking if you want to get rid of the seventh parameter from the constructor. This makes sense since you've only passed in six items.

If you go back to **Address.kt**, you'll see the country parameter is the 7th parameter, but it has a default value provided. So why isn't that default value showing up?

This is because, by default, the Kotlin compiler only generates a single constructor with all available parameters. Java doesn't support default parameters in the same way that Kotlin does. If you want to allow default values, you have to create constructors that do not include the various default values.

That sounds really boring. Fortunately, the Kotlin compiler can be told to do this for you! Go to **Address.kt** and update the declaration of the `Address` class:

```
data class Address @JvmOverloads constructor
```

The `@JvmOverloads` annotation tells the compiler that it should generate those boring extra methods for you which omit any parameters that have default values.

In Kotlin, the `constructor` keyword is implied in the declaration of the class when you're adding a bunch of `val` and `var` declarations that can be passed in when the object is created.

However, if you want to add `@JvmOverloads` for the default constructor, you have to explicitly use the `constructor` keyword in order for the proper overloaded constructors to be generated.

Go back to **main.java**, and your build error should now be resolved. Run the Java program using the Play button in the upper-left corner next to the `main()` method.

When you do, the following will print out:

```
-----
Testy McTesterson
345 Nonexistent Avenue NW
Washington, DC 20016
UNITED STATES
-----
```

> **Note**: As you continue through the chapter, make sure to use the Play button in the upper-left of either the **main.kt** or **main.java** files rather than the Play button at the top-right of the IDE window or the one in the **Run** tab at the bottom of the IDE. The button and the tab on the IDE will run whichever program you ran most recently, Java or Kotlin, whereas the one in the top-left of each file will always run the program in that specific file.

Next, in **main.java**, directly under where the address is constructed, start typing `address.get` and you'll see something cool in the auto-complete offered by IntelliJ:

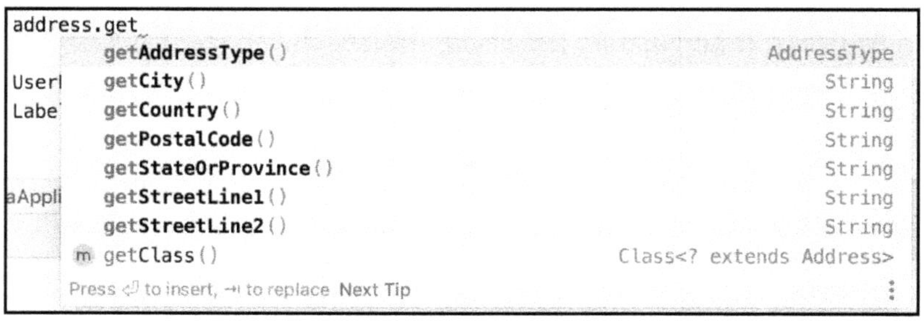

Those getters that were so annoying to write in Java have been automatically generated by the Kotlin compiler for the `Address` class. Sweet! What about the setters?

Start typing `address.set` and you'll notice something:

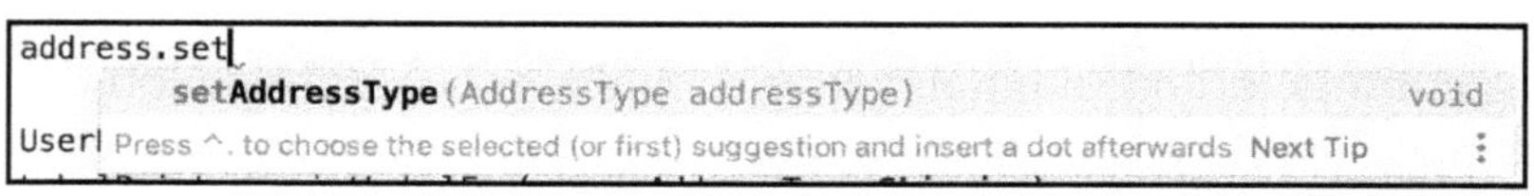

Only one setter was automatically generated for the `Address` properties. Why?

Recall that, in Kotlin, anything which is a `val` is supposed to be set by the constructor and then never changed. This means that a setter is completely unnecessary and, therefore, won't be generated.

The only property of `Address` that is a `var` property is the `AddressType`, so that's the only Java setter that gets generated.

Let that setter auto-complete and update the address type to `Billing`:

```
address.setAddressType(AddressType.Billing);
```

Run **main.java**. Since you're trying to print the label for a Shipping address but you've changed it to a Billing address, you'll see:

```
!! Testy McTesterson does not have a Shipping address set up !!
```

You're trying to print a Shipping address label, but you've changed the type on `address` to Billing!

Delete the line setting the address type and run **main.java** again. You will again see:

```
-----
Testy McTesterson
345 Nonexistent Avenue NW
Washington, DC 20016
UNITED STATES
-----
```

Since you're probably going to print Shipping labels, it makes sense to add a default value to the functions in **LabelPrinter.kt**. Open up that file, and add a default `type` value to the `printLabelFor()` function:

```
fun printLabelFor(user: User, type: AddressType =
AddressType.Shipping) {
```

Now, try to use that in Kotlin by going to **main.kt** and updating the `printLabelFor()` line to remove the type:

```
printLabelFor(user)
```

Run **main.kt**, and you'll see the same data print out as before:

```
Shipping Label:
-----
Bob Barker
987 Unreal Drive
Burbank, CA 91523
UNITED STATES
-----
```

That was easy. Next, update the line printing a label at the end of **main.java** to remove the parameter, which has a default value:

```
LabelPrinter.printLabelFor(user);
```

When you do this, you'll see an error:

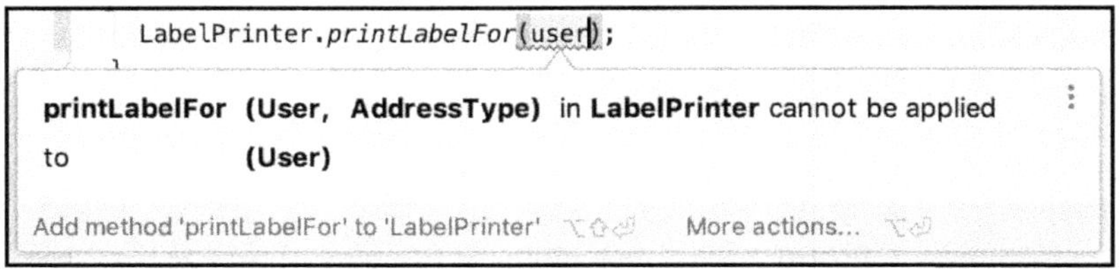

Similarly to the `constructor`, without a hint, this function doesn't know it needs to generate multiple Java methods to account for anything that has a default value for a given parameter. Time to give it that hint!

In **LabelPrinter.kt**, add the `@JvmOverloads` annotation directly above where `printLabelFor()` is declared:

```
@JvmOverloads
fun printLabelFor(user: User, ....
```

Now, go back to **main.java**, and the error should be resolved. Run **main.java**, and the output should be the same as it was previously:

```
-----
Testy McTesterson
345 Nonexistent Avenue NW
Washington, DC 20016
UNITED STATES
-----
```

Now, it's time to learn how to deal with class non-companion objects in Java!

Accessing nested Kotlin objects

In Kotlin, you can create objects that are not necessarily classes within a class. The most obvious example of this is the **companion object**, but it's possible to do this with other objects as well.

How do you access these in Java? Let's turn an `Address` into a `HashMap`, which can eventually be turned into JSON to be sent back and forth to a server, to find out.

In **Address.kt**, below the last function but still within the `Address` class, add an `object` with the JSON keys you'll be using to distinguish between the items in the `HashMap`:

```
object JSONKeys {
  val streetLine1 = "street_1"
  val streetLine2 = "street_2"
  val city = "city"
  val stateOrProvince = "state"
  val postalCode = "zip"
  val addressType = "type"
  val country = "country"
}
```

Next, go to **main.java** and attempt to access the keys that you've just created:

```
Address.JSONKeys keys = Address.JSONKeys;
```

You'll get the following error:

Expression expected

What this error is rather obtusely trying to tell you is that, when using interoperability with a nested Kotlin object, there needs to be an instance of that object to work with before doing anything.

Fortunately, Kotlin generates a Java `INSTANCE` variable, which can be accessed on non-companion nested objects for Java access.

In **main.java**, use the `INSTANCE` generated for a non-companion object to grab a reference to the keys:

```
Address.JSONKeys keys = Address.JSONKeys.INSTANCE;
```

And the error should now be gone. Now, add code to create a `HashMap`, which is an object with keys and values:

```
HashMap<String, Object> addressJSON = new HashMap<>();
addressJSON.put(
  keys.getStreetLine1(), address.getStreetLine1());
```

This code creates the `HashMap` in Java with the appropriate types, then uses the `put()` method to add a key and its value. However, this is a bit verbose.

The getter and setter methods create a lot of noise. What if you'd prefer not to use them? Good news! You can tell the Kotlin compiler to not to create these methods on properties of a class with (you guessed it!) an annotation.

Go back to **Address.kt** and update the `val`s and `var`s in the `constructor` to use the `@JvmField` annotation:

```
data class Address @JvmOverloads constructor (
    @JvmField val streetLine1: String,
    @JvmField val streetLine2: String?,
    @JvmField val city: String,
    @JvmField val stateOrProvince: String,
    @JvmField val postalCode: String,
    @JvmField var addressType: AddressType,
    @JvmField val country: String = "United States") {
```

The `@JvmField` annotation tells Kotlin that for JVM languages, it doesn't need to generate getter and setter methods — it just creates a **field**, or a property variable, and uses that directly. The `@JvmField` annotation can be used on all sorts of types, and is generally advisable to use on properties of a Kotlin object if you wish to avoid generating getters and setters, no matter what their type.

For constants that are basic types on independent Kotlin objects, such as `String` and `Int`, you can use the `const` keyword in Kotlin to achieve the same effect without littering your code with `@` symbols.

Scroll down to the `JSONKeys` object and update each variable to use `const`:

```
object JSONKeys {
  const val streetLine1 = "street_1"
  const val streetLine2 = "street_2"
  const val city = "city"
  const val stateOrProvince = "state"
  const val postalCode = "zip"
  const val addressType = "type"
  const val country = "country"
}
```

Now, you can go back to **main.java**; update the first line that you've already added to use the field and `const` you've defined.

```
addressJSON.put(keys.streetLine1, address.streetLine1);
```

That looks a little nicer! Now, add code to put the rest of the properties for the address into the `HashMap`, then print the `HashMap` out:

```
addressJSON.put(keys.streetLine2, address.streetLine2);
addressJSON.put(keys.city, address.city);
addressJSON.put(keys.stateOrProvince, address.stateOrProvince);
addressJSON.put(keys.postalCode, address.postalCode);
addressJSON.put(keys.country, address.country);
addressJSON.put(keys.addressType, address.addressType.name());

System.out.println("Address JSON:\n" + addressJSON);
```

Try to run **main.java**, and you'll see a couple errors in **User.java** — since you've told the compiler it doesn't need to use getter and setter methods, the methods you were using to get the address type are now gone.

Replace the getters causing the errors with field access:

```
builder.append(address.addressType.name() + " address:\n");
builder.append(LabelPrinter.labelFor(this,
address.addressType));
```

Now, go back and run **main.java** and at the bottom you'll see:

```
Address JSON:
{zip=20016, country=United States, street_1=345 Nonexistent
Avenue NW, city=Washington, street_2=null, state=DC,
type=Shipping}
```

Your Java code is now accessing the properties of your Kotlin code without getter or setter methods, and it's much cleaner to boot. Hooray!

Now it's time to see how you would set up things you'd normally use as `static` in Java.

"Static" values and functions from Kotlin

In Java, a `static` member in a class means that it can be accessed without an instance of the class. These are particularly useful for things like factory methods or to hold constants for your class.

Having used companion objects in Kotlin before, this probably sounds pretty familiar. But using companion objects from Java requires a little bit of help from the compiler.

In **Address.kt**, below the `JSONKeys` object but still within the `Address` class, add a new companion object with a single constant value:

```
companion object {
  val sampleFirstLine = "123 Fake Street"
}
```

In **main.kt**, add a line to print out this new value from the companion object:

```
println("Sample First Line: ${Address.sampleFirstLine}")
```

Run **main.kt**, and you'll see at the end of the console printout:

```
Sample First Line: 123 Fake Street
```

Nice — that was easy! Let's see how that works in Java. In **main.java**, add a similar line:

```
System.out.println("Sample first line of address: " +
Address.sampleFirstLine);
```

You'll immediately see an error, because nothing's told the compiler that Java should be able to see this particular value:

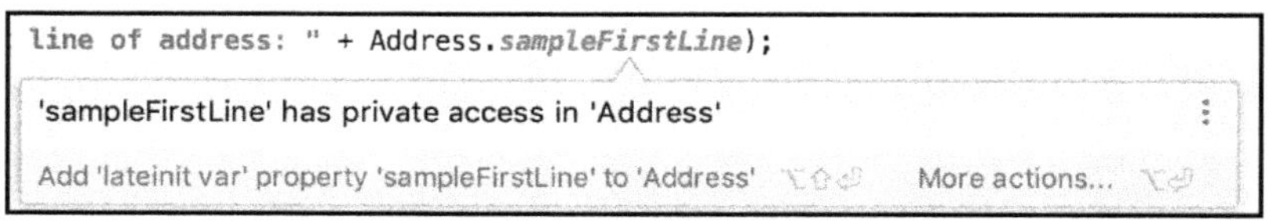

'sampleFirstLine' has private access in 'Address'

The error is slightly misleading - the property isn't `private`, but the compiler does need to know that it won't be changing in order to generate a static accessor.

Since `sampleFirstLine` is a simple `String` type, you can use the `const` keyword just as you did with the `JSONKeys` object in order to make it visible to Java.

Go to **Address.kt** and update the declaration to include `const`:

```
const val sampleFirstLine = "123 Fake Street"
```

Now, go back to **main.java**, and the error should have disappeared. Run **main.java** and you'll now see:

```
Sample first line of address: 123 Fake Street
```

Hooray! Now your Java code can access "static" variables on your Kotlin companion object. What about accessing a function which doesn't need an instance of the class?

Go back to **Address.kt**, and in the companion object, add a function that creates a sample Canadian address:

```
fun canadianSample(type: AddressType): Address {
  return Address(sampleFirstLine,
    "4th floor",
    "Vancouver",
    "BC",
    "A3G 4B2",
    type,
    "Canada")
}
```

Again, this is pretty straightforward to access in Kotlin. Go to **main.kt** and add the line:

```
println("Sample Canadian Address:\n$
{Address.canadianSample(AddressType.Billing)}")
```

Run **main.kt**, and you'll see printed at the end of the console:

```
Sample Canadian Address:
123 Fake Street
4th floor
Vancouver, BC A3G 4B2
CANADA
```

Now, go to **main.java**, and try to add something similar:

```
Address canadian = Address.canadianSample(AddressType.Shipping);
System.out.println(canadian);
```

Again, you'll see an error, although a slightly different one than you saw for the `val` in the companion object:

Cannot resolve method 'canadianSample'

Java can't see this method, but you can fix that using one of two approaches. You could update the call in Java to be:

```
Address canadian =
Address.Companion.canadianSample(AddressType.Shipping);
System.out.println(canadian);
```

Here, you're using the default `Companion` name of the Kotlin companion object to allow Java to access the method. Alternatively, you can fix the error with a simple annotation. Go back to **Address.kt**, and above the declaration of `canadianSample`, add a `@JvmStatic` annotation:

```
@JvmStatic
fun canadianSample(type: AddressType): Address { ... }
```

This tells the Kotlin compiler that, when generating Java code for the `Address` class, it should make `canadianSample()` a `static` method on the class for Java, and so you avoid needing to use the `Companion` name. Go back to **main.java**, and your error should now be cleared up. Run **main.java**, and at the bottom it'll print out:

```
123 Fake Street
4th floor
Vancouver, BC A3G 4B2
CANADA
```

Phew! You're now able to use both Kotlin code from Java and Java code from Kotlin. You can now go forth and conquer the Java Virtual Machine!

Challenge

For this chapter's challenge, you'll create an insecure way to store credit card information and access it from Java:

- Create a class in Kotlin for credit cards with properties for the card number, expiration month, expiration year and an optional security code (a.k.a., the CVV), which defaults to `null`. Make sure that you can use a constructor from Java, which takes advantage of the default value.
- Create a way to compare the current card to the passed-in card and determine if they are the same based on expiration year, expiration month and card number.
- Using one of the annotations you've already used in this chapter, suppress the creation of getter and setter methods for Java.
- Add a `List` of credit cards the user has stored to the `User` class.
- Add a function you can call statically from Java to validate whether or not an expiration date is valid (meaning, the expiration is in the future).
- Add an extension function on `User` to attempt to add a credit card to the user's list, but that rejects the card if it (a) is identical to another card or (b) has expired.
- Attempt to add these cards to the user's list of cards. How many cards does the user have when you're done?

> **Note**: In the real world, **do not** store credit card details like number/expiration/CVV, because that increases the probability of them getting stolen. Most payment processing companies have an API which will exchange this information for a token that represents the credit card. The token is very easy for the payment company to invalidate without having to cancel the underlying credit card should there be a security breach. The token is what you should generally store instead.

Key points

- Kotlin was designed from the beginning to be compatible with the JVM, and **Kotlin bytecode** can run anywhere that Java bytecode runs.
- You can intermix Kotlin and Java code within one project.
- It's possible to add Kotlin **extension functions** to classes written in Java, and also to call Kotlin **free functions** from Java code.
- Annotations like `@JvmOverloads` and `@JvmStatic` help you integrate your Java and Kotlin code.

Where to go from here?

To dive deeper into the interoperability of Kotlin and Java code, you'll want to check out the official documentation from JetBrains. If you're an Android developer, you'll also want to check out the interop guide created by Google:

- Android Kotlin Guide for writing cross-language code: https://android.github.io/kotlin-guides/interop.html

Like in life, no matter how careful you are as a developer, things will not always go as planned in your software. Next up, you'll see how you can handle unexpected conditions using Exceptions.

Chapter 20: Exceptions

By Irina Galata

People interact with software as developers and as users, and sometimes they make mistakes. A user could, for example, input invalid data, and a developer could forget to validate it. It's important to notice and handle defects and potential weaknesses in your code in order to avoid unpredictable behavior of your app and unsatisfying experiences for its users.

Exceptions are a convenient way to detect errors in software. This concept is used in a wide variety of programming languages, including Kotlin.

What is an exception?

An exception is primarily an event which signals that something went wrong during program execution. Exceptions are represented by the `Exception` Java class, which is a superclass of all exceptions in Java and Kotlin programs — e.g., `NullPointerException`, `IOException`, etc. Depending on their nature, these events should be **caught** at runtime or fixed to prevent the exception from happening in the first place. This chapter will discuss catching exceptions later.

Conversely, another type of critical event, an **error** — represented by `Error` and its subclasses — should not be handled but should instead be fixed, because it's the result of serious problems in a program, like inappropriate memory usage, for example.

Both `Exception` and `Error` extend `Throwable` and, therefore, could be **thrown** by the JVM or manually from code using the keyword `throw`, in order to notify the user of the code that a problem occurred. Every `Throwable` object can contain a message and a cause — another `Throwable` instance that caused this error or exception, and a **stacktrace**.

Let's see how a program behaves when an exception occurs and you don't handle it. Create a `main()` function that calls `someFunction()`, which calls `anotherFunction()`, which in turn calls `oneMoreFunction()` that throws an exception with the message "Some exception".

main.kt

```
fun main() {
  someFunction()
}

fun someFunction() {
  anotherFunction()
}

fun anotherFunction() {
  oneMoreFunction()
}

fun oneMoreFunction() {
  throw Exception("Something went wrong")
}
```

Your program can be represented as a long chain of function invocations. When something goes wrong somewhere in `oneMoreFunction()`, an exception gets thrown and the normal execution flow interrupts.

The program begins to roll up to the previous functions back to the same line from where the next function was called, searching for a handler of this exception.

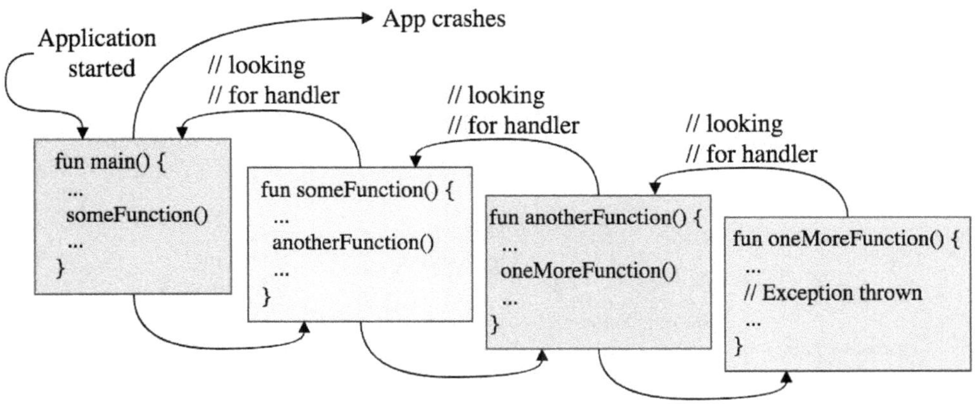

Without handling the exception, the process ends up in the entry point of your app — the `main()` function — and then the app crashes, your user sees an annoying error message.

Run the code and you will see the stacktrace of this exception in your terminal:

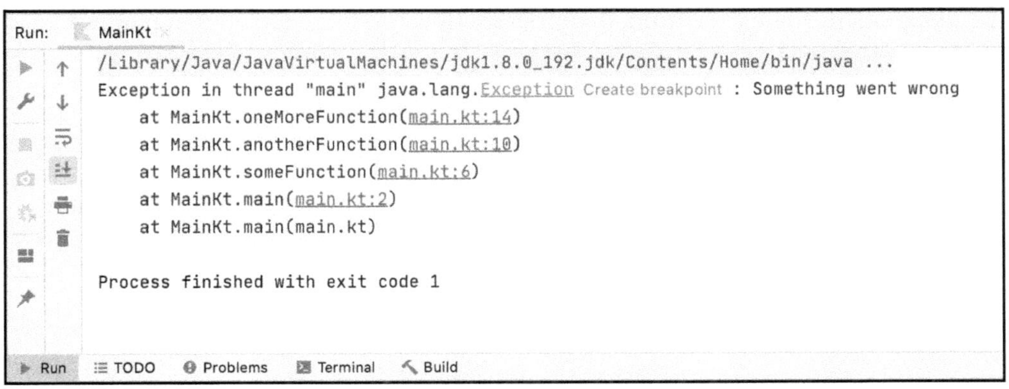

Something went wrong at oneMoreFunction

A **stacktrace** is a detailed description of an exception that occurred in your program. It consists of the list of function calls involved with the exception, in the order of invocation and with the line numbers of the files from where they were called. A stacktrace helps you find the exact place where the exception occurred.

To prevent the app from crashing, you should **handle** an exception; you can do that in any function in the chain that led to the exception. Now look how things change if you handle an exception:

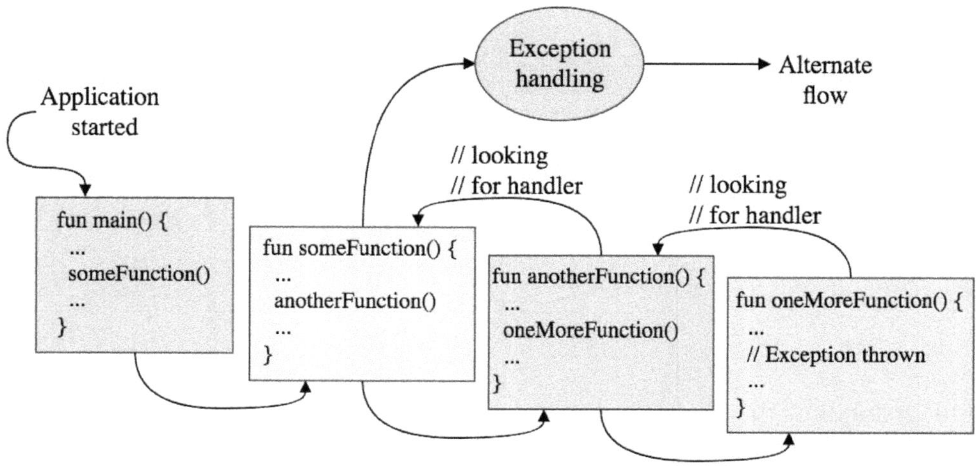

While rolling up your program, it finds a handler inside `someFunction()` and, after handling an alternate execution, the program flow re-starts and your app doesn't crash.

You'll learn how to handle errors later in this chapter. In the meantime, remove or comment out your call to `someFunction()`

For the project that follows, you will use exceptions to troubleshoot launch issues, mechanical failures and encounters with aliens!

Throwing exceptions

Imagine you're a spacecraft engineer and your main responsibility is to launch a craft for investigation of deep space. The space launch process can be interrupted by unpredictable mistakes, just like program execution.

Create a `SpaceCraft` class in the chapter starter project:

```
class SpaceCraft {

  private var isConnectionAvailable: Boolean = false
  private var isEngineInOrder: Boolean = false
  private var fuel: Int = 0
  var isInSpace: Boolean = false

  fun launch() {
    if (fuel < 5) {
      sendMessageToEarth("Out of fuel. Can't take off")
      return
    }

    if (!isEngineInOrder) {
      sendMessageToEarth("The engine is broken. Can't take off")
      return
    }

    if (!isConnectionAvailable) {
      sendMessageToEarth("No connection with Earth. Can't take
off")
      return
    }

    sendMessageToEarth("Trying to launch...")
    fuel -= 5
    sendMessageToEarth("I'm in space!")
    sendMessageToEarth("I've found some extraterrestrials")
    isInSpace = true
  }

  fun sendMessageToEarth(message: String) {
    println("Spacecraft to Earth: $message")
  }
}
```

In `launch()`, this `SpaceCraft` checks the fuel level, engine state and connection to Earth before being able to take off. If everything looks good, it sends some messages back to Earth from space. Otherwise, the method returns without sending the `SpaceCraft` to space.

All `sendMessageToEarth()` is doing is printing out the message.

Obviously, you cannot navigate your spacecraft from your room — create a `SpacePort` for this purpose:

```
object SpacePort {
  fun investigateSpace(spaceCraft: SpaceCraft) {
    spaceCraft.launch()
  }
}
```

Your spacecraft can now launch and find some aliens, but there are potential problems, e.g., a broken engine or lost connection. To check if they actually appear, create a `SpaceCraft` in your `main()` function and launch the spacecraft using the `Spaceport`:

```
val spaceCraft = SpaceCraft()
SpacePort.investigateSpace(spaceCraft)
```

Here, you create your a `SpaceCraft` and send it through the `SpacePort` to investigate space.

Run the program. How likely are you to launch a spacecraft on the first try? Not a chance! You'll get the following message in your terminal:

```
Spacecraft to Earth: Out of fuel. Can't take off.
```

When facing any critical situation while launching, you should consider the proper way to send alerts should a problem occur. Exceptions are a good way to do so. Replace the `sendMessageToEarth()` function invocations within `launch()` with throwing an exception when a problem occurs:

```
if (fuel < 5) {
  throw Exception("Out of fuel. Can't take off.")
}

if (!isEngineInOrder) {
  throw Exception("The engine is broken. Can't take off.")
}

if (!isConnectionAvailable) {
  throw Exception("No connection with Earth. Can't take off.")
}
// remaining launch code
```

To throw an exception, you use the `throw` keyword. Now, whenever a problem occurs, you communicate it with an exception.

Run the program again. Now the report is more detailed. You will see the following:

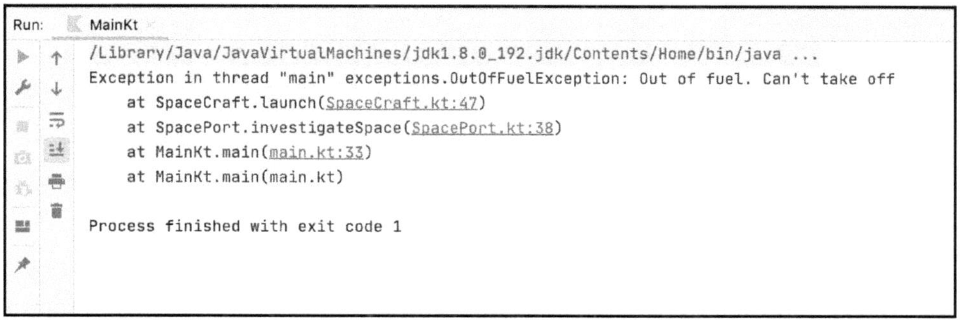

Out of fuel. Can't take off at SpaceCraft.launch

Handling exceptions

As you throw exceptions, as long as you can recover from them, you should handle them. You are not obliged to handle exceptions only where you've thrown them — you can do so on any level on the stack of function calls.

Obviously, a spaceship cannot refuel or fix an engine by itself. Therefore, you should handle exceptions thrown from the spacecraft at the spaceport.

In the `SpacePort` object, update the `investigateSpace()` function to *catch* exceptions:

```
fun investigateSpace(spaceCraft: SpaceCraft) {
  try {
    spaceCraft.launch()
  } catch (exception: Exception) {
    spaceCraft.sendMessageToEarth(exception.localizedMessage)
  }
}
```

A **try-catch** expression is used to wrap a potentially problematic piece of code to avoid crashes and to handle exceptions. In the parentheses after the `catch` keyword, you should specify the exact type of the expected exception or its superclass. By using try-catch, an exception still gets thrown and you get notified, but the program doesn't terminate.

But remember that you have different problems and you should handle all of them separately — e.g., you won't fix the engine if the fuel tank is just empty. You need to distinguish the exceptions thrown from the spacecraft. In this case, it's not enough to use standard exceptions — you need to create custom ones.

> **Note**: It's a bad practice to specify the parent `Exception` class in a `catch` statement since all thrown exceptions would be caught in this `catch` block. Always create separate `catch` blocks for every expected exception, like in the example below.

Creating custom exceptions

You already know that every child of `Exception` is an exception, too. Therefore, you just need to create subclasses of `Exception`. Add these to your project:

```
class OutOfFuelException :
        Exception("Out of fuel. Can't take off.")
```

```
class BrokenEngineException :
        Exception("The engine is broken. Can't take off.")
```

```
class SpaceToEarthConnectionFailedException :
        Exception("No connection with Earth. Can't take off.")
```

Here, you're inheriting from `Exception` to make your own, specialized exceptions.

Update the `launch()` function in `SpaceCraft`:

```
if (fuel < 5) {
  throw OutOfFuelException()
}

if (!isEngineInOrder) {
  throw BrokenEngineException()
}

if (!isConnectionAvailable) {
  throw SpaceToEarthConnectionFailedException()
}
// remaining launch code
```

Now you're using your custom exceptions rather than the generic one.

Modify the `investigateSpace()` function in `SpacePort` to look like the following:

```
fun investigateSpace(spaceCraft: SpaceCraft) {
  try {
    spaceCraft.launch()
  } catch (exception: OutOfFuelException) {
    spaceCraft.sendMessageToEarth(exception.localizedMessage)
  } catch (exception: BrokenEngineException) {
    spaceCraft.sendMessageToEarth(exception.localizedMessage)
  } catch (exception: SpaceToEarthConnectionFailedException) {
    spaceCraft.sendMessageToEarth(exception.localizedMessage)
  }
}
```

To catch multiple exceptions, you use several `catch` blocks. Within these blocks, you're using `localizedMessage` to get a message detailing what the exception is.

When there are several `catch` blocks, an exception is caught by the first matching block, and then program flow continues after the full try-catch expression.

Since you can now differentiate the exceptions, you need to take action when they occur. Add the following functions in the `SpaceCraft` class:

```
fun refuel() {
  fuel += 5
  sendMessageToEarth("The fuel tank is filled.")
}

fun repairEngine() {
  isEngineInOrder = true
  sendMessageToEarth("The engine is in order.")
}

fun fixConnection() {
  isConnectionAvailable = true
  sendMessageToEarth("Hello Earth! Can you hear me?")
  sendMessageToEarth("Connection is established.")
}

fun land() {
  sendMessageToEarth("Landing...")
  isInSpace = false
}
```

Now you have ways to fix any issues you might have with your spacecraft.

Move back to SpacePort and update the exception handling. It should now look like this:

```
try {
  spaceCraft.launch()
} catch (exception: OutOfFuelException) {
  spaceCraft.sendMessageToEarth(exception.localizedMessage)
  spaceCraft.refuel()
} catch (exception: BrokenEngineException) {
  spaceCraft.sendMessageToEarth(exception.localizedMessage)
  spaceCraft.repairEngine()
} catch (exception: SpaceToEarthConnectionFailedException) {
  spaceCraft.sendMessageToEarth(exception.localizedMessage)
  spaceCraft.fixConnection()
} finally {
  if (spaceCraft.isInSpace) {
    spaceCraft.land()
  } else {
    investigateSpace(spaceCraft)
  }
}
```

In addition to calling different functions in each catch block, you've also added a **finally** block to the try-catch. As opposed to the catch block, the code inside the finally block will be executed regardless of whether an exception occurs or not.

In this block, you check if your spaceship is in space or not. Depending on the result of this check, you either return the craft to Earth or relaunch it.

Run the program. You will see the following:

```
Spacecraft to Earth: Out of fuel. Can't take off
Spacecraft to Earth: The fuel tank is filled
Spacecraft to Earth: The engine is broken. Can't take off
Spacecraft to Earth: The engine is in order
Spacecraft to Earth: No connection with Earth. Can't take off
Spacecraft to Earth: Hello Earth! Can you hear me?
Spacecraft to Earth: Connection is established
Spacecraft to Earth: Trying to launch...
Spacecraft to Earth: I'm in space!
Spacecraft to Earth: I've found some extraterrestrials
Spacecraft to Earth: Landing...
```

Apparently, you've managed to overcome all of the difficulties and launched your spacecraft to space! Send greetings to the aliens for me.

Difference between Java and Kotlin exceptions

Checked exceptions

If you're familiar with Java, you may remember that there are two types of exceptions — **checked** and **unchecked**. Checked exceptions must be either handled or declared after your method signature with the `throws` keyword. Unchecked exceptions can be ignored, but then crash your app when not handled. Conversely, all exceptions in Kotlin are unchecked and, therefore, you're not forced to handle them or declare them. Your program still terminates when exceptions get thrown.

try as an expression

In Kotlin, the `try-catch` construction is an expression. This means that you can get a value from a `try-catch` block and can equate it to some variable:

```
val date: Date = try {
      Date(userInput) // try to parse user input
   } catch (exception: IllegalArgumentException) {
      Date() // otherwise use current date
   }
```

The value of the expression is equal to the last expression of the `try` block or the last expression of the `catch` block.

Challenges

1. Create a `testSetup(spaceCraft: SpaceCraft)` function in `SpacePort` which will launch your spacecraft. If it takes off successfully, this function will return true; if it fails, it will return false. Create a class `SpaceCraftException` and make it a superclass of `OutOfFuelException`, `BrokenEngineException` and `SpaceToEarthConnectionFailedException` to simplify your `try-catch-finally` expression. Don't forget to get your ship back to Earth after the test.

2. Create an `overhaul()` function in `SpaceCraft`, which will perform all necessary checks and fixes to make sure your spacecraft is ready to relaunch. Additionally, modify `investigateSpace()` in `SpacePort` so that, when an exception occurs, the spacecraft is repaired and takes off again. Use `SpaceCraftException` to simplify handling.

3. Create one more exception class called `AliensAttackException`. Throw an instance of the new exception when your spacecraft faces extraterrestrials. Handle it in `investigateSpace()`, and make sure that, after the alien confrontation, your spacecraft sends an SOS message to Earth and immediately returns to its home planet.

Key points

- **Exceptions** are the events that happen when something goes wrong in your program.
- Extend the `Exception` class or its subclasses to create custom exceptions.
- Throw an exception using the `throw` keyword.
- Do not catch the base class `Exception`, use the most specific exception class you can.
- Create custom exceptions for uncommon cases to differentiate them.
- When handling exceptions, place the code that should be executed whether an exception occurs or not in the `finally` block.
- All exceptions in Kotlin are **unchecked**.
- Don't ignore exceptions.
- Try-catch is an expression.

Where to go from here?

Exception throwing and handling can be a bit of an art. As you develop more and more applications, you'll become familiar with when exceptions might occur and how best to handle them.

In the next chapter, you'll shift from focusing on classes and object-oriented programming to instead looking at the other primary programming approach supported by Kotlin, **functional programming**.

Chapter 21: Functional Programming

By Irina Galata

The evolution of programming as an engineering discipline includes improvement of languages and tools. There are also different fundamental approaches you can use to develop your programs, often called **paradigms**. There are various programming paradigms, but don't be intimidated, since all of them have strengths and weaknesses.

The more comfortable you become with the different approaches, the easier it will be able to apply them. Plus, you already know at least one of them: object-oriented programming aka OOP. In this chapter, you'll get acquainted with another type of programming — **functional programming** — and learn its technical details.

What is functional programming?

You may remember that a key feature of OOP is that classes and their instances contain properties and methods. Functional programming is instead based around the use of functions, which ideally don't have **side effects**.

A side effect is any change to the state of a system. A simple example of a side effect is printing something to the screen. Another is changing the value of the property of an object. Side effects are typically rampant in OOP, as class instances send messages back and forth to one another and change their internal state.

Another key feature of functional programming making functions **first-class** citizens of the language, as you'll see in a future section.

Most functional programming languages also rely on a concept called **referential transparency**. This term effectively means that given the same input, a function will always return the same output. When a function has this property it is called a **pure function**.

Functions in functional programming languages are more like their mathematical namesake functions than typical functions in non-functional programming approaches.

Unlike versions of Java prior to Java 8, Kotlin allows you to use both the OOP and functional approaches to building software, either separately or by combining them to make your code more efficient and flexible. In this chapter, you'll see an example of the combination of the ideas of OOP and functional programming.

Getting started

Before diving into using functional programming, you'll setup a system that will let you explore the details. Open up the starter project and keep reading.

In this chapter, you're going to write a program to conduct a battle between two robots. First of all, you need to create those battle robots.

Create a class called `Robot` with the following definition:

```
import java.util.*

class Robot(val name: String) {
  var strength: Int = 0
```

```
  private var health: Int = 100

  init {
    strength = Random().nextInt(100) + 10
    report("Created (strength $strength)")
  }

  fun report(message: String) {
    println("$name: \t$message")
  }
}
```

You've created a robot class for robots that have some amount of strength and health and can report messages.

To take part in a battle, your robot should be able to take damage from another robot. Add the following code to the `Robot` class:

```
// 1
var isAlive: Boolean = true

private fun damage(damage: Int) {
  // 2
  val blocked = Random().nextBoolean()

  if (blocked) {
    report("Blocked attack")
    return
  }

  // 3
  health -= damage
  report("Damage -$damage, health $health")

  // 4
  if (health <= 0) {
    isAlive = false
  }
}
```

Here's what's going on above:

1. The `isAlive` property keeps track of if a robot is able to continue the battle.
2. In the `damage()` function, you give a robot a chance to block the attack of another robot using the `nextBoolean()` function on a new `Random()`.
3. If an attacked robot couldn't defend itself, you decrease its health.
4. And, finally, you check to see if it's still alive after the attack.

Your robot also needs to be able to cause damage to another robot. Add the following code to the `Robot` class:

```
// 1
fun attack(robot: Robot) {
  // 2
  val damage = (strength * 0.1 + Random().nextInt(10)).toInt()

  // 3
  robot.damage(damage)
}
```

In this code you:

1. Define the `attack()` function, which receives another robot as an argument.
2. Calculate a damage value depending on the strength of the current robot and its luck.
3. Do damage to the other robot.

Now that you have a robot that can cause damage, your robots need a space to conduct the battle.

Next, create a `Battlefield` object:

```
object Battlefield {
  // 1
  fun beginBattle(firstRobot: Robot, secondRobot: Robot) {
    // 2
    var winner: Robot? = null
    // 3
    battle(firstRobot, secondRobot)
    // 4
    winner = if (firstRobot.isAlive) firstRobot else secondRobot
  }

  fun battle(firstRobot: Robot, secondRobot: Robot) {
    // 5
    firstRobot.attack(secondRobot)
    // 6
    if (secondRobot.isAlive.not()) {
      return
    }
    // 7
    secondRobot.attack(firstRobot)

    if (firstRobot.isAlive.not()) {
      return
    }
```

```
      // 8
      battle(firstRobot, secondRobot)
    }
  }
```

Above, you do the following:

1. Declare a function that will initiate a battle between two participants.
2. Declare a variable to define the winner of the fight.
3. Perform the battle.
4. Check which robot has won.
5. In `battle()`, force the first robot to attack the second one.
6. Check if the second robot is alive. If not, finish the fight.
7. Repeat the previous steps for the second robot, letting it fight back.
8. Call the `battle()` function from itself to continue the battle while the robots are still alive.

The `battle()` function is an example of a **recursive function**: a function that calls itself. Recursive functions are common in strict functional programming languages, since they are used to replace loops. Recursive functions are susceptible to a condition known as **stack overflow**, where the function call stack exceeds a limit, if they call themselves too many times. You'll see near the end of chapter how, in certain cases, you can avoid stack overflow in Kotlin while still coding with recursive functions.

To create a battle, in the `main()` function, add the following lines of code:

```
val firstRobot = Robot("Experimental Space Navigation Droid")
val secondRobot = Robot("Extra-Terrestrial Air Safety Droid")

Battlefield.beginBattle(firstRobot, secondRobot)
```

Your robots are ready to fight! Run the application. You'll get a similar output:

```
Run:    MainKt
/Library/Java/JavaVirtualMachines/jdk1.8.0_192.jdk/Contents/Home/bin/java ...
Experimental Space Navigation Droid:    Created (strength 104)
Extra-Terrestrial Air Safety Droid:     Created (strength 72)
Extra-Terrestrial Air Safety Droid:     Damage -18, health 82
Experimental Space Navigation Droid:    Damage -12, health 88
Extra-Terrestrial Air Safety Droid:     Blocked attack
Experimental Space Navigation Droid:    Blocked attack
Extra-Terrestrial Air Safety Droid:     Damage -15, health 67
Experimental Space Navigation Droid:    Blocked attack
Extra-Terrestrial Air Safety Droid:     Damage -16, health 51
Experimental Space Navigation Droid:    Blocked attack
Extra-Terrestrial Air Safety Droid:     Blocked attack
Experimental Space Navigation Droid:    Blocked attack
Extra-Terrestrial Air Safety Droid:     Blocked attack
Experimental Space Navigation Droid:    Damage -7, health 81
Extra-Terrestrial Air Safety Droid:     Damage -10, health 41
Experimental Space Navigation Droid:    Damage -16, health 65
Extra-Terrestrial Air Safety Droid:     Damage -17, health 24
Experimental Space Navigation Droid:    Damage -13, health 52
Extra-Terrestrial Air Safety Droid:     Damage -15, health 9
Experimental Space Navigation Droid:    Blocked attack
Extra-Terrestrial Air Safety Droid:     Damage -16, health -7

Process finished with exit code 0
```

From the output above, it looks like "Experimental Space Navigation Droid" won.

First-class and higher-order functions

One of the main ideas of functional programming is **first-class** functions. This means that you can operate with functions in the same ways you can other elements of the language — you can pass functions as arguments to other functions, return functions from functions, and assign functions to a variable. Functions that receive a function as a parameter or return functions are called **higher-order** functions.

Function types

To declare a function which receives a function parameter or returns another function, it's necessary to know how to specify a **function type**.

As an example, a function of type `(Int, Int) -> Float` receives two `Int` parameters and returns a `Float`. In parentheses, you define the types of the function parameters separated by a comma. After the -> symbol, you give the function return type. This function type would be read as something like "Int, Int to Float".

The function type for a function that takes no parameters and returns no meaningful value is `() -> Unit` in Kotlin.

Passing a function as an argument

Update `beginBattle()` to receive another function as a parameter, which will be executed when the battle is finished. That way, you'll know exactly which robot has won:

```
fun beginBattle(
  firstRobot: Robot,
  secondRobot: Robot,
  onBattleEnded: (Robot) -> Unit
) {
  var winner: Robot? = null
  battle(firstRobot, secondRobot)
  winner = if (firstRobot.isAlive) firstRobot else secondRobot
  onBattleEnded(winner)
}
```

As you see, `beginBattle()` now receives `onBattleEnded`, a function of type `(Robot) -> Unit`, which means that it receives an instance of `Robot` and returns `Unit`. Once the winner is known, you invoke it by passing a robot `winner` to `onBattleEnded()`.

Update the `main()` function and add `onBattleEnded()`:

```
fun main() {
  val firstRobot = Robot("Experimental Space Navigation Droid")
  val secondRobot = Robot("Extra-Terrestrial Air Safety Droid")
  Battlefield
    .beginBattle(firstRobot, secondRobot, ::onBattleEnded)
}

fun onBattleEnded(winner: Robot) {
  winner.report("Win!")
}
```

To pass a named function as an argument to another function, you use the `::` operator.

Run the app again.

```
Run:    MainKt
/Library/Java/JavaVirtualMachines/jdk1.8.0_192.jdk/Contents/Home/bin/java ...
Experimental Space Navigation Droid:    Created (strength 86)
Extra-Terrestrial Air Safety Droid:     Created (strength 78)
Extra-Terrestrial Air Safety Droid:     Damage -16, health 84
Experimental Space Navigation Droid:    Blocked attack
Extra-Terrestrial Air Safety Droid:     Damage -14, health 70
Experimental Space Navigation Droid:    Damage -15, health 85
Extra-Terrestrial Air Safety Droid:     Damage -15, health 55
Experimental Space Navigation Droid:    Damage -11, health 74
Extra-Terrestrial Air Safety Droid:     Blocked attack
Experimental Space Navigation Droid:    Blocked attack
Extra-Terrestrial Air Safety Droid:     Blocked attack
Experimental Space Navigation Droid:    Blocked attack
Extra-Terrestrial Air Safety Droid:     Damage -11, health 44
Experimental Space Navigation Droid:    Blocked attack
Extra-Terrestrial Air Safety Droid:     Blocked attack
Experimental Space Navigation Droid:    Blocked attack
Extra-Terrestrial Air Safety Droid:     Damage -16, health 28
Experimental Space Navigation Droid:    Blocked attack
Extra-Terrestrial Air Safety Droid:     Damage -17, health 11
Experimental Space Navigation Droid:    Blocked attack
Extra-Terrestrial Air Safety Droid:     Damage -16, health -5
Experimental Space Navigation Droid:    Win!

Process finished with exit code 0
```

Now, you can see the winner of the battle directly.

Returning functions

Similar to passing functions as arguments, you can return a function from another function, as in the following code:

```
fun someFunction(): () -> Int {
  return ::anotherFunction
}

fun anotherFunction(): Int {
  return Random().nextInt()
}
```

`someFunction()` returns a function of type `() -> Int`, which fits `anotherFunction()`, so you can return `anotherFunction` from `someFunction()` using the `::` operator.

Lambdas

As you learned about in Chapter 10, a **lambda** is a function literal, which can be invoked, passed as an argument or returned just like ordinary functions. In this chapter, you'll learn a bit more about lambdas in the context of functional programming.

Recall the lambda syntax, using a lambda assigned to a variable `pow`:

```
val pow = { base: Int, exponent: Int ->
  Math.pow(base.toDouble(), exponent.toDouble())
}
```

A lambda expression is always defined in curly brackets. First, you declare the names and types of the lambda parameters, and, after the -> sign, you place the body of your lambda.

You don't have to use the `return` keyword inside a lambda, nor do you have to specify its return type. The last expression in a lambda body determines the return type and the value that is returned — `Math.pow(base.toDouble(), exponent.toDouble())` of type `Double` in this case.

Once defined into a variable, you can use a lambda by calling it as if it were a function:

```
pow(2, 4)
```

There's also another way to declare a lambda:

```
val pow: (Int, Int) -> Double = { base, exponent ->
  Math.pow(base.toDouble(), exponent.toDouble())
}
```

You can explicitly declare the type of a lambda but not have to specify the types of parameters inside the brackets. Just like in the previous example, the lambda receives two parameters of type `Int` and returns a `Double`.

If a lambda has only one parameter, you don't need to specify its name. You can access it by using `it` as a name:

```
val root: (Int) -> Double = { Math.sqrt(it.toDouble()) }
```

Using a lambda, you can update your call to `beginBattle()` in the `main()` function in the following way:

```
val onBattleEnded = { winner: Robot -> winner.report("Win!") }
Battlefield.beginBattle(firstRobot, secondRobot, onBattleEnded)
```

Or even more conveniently:

```
Battlefield.beginBattle(firstRobot, secondRobot) {
  it.report("Win!")
}
```

In Kotlin, if a lambda is the *last* parameter of a function, it can be placed outside of the parentheses of a higher-order function.

In this example, the lambda being passed to `beginBattle()` is:

```
{ it.report("Win!") }
```

How do lambdas work?

When you defined the `onBattleEnded` lambda, it was compiled to the equivalent of the following Java code:

```
final class MainKt$main$onBattleEnded$1 extends Lambda
        implements Function1 {

  public static final MainKt$main$onBattleEnded$1 INSTANCE =
      new MainKt$main$onBattleEnded$1;

  public bridge invoke(Object arg0) {
    MainKt$main$onBattleEnded$1.invoke((Robot)arg0);
  }

  public final invoke(Robot robot) {
    robot.report("Win!");
  }
}
```

For every lambda, the Kotlin compiler generates a separate class, which extends an abstract class `Lambda` and implements an interface like `Function1`. The `Function1` interface is replaced by its alternatives (`Function0`, `Function2`, etc.) depending on the number of parameters of your lambda.

Take a look at the Kotlin source code of `Function1`:

```
/** A function that takes 1 argument. */
public interface Function1<in P1, out R> : Function<R> {
  /** Invokes the function with the specified argument. */
  public operator fun invoke(p1: P1): R
}
```

It's an interface with the single function `invoke()`, which receives a parameter of type `P1` and return type of `R`.

Let's find out what happens when you invoke your lambda in the equivalent Java code:

```
Function1 onBattleEnded =
    (Function1)MainKt$main$onBattleEnded$1.INSTANCE;
onBattleEnded.invoke(winner);
```

The lambda is converted to an instance of the generated `Lambda` sublass with the `Function1` type and its `invoke()` function is called and passed the arguments that were passed into the lambda.

Closures

Lambas (as well as local functions) act as **closures**, which means that they can access and modify variables defined outside of their own scope. Unlike Java, variables declared in the outer scope can be modified within the closure.

Take a look at the following example:

```
var result = 0

val sum = { a: Int, b: Int ->
  result = a + b
}

sum(5, 18)
```

The `result` value changes inside the `sum` lambda. Here's what happens under the hood in the equivalent Java code:

```
final IntRef result = new IntRef();
result.element = 0;
Function2 sum = (Function2)(new Function2() {
  public Object invoke(Object var1, Object var2) {
    this.invoke(((Number)var1).intValue(),
        ((Number)var2).intValue());
    return Unit.INSTANCE;
  }

  public final void invoke(int a, int b) {
    result.element = a + b;
  }
});
sum.invoke(Integer.valueOf(5), Integer.valueOf(18));
```

`IntRef` is a wrapper around the `result` variable, allowing you to access it inside the lambda:

```
public static final class IntRef implements Serializable {
  public int element;

  @Override
  public String toString() {
    return String.valueOf(element);
  }
}
```

There are wrappers available for all primitives and the `Object` base class.

You are already familiar with what is happening with `sum(5, 18)`. The Kotlin compiler generates an instance of `Function2` (as `sum` is a lambda with two parameters) and calls its `invoke()` function.

Extension functions

You learned about extension methods on classes in Chapter 14. Let's look at them again from the perspective of functional programming.

Sometimes you need to extend the functionality of a specific class. And, quite often, direct inheritance is not an option — your class could already extend another class, for example, or the required class isn't open for inheritance.

Take a look at the following example:

```
fun String.print() = System.out.println(this)
```

`String` is now a **receiver** type for the extension function.

You can use the function like this:

```
val string = "Hello world"
string.print()
```

The `String` class is final in Java, so you can't extend it. But, now you can call the new `print()` function on `String` instances. See what's generated from the above function:

```
public static final void print(@NotNull String $receiver) {
  System.out.println($receiver);
}
```

So, it's an ordinary function but, as a first argument, it implicitly *receives* an instance of the extended class on which this function was called. You can access it without any qualifiers or using `this` keyword.

It's time to further develop your battle robots. Create the following extension functions for `Random` in the `extensions.kt` file:

```
fun Random.randomStrength(): Int {
  return nextInt(100) + 10
}

fun Random.randomDamage(strength: Int): Int {
  return (strength * 0.1 + nextInt(10)).toInt()
}

fun Random.randomBlock(): Boolean {
  return nextBoolean()
}
```

You'll use these functions to calculate the strength of a robot, calculate the the damage it can do, and determine whether it can defend itself.

Update the Robot class to use the newly created functions:

```
private var random: Random = Random()

init {
  strength = random.randomStrength()
  report("Created (strength $strength)")
}

fun damage(damage: Int) {
  val blocked = random.randomBlock()

  if (blocked) {
    report("Blocked attack")
    return
  }

  health -= damage
  report("Damage -$damage, health $health")

  if (health <= 0) {
    isAlive = false
  }
}

fun attack(robot: Robot) {
  val damage = random.randomDamage(strength)
  robot.damage(damage)
}
```

You've added new functionality to the Random class without inheritance and used the new functionality within the Robot class.

Lambdas with receivers

Just as you can specify a receiver for an extension function, you can do so for a lambda as well.

Look at the onBattleEnded lambda parameter you created earlier and change its type from (Robot) -> Unit to Robot.() -> Unit. Note the subtle difference: all you added was .(). Here's what beginBattle() looks like now:

```
fun beginBattle(
  firstRobot: Robot,
  secondRobot: Robot,
  onBattleEnded: Robot.() -> Unit
) {
  var winner: Robot? = null
```

```
    battle(firstRobot, secondRobot)
    winner = if (firstRobot.isAlive) firstRobot else secondRobot
    winner.onBattleEnded()
  }
```

Now the type of the `onBattleEnded` lambda is `Robot.() -> Unit`. You invoke the lambda on the receiver `winner` using `winner.onBattleEnded()`.

Recall that an extension function implicitly receives an instance of the extended class. This means that you can still use this lambda in the following way:

```
onBattleEnded(winner)
```

However, using the lambda with receiver syntax `winner.onBattleEnded()` gives a clearer indication of which robot instance is handling the code within the `onBattleEnded` lambda.

Anonymous functions

Anonymous functions are more or less the same as ordinary ones, but they don't have a name. To invoke them, you need to assign them to a variable or pass them as an argument to another function. Consider the following snippet of code:

```
fun(robot: Robot) {
  robot.report("Win!")
}
```

This function can be used in the same way that you use regular functions — to invoke, pass as an argument, assign to a variable, etc.

Therefore, you can pass this function to the `beginBattle()` function instead of the lambda expression you used before:

```
val reportOnWin = fun(robot: Robot) { robot.report("Win!") }
Battlefield.beginBattle(firstRobot, secondRobot, reportOnWin)
```

You must reset your `beginBattle()` function signature to be the earlier version:

```
fun beginBattle(
  firstRobot: Robot,
  secondRobot: Robot,
  onBattleEnded: (Robot) -> Unit
)
```

You can also use a more concise form when passing in the anonymous function by omitting the type of a parameter if it can be inferred from the context:

```
Battlefield.beginBattle(firstRobot, secondRobot, fun(robot) {
  robot.report("Win!")
})
```

Returning from lambdas

If you use a regular `return` expression inside a lambda, you'll return to the call site of the outer function. That is, the `return` in the lambda also returns from the outer function.

Consider the code snippet below, where a lambda is passed to `forEach()`:

```
fun calculateEven() {
  var result = 0

  (0..20).forEach {
    if (it % 3 == 0) return

    if (it % 2 == 0) result += it
  }

  println(result)
}
```

You'll never get `result` printed as the `return` statement in the lambda stops the execution of `calculateEven()`. But if you only need to return from the lambda expression, you can use a **qualified return**:

```
fun calculateEven() {
  var result = 0

  (0..20).forEach {
    if (it % 3 == 0) return@forEach

    if (it % 2 == 0) result += it
  }

  println(result)
}
```

This way, as soon as an element is a multiple of three, the current iteration of the loop will be interrupted, and the next one will start. This behavior is similar to the use of a `continue` statement.

So the `result` variable will be equal to the sum of all *even* elements from 0 to 20, except for multiples of three.

The code above could also be rewritten in the following way:

```
fun calculateEven() {
  var result = 0

  (0..20).forEach loop@{
    if (it % 3 == 0) return@loop

    if (it % 2 == 0) result += it
  }

  println(result)
}
```

`loop` is just an explicit label, and you can use any of them to return to the place you need.

If you replace the lambda above with an anonymous function, you could use a regular `return` to return from the function and get the same result:

```
fun calculateEven() {
  var result = 0

  (0..20).forEach(fun(value) {
    if (value % 3 == 0) return

    if (value % 2 == 0) result += value
  })

  println(result)
}
```

Inline functions

Remember that, for each lambda that you create to pass to another function, the Kotlin compiler generates an appropriate class extending `FunctionN`. In some cases, that might not be a good solution, especially when you do it multiple times, as this will increase memory usage and have a performance impact on your application.

To avoid such behavior, you can mark your function with the `inline` keyword, which replaces the function call at the call site with the body of the function. Using `inline`, no additional classes are generated, and invocations of this function and received lambdas are replaced by their body.

Let's see how inlining works. Make the `beginBattle()` function `inline`:

```
inline fun beginBattle(
  firstRobot: Robot,
  secondRobot: Robot,
  onBattleEnded: Robot.() -> Unit
)
```

Now, the `main()` function body will be generated into the following equivalent Java code:

```
public static final void main(@NotNull String[] args) {
  Robot firstRobot =
    new Robot("Experimental Space Navigation Droid");
  Robot secondRobot =
    new Robot("Extra-Terrestrial Air Safety Droid");
  Battlefield this_$iv = Battlefield.INSTANCE;
  Robot winner$iv = (Robot)null;
  this_$iv.battle(firstRobot, secondRobot);
  winner$iv = firstRobot.isAlive() ? firstRobot : secondRobot;
  winner$iv.report("Win!");
}
```

As you can see, there are no invocations of the `beginBattle()` function; it's replaced by its body. The `onBattleEnded` lambda invocation also disappeared; now you can only see its body.

That may seem like a nice workaround for the overhead of Kotlin lambdas, and so it is. But this solution causes growth in the size of your generated code. You'll need to decide whether to inline your function or not based on a code size versus performance tradeoff.

If you try to inline a function which doesn't receive any lambdas as parameters, then inlining has a high probability of being useless; no extra classes get generated and there's no need to inline the function. In this case, you'll see the following warning in the IDE:

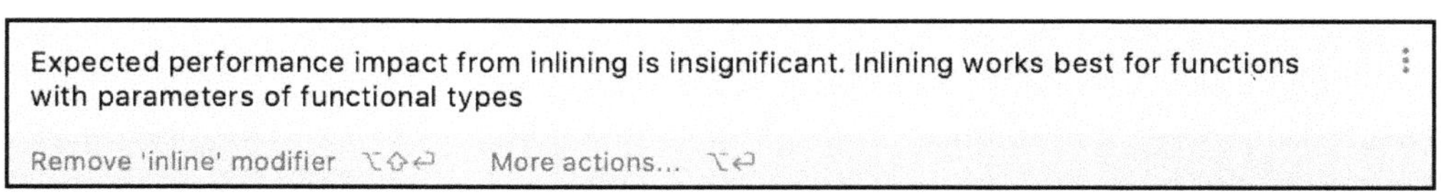

Expected performance impact from inlining is insignificant. Inlining works best for functions with parameters of functional types.

But if you're sure that inlining is necessary, use the `@Suppress("NOTHING_TO_INLINE")` annotation to hide the warning from the compiler:

```
@Suppress("NOTHING_TO_INLINE")
inline fun someFunction() {

}
```

Also, it's not a good idea to inline large functions, as it'll cause your generated code to grow significantly. Try to split the large function into several smaller functions, and inline only what's needed.

noinline

If you don't want some of the lambda parameters to be inlined along with the higher-order function, you can mark the lambda as `noinline`. A `FunctionN` instance will still be generated for `noinline` lambda:

```
inline fun someFunction(
  inlinedLambda: () -> Unit,
  noinline nonInlinedLambda: () -> Unit
)
```

If all lambda parameters of your function are marked with the `noninline` keyword, then inlining is probably pointless because of the reasons mentioned in the previous paragraph — the Kotlin compiler doesn't generate any extra classes, so it's not necessary to inline the function.

crossinline

The `crossinline` keyword is used to mark a lambda parameter which shouldn't allow a non-local return (i.e., `return` without a label). This is useful when a function, which receives a lambda, will call it inside another lambda. In this case, it's not allowed to return from such a lambda. Take a look at the example below:

```
inline fun someFunction(body: () -> Unit) {
  yetAnotherFunction {
    body()
  }
}

fun yetAnotherFunction(body: () -> Unit) {

}
```

If you insert this snippet, you'll get the following compiler error:

Can't inline 'body' here: it may contain non-local returns. Add 'crossinline' modifier to parameter declaration 'body'

To avoid usage of a non-local return in the function parameter, and to make your project compile, you can use the `crossinline` keyword:

```
inline fun someFunction(crossinline body: () -> Unit) {
  yetAnotherFunction {
    body()
  }
}
```

After that, the compiler will issue a warning if you use a non-local return inside the `body` parameter:

```
fun oneMoreFunction() {
  someFunction {
    return
  }
}
```

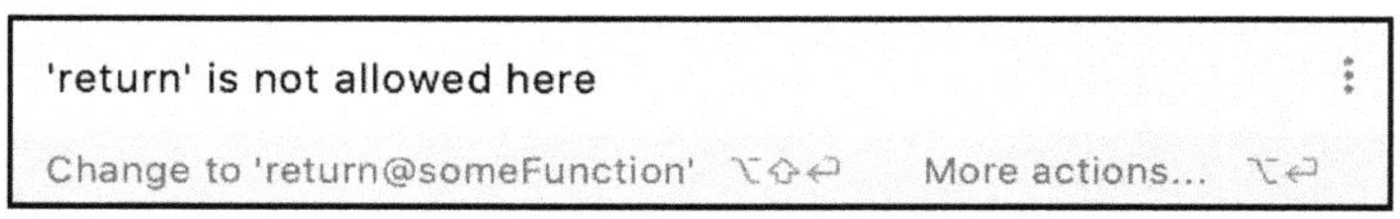

'return' is not allowed here

Tail recursive functions

The last expression in a function is called the **tail call.** If, in some cases, the function gets called again in the tail call expression, this function is called **tail-recursive.** In Kotlin, you can mark such functions as `tailrec`, and the Kotlin complier will replace the recursion by an appropriate loop for the sake of performance optimization. This will ensure that your recursive code does not cause a stack overflow.

Add the `tailrec` keyword to the `battle()` function declaration:

```
tailrec fun battle(firstRobot: Robot, secondRobot: Robot)
```

To check how this works, take a look at the equiavlent Java code:

```
public final void battle(@NotNull Robot firstRobot, @NotNull
Robot secondRobot) {
  do {
    firstRobot.attack(secondRobot);
    if (!secondRobot.isAlive()) {
      return;
    }

    secondRobot.attack(firstRobot);
  } while (firstRobot.isAlive());
}
```

Using `tailrec`, the function is now based on the loop, and not on a recursive call.

Collections standard library

The use of standard library functions on collections that you saw in Chapter 10 are further examples of functional programming. The Kotlin standard library offers you a huge amount of useful functions for collection processing.

For example, define a list of robots which are expected to take part in the robot battle:

```
val participants = arrayListOf<Robot>(
  Robot("Extra-Terrestrial Neutralization Bot"),
  Robot("Generic Evasion Droid"),
  Robot("Self-Reliant War Management Device"),
  Robot("Advanced Nullification Android"),
  Robot("Rational Network Defense Droid"),
  Robot("Motorized Shepherd Cyborg"),
  Robot("Reactive Algorithm Entity"),
  Robot("Ultimate Safety Guard Golem"),
  Robot("Nuclear Processor Machine"),
  Robot("Preliminary Space Navigation Machine")
)
```

It's important to separate them into several categories by strength to avoid unfair fights. The first fight will be conducted for the top category of robots, so you need to find the strongest among them.

With Kotlin, you can do that by applying the following code:

```
val topCategory = participants.filter { it.strength > 80 }
```

That's much more concise than applying a loop. The `filter()` function is an example of a higher-order function, taking a function as its parameter. Of course, under the hood, the `filter()` function uses a loop to find all the appropriate elements in the list.

But that's not even the best thing about collection handling with functional programming. Quite often, it's necessary to apply several transformations at the same time:

```
val topCategory = participants
  // 1
  .filter { it.strength > 80 }
  // 2
  .take(3)
  // 3
  .sortedBy { it.name }
```

Here, you do the following:

1. Filter robots by their strength to find the strongest ones.
2. Take only first the three robots.
3. Sort the remaining robots by their names alphabetically.

Recall that functional programming is about functions without side effects. The code above fits this criterion. All of the functions you applied (`filter()`, `take()`, etc.) don't modify the original list in any way; they return a new list each time. Therefore, you can process the initial list as much as you need.

Infix notation

If a function is a member function or an extension function and receives only one argument, you can mark it with the `infix` keyword. That way you can invoke it without a dot and parentheses.

Mark the `attack()` function in the `Robot` class with the `infix` keyword:

```
infix fun attack(robot: Robot) {
  val damage = random.randomDamage(strength)
  robot.damage(damage)
}
```

Now, you can invoke it in the following way:

```
firstRobot attack secondRobot
```

Using the infix notation makes the code a bit more readable in certain cases.

Sequences

In Kotlin, you can use **Sequence** to create a lazily evaluated collection so that you can operate on collections of unknown size, which can be potentially infinite.

Here's an example of creating a sequence using `generateSequence()` from the standard library:

```
val random = Random()
// 1
val sequence = generateSequence {
  // 2
  random.nextInt(100)
}

sequence
  // 3
  .take(15)
  // 4
  .sorted()
  // 5
  .forEach { println(it) }
```

Here's what's going on in the code above:

1. You a create a sequence using `generateSequence()`, which receives a lambda of type `() -> T?` as an argument.
2. You return a random number from 0 to 100 from the lambda.
3. You take only the first 15 elements of the sequence.

4. You sort the elements.

5. You print each of them.

The lambda you passed to `generateSequence()` will be executed 15 times to evaluate the first 15 elements of the sequence.

If you run the app, you'll get a similar result:

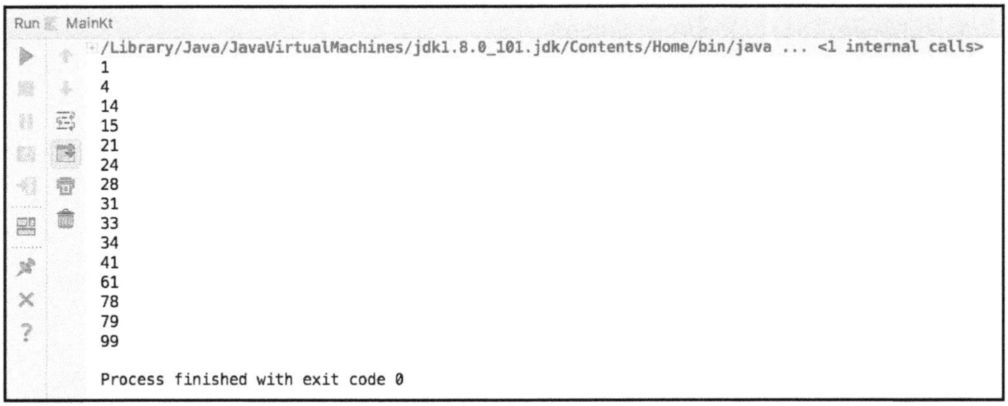

Sequences can also be used to solve different kinds of mathematical tasks using functional programming. For example, you can find the factorial of 10 as follows:

```
val factorial = generateSequence(1 to 1) {
  it.first + 1 to it.second * (it.first + 1)
}

println(factorial.take(10).map { it.second }.last())
```

As the value of the factorial of N cannot be evaluated as a one-time operation, and you need to perform N - 1 multiplications, it's convenient to store the previous result to evaluate the next one.

In this case, you can use a `Pair` class, and you can use its `first` field to store the index, and the `second` to store the factorial for the current index. That way, when you calculate the factorial for the next index, you can access the value of the factorial for the previous one and multiply it by the incremented index. The above is an example of the technique known as **memoization**.

Challenges

1. Using the list of robot `participants` in the "Collections standard library" section, arrange a series of fights for the intermediate category of robots (i.e., their strength is around 40-80 points) between four participants. For example, you have the following list of robots: A, B, C, D. Therefore, you start from two battles A - B and C - D. The last fight will be conducted between the winners of those first two fights. **Note:** if you use random initial strengths, you may need to run the battle a few times to make sure you have enough intermediate participants.

2. Write a function to evaluate the first N elements of the **Fibonacci sequence** using memoization. Each of the elements of the Fibonacci is equal to the sum of the two previous ones. Start from 1, 1, 2, 3...

Key points

- Functional programming uses **first-class** functions, which can be passed as arguments, returned or assigned to variables.
- A **higher-order function** is a function that receives another function as a parameter and/or returns one.
- A **lambda** is a function literal defined in curly brackets, and can be invoked, passed to a function, returned or assigned to a variable.
- When you create a lambda, an implicit class is created that implements a `FunctionN` interface, where `N` is number of parameters that the lambda receives.
- Kotlin lambdas act as **closures**, with access variables defined in the outer scope of the lambda.
- Extension functions implicitly receive an instance of the extended class as the first parameter.
- **Lambdas with receivers** are similar to extension functions.
- Mark a lambda that shouldn't support a non-local return with the `crossinline` keyword.

- Use the `tailrec` keyword to optimize tail-recursive functions.
- Use the `inline` keyword to replace a function invocation with its body.
- If a function is a member function or extension function, and it receives only one argument, you can mark it with an `infix` keyword and call it without the dot operator or parentheses.
- Use **sequences** to create lazily evaluted collections.

Where to go from here?

Functional programming opens a world of possibilities, which are difficult to cover entirely in a single chapter. But to deepen your knowledge after understanding the basics, you can move on to more advanced concepts, such as function **composition**, **Either**, **Option**, **Try**, and more.

You can start by investigating the great library funKTionale (https://github.com/MarioAriasC/funKTionale), where you can find implementations of the concepts mentioned above, as they're not a part of the Kotlin standard library.

In the next chapter, you'll learn about the concept of **conventions** in Kotlin and see how they're used to allow **operator overloading**.

Chapter 22: Conventions & Operator Overloading

By Irina Galata

Kotlin is known for its conciseness and expressiveness, which allows you to do more while using less code. Support for user-defined operator overloading is one of the features that gives Kotlin, and many other programming languages, this ability. In this chapter, you'll learn how to efficiently manipulate data by overloading operators.

What is operator overloading?

Operator overloading is primarily *syntactic sugar*, and it allows you to use various operators, like those used in mathematical calculations (e.g., +, −, *, +=, >=, etc.) with your custom-defined data types. You can create something like this:

```
val fluffy = Kitten("Fluffy")
val snowflake = Kitten("Snowflake")

takeHome(fluffy + snowflake)
```

You have two instances of the `Kitten` class, and you can take them both home using the + operator. Isn't that nice?

Getting started

For this tutorial, imagine that you run a startup IT company and that you want to build an application to manage your employee and department data.

Open the starter project for this chapter. It has shell classes for `Company`, `Department` and `Employee`. To start, add a list of departments to your `Company` class:

```
private val departments: ArrayList<Department> = arrayListOf()
```

Similarly, add a list of employees to your `Department` class:

```
val employees: ArrayList<Employee> = arrayListOf()
```

And update the `Employee` constructor to track the employee company:

```
class Employee(
  val company: Company,
  val name: String,
  var salary: Int
)
```

Now, update the `main()` function in the starter project to add `company` to each of the employees:

```
fun main(args: Array<String>) {
  // your company
  val company = Company("MyOwnCompany")

  // departments
```

```
  val developmentDepartment = Department("Development")
  val qaDepartment = Department("Quality Assurance")
  val hrDepartment = Department("Human Resources")

  // employees
  var Julia = Employee(company, "Julia", 100_000)
  var John = Employee(company, "John", 86_000)
  var Peter = Employee(company, "Peter", 100_000)

  var Sandra = Employee(company, "Sandra", 75_000)
  var Thomas = Employee(company, "Thomas", 73_000)
  var Alice = Employee(company, "Alice", 70_000)

  var Bernadette = Employee(company, "Bernadette", 66_000)
  var Mark = Employee(company, "Mark", 66_000)
}
```

You have a company consisting of three small departments. As you plan to grow your startup, you'll need to think of the most efficient way of the handling all of the company data, such as departments and staff list, and its processes like hiring, raises or dismissals.

Using conventions

The ability to use overloaded operators in Kotlin is an example of what's called a **convention**. In Kotlin, a convention is an agreement in which you declare and use a function in a specific way, and the prototypical example is being able to use the function with an operator.

In this book, you've already used conventions when you marked a function with the `infix` keyword; in this way, *by convention*, you could omit the function parentheses and call the function without the dot symbol.

Unary operator overloading

You're likely familiar with unary operators in programming languages — `+a`, `--a` or `a++`, for example. If you want to use an increment operator like ++ on your custom data type, you need to declare the `inc()` function as a member of your class, either inside the class or as an extension function. Here, you'll create a function to give your employees a raise. Add the following function to your `Employee` class:

```
operator fun inc(): Employee {
  salary += 5000
  println("$name got a raise to $$salary")
```

```
    return this
  }
```

You mark the function with the `operator` keyword, name it `inc()` and make it return `Employee`. Inside the function, you add 5,000 to the employee `salary`, using the += operator on the `Int`, and you return `this` from the function to return the same instance.

You can now execute employee raises by convention:

```
++Julia // now Julia's salary is 105_000
```

This will be compiled to:

```
Julia = Julia.inc();
```

The decrement operator can be used in a similar way. Add this to `Employee`:

```
operator fun dec(): Employee {
  salary -= 5000
  println("$name's salary decreased to $$salary")
  return this
}
```

For example, you can cut down Peter's salary via:

```
--Peter // now Peter's salary is 95_000
```

Take a look at the convention functions for all the various unary operators:

Operator	Necessary function
++a	inc()
--a	dec()
-a	unaryMinus()
+a	unaryPlus()
!a	not()

You can use these operators to give a meaning to incrementing or decrementing a data type, changing the sign of a data type using – or affirming it with +, and negating it using the not operator `!`.

Binary operator overloading

Similarly, you can use binary operators to combine your custom data types with other values in some kind of meaningful way. An example for our `Employee` class is for employee raises and pay cuts of a specified amount.

Update the `Employee` class by adding the following functions, which will use assigment the operators += and -=:

```
operator fun plusAssign(increaseSalary: Int) {
  salary += increaseSalary
  println("$name got a raise to $$salary")
}

operator fun minusAssign(decreaseSalary: Int) {
  salary -= decreaseSalary
  println("$name's salary decreased to $$salary")
}
```

Inside these functions, you add or subtract the amount passed in as an argument to the employee salary. Since the parameter on the functions is an `Int`, you'll need to combine an `Employee` object with an `Int` using the operators.

Now you can manage the salary of your employees using the corresponding operators:

```
Mark += 2500
Alice -= 2000
```

Kotlin's compilier will translate the code above to the following, as expected:

```
Mark.plusAssign(2500);
Alice.minusAssign(2000);
```

In the same way, you can manage your department and employee lists. Add these functions to the `Company` class:

```
operator fun plusAssign(department: Department) {
  departments.add(department)
}

operator fun minusAssign(department: Department) {
  departments.remove(department)
}
```

And these to the `Department` class:

```
operator fun plusAssign(employee: Employee) {
  employees.add(employee)
  println("${employee.name} hired to $name department")
}

operator fun minusAssign(employee: Employee) {
  if (employees.contains(employee)) {
    employees.remove(employee)
    println("${employee.name} fired from $name department")
  }
}
```

Now, you can concisely manage your company data with the overloaded operators:

```
company += developmentDepartment
company += qaDepartment
company += hrDepartment

developmentDepartment += Julia
developmentDepartment += John
developmentDepartment += Peter

qaDepartment += Sandra
qaDepartment += Thomas
qaDepartment += Alice

hrDepartment += Bernadette
hrDepartment += Mark

qaDepartment -= Thomas
```

These assignments via operator are equivalent to the code below:

```
company.plusAssign(developmentDepartment);
company.plusAssign(qaDepartment);
company.plusAssign(hrDepartment);

developmentDepartment.plusAssign(Julia);
developmentDepartment.plusAssign(John);
developmentDepartment.plusAssign(Peter);

qaDepartment.plusAssign(Sandra);
qaDepartment.plusAssign(Thomas);
qaDepartment.plusAssign(Alice);

hrDepartment.plusAssign(Bernadette);
hrDepartment.plusAssign(Mark);

qaDepartment.minusAssign(Thomas);
```

Build and run the `main()` function and check your console to see the results:

```
Run: MainKt
/Library/Java/JavaVirtualMachines/jdk1.8.0_192.jdk/Contents/Home/bin/java ...
Julia hired to Development department
John hired to Development department
Peter hired to Development department
Sandra hired to Quality Assurance department
Thomas hired to Quality Assurance department
Alice hired to Quality Assurance department
Bernadette hired to Human Resources department
Mark hired to Human Resources department
Thomas fired from Quality Assurance department
Thomas no longer works here
Julia got a raise to $105000
Peter's salary decreased to $95000
Mark got a raise to $68500
Alice's salary decreased to $68000

Process finished with exit code 0
```

By using the binary assignment operators, you've given yourself an intuitive way to add employees to departments and departments to your startup.

Handling collections

Operator overloading is also quite helpful for when working with collections. For example, if you want to be able to access an employee by its index within a department, declare the following `get()` operator function in the `Department` class:

```
operator fun get(index: Int): Employee? {
  return if (index < employees.size) {
    employees[index]
  } else {
    null
  }
}
```

You first check that the supplied `index` is within the range of employees in the department, and if so, you return that employee from your internal list. Otherwise, you return null. The operator corresponding to this function is the indexing operator:

```
val firstEmployee = qaDepartment[0]
```

Note that this new operator function returns a nullable `Employee`. If you wanted to give that employee a raise, you'd do so as follows:

```
qaDepartment[0]?.plusAssign(1000)
```

Since the return type of the `get()` function is a nullable `Employee?`, you cannot use the += operator directly. You also need to use a safe call operator `?.` to avoid a possible `KotlinNullPointerException` from the code.

If you add the `set()` function to the `Department` class, you'll also be able to set an employee by index:

```
operator fun set(index: Int, employee: Employee) {
  if (index < employees.size) {
    employees[index] = employee
  }
}
```

To update the employee at the second index to Thomas you use the following code:

```
qaDepartment[1] = Thomas
```

To check if an employee works in a given department, you can define the `contains()` operator function in the `Department` class.

Here, you need to confirm if an employee is in the underlying list:

```
operator fun contains(employee: Employee) =
  employees.contains(employee)
```

After adding the function above, you can use `in` and `!in` operators with `Employee` and `Department` objects:

```
if (Thomas !in qaDepartment) {
  println("${Thomas.name} no longer works here")
}
```

Using the indexing and `in` operators makes the logic of your employee and department code much more evident and readable.

Adding ranges

You can also get a list of employees in a given range using the `..` operator. To implement such functionality, first define how to sort the employee list so that you always get the same result from this operator.

Update the `Employee` class to implement the `Comparable` interface:

```
data class Employee(
  val company: Company,
  val name: String,
  var salary: Int
) : Comparable<Employee>
```

Then, override its function `compareTo()`:

```
override operator fun compareTo(other: Employee): Int {
  return when (other) {
    this -> 0
    else -> name.compareTo(other.name)
  }
}
```

By marking the `compareTo()` function with the keyword `operator`, you've ensured that you can use the comparison operators >, <, >=, etc. This function should return `-1`, `0` or `1` if another object is larger, equal to or less than the current one, respectively. You've also marked the class with the keyword `data` to override the `equals()` function so that you can implicitly use it in the`compareTo()` function.

You can now compare employees by their names, which will help you sort them alphabetically. To iterate through the list of employees in a department, update the `Department` class to implement an `Iterable` interface and its function `iterator()`.

Start by updating the class declaration:

```
class Department(
  val name: String = "Department"
) : Iterable<Employee>
```

Then, override `iterator()` to conform to the interface:

```
override fun iterator() = employees.iterator()
```

After that, you can use the following construction on a department:

```
developmentDepartment.forEach {
 // do something
}
```

To access the list of all employees sorted by name in your company, add the following property with custom getter to the `Company` class:

```
val allEmployees: List<Employee>
  get() = arrayListOf<Employee>().apply {
    departments.forEach { addAll(it.employees) }
    sort()
  }
```

Now you can add the `rangeTo()` operator function on the `Employee` class, which corresponds to the `..` operator:

```
operator fun rangeTo(other: Employee): List<Employee> {
  val currentIndex = company.allEmployees.indexOf(this)
  val otherIndex = company.allEmployees.indexOf(other)

  // start index cannot be larger or equal to the end index
  if (currentIndex >= otherIndex) {
    return emptyList()
  }

  // get all elements in a list from currentIndex to otherIndex
  return company.allEmployees.slice(currentIndex..otherIndex)
}
```

Now you can create a range of `Employees`:

```
print((Alice..Mark).joinToString { it.name }) // prints "Alice,
Bernadette, John, Julia, Mark"
```

With the code above, you receive a list of employees from `Alice` to `Mark`, sorted alphabetically. You then join their names to one string and print the result.

You've seen a number of examples of binary and other operators (such as indexing) for custom data types. Below, you can find a list of conventions for the functions corresponding to these and other operators:

Operator	Necessary function	Operator	Necessary function
`a + b`	`plus(b)`	`a(i, j)`	`invoke(i, j)`
`a - b`	`minus(b)`	`a..b`	`rangeTo(b)`
`a * b`	`times(b)`	`a += b`	`plusAssign(b)`
`a / b`	`div(b)`	`a -= b`	`minusAssign(b)`
`a % b`	`rem(b)`	`a *= b`	`timesAssign(b)`
`a in b`	`contains(a)`	`a /= b`	`divAssign(b)`
`a[i]`	`get(i)`	`a %= b`	`remAssign(b)`
`a[i, j]`	`get(i, j)`	`a == b`	`equals(b)`
`a[i] = b`	`set(i, b)`	`a > b`	`compareTo(b)`
`a[i, j] = b`	`set(i, j, b)`	`a < b`	`compareTo(b)`
`a()`	`invoke()`	`a >= b`	`compareTo(b)`
`a(i)`	`invoke(i)`	`a <= b`	`compareTo(b)`

As you review this table, it's important to note that you should be judicious in your use of operator overloading. Any operators that you decide to overload in your data types should be intuitive and recognizable for the given use case, so that they actually make the resulting code not simply more consise but also easier to read and interpret than the more verbose code you would have otherwise used.

Operator overloading and Java

Unlike Kotlin, Java doesn't support user-defined operator overloading. However, the + operator is actually overloaded in standard Java; you not only use it to sum two numbers but also to concatenate strings:

```
String a = "a";
String b = "b";
System.out.print(a + b); // prints "ab"
```

Why doesn't Java allow developers to overload operators themselves?

While overloaded operators can simplify your code, they can also misleading. Since any given operator can have multiple meanings, it can be unclear what's exactly happening in a specific line of code.

As was mentioned at the end of the last section, you should always overload operators attentively, and don't make them behave unexpectedly; for example, the + operator should always be used to "add" two things together in whatever context it is used, and not perform an operation that would correpsond to the equivalent of subtracting, multiplying or dividing.

Delegated properties as conventions

In Chapter 13: "Properties," you were introduced to various types of **delegated propeties**. You can delegate the initialization of a property to another object by using conventions for the `getValue()` and `setValue()` functions in a delegate class:

```
class NameDelegate {
  operator fun getValue(
    thisRef: Any?,
    property: KProperty<*>
  ): String {
    // return existing value
  }
  operator fun setValue(
    thisRef: Any?,
    property: KProperty<*>,
    value: String
  ) {
    // set received value
  }
}
```

In conjunction with the above, you use the construction below to delegate the `name` property to a `NameDelegate` object:

```
var name: String by NameDelegate()
```

In this way, all calls to get or set the `name` property will be delegated to the `getValue()` and `setValue()` functions in `NameDelegate`. This is useful for consolidating complex logic or operations into the delegate class.

Challenges

1. Modify theEmployee class so that you can add several employees to a department simultaneously using the + operator:

   ```
   developmentDepartment.hire(Julia + John + Peter)
   qaDepartment.hire(Sandra + Thomas + Alice)
   hrDepartment.hire(Bernadette + Mark)
   ```

   You'll also need to add a `hire()` function to `Department` that takes a list of employees `List<Employee>` as a parameter.

2. Using the Kotlin Bytecode Viewer in IntelliJ IDEA (**Tools ▸ Kotlin ▸ Show Kotlin Bytecode ▸ Decompile**), review exactly what happens when the code above gets executed.

Key points

- To use **overloaded operators**, it's necessary to follow the specific **conventions** for the operator.
- Conventions manage multiple features in Kotlin, such as operator overloading, infix functions and delegated properties.
- Operators should always behave predictably; don't overload operators in a way that makes their behavior unclear for other developers who might use or read your code.

Where to go from here?

In this chapter, you learned how to add custom behaviors to different operators. Now, you're ready to use them in a real project. Try to replace the routine and repetitive code in your own projects with overloaded operators to make your code more elegant and concise. But don't forget about **predictability** and **clarity**!

In the next chapter, you'll see how to include long-running operations in your code that don't block the rest of your code from running but that still allow you to write your code in a sequential fashion, using **Kotlin Coroutines**.

Chapter 23: Kotlin Coroutines

By Irina Galata

While working through the previous chapters, you've run **synchronous** code only. That means that one command was executed after another by your CPU, sequentially, and no code in your projects were running simultaneously on different computing cores (in the case that your CPU has them, which they tend to these days).

Consequently, if you decided to perform any long-running, time-consuming operations (e.g., sending a request over a network to a server, or processing a large file), your program would appear to freeze until the operation finished, and a user would have to wait. That's less than ideal — a user should be able to interact with your program even while it's executing a difficult task. That expectation leads to the concept of the *asynchronous programming*.

Asynchronous programming

As opposed to the synchronous approach, **asynchronous programming** allows for the execution of several tasks in parallel at the same time. That way, you can render a beautiful loader animation while your app is also retrieving the necessary data from a server, for example. Or you could break up a non-trivial task into a few easier ones and execute them simultaneously to decrease the processing time.

Threads

In Java — and accordingly in Kotlin on the JVM — you can parallelize your program using **threads**. Each `java.lang.Thread` object represents one execution flow, which sequentially performs the commands within the single thread.

You can operate on threads in various ways — create them, start, pause, join, etc. By creating several threads, you can perform multiple tasks simultaneously.

Take a look at the example below:

```
fun main() {
  thread(start = true, name = "another thread") {
    (0..10).forEach {
      println(
        "Message #$it from the ${Thread.currentThread().name}")
    }
  }

  (0..10).forEach {
    println(
      "Message #$it from the ${Thread.currentThread().name}")
  }
}
```

In the above, you first create a thread named "another thread" using the function `thread()` from the `kotlin.concurrent` package. You pass `true` for the `start` parameter, so the thread will start executing commands immediately. A message with the thread name and a number will be printed 11 times.

In the code below that, you perform the same work on the main, default thread for your project, without creating a new one.

If you run the code below, you'll see a similar output:

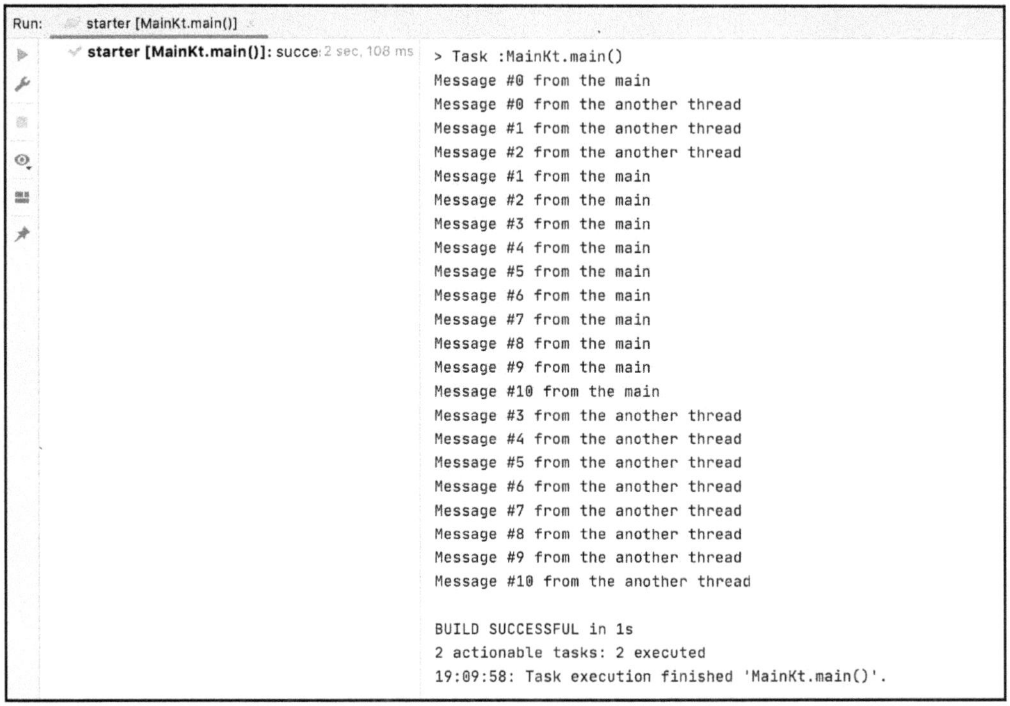

The exact ordering of the parallel `println()` results from the two threads is indeterminate, and it depends on whatever is going on in your CPU at the time you run. You can see that your main thread, along with "another thread," are executing at the same time without waiting for each other to complete, which is expected and is the desired behavior.

Everything seems fine with threads until you need to manipulate a large number of them or pass data back and forth between them. Also, it's important to note that Java threads are based on OS-level threads and, therefore, consume a significant amount of system resources. You can't create thousands of threads as you'll likely end up with an `OutOfMemoryError` thrown by the JVM.

Is there any other option, then?

Coroutines

There isn't an immediate better option in the Java language but, in Kotlin, you receive **coroutines** right out of the box! A coroutine is primarily a *computation*. Its defining feature is that it can be *suspended* and *resumed* at specified points of the computation without blocking a thread. Suspension is an extremely efficient operation. You can create hundreds and even thousands of coroutines and run them concurrently, as they are lightweight and don't require many extra resources for their execution.

Coroutines can be suspended at specified suspension points. These points are calls to functions marked with the `suspend` modifier. These suspending functions can only be invoked from coroutines or other suspending functions, as well as functions inlined in either coroutines or suspending routines.

Getting started

Open up the starter project for this chapter. The starter project contains a non-coroutine version of the example project you'll build below using coroutines. The `main()` function in **main.kt** looks as follows:

```
fun main() {
  BuildingYard.startProject("Smart house", 20)
}
```

Go ahead and run the `main()` function the same way you've done in previous chapters. You'll see a virtual building being constructed in the console.

One thing you'll notice is that it takes a *long* time to construct the building in a sequential manner, with each task being done one after another. When we switch to using coroutines in our project below, you'll see how asynchronous code makes the virtual building construction go much, much faster!

To get started with coroutines, add `dependencies {}` block and the coroutine dependency to your **build.gradle.kts** file:

```
dependencies {
  implementation("org.jetbrains.kotlinx:kotlinx-coroutines-core:
1.4.0")
}
```

After that, you can write the earlier example like this:

```
fun main() = runBlocking {
  launch(Dispatchers.Default) {
    (0..10).forEach {
      println("Message #$it from the $
{Thread.currentThread().name}")
    }
  }

  (0..10).forEach {
    println("Message #$it from the $
{Thread.currentThread().name}")
  }
}
```

You will need to include the following imports to make the code above compile:

```
import kotlinx.coroutines.Dispatchers
import kotlinx.coroutines.launch
import kotlinx.coroutines.runBlocking
```

That code is the coroutine analog of the thread code at the beginning of this chapter. If you run this code, you'll get a similar result:

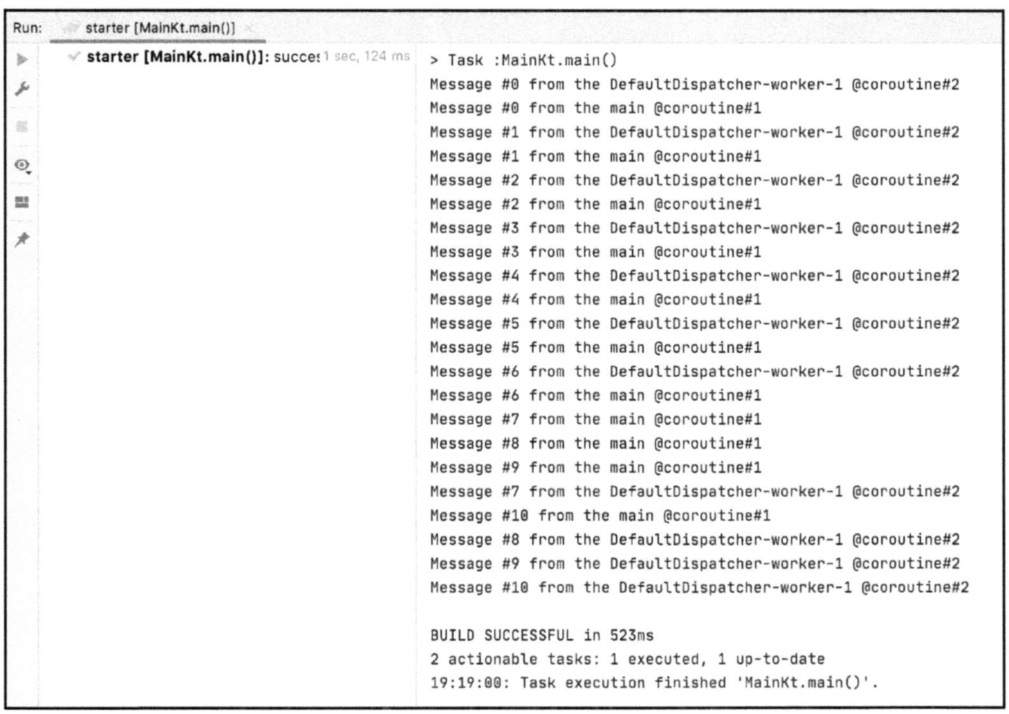

> **Note**: You should remember that, when using coroutines, threads are still used under the hood. But one thread can execute thousands of coroutines. Therefore, you don't spend precious memory resources to manipulate a large number of coroutines.

Configuring coroutines

Kotlin coroutines are an extremely flexible solution for the wide variety of cases you may have. And the way a coroutine behaves is pretty much defined by its *context*. Any coroutine gets executed inside some `CoroutineScope` containing an instance of `CoroutineContext`, which is represented by a collection containing important configurations. You're going to get acquainted with the most important of them - `Job`, `Dispatcher` and, later in this chapter, `CoroutineExceptionHandler`.

Job

`Job` basically represents a background job, which has a state (active, cancelled, completed, etc.), optionally has children, and can be started and cancelled. You'll learn more about `Job` in this chapter.

Dispatchers

Dispatchers are responsible for the threads where your coroutines are executed. There are some ready-to-use dispatchers in the Kotlin core library:

1. `Dispatchers.Default` uses a pool of background threads for resource-demanding operations. The number of threads is equal to the number of cores on your machine, but at least two if it's a single-core CPU, which is highly unlikely nowadays.

2. `Dispatchers.IO` is useful when you need to perform input/output operations, e.g., saving user data to local storage or uploading files to a server. Use this dispatcher when a thread is supposed to be blocked while waiting for a response. It uses a pool of 64 threads.

3. `Dispatchers.Unconfined` is not limited to any thread. Don't use it unless you're sure that other dispatchers don't fit your case.

4. Optionally, you may use the single-threaded `Dispatchers.Main` for a UI-related Kotlin library (Android, JavaFx or Swing). You'll use it to perform operations on the UI thread and access UI objects.

CoroutineScope

`CoroutineScope` is an interface which does nothing except provide an associated `CoroutineContext`:

```
public interface CoroutineScope {
  public val coroutineContext: CoroutineContext
}
```

It's necessary to bind your coroutines to some *lifecycle* (if you're familiar with Android, the lifecycle of an `Activity` is a great example). That way, all jobs get cancelled as soon as your component/program completes and they're not necessary anymore.

Obtaining a scope

There are multiple ways to get `CoroutineScope` to launch a coroutine. Some of them are mentioned here:

1. Using `GlobalScope`, which is accessible from anywhere in your code. You can use it to execute top-level coroutines that shouldn't be bound to the lifecycle of some specific component, but rather the whole application. Always consider the options below before using this one.

2. The `MainScope()` function returns a scope which, like the `Main` dispatcher, is handy when you work with UI components.

3. You can use the `CoroutineScope(context: CoroutineContext)` function to wrap a specific context (Hint: You can use the dispatchers mentioned above, as `CoroutineDispatcher` is a `CoroutineContext` too).

Coroutines builders

In order to use coroutines and therefore parallelize the execution of your code, you need to use *coroutine builders*. They're regular functions that create a new coroutine inside a specified `CoroutineContext`. You've already seen some of them in the code snippet above — `runBlocking()` and `launch()`. Let's find out how they work.

runBlocking()

The declaration of the `runBlocking()` function in the coroutine library code is as follows:

```
public fun <T> runBlocking(
  context: CoroutineContext = EmptyCoroutineContext,
  block: suspend CoroutineScope.() -> T
): T
```

`runBlocking()` is a regular, non-coroutine function that creates a new coroutine to execute the *suspending* lambda you pass it as the parameter `block`. It *blocks* the current thread until the new coroutine execution finishes. That way, program execution won't stop and the coroutine will have time to complete. It's supposed to be used for testing purposes and in the `main()` function; in any other case, use other mentioned functions in order to avoid thread blocking and to use all the benefits of Kotlin coroutines.

launch()

The example code also used the `launch()` function, which has the following signature:

```
public fun CoroutineScope.launch(
  context: CoroutineContext = EmptyCoroutineContext,
  start: CoroutineStart = CoroutineStart.DEFAULT,
  block: suspend CoroutineScope.() -> Unit
): Job
```

Similar to `runBlocking()` this function creates a new coroutine, but it doesn't block the current thread. Instead, it returns a `Job` object, which lets you control your coroutine execution. In the example above, you were not interested in sequential execution of the code, but parallel.

In case you need to wait for the execution of your newly created coroutine, you use the `join()` method of `Job` to *suspend* the current coroutine/suspend function until the job is done:

```
public suspend fun join()
```

That way you can call the `join()` function on a coroutine to wait until the result is ready:

```
launch { postVideoToFeed() }.join()
```

> **Note**: All exceptions thrown during execution of a coroutine created with `launch()` are treated as *uncaught* exceptions and will fail the parent coroutine.

CoroutineStart

As you can see from the `launch` function declaration, you can specify not only the threads on which your coroutine will be launched, but also the moment when it should happen. There are four options:

1. `DEFAULT` corresponds to the immediate start of a coroutine.
2. `LAZY` — a coroutine won't be launched until it's necessary. You can do so by calling `start()` on the corresponding `Job` (or `Deferred`) object.
3. `ATOMIC` is similar to the default one, but the coroutine is not cancellable in that case.
4. If you use `UNDISPATCHED` start, the coroutine will be launched immediately until its first suspension point in the current thread.

async()

There will be numerous cases where you are interested not only in waiting for the coroutine to be executed, but also in getting a *result* from it. The most common case is getting data from a server—for example, loading a user profile or getting a list of chat messages. `async()` is a definite solution for this case:

```
public fun <T> CoroutineScope.async(
  context: CoroutineContext = EmptyCoroutineContext,
  start: CoroutineStart = CoroutineStart.DEFAULT,
  block: suspend CoroutineScope.() -> T
): Deferred<T>
```

It's quite similar to `launch()`, but it returns a `Deferred` object, which is actually a `Job` itself (interface `Deferred` extends the `Job` interface), but it contains a *result* of the execution. In order to wait for the result, use the `await()` function:

```
public suspend fun await(): T
```

The `await()` function suspends the coroutine where this function is invoked until the result is ready and returns it without blocking the current thread:

```
val userData = async { getUserDataFromServer() }.await()
```

withContext()

The `withContext()` function gets the result of the execution as well. However, it's optimized for more straightforward cases, when you don't need the `Deferred` instance but just the *result* itself:

```
public suspend fun <T> withContext(
  context: CoroutineContext,
  block: suspend CoroutineScope.() -> T
): T
```

`withContext()` switches the coroutine to the specified `context` and *suspends* until the `block` is executed and the result of the job is available.

The various different builder functions associated with coroutines and their usage may seem overwhelming at first, and they're best understood by looking at an example.

Example: A high-rise building

To illustrate all the niceties of coroutines, it's necessary to imagine a process or task, some parts of which could be executed simultaneously, while other parts should be completed strictly one after another. The process of constructing a high-rise building is a good example.

The starter project contains a class named `Building` that represents the activities involved in building a new high-rise:

```
class Building(val name: String) {

  fun makeFoundation() {
    Thread.sleep(300)
    speakThroughBullhorn("The foundation is ready")
  }

  fun buildFloor(floor: Int) {
    Thread.sleep(100)
    speakThroughBullhorn("The $floor'th floor is raised")
  }

  fun placeWindows(floor: Int) {
    Thread.sleep(100)
    speakThroughBullhorn("Windows are placed on the $floor'th
floor")
  }

  fun installDoors(floor: Int) {
    Thread.sleep(100)
    speakThroughBullhorn("Doors are installed on the $floor'th
floor")
  }

  fun provideElectricity(floor: Int) {
    Thread.sleep(100)
    speakThroughBullhorn("Electricity is provided on the
$floor'th floor")
  }

  fun buildRoof() {
    Thread.sleep(200)
    speakThroughBullhorn("The roof is ready")
  }

  fun fitOut(floor: Int) {
    Thread.sleep(200)
    speakThroughBullhorn("The $floor'th floor is furnished")
  }

  fun speakThroughBullhorn(message: String) = println(message)

}
```

In each function in `Building` in the starter project, we sleep the current thread for a certain number of milliseconds, and then call `speakThroughBullhorn()` to print a message.

To switch from using threads to working with coroutines and the associated functions, make the following changes to the `Building` class:

- Mark all functions except `speakThroughBullhorn()` in `Building` with the `suspend` modifier so that they can be called from coroutines and other suspending functions
- Wrap the body of each function except `speakThroughBullhorn()` with the launch function
- Change the `Thread.sleep()` calls to instead be the coroutine function `delay()`
- Prepend the strings that are printed with `[${Thread.currentThread().name}]`
- Add a `var floors: Int = 0` parameter to the `Building` constructor
- Increment the floor count using `++floors` at the end of the `buildFloor()` function

The result should be the following:

```
class Building(
  val name: String,
  var floors: Int = 0,
  private val scope: CoroutineScope
) {

  suspend fun makeFoundation() = scope.launch {
    delay(300)
    speakThroughBullhorn("[${Thread.currentThread().name}] The
foundation is ready")
  }

  suspend fun buildFloor(floor: Int) = scope.launch {
    delay(100)
    speakThroughBullhorn("[${Thread.currentThread().name}] Floor
number $floor floor is built")
    ++floors
  }

  suspend fun placeWindows(floor: Int) = scope.launch {
    delay(100)
    speakThroughBullhorn("[${Thread.currentThread().name}]
Windows are placed on floor number $floor")
  }
```

```
  suspend fun installDoors(floor: Int) = scope.launch {
    delay(100)
    speakThroughBullhorn("[${Thread.currentThread().name}] Doors
are installed on floor number $floor")
  }

  suspend fun provideElectricity(floor: Int) = scope.launch {
    delay(100)
    speakThroughBullhorn("[${Thread.currentThread().name}]
Electricity is provided on floor number $floor")
  }

  suspend fun buildRoof() = scope.launch {
    delay(200)
    speakThroughBullhorn("[${Thread.currentThread().name}] The
roof is ready")
  }

  suspend fun fitOut(floor: Int) = scope.launch {
    delay(200)
    speakThroughBullhorn("[${Thread.currentThread().name}] Floor
number $floor is furnished")
  }

  fun speakThroughBullhorn(message: String) = println(message)
}
```

In the `Building` class, you have functions that represent single tasks that should be completed during the building process.

For each of the tasks, you need a new coroutine to optimize the process. As you don't need a result from these tasks, you use the `launch()` function to create the coroutine. And, much like in the real world, a task can take some time to complete. You simulate waiting using the `delay()` function, which just suspends a coroutine for a specific amount of time. To build the high-rise, you need some physical space to place it. Update the contents of the file **BuildingYard.kt** from the starter project with a `BuildingYard` class that has a suspending function `startProject()`:

```
class BuildingYard {
  suspend fun startProject(name: String, floors: Int) {

  }
}
```

You initiate the process of building a twenty-floor high-rise in the `main()` function in **main.kt** as follows:

```
fun main() = runBlocking {
  BuildingYard().startProject("Smart house", 20)
}
```

As you don't want your program to shut down before the high-rise is ready, use the `runBlocking()` function.

Now, it's time to start the planning stage of building. Which task should come first? It's necessary to prepare the foundation, as it's an essential phase before starting any other one. Update the `startProject()` function in `BuildingYard` class as follows:

```
suspend fun startProject(name: String, floors: Int) {
  val building = withContext(Dispatchers.Default) {
    val building = Building(name, scope = this)
    val cores = Runtime.getRuntime().availableProcessors()
    building.speakThroughBullhorn(
      "The building of $name is started with $cores building
machines engaged")
    building.makeFoundation().join()
    building
  }
  if (building.floors == floors) {
    building.speakThroughBullhorn("${building.name} is ready!")
  }
}
```

In entering the above, you expect to get a completed building as a result, so you wrap the whole building process in a lambda to pass it to `async()` and then call `await()` to suspend the current coroutine and wait for the result.

The `availableProcessors()` function on the `Runtime` returns the number of cores in the CPU of your computer. A *core* is responsible for performing the operations on the CPU. You have probably heard the term *multi-core processor*; this means that the CPU can perform multiple operations simultaneously. It's not uncommon for processors to have four cores or even eight. Don't worry though, you can still have more threads than cores as multiple threads can run on the same core!

You use the `join()` function in order to wait until the foundation is ready, as any other phase couldn't be started before that.

If you run the project now, you'll get the following result:

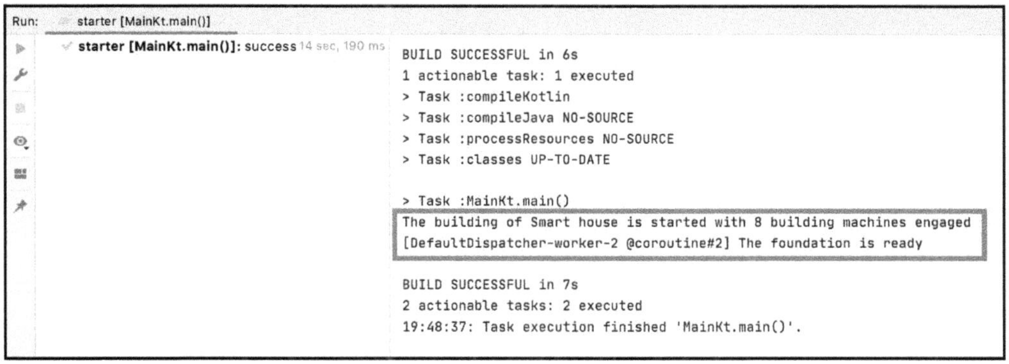

The first line of output will be report the number of cores in your CPU.

With the foundation of the building ready, now it's possible to start working on the floors. Update the `startProject()` function to add a loop over the floors, within which you'll decorate the floor with windows, doors, etc. Add this code right after `building.makeFoundation().join()` and before the line `building`:

```
(1..floors).forEach {
  // A floor should be raised before we can decorate it
  building.buildFloor(it).join()

  // These decorations could be made at the same time
  building.placeWindows(it)
  building.installDoors(it)
  building.provideElectricity(it)
  building.fitOut(it)
}

building.buildRoof().join()
```

Inside the loop over the floors, before decorating a floor, it's vital to build it, so you use the `join()` function on `building.buildFloor(it)` to wait. After that, all decorative tasks can be performed simultaneously so there's no need to suspend the current coroutine.

When all the floors are ready, you can build the final part of your building — a roof.

Build and run the latest version of your program.

You'll see that the construction of your building performs successfully:

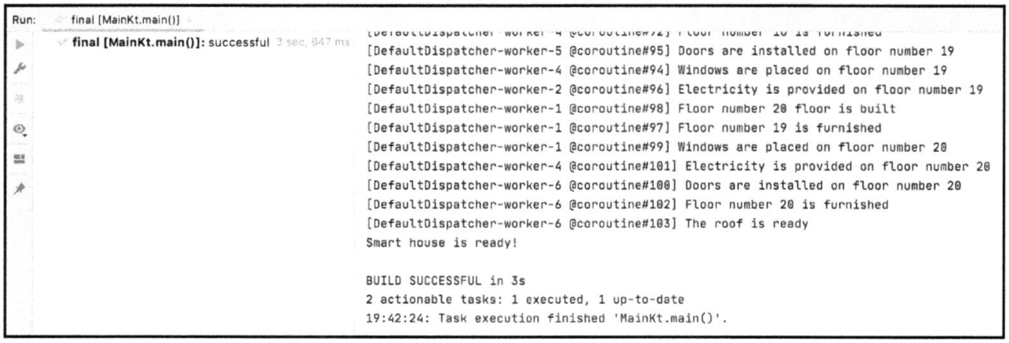

If you look in detail at the output, you see that your program executed the coroutines on different threads within the `CommonPool`. Also, the construction process of different floors overlaps, just like in real life (e.g., when the building of the 20th floor is started, the decorating of the 19th wasn't finished yet).

Error handling

The common approach to handle exceptions while using coroutines is a well-known `try-catch` block. The way you catch exceptions in synchronous code is still applicable here:

```
try {
  val userProfile = scope.withContext(Dispatchers.IO) {
    getProfile()
  }
} catch (e: NoSuchUserException) {
  // handle exception
}
```

Using CoroutineExceptionHandler

There could be a case when you need to have a global exception handler for all your coroutines, and `CoroutineExceptionHandler` is designed for this purpose:

```
val scope = CoroutineScope(Dispatchers.Default)
val handler = CoroutineExceptionHandler { context, exception ->
  println(exception.message)
}
scope.launch(handler) {
  uploadData()
}
```

> **Note**: `CoroutineExceptionHandler` won't be triggered if it's not set to the scope of the parent coroutine, as it's supposed to be used for global handling of unexpected exceptions.

Understanding coroutines

Coroutines aren't a new concept in software development; several programming languages — such as C#, Ruby and Python — have supported them for a long time. In many languages, coroutines are based on *state machines*, and Kotlin isn't an exception.

The Kotlin compiler generates a class that represents a state machine for each of your coroutines. When your coroutine execution reaches the suspension point (i.e., invocation of a suspending function), its state machine stores the current state of the coroutine in order to easily resume the execution later. In this way, coroutines are extremely efficient, since they don't block threads and they require only one class for the execution of each of them, which is cheap and lightweight at the same time.

Challenges

Challenge 1

Modify the `BuildingYard` class in such way that you could build several buildings simultaneously, not one by one. (Hint: Consider using `Collection<Deferred<T>>.awaitAll()`)

Challenge 2

Modify the `Building` class in such way so the `buildFloor()` function could fail randomly (i.e., throw an exception). In the `BuildingYard` class, after this function execution completes, check whether it executed successfully. If it is unsuccessful, start the execution of the task again.

Key points

- The **asynchronous** approach to programming focuses on allowing you to execute several operations at the same time.
- **Threads** are used when you don't need a lot of them to perform the necessary tasks.
- **Coroutines** are like "lightweight threads", since they don't require as much memory resources and they're not based on OS level threads like Java threads.
- A large number of coroutines could be executed on a single thread without blocking it.
- Each coroutine is bound to some `CoroutineContext`.
- `CoroutineContext` is responsible for many important parts of a coroutine such as its `Job`, `Dispatcher` and `CoroutineExceptionHandler`.
- Use coroutines builders (`runBlocking()`, `withContext()`, `launch()`, `async()`) to create and launch coroutines.

- You can decide when to launch your coroutine using `CoroutineStart`.
- Use **dispatchers** to define the threads for your coroutine execution.
- Coroutines are based on the concept of a state machine, with each state referring to a suspension point. It doesn't require extra time or resources to switch between coroutines and to restore their state.

Where to go from here?

To continue your coroutines learning journey you may find it exciting to get to know some more advanced, topics, like **Channels** and **Flows**. The official documentation would be a great departing point! Those will help you to make use of *streams* of data, not just a single value. You can learn about Channels at https://kotlinlang.org/docs/reference/coroutines/channels.html and Flows at https://kotlinlang.org/docs/reference/coroutines/flow.html.

Moreover, there are several ways you could parallelize your code execution in Kotlin. One example is the reactive approach, which is becoming quite popular. **ReactiveX** or **Rx** is an API for asynchronous programming implemented by a wide variety of platforms and programming languages (e.g., Kotlin, Java, Swift, Python, etc.).

You can find out more about by reading the official RxKotlin documentation at https://github.com/ReactiveX/RxKotlin.

But the existence of different solutions doesn't mean that you need to choose only one. Kotlin coroutines and RxKotlin can successfully coexist in your project, as the APIs are designed to solve somewhat different programming problems. In different parts of your application, you can select the most appropriate one.

Also, you may want to get acquainted with other coroutine APIs available, such as:

- **kotlinx-coroutines-rx**: https://github.com/Kotlin/kotlinx.coroutines/tree/master/reactive/kotlinx-coroutines-rx2
- **kotlinx-coroutines-jdk8**: https://github.com/Kotlin/kotlinx.coroutines/tree/master/integration/kotlinx-coroutines-jdk8

In the next chapter, you'll have a chance to investigate the use of Kotlin away from the JVM, as a scripting tool.

Chapter 24: Scripting with Kotlin

By Ellen Shapiro

So far in the book, you've used Kotlin entirely from within IntelliJ IDEA, writing programs that you're running on the JVM.

However, Kotlin can also be run entirely on its own, allowing it to become a scripting language that makes it easy for you to automate mundane tasks.

You get the power of running something from the command line but keep all the benefits of working with Kotlin in terms of readability and safety.

> **IMPORTANT**: The remainder of this chapter assumes that you are running either macOS, Linux or some other Kotlin-supported Unix operating system (ex., FreeBSD or Solaris). If you're running Windows, you'll want to use either Cygwin (https://www.cygwin.com/) or the Windows 10 Subsystem for Linux (https://docs.microsoft.com/en-us/windows/wsl/install-win10) to be able to use the same commands shown here. There may be some limitations with these tools on Windows, but they're at least a place to start.

What is scripting?

Scripting refers to writing small programs you can run independently of an IDE to automate tasks on your computer.

A **script** is the small program that you write and run. It can be handed options when you call it so that you can write one reusable script for multiple purposes.

You'll often hear people talk about **shell scripting**, which is using `.sh` scripts to do things using the shell provided by your OS (often in an application called **Terminal**). Common shells are **bash**, **zsh**, and **fish**.

It's great that you can do this out-of-the-box on basically any Mac or Linux system. However, there are a number of issues with shell scripting that have led developers to pursue alternatives:

- Shell scripting is **not type-safe**. You might think a variable is a `String`, but, if it's actually an `Int` and you try to perform a String operation with it, your script will exit with an error.
- Shell scripting is **not compiled**. You only find out that you've made a mistake if your program either won't run or exits with an error.
- Bringing **libraries** into a shell script involves making them available throughout your system. This may not be behavior you want for many reasons, including security.
- Shell scripts can be very **difficult to read**. Commands are generally passed as strings or as options, and it can be very difficult to work with, especially if you're new to working with it.

Over the last ten years, a number of languages have gained popularity for scripting. **Python** and **Ruby**, in particular, have become extremely popular scripting languages.

However, while scripts written in either of those languages are vastly more readable than shell scripts, and they make bringing in libraries far safer, neither Python nor Ruby are type-safe in the way that Kotlin is. Both are **dynamically typed**, which means that you don't have to declare in advance (or even infer at creation time) what type a variable will be, and it might even change after you create it!

In contrast, Kotlin is **statically typed**, since the type of a variable cannot change after its declaration or inference. For example, when you write the following:

```
val three = 3
```

The variable `three` is *inferred* to have a type of `Int`. If you were to write:

```
val three: String = 3
```

You'd get an error, since you've explicitly declared the type of `three` to be a `String`, and the value `3` is not a `String`, it's an `Int`. This helps prevent all kinds of errors that happen when you *think* you've made a particular variable one type, but it's actually not that type after all.

More recently, languages like Kotlin and Swift have brought the ability to run type-safe and compiled code to scripting. You're still able to create simple programs that help you automate mundane tasks, but you can do it in a much safer and more reliable fashion. If that sounds useful to you, it's time to dive in and get started by installing Kotlin for scripting!

Installing Kotlin for scripting

Up to this point, your computer has been accessing Kotlin through your IDE, IntelliJ IDEA. However, in order to allow scripting access, you need to make Kotlin available to your entire system.

To do this, you're going to use a tool that allows management of SDKs for macOS and Linux called SDKMan! (https://sdkman.io) to install Kotlin for the command line.

> **Note**: Alternatively, there's a tutorial on the Kotlin website that helps walk you through other ways to install for macOS (such as Homebrew and MacPorts) and Ubuntu systems (Snap), and that also gives you instructions for a manual install. You can find the tutorial at https://kotlinlang.org/docs/tutorials/command-line.html and at https://brew.sh.

You **will** need an Internet connection for the rest of these installation steps.

Installing SDKMan!

> **Note**: If you've already got SDKMan! installed, skip to the "Installing Kotlin" section below.

If you're on macOS or Ubuntu Linux, open up the **Terminal** program. When it finishes loading, type in:

```
curl -s https://get.sdkman.io | bash
```

Press **Return** on Mac or **Enter** on PC (we'll call this "Press Enter" for the rest of the chapter). This will go to https://get.sdkman.io and install the latest version, which works with `bash` — the main command line shell on many Unix systems, including macOS and Linux.

> **Note**: If you're on non-Ubuntu flavors of Linux, any time this chapter references `Terminal`, it's referring to a `bash` shell. If you're running a flavor of Linux other than Ubuntu, you're most likely familiar with how your system allows input into a `bash` shell. Please use that instead of the `Terminal` application whenever `Terminal` is referenced.

> **IMPORTANT**: There may be some instructions that print out when the `curl` command finishes — these differ a bit from system to system. If there are any instructions printed out, please follow them before considering the installation complete and proceeding.

Once your installation of SDKMan! is complete, it's time to actually install Kotlin.

Installing Kotlin

Open a new Terminal — either a new window or a new tab if your shell program allows it — and install Kotlin using SDKMan! by typing the following command and pressing Enter:

```
sdk install kotlin
```

This will use SDKMan! to fetch the most recent binary of Kotlin, install it on your machine and make it available within your shell `$PATH`, which means that you will be able to execute Kotlin from any directory in your system.

Once the installation is complete, enter the following at the command line to validate that Kotlin is installed and available to your entire system:

```
which kotlin
```

This should print out a path similar to this one, replacing `[username]` with your actual username:

```
/Users/[username]/.sdkman/candidates/kotlin/current/bin/kotlin
```

Or this one:

```
/usr/local/bin/kotlin
```

Seeing this confirms that Kotlin was installed using SDKMan! and that it should be accessible to you whenever you're using `Terminal`.

To make sure everything is working correctly, type the following at the command line:

```
kotlinc-jvm
```

This will launch a **Read-Evaluate-Print-Loop**, or REPL.

Using the REPL

A REPL is essentially a tiny Kotlin program in which you can type things and have them execute immediately. When it launches, you'll see something like this:

```
ellen@MacBook-Pro Book % kotlinc-jvm
Welcome to Kotlin version 1.4.21 (JRE 1.8.0_91-b14)
Type :help for help, :quit for quit
>>>
```

Next to the >>> prompt where you see a blinking cursor, type in the following, then press Enter:

```
println("Hello, world!")
```

The way that a REPL works is fairly straightforward:

- It **reads** whatever you've entered at the prompt.
- It then **evaluates** whatever you've typed as if it were the contents of a Kotlin function.
- It then **prints** the results of the evaluation.
- Finally, it **loops** back around to the beginning, so it can start reading again when you enter something new.

In this case, printing the results of the evaluated `println` statement results in (surprise!) that statement being printed out:

```
ellen@MacBook-Pro Book % kotlinc-jvm
Welcome to Kotlin version 1.4.21 (JRE 1.8.0_91-b14)
Type :help for help, :quit for quit
>>> println("Hello, world!")

Hello, world!
>>>
>>> 
```

The REPL is also capable of more complex operations, and it has the full ability of the compiler to use type inference, though you'll notice very quickly that it lacks autocomplete.

It also has the ability to hold on to defined variables and constants that are used throughout a single session — from when you launch the REPL to when you quit it.

Type in the following to define a `val` that will be used throughout the current REPL session:

```
val groceries = listOf("apples", "ground beef", "toilet paper")
```

You'll note that, since you've stored the output into a `val`, it doesn't immediately print out when you press Enter. If you don't assign to a `val` or `var`, the result of the print portion of the REPL will print directly to the console.

As an example, enter the following:

```
groceries.joinToString("\n")
```

Immediately, a newline-separated list of your `groceries` strings will print out:

```
apples
ground beef
toilet paper
```

You can perform any operation in the REPL that you can do with the standard library, including using lambdas and the `it` parameter. Enter the following to count how many characters are in each word of your `groceries` list:

```
groceries.map { it.count() }
```

Immediately, you'll see print out:

```
[6, 11, 12]
```

You can even define a class in the REPL. Enter the following to create a super-basic `data class` to hold the name and cost of a grocery item:

```
data class Grocery(val name: String, val cost: Float)
```

Press Enter. At the next prompt, create a list of groceries with their costs:

```
val moreGroceries = listOf(Grocery("apples", 0.50f),
Grocery("ground beef", 5.25f), Grocery("toilet paper", 2.23f))
```

In addition to using the default `it` lambda parameter, you can also use Kotlin's ability to have named parameters in lambdas directly in the REPL.

Store the total cost into a variable by adding the following:

```
val cost = moreGroceries.fold(0.0f) { running, next ->
  running + next.cost
}
```

Finally, you can use Kotlin's string interpolation syntax the same way as you can in a normal class. Add the following to print out the total cost of your groceries:

```
println("Your groceries cost $cost")
```

When you press Enter, it will print out:

```
Your groceries cost 7.98
```

Now, exit the current REPL by typing:

```
:quit
```

When you press Enter, you'll see Terminal go back to its normal state rather than using >>> prompt in front of everything you're typing in. You can also press **Ctrl-D** on most systems to exit the REPL.

To see that nothing persists between sessions, launch the REPL again by typing:

```
kotlinc-jvm
```

When the REPL finishes launching and you see the >>> prompt again, try to print out the `groceries` constant from the previous session by entering:

```
println("$groceries")
```

When you press Enter, you'll see the following:

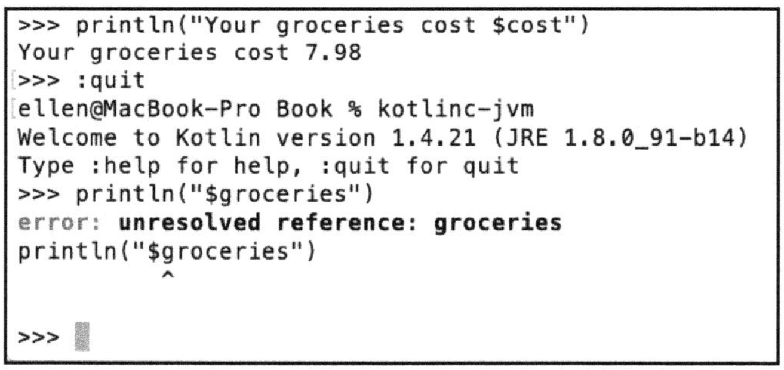

```
>>> println("Your groceries cost $cost")
Your groceries cost 7.98
>>> :quit
ellen@MacBook-Pro Book % kotlinc-jvm
Welcome to Kotlin version 1.4.21 (JRE 1.8.0_91-b14)
Type :help for help, :quit for quit
>>> println("$groceries")
error: unresolved reference: groceries
println("$groceries")
          ^

>>>
```

error: unresolved reference: groceries

The error means that the REPL doesn't know what `groceries` is — which it shouldn't, since that was in the previous run of the REPL, before you typed in `:quit`. As long as a single REPL is running, it can hold information in memory and reference that information. But as soon as you quit that REPL, all the information it was holding disappears along with it.

Now, you can type `:quit` again to get out of the second REPL you started. Being able to try stuff out in the REPL is really helpful if you just want to investigate something quickly from the standard library. But what if you want to do something more complex — or make it reusable? This is where using files for your Kotlin scripts comes in.

Creating script files

Kotlin script files are a unique type of Kotlin file. They compile as if the entire file is the `main()` function for a Kotlin program.

This difference is emphasized by the fact that they have a different file extension. Normal Kotlin files end in a `.kt` extension and require a `main()` function to begin a running program. Kotlin script files, on the other hand, end in `.kts`. You'll read a bit more about when to use which one a bit later in the chapter.

You can run either type of file via either IntelliJ IDEA or the command line. In fact, compiling and running from the command line is actually what IntelliJ IDEA has been doing under the hood the entire time you've been using it. The user interface simply boils this down into the happy green Play button since that's much easier to understand.

Running via the command line might seem more complicated, but, as you'll see with `.kts` files, it's actually easy. So let's get started!

Running a script from the command line

First, go in your computer's file browser to the **starter** directory for this chapter. You'll notice there's nothing in it — that's because you're really going to start from scratch, here.

Open a new **Terminal** instance, and `cd` into the **starter** directory. Once there, run the following command to create a new, empty Kotlin script file:

```
touch script.kts
```

Leave your **Terminal** open, as you're going to come back to it once or twice. Open up the **script.kts** file that was just created in any text editor (e.g., **Sublime Text**, **Atom**, **VS Code**, **vim** or **emacs**) — you'll get to editing it with IntelliJ IDEA, shortly. Update the file to add the following line:

```
println("Hello, scripting!")
```

> **Note**: If you're on macOS and using TextEdit, watch out that the system doesn't try to use "smart quotes" with your script because that can cause compilation issues. Make sure you're in text mode and not rich-text mode.

Save the **script.kts** file. Back in your **Terminal** window, enter the following command to run the script you just created:

```
kotlinc -script script.kts
```

Under the hood, the compiler will take your `.kts` file, compile it as if its contents were in a `main()` method that received the `args: List<String>` parameter, and then print out:

```
Hello, scripting!
```

Nice! But at this point, you're essentially back where you were with Python and Ruby. Easy to read and run, but you don't find out if anything is wrong until you fully compile the script.

If you really want to combine the power of scripting and the safety of a compiled language, you'll want to edit the `.kts` file in the same IDE you've been using all along — IntelliJ IDEA.

Running a script with IntelliJ IDEA

Quit your generic text editor and open up IntelliJ IDEA. If you close your other projects, you should land on this screen:

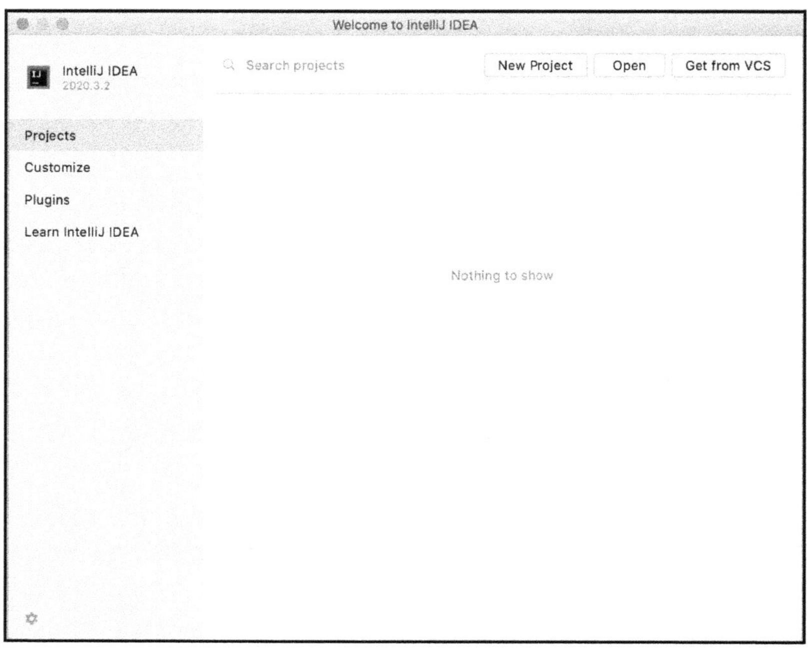

Select the **Open** option. You'll need to select the **starter** folder rather than the script itself:

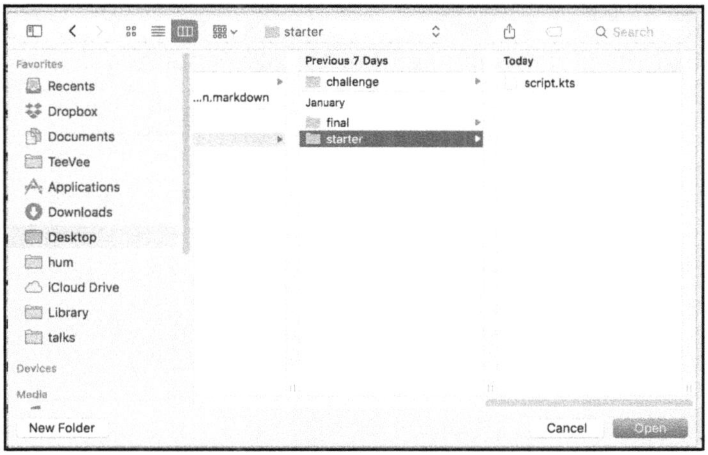

Your project will open and, in the sidebar, you'll see that you can now see your `.kts` file:

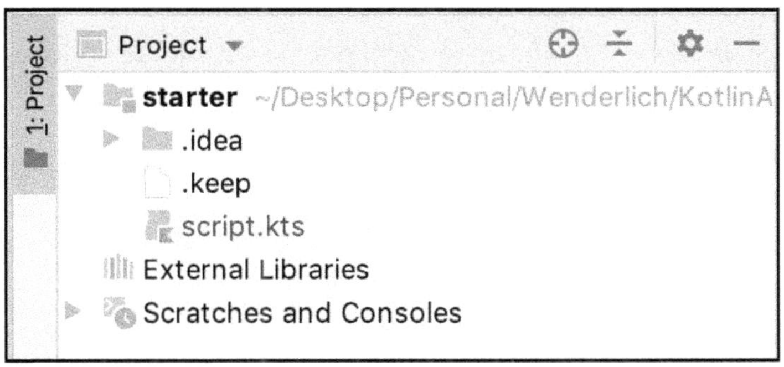

Open up the file, and you'll see the same thing you had previously, but with nice pretty syntax highlighting:

Note: You may see an error on the `println` function that says "Unresolved reference: println." Fear not, this will go away when you edit the project structure as you'll read in a bit.

You'll also probably notice that, since there is no `main` method, there is no Play button next to your line. You know this runs from running it on the command line — but how do you run it in IntelliJ IDEA?

In the upper right-hand corner of IntelliJ IDEA, there's a button that says **Add configuration:**

Click on it, and you'll see a screen where you can edit existing configurations or add new configurations that will run scripts for you.

In the top left-hand corner of this screen, there is a + button:

When you click on the +, a small window will pop up with some options for configurations. Select the **Kotlin script** option.

It will look like this:

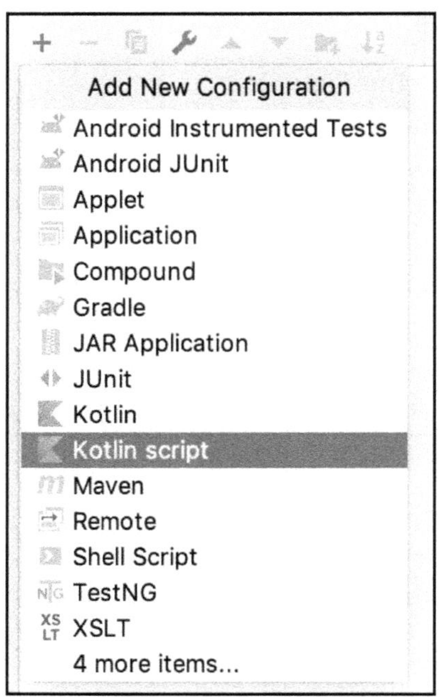

IntelliJ IDEA will create a configuration, and you'll be able to name it and select a script to run with it:

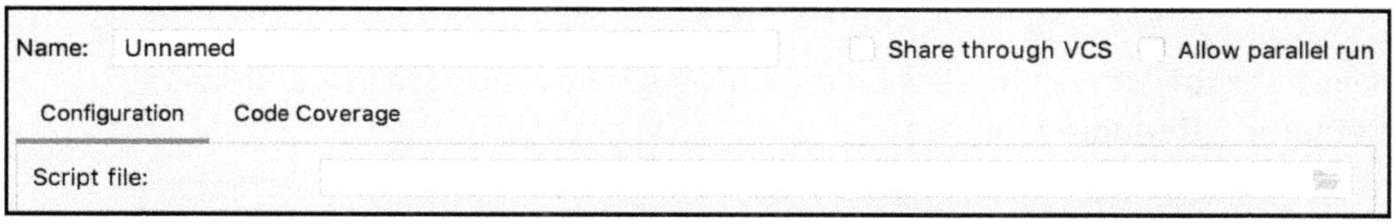

Name your configuration **Run Script**. Then, click the button on the far right of the **Script File:** text entry area. This will launch a file selector so you can choose what Kotlin script is run when this configuration is run.

Select your **script.kts** file and click **Open**:

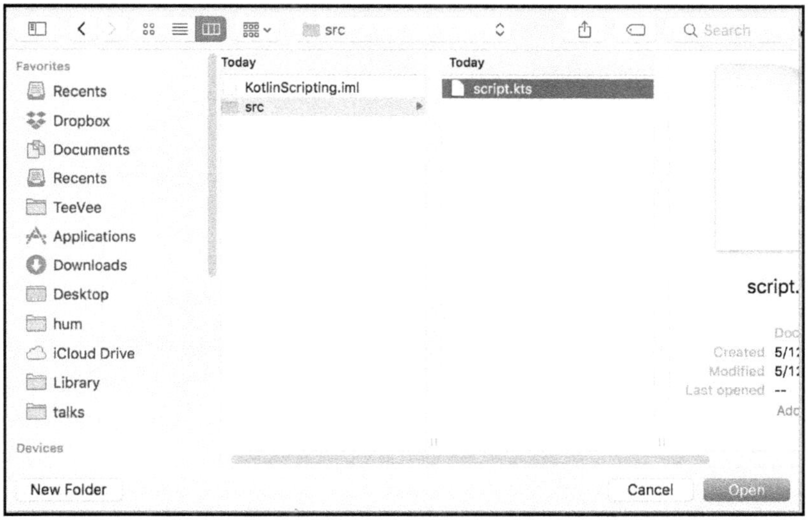

Once you've selected the file, you'll get kicked back to the configuration editor, and the path to the selected file will be filled in. Click the **Apply** button on the configuration editor, then click the **OK** button.

This will close the configuration editor, and you'll see that the configuration you just created is now displayed next to the Run/Play button in the top-right of IntelliJ IDEA:

Click the Run button, and you'll see in the console:

```
Hello, scripting!
```

One thing you may notice if you add to your script is that auto-completion is either very slow or not working at all – which defeats some of the point of using IntelliJ to edit the script. The good news is, a naming trick and some quick resets can fix this.

Select `script.kts`, right-click on it to bring up the context menu, and select **Refactor > Rename File**:

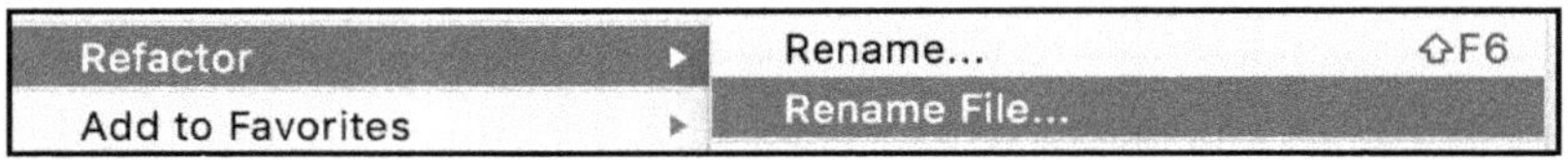

Update the name of the file to `script.main.kts` to help IntelliJ understand that this is a script meant to be run as the `main` of a program:

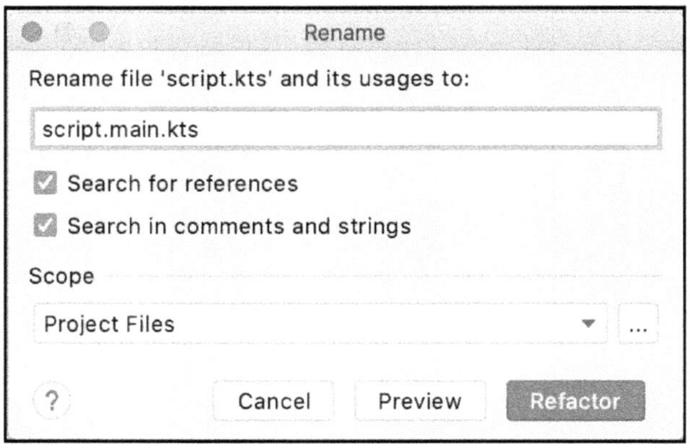

Click the **Refactor** button to finish renaming the file. Next, you'll need to manually clear the context of the script by going to **Tools > Tasks and Contexts > Clear Context**.

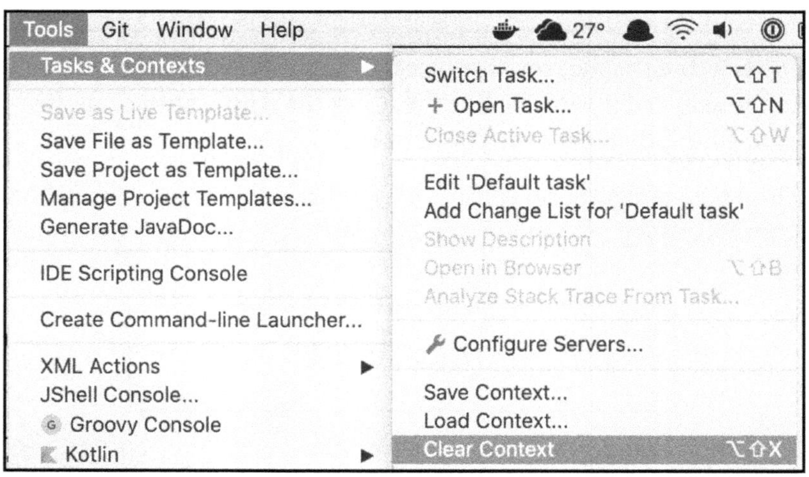

This will automatically close any open file. When you reopen `script.main.kts`, you should see a banner at the top that lets you know a new script context is available:

> **Note**: If this banner doesn't show up immediately, you may need to clear the context again – it can be a little tempermental.

Click **Apply Context**, and you'll now get syntax highlighting and autocomplete in your script without issue.

Woo hoo! Now it's time to figure out how to give your script the information it needs to be flexible: User input!

Handling arguments

An **argument**, when it comes to running a Kotlin script, is a string that you enter into the command line. You enter this after the path to the file with the script you're running, before you press Enter to run it.

You can separate multiple arguments with spaces, and they'll automatically be turned into a `List`. If you want to pass in a string with spaces as a single argument, you can put it in quotation marks.

As you'll recall, a `.kts` file essentially treats the entire contents of the file as the contents of a `fun main(args: List<String>)` method. If you'd been wondering what `args` is short for, now you know: arguments!

Even though you don't see the `args` declaration directly in your script, you can still access the arguments from the script.

Add the following lines to **script.main.kts** to print out a list of the arguments if any were received; this will also let you know if there weren't any arguments received:

```
if (args.isEmpty()) {
  println("[no args]")
} else {
  println("Args:\n ${args.joinToString("\n ")}")
}
```

Save the file, then click the Run button again. You'll see the script print out:

```
[no args]
```

So, how do you add arguments when running in IntelliJ IDEA? By using the configuration you created earlier. Click the drop-down where the run script is displayed, and select **Edit Configurations...**:

You'll see the configuration editor, and your current configuration — the one you created earlier — is selected by default.

You'll notice that one of the inputs is named **Program arguments**:

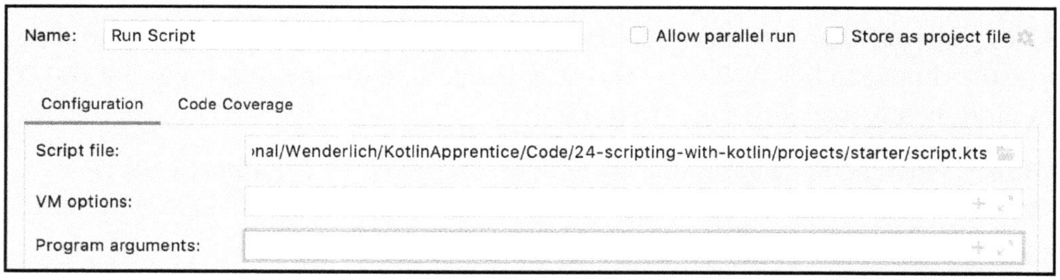

Into this input line, type:

```
hello
```

Then click the **OK** button to save your changes and dismiss the configuration editor. Run the configuration again, and you'll see the following included in the console output:

```
Args:
 hello
```

Excellent! Now, go back and select **Edit Configurations...** again. Update the program arguments to include your first and last name as a single argument, by putting both in quotation marks:

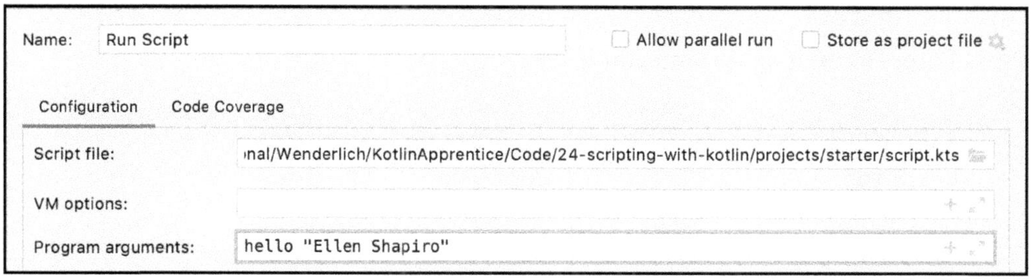

Run the program again, and you'll see:

```
Args:
 hello
 Ellen Shapiro
```

...although it'll be with your name instead of "Ellen Shapiro"!

You've probably noticed that making all these changes to the configuration is a real hassle. One of the ways you can improve the iteration time for changing parameters on your script is to continue to run it using the command line.

Remember that Terminal window you had open earlier, where you'd `cd`'d into the `starter` folder? Find that window again — or open a new Terminal window and `cd` into the `starter` folder again if you can't find the one you used before.

Previously, you ran `kotlinc -script script.kts` to run your script, but remember you changed the filename. Enter the same command using the new filename:

```
kotlinc -script script.main.kts
```

Press Enter. Here, it's much clearer that there are no arguments passed in, since there's nothing after the `script.main.kts` path. Indeed, the following will print:

```
[no args]
```

Press the Up Arrow key to bring up the last command, then type in some additional parameters, as shown here:

```
kotlinc -script script.main.kts Kotlin scripting is awesome
```

Press Enter to run it again, and you'll see:

```
Args:
 Kotlin
 scripting
 is
 awesome
```

Now, press the Up Arrow again. Use the Left and Right Arrow keys to go back and forth at the command line, adding quotes around the four arguments to turn them into one single argument:

```
kotlinc -script script.main.kts "Kotlin scripting is awesome"
```

Now, your output will only have a single argument:

```
Args:
 Kotlin scripting is awesome
```

As you can see, you get a much clearer and faster iteration than having to muck around with a configuration file. For the rest of these examples, you should keep IntelliJ IDEA open as a text editor to work on the script, so that you get the benefits of compile-time type checking. But you should run the program using a Terminal shell, after saving any changes using **File ▸ Save All** or pressing **Command-S** on Mac or **Ctrl-S** on PC.

Now, it's time to try to do something a little more useful: get and print out information about the filesystem.

Getting information from the system

Getting information about the filesystem is really helpful because you can use it in many different ways: moving files around, copying files, and figuring out how large files are or where they're located.

You're going to do something relatively simple here: print out the names of the files in a passed-in folder. It's a great example of how you can work with existing Kotlin and Java APIs for something that runs at the command line.

Even though with your script you're effectively in the `main()` function of a program, you can still add other functions and use things from the standard library really easily.

Here, since you're working with the filesystem, you're going to want to take advantage of some functionality which is built into the JDK: Its handling of files and folders through the **File** class.

`File` is actually a little bit misleading as a name for this class, because a `File` object could be either a file or a folder. In fact, it's quite easy using `File` to get the current working directory, which is a folder.

In **script.main.kts**, add a function below your argument parser:

```
fun currentFolder(): File {
  return File("").absoluteFile
}
```

You'll notice that, when you add the `File` return type, IntelliJ IDEA might automatically import the Java class at the top of your **script.main.kts** file:

```
import java.io.File
```

If it does not, you should be able to press **Option-Return** on Mac or **Alt-Enter** on PC to pull in the `import` statement. Even though you're already in a `main()` function, you can still import the libraries you need to make everything work. Neat!

Since the method you created passes in an empty string to the `File` object, by default, it will return the current working directory from which this script is called. Add a couple of lines to print the name of the current folder:

```
val current = currentFolder()
println("Current folder: $current")
```

Save the script in IntelliJ IDEA and then run the script again by pressing the Up Arrow key in Terminal and pressing Enter. At the bottom of the printout, you'll see (with `[fullpath]` replaced by the full path to wherever you've put the *Kotlin Apprentice* code):

```
Current folder: [fullpath]/KotlinApprentice/24-scripting-with-
kotlin/projects/starter
```

Excellent — your script now knows where you are. Now, it's time to find out a bit more about what's around you.

You've seen that you can add functions within a `.kts` script even though it's already inside a `main()` function. You can also use extension functions to add functionality to existing Kotlin or Java classes.

Add an extension function to `File` to get a `List<File>` of the contents of the current `File` object, which, as a reminder, is actually a folder:

```
fun File.contents(): List<File> {
  return this.listFiles().toList()
}
```

Update your line printing out the folder to the following, printing out the folder's contents instead, then save the script:

```
val current = currentFolder()
println("Current folder contents:\n $
{current.contents().joinToString("\n ")}")
```

Go back to Terminal and press the Up key to bring up the previous command, then press Enter. You'll see something like this:

```
Current folder contents:
 [fullpath]/KotlinApprentice/scripting-with-kotlin/projects/
starter/.DS_Store
 [fullpath]/KotlinApprentice/scripting-with-kotlin/projects/
starter/script.main.kts
 [fullpath]/KotlinApprentice/scripting-with-kotlin/projects/
starter/.idea
```

Note: If you're not on a system using macOS, you won't see the `.DS_Store` file — that's a type of file that's specific to the Mac filesystem.

If you've got your folder for this book buried deep in your filesystem, you'll probably realize that this is not giving you exceptionally useful information since there's so much other noise being printed.

Instead, below your extension function to get the `contents()` of a folder, add another extension function to get just the names of the files within the folder:

```
fun File.fileNames(): List<String> {
  return this.contents().map { it.name }
}
```

Next, update the line printing out the contents of the folder to use this new method:

```
println("Current folder contents:\n $
{current.fileNames().joinToString("\n "))}")
```

Save the script, go back to Terminal and press the Up key again to bring up the previous command, then press Enter. You'll now see something far shorter than you were seeing previously:

```
Current folder contents:
 .DS_Store
 script.main.kts
 .idea
```

Aha! Now, it's just the file names. But there aren't just file names in there — there are also folder names. Again, a `File` object could be a file or a folder. So how do you tell the difference?

`File` has two convenience properties to help with this: `isDirectory` and `isFile`. Using those, create two new extension methods to list out the folders and the files of a given `File` object:

```
fun File.folders(): List<File> {
  return this.contents().filter { it.isDirectory }
}

fun File.files(): List<File> {
  return this.contents().filter { it.isFile }
}
```

Update your `fileNames()` extension method to only return the names of files:

```
fun File.fileNames(): List<String> {
  return this.files().map { it.name }
}
```

Next, add another extension method that only returns the names of folders:

```
fun File.folderNames(): List<String> {
  return this.folders().map { it.name }
}
```

Now, it's time to pull everything into a convenience method so that you can access it more easily.

Add the following method:

```
fun File.printFolderInfo() {
  // 1
  println("Contents of `${this.name}`:")

  // 2
  if (this.folders().isNotEmpty()) {
    println("- Folders:\n   $
{this.folderNames().joinToString("\n   ")}")
  }

  // 3
  if (this.files().isNotEmpty()) {
    println("- Files:\n   ${this.fileNames().joinToString("\n
")}")
  }

  // 4
  println("Parent: ${this.parentFile.name}")
}
```

What's going on here?

1. You print the name of the current folder, so you know what you're printing information about.
2. You print a list of the names of the folders within the current folder, if there are any.
3. You print a list of the names of the files within the current folder, if there are any.
4. You print information about the parent `File` object — which, again, is actually a folder.

Now, remove the existing line in your code printing information about `current` and replace it with a line that calls this new convenience method:

```
current.printFolderInfo()
```

Save the script, go back to Terminal, press the Up key once more to bring up the last command, and then press Enter. You should see something like:

```
Contents of `starter`:
- Folders:
   .idea
- Files:
   .DS_Store
   script.main.kts
```

```
Parent: projects
```

Now that you're successfully printing the contents of the current folder, it's time to start using the power of command line arguments so that you can print the information of any arbitrary folder in your system!

Adding arguments

Often, arguments are passed in with the format `name=Value`. This makes it easy to detect which argument is for what purpose, no matter what the order of arguments is.

At the bottom of **script.main.kts**, create a function to check for an argument prefix, then return the value for that argument if something was actually passed in for the argument:

```
fun valueFromArgsForPrefix(prefix: String): String? {
  val arg = args.firstOrNull { it.startsWith(prefix) }

  if (arg == null) return null

  val pieces = arg.split("=")
  return if (pieces.size == 2) {
    pieces[1]
  } else {
    null
  }
}
```

Next, below the function `valueFromArgsForPrefix()`, add some lines to look for a particular prefix for an argument:

```
val folderPrefix = "folder="
val folderValue = valueFromArgsForPrefix(folderPrefix)
```

Then, add code to print info about either the passed-in folder or the current working directory if no folder was passed in:

```
if (folderValue != null) {
  val folder = File(folderValue).absoluteFile
  folder.printFolderInfo()
} else {
  println("No path provided, printing working directory info")
  currentFolder().printFolderInfo()
}
```

Next, save the script then go back to **Terminal** and type in:

```
pwd
```

Press Enter. This will print out something similar to:

```
/Users/ellen/Desktop/Wenderlich/KotlinApprentice/scripting-with-
kotlin/projects/starter
```

It will, however, have a different prefix based on the location of the code for this book depending on where you put it on your hard drive. Copy this value by selecting it and pressing **Command-C** on Mac or **Ctrl-Shift-C** on PC.

Next, press the Up button on your keyboard twice — once to get `pwd` and then another time to get your parameters back. You should see:

```
kotlinc -script script.main.kts "Kotlin scripting is awesome"
```

Press Enter to see what happens now if you don't pass a folder in, and you'll see the same folder information you saw before:

```
No path provided, printing working directory info
Contents of `starter`:
- Folders:
   .idea
- Files:
   .DS_Store
   script.main.kts
Parent: projects
```

Now, it's time to actually pass in a folder. Press Up one more time to bring up the command and parameters. This time, add the folder parameter by typing `folder=`, then pasting in the path you printed out earlier of the current working directory.

You should see something like this, though with your own path to the *Kotlin Apprentice* folder:

```
kotlinc -script script.main.kts "Kotlin scripting is awesome"
folder=/Users/ellen/Desktop/Wenderlich/KotlinApprentice/
scripting-with-kotlin/projects/starter
```

Delete the `/starter` at the end of this line so that the `folder` parameter ends with `/projects` — this will give you the contents of the `projects` folder. Press Enter again, and you'll see:

```
Contents of `projects`:
- Folders:
   starter
   final
   challenge
- Files:
   .DS_Store
```

You can continue altering the path for the folder to be whatever you want it to be — and the contents of the folder will always print out. You'll run into an issue if you try to pass in the root folder of your filesystem using `folder=/`; see if you can find the cause of the error in the script and fix it.

Congratulations! You've now learned how to write a Kotlin script, how to run it from both IntelliJ IDEA and the command line, and how to make your script do different things based on the arguments passed in when the script is run.

Challenges

1. In the script you created to list the contents of a directory, add a way to decide from a passed-in parameter whether hidden files (i.e., files that start with a `.` and so are not normally rendered visible in your filesystem browser) should be included in the list of things printed out or not. You should default to not showing hidden files in the list.
2. Create a Kotlin script to take a string and change its letters by using a **ROT-n** encoder: offset each letter by `n` places in the 26-letter English alphabet, then print out the scrambled string.
3. In your ROT-n script, add handling for an argument that tells you how many letters your script should rotate by.
4. Figure out a way to call your your ROT-n script repeatedly in order to get back the same string you put in. No, you may not use ROT-26, smarty-pants.

Key points

- **Scripting** is writing small programs in a text editor that can be run from the command line and be used to do various types of processing on your computer.
- As a scripting language, Kotlin gives you the **static-typing** lacking in other scripting languages like Python and Ruby.
- Kotlin comes with a **Read-Evaluate-Print Loop** or REPL that can be used to investigate Kotlin code in an interactive manner.
- Kotlin scripts end with the extension `.kts`, as opposed to normal Kotlin code that ends with `.kt`.
- You can use IntelliJ IDEA as a script editor, and then either run your scripts within the IDE or from a command line shell on your OS.
- Kotlin scripts run inside a hidden `main()` function and can access `args` passed into the script at the command line. Scripts can also import Kotlin and Java libraries to access their features.
- You can use Kotlin scripts to read and write to the files and folders on your filesystem, and much more!

Where to go from here?

The tool `kscript` (https://github.com/holgerbrandl/kscript) provides a convenient wrapper around Kotlin scripting. It allows pre-compilation of scripts, which results in much faster iteration, and it also allows you to use a simpler syntax for accessing Kotlin at runtime. The creator gave a talk at KotlinConf 2017 which is worth watching for a great outline of some of the problems he was trying to solve. You can watch it at https://www.youtube.com/watch?v=cOJPKhlRa8c.

In the next chapter, you'll see an alternative to Kotlin scripting: building native command-line programs with Kotlin. You'll also begin to prepare yourself to work with Kotlin on multiple platforms!

Chapter 25: Kotlin/Native

By Victoria Gonda

While Kotlin began its existence focused on the JVM, it has since expanded in scope to include native and web development. In fact, as you'll see in the next chapter "Kotlin Multiplatform", alongside its popularity in Android development, you can even use Kotlin to assist in building iOS apps.

The technology used to bring Kotlin beyond the JVM is called **Kotlin/Native**. Kotlin/Native allows you to compile Kotlin code outside of virtual machines, resulting in self-contained binaries that are native to the environment in which they're run. The Kotlin/Native compiler was announced in 2017, and in late 2018 reached version 1.0.

While this chapter looks at **Kotlin/Native** specifically, You can also use **Kotlin/JS** to compile Kotlin code to JavaScript.

> **Note**: If you want to learn more about Kotlin/JS, you can check out the docs at https://kotlinlang.org/docs/reference/js-overview.html.

In previous chapters, you've used IntelliJ IDEA to create and run Kotlin code. IntelliJ utilized the version of the Kotlin compiler for the JVM to build and run Java bytecode. In this chapter, you'll see how to install and use the Kotlin/Native compiler outside of IntelliJ in order to create native binaries that can be run outside the JVM.

Konan and LLVM

This diagram below shows the process through which Kotlin/Native takes Kotlin code and turns it into native code.

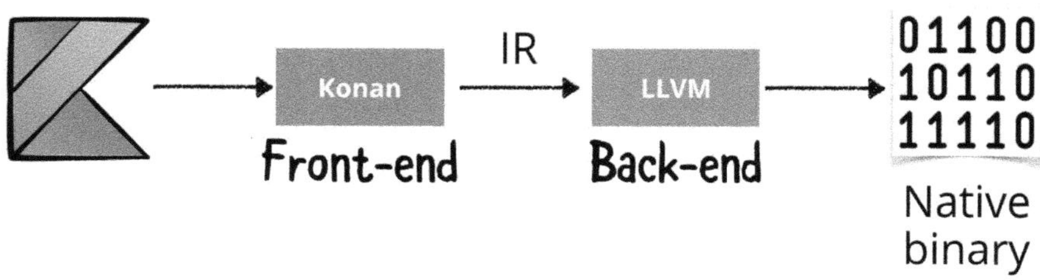

The Kotlin/Native compiler itself is named **Konan**. Konan handles the **front-end** of the process, compiling the Kotlin source code into an **Intermediate Representation (IR)** that is the input to the **back-end** of the process. Kotlin/Native leverages the **LLVM compiler** for the back-end.

If you're not familiar with LLVM, at one point it stood for "Low-Level Virtual Machine", but it actually has nothing to do with virtual machines as the term is used today. The name is now just a stand-alone acronym.

LLVM was created initially by a team led by Chris Lattner, who also led the team that created the Swift language at Apple. LLVM is a set of components that optimize IR code and compile it to machine-dependent binaries.

By combining Konan with LLVM, Kotlin/Native lets you produce native executables from your Kotlin code. In theory, Kotlin/Native can be used on any platform supported by LLVM.

Installation

You can download v1.4.20 or later of Kotlin/Native from GitHub: https://github.com/JetBrains/kotlin-native/releases. There are a number of development builds released there, and you may want to stick to downloading the latest stable version. Distributions are available for macOS, Windows, and Linux.

> **Note**: This chapter uses the macOS compiler. If you're not using macOS, make sure you're downloading the correct compiler for your machine.

For example, go to the download page https://github.com/JetBrains/kotlin/releases/tag/v1.4.20. At the bottom of the page, you can download a tarball of Kotlin/Native for macOS: **kotlin-native-macos-1.4.20.tar.gz**.

If you do a web search instead, be careful searching for things like "install kotlin compiler macos" or using **Homebrew** with "brew install kotlin". That will lead you to installing the same **kotlin-jvm** compiler that you used with SDKMan! in Chapter 24, "Scripting with Kotlin." to install in Chapter 24, "Scripting with Kotlin." That version of the Kotlin compiler turns Kotlin source code into Java bytecode, and not the Kotlin/Native compiler Konan uses for making native executables.

You'll see another example of using the kotlin-jvm compiler in this chapter's challenges, but the rest of the chapter itself is focused on using Kotlin/Native.

In a terminal window, navigate to wherever you downloaded the compiler:

```
cd ~/Downloads/
```

Then, untar and unzip the file.

```
tar -xzvf kotlin-native-macos-1.4.20.tar.gz
```

> **Note**: If you're directly copying the command from above, make sure the file name is correct for the version you downloaded. You may need to modify the command to match.

Then, move the resulting folder to a location in your home directory, for example, a **bin** folder.

For example:

```
mv kotlin-native-macos-1.4.20 /usr/local/bin
```

Next `cd` into that folder and take a look at what's inside using `tree -L 2`:

```
cd /usr/local/bin/kotlin-native-macos-1.4.20
tree -L 2
```

> **Note**: If you're on macOS, you may need to install tree using `brew install tree`

```
→ kotlin-native-macos-1.4.20 tree -L 2
.
├── README.md
├── RELEASE_NOTES.md
├── bin
│   ├── cinterop
│   ├── generate-platform
│   ├── jsinterop
│   ├── klib
│   ├── konan-lldb
│   ├── konanc
│   ├── kotlinc
│   ├── kotlinc-native
│   └── run_konan
├── klib
│   ├── cache
│   └── common
├── konan
│   ├── konan.properties
│   ├── lib
│   ├── nativelib
│   ├── platformDef
│   ├── platforms
│   └── targets
├── licenses
│   ├── LICENSE.txt
│   ├── NOTICE.txt
│   └── third_party
├── sources
│   ├── kotlin-stdlib-common-sources.zip
│   ├── kotlin-stdlib-native-sources.zip
│   ├── kotlin-test-annotations-common-sources.zip
│   ├── kotlin-test-common-sources.zip
│   ├── org.jetbrains.kotlinx.kotlinx-cli-common-sources.zip
│   └── org.jetbrains.kotlinx.kotlinx-cli-native-sources.zip
└── tools
    ├── env_blacklist
    └── konan_lldb.py

14 directories, 22 files
```

You see a few different items in the **bin** subfolder including **konanc** and **kotlinc**, the compilers you need for Kotlin/Native code. If you run a `diff` command on the two files, you see that they are in fact identical.

```
diff bin/kotlinc bin/konanc
```

Doing a `less` on either file, you can see that both reference a shell script named **run_konan**:

```
less bin/konanc
```

You'll want to add the **bin** subfolder of the Kotlin/Native distribution into your path by adding an export like this to your **.bashrc** file (or the equivalent for your shell):

```
export PATH="$PATH:/usr/local/bin/kotlin-native-macos-1.4.20/
bin"
```

Then run a `source` command on your **.bashrc** file to make the path update take effect in your current terminal session.

```
source ~/.bashrc
```

If you've also installed the kotlin-jvm compiler, for example, like in Chapter 24 using SDKMan! or by using Homebrew on macOS, then you need to be careful to make sure you're using the right version of the Kotlin compiler when you want to compile code to native binaries and not to Java bytecode. If you stick to using **konanc** and not **kotlinc**, then you'll be sure to be using the Kotlin/Native version and not the kotlin-jvm version.

Another important point to make is that when you use Kotlin/Native with IDEs such as **IntelliJ IDEA** and **Android Studio**, the build plugins you use with **Gradle** will install a separate version of the Kotlin/Native compiler than the one you just installed. So in that case you don't need to associate the downloaded compiler with your IDE in any way; the IDE will use its own version of the compiler, based on settings in the build files.

Hello, Kotlin/Native

With a Kotlin/Native compiler in place, you can now proceed to write your first native program in Kotlin.

You can use IntelliJ IDEA to create and run Kotlin/Native code, or you can use a plain text editor. Creating a Kotlin/Native project in IntelliJ usually uses Gradle as the build system. In this chapter, you're working outside of Gradle and manually compiling the Kotlin code yourself.

Modern text editors will often have plugins for coding in languages like Kotlin, adding features such as syntax highlighting and code completion. For example, **Visual Studio Code** has a “Kotlin Language” extension. That extension does not provide code completion at this time, but does do syntax highlighting.

Create a new file in your text editor of choice and save it as **hello.kt**.

In the file, create a `main` function just like you have in previous chapters for code that ran on the JVM:

```
fun main() {

}
```

In earlier versions of Kotlin prior to 1.3, you had to supply `main` with an `args` parameter of type `Array<String>`, but now that's no longer necessary if you aren't going to use command-line arguments.

Add a single print statement to `main()`, and print the string “Hello, Kotlin/Native!”.

```
println("Hello, Kotlin/Native!")
```

Save the file then switch to a terminal window and enter the command to compile the code into a native executable.

```
konanc -o hello hello.kt
```

The `-o` option lets you specify the name of the output executable. The command as written must be run in the same directory as the **hello.kt** file.

Go ahead and run the compiler command. The first time you compile a file with `konanc`, it's going to take a few minutes, since the Kotlin compiler will download the files it needs to do the compilation, including the LLVM compiler. After your first run of `konanc`, compiles will take much less time.

When the command is done, do an `ls -l` command to see the output file, **hello.kexe**. The **kexe** extension denotes “Kotlin executable”. Typically you'll want to remove that extension since it's not a standard Unix convention.

If you don't use the `-o` option, the default output filename is **program.kexe**.

Next, run `./hello.kexe` and see the native executable run:

```
Hello, Kotlin/Native!
```

The file **hello.kexe** is a native binary for macOS. The file was produced using Konan and LLVM. There is no Java bytecode to be found as far as the native binary is concerned, and you do not need the JVM to run the file.

Kotlin Standard Library

One thing you may notice is that, when compiled with v1.4.20 of Kotlin/Native, the executable file **hello.kexe** is about 945 KB on macOS, which is over 100 times larger than the executable for an equivalent program written in C would be. That large size is because the **Kotlin standard library** is statically linked in to the executable file.

This means that you're free to use anything in the standard library in your program.

You can see that by adding something like a list into the program using the standard library `listOf()` function.

```
val numbers = listOf(1, 2, 3)
```

Then you can print out the size of the list.

```
println(numbers.size)
```

Go ahead and add that code and recompile the executable using the same command as before:

```
konanc -o hello hello.kt
```

Then run the executable file again. You'll see the size of the small list printed to the console.

Notice that, when including the standard library call to `listOf()`, you don't need to do any imports or do any special link command when you re-compile the file.

Challenges

1. Create a Kotlin/Native program similar to the first one you wrote, but this time with some more standard library code. In particular, try printing out the squares of all even integers less than or equal to 100.

   As a hint, you can use the `map` and `filter` functions to do this. Also, you can use a range operator and the `toList()` function to make a list of numbers:

   ```
   val numbers = (1..100).toList()
   ```

2. Compile the code from the last challenge with the kotlin-jvm compiler instead of Kotlin/Native. Remember that the `kotlinc` here needs to be different than the version that comes with Kotlin/Native. You can get this one via Homebrew using `brew install kotlin`.

   Watch out on setting up your path correctly so that you know which version of the compiler you are using, Kotlin/Native or kotlin-jvm. Homebrew will typically install in **/usr/local/bin**, so you can use that full path in order to make sure you're using the kotlin-jvm version.

   A hint here is that you can compile using:

```
/usr/local/bin/kotlinc evensquares.kt
```

This will produce Java bytecode in a file named **EvenSquaresKt.class**. You can then run that bytecode on the JVM using:

```
/usr/local/bin/kotlin EvensquaresKt
```

This is similar to the process you would use when compiling Java code with the `javac` compiler and running with the `java` command.

Key points

- **Kotlin/Native** is used to compile Kotlin code to native binaries that can be run without virtual machines and Kotlin runtimes.
- The name of the Kotlin/Native compiler is **Konan**. The command to run Konan is `konanc`.
- Kotlin/Native leverages the **LLVM** compiler to produce native binaries. Konan acts as a front-end for LLVM, producing an Intermediate Representation for LLVM.
- The Kotlin/Native compiler can be installed from it's GitHub page at https://github.com/JetBrains/kotlin-native/releases.
- When installing the Kotlin/Native compiler, be sure to distinguish it from the kotlin-jvm compiler used to create Java bytecode.
- Kotlin/Native code starts with a `main` function, similar to other C-like languages.
- The Kotlin standard library is statically linked to Kotlin/Native executables.

Where to go from here?

Now that you've got a handle on the use of Kotlin/Native and what it's for, the next chapter will utilize Kotlin/Native in the context of a Kotlin Multiplatform project. Kotlin/Native will be used by your IDE to compile shared Kotlin code for use on iOS.

If you want to dig deeper into Kotlin/Native, a good place to start is the Kotlin/Native page on the Kotlin language web site: https://kotlinlang.org/docs/reference/native-overview.html.

Chapter 26: Kotlin Multiplatform

By Victoria Gonda

As of 2019, Kotlin is the preferred language to use for Android development. On iOS, the Swift language has replaced Objective-C as the de facto development language.

Swift and Kotlin have a multitude of similarities, including static typing, type safety, support for the functional and OOP paradigms, and safe-handling of null values. The languages are also syntactically very similar.

The advent of Kotlin/Native has opened up the possibility of integrating Kotlin code into your iOS projects. In fact, the **Kotlin Multiplatform (KMP)** approach is beginning to take off as a cross-platform toolset for iOS, Android, and beyond.

In this chapter, you'll use **Android Studio** and **Xcode** to create a KMP project.

> **Note**: Because KMP can also be used with JavaScript, in documentation you might also see reference to **KMM** which is Kotlin Multiplatform Mobile, KPM specifically used for Android and iOS.

The KMP Approach

Typical apps on iOS and Android pull down data from the Internet, parse the data into objects within the app code, and cache some of the network data locally in a database.

For iOS, you might use a library like **Alamofire** for networking and something like **JSONSerialization** to parse the data received from the network into objects. You'd use **Core Data** to store the data locally in a database.

You'd implement an architecture pattern like **MVVM** to structure your app code. You might use a library like **RxSwift** to make your code more declarative. And you'd have tests for the view models and other parts of the app. You'd show lists of data in a **UITableView** in a **UIViewController**.

On Android, you'd have analogs of all of that code. You might use **Retrofit** for networking, **Gson** or **Moshi** for parsing the JSON, **Room** for storing the data in a database, a pattern like **MVP** or **MVVM** for the architecture, and maybe use **RxJava** in the app. You'd repeat similar tests. And you'd show list data in a **RecyclerView** in an **Activity** or **Fragment** using an adapter.

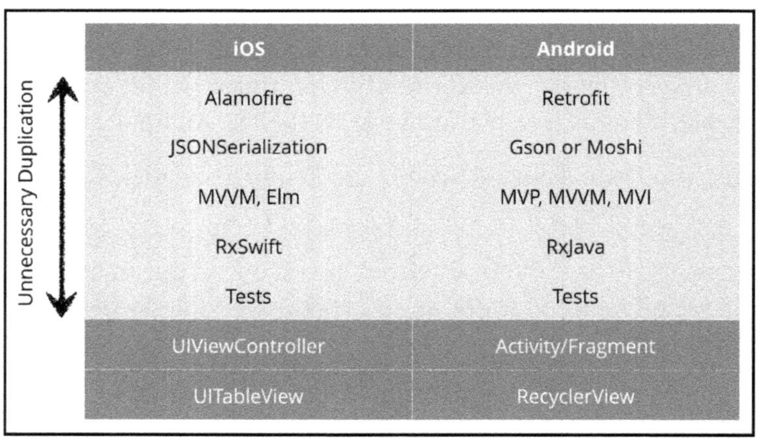

That's a lot of duplication even for a simple app. Imagine that there were numerous screens in your app, with more data, networking calls, and local caching of the remote data, as there would be in a full-featured app. The amount of code duplication would grow essentially linearly with the size of the app, as would the amount of time and effort to first produce and then maintain the two apps for the two platforms.

Other Cross-Platform Frameworks

Reducing this duplication in targeting both iOS and Android has long been a vision of many developers and organizations in the mobile world. Early attempts included web frameworks such as **PhoneGap**.

Organizations like Microsoft have produced tools like **Xamarin**, which uses C# and .NET to target iOS and Android. **React Native**, a derivative of the **React** web framework from Facebook, has become a popular modern framework for mobile. Most recently, Google has released the cross-platform framework **Flutter**, which uses its own runtime to allow apps written in **Dart** to perform at native speeds on iOS and Android.

These and other cross-platform toolkits have had great promise, but none have truly taken hold in the mobile development world. There are many reasons for this, some technical, others, less technical. Just a few of the reasons are poor performance of the resulting apps, inconsistencies with the native user interfaces, an inability to stay up-to-date with the latest iOS and Android features, and developer loyalty to and expertise with the native SDKs.

This is where Kotlin Multiplatform comes in. It's not a cross-platform framework. In fact, it's not a framework at all. It's more of an approach to mobile app development that in some ways gives you the best of all possible worlds.

Kotlin Multiplatform has a number of distinct advantages over the other approaches:

- Android developers can leverage their Kotlin skills within shared code used by both the iOS and Android apps.
- iOS developers can use their knowledge of Swift to quickly get up to speed with Kotlin and contribute to the shared Kotlin code.
- The Android UI code remains Kotlin, and the iOS UI code remains in Swift, so the user interfaces can take advantage of the latest improvements on both platforms.
- Performance of both the iOS and Android apps matches the performance of purely platform-specific native apps.

Like the other approaches to cross-platform, Kotlin Multiplatform promises to cut down on the time and effort required to produce apps for both iOS and Android.

Sharing Code

With Kotlin Multiplatform, you reduce code duplication by putting code common to all front-end apps into one module or shared project. This includes business logic, and things like networking code, data parsing, data persistence, and more.

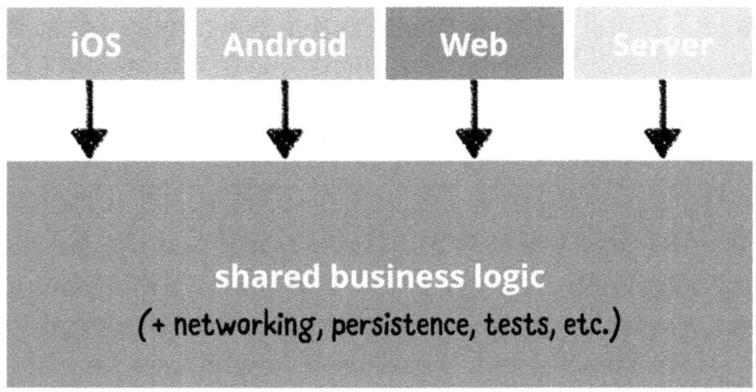

You can use various architectural patterns, and in a large app, you might consider something like **Clean Architecture**, where all the inner layers of the software are shared between front-ends, and only the outermost layer is unique to a given platform such as iOS, Android, Web, or Server. This significantly reduces the amount of duplication in the software, as most or all of the logic and functionality is only written in one place.

Another benefit of KMP, especially on a larger app development project, is that you can divide your team up into groups that work in different areas. You can have a group dedicated to the shared code, a group dedicated to the Android user interface, and a group dedicated to the iOS user interface. Each of these groups can have subgroups for a larger app.

An additional possible benefit, if your team's expertise is favored towards Kotlin, is that you can even write the iOS user interface code in Kotlin instead of Swift. This is not recommended in general, as it goes somewhat against the grain of what can be achieved with Kotlin Multiplatform. But it may be a good approach for an independent Android developer looking to create an iOS version of their app.

HelloKMP

You're going to build a simple app named **HelloKMP** that shares Kotlin code between iOS and Android apps. You'll start in Android Studio and first setup the Android app project and the project level build files for the entire KMP project.

You'll want to use Android Studio 4.1 or later with SDK 30 or later installed and Kotlin plugin 1.4.20 in order to follow along.

> **Note**: If you don't have Android Studio installed, you can get it at https://developer.android.com/studio/.

Open Android Studio and click the **Create New Project** link on the welcome screen.

Then choose **Empty Activity** and hit **Next**.

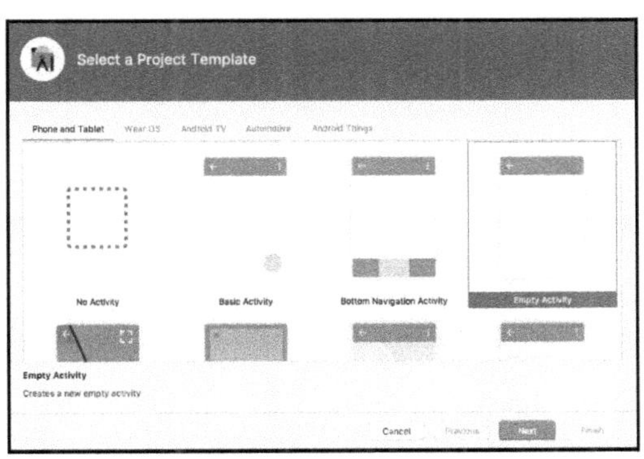

Name the project **HelloKMP**. The package name should be something like `com.raywenderlich.hellokmp`, and the language is Kotlin. Choose a location for the project and use API 21 for the minimum Android SDK level supported. Then click **Finish**.

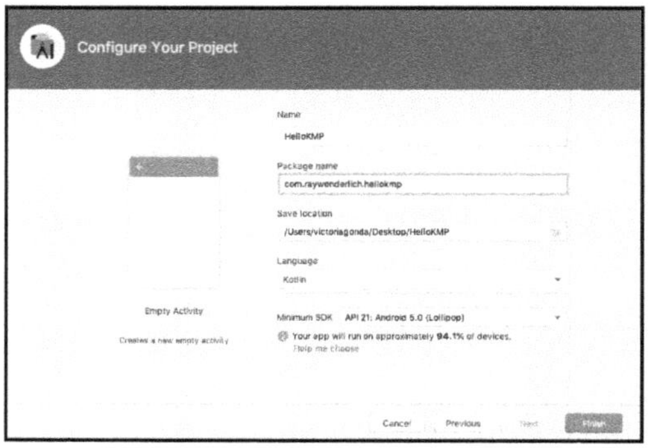

The project will open and a **Gradle** build will run.

In an Android emulator, run the initial Android app to make sure it builds and runs.

Renaming the app folder

The name of the android **app** folder is ideally something like **androidApp** instead of just the default **app**, in order to distinguish that part of the project as being the Android app.

To rename the folder, right click on the folder name and select **Refactor ▸ Rename.**

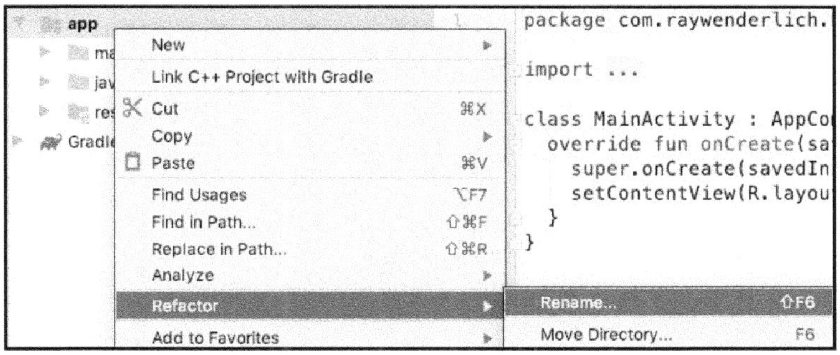

When prompted, select **Rename module**.

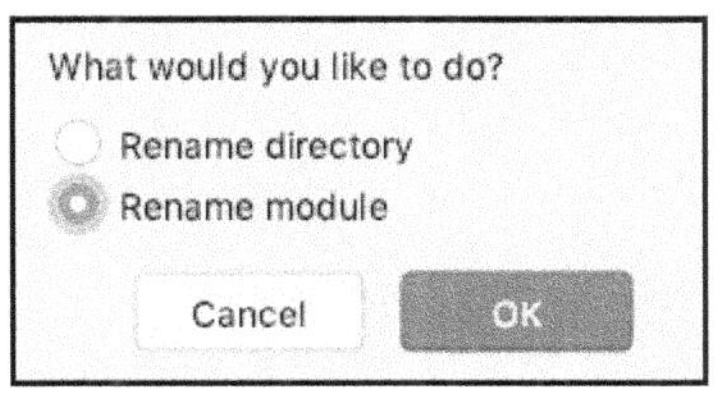

Then, enter **androidApp** as the name.

Finally, build and run the Android app in an emulator to make sure all is good after these changes.

Shared project

You're going to build up the shared project more or less by hand. That way, you'll see all that goes into creating the shared project.

In a terminal window and from the root of the HelloKMP project, first make directories for the shared project, using the -p option which creates parent directories as needed:

```
mkdir -p shared/src/androidMain/kotlin
mkdir -p shared/src/commonMain/kotlin
mkdir -p shared/src/iosMain/kotlin
```

You've made **commonMain**, **androidMain**, and **iosMain** folders.

Next, use the touch command to add the Kotlin source files you'll start with, along with a **build.gradle.kts** file for the shared project:

```
touch shared/src/commonMain/kotlin/common.kt
touch shared/src/androidMain/kotlin/android.kt
touch shared/src/iosMain/kotlin/ios.kt
touch shared/build.gradle.kts
```

Back in Android Studio, switch the **Project** panel to **Project** view to see the folder and file structure of the project, including the folders and files you just added.

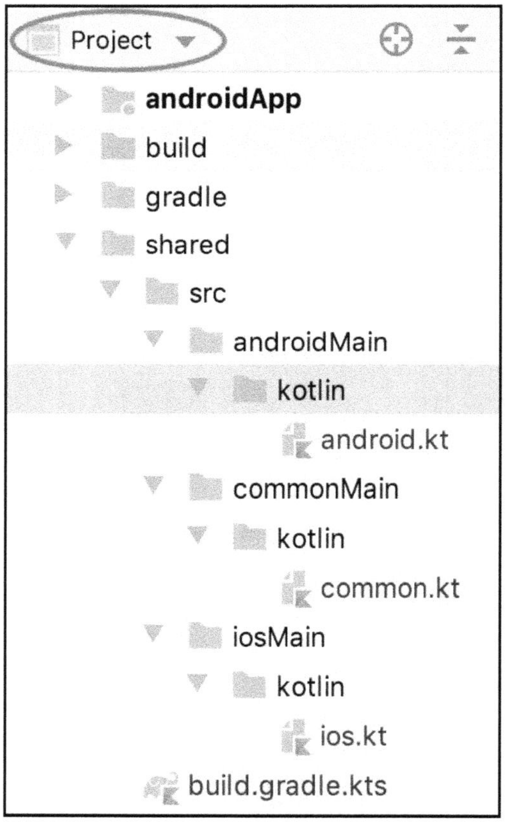

Configuring your environment

To work with Kotlin Multiplatform projects in Android Studio, you need to download the Kotlin Multiplatform Mobile plugin. Open **Preferences ▸ Plugins ▸ Marketplace** and search for **Kotlin Multiplatform Mobile**.

Install the plugin and restart Android Studio.

> **Note**: There are generators to create Kotlin Multiplatform modules and apps included in this plugin. This chapter is not using them so you can learn the individual parts.

Shared code build file

The shared code will be turned into the a **jar** file for running with the Android app, and an iOS **framework** for running with the iOS app. The shared project **build.gradle.kts** file is a Kotlin file where you will specify how that is done.

First, update the **settings.gradle** file at the project root to include building the shared code. Before the include for **androidApp**, add:

```
include ':shared'
```

Next, you turn to writing the build file for the shared project, **shared/build.gradle.kts**.

First, set up the **multiplatform** plugin in order to pull in the compilers you need, such as the Kotlin/Native compiler.

```
plugins {
  kotlin("multiplatform")
  id("com.android.library")
}
```

If you see a popup indicating that there is a new build context, be sure to accept the proposed change.

Add a `kotlin` section to define your targets:

```
kotlin {

}
```

Inside the `kotlin` section, first define some targets:

```
android()
ios {
  binaries {
    framework {
      baseName = "shared"
    }
  }
}
```

This means you're targeting both iOS and Android.

Then, add `sourceSets` sections to the `kotlin` section, in which you define dependencies for the shared code:

```
sourceSets {
  val commonMain by getting
  val androidMain by getting {
    dependencies {
      implementation("com.google.android.material:material:
1.2.1")
    }
  }
  val iosMain by getting
}
```

Having made changes to Gradle files in the project, you can finish up by syncing the project files to make sure there are no errors. The first sync will take awhile, since Android Studio needs to pull down the Kotlin/Native compiler.

expect and actual

Compiling the entire shared project for all platforms is not the approach taken by Kotlin Multiplatform. Instead, a certain amount of code is common to all platforms, but some amount of the shared code is unique to each platform. Kotlin includes the **expect/actual** mechanism to allow for this.

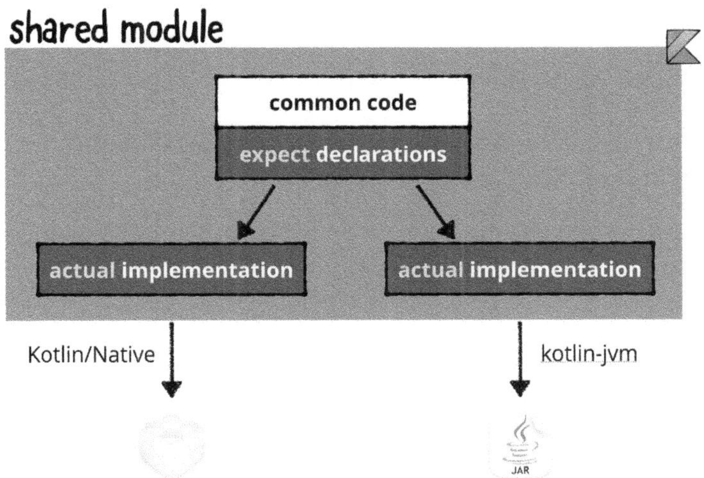

You can think of `expect` as defining something like an **interface** in Kotlin or a **protocol** in Swift. You use `expect` to say that the shared common code *expects* something to be available in the compiled code for all platforms. You then use `actual` to give the *actual* version of that something for each separate platform.

In the usage of `expect` and `actual` for HelloKMP, you're going to expect that each platform can tell the shared code what its name is as a string using a `platformName()` function. You can then use that `platformName()` function in other parts of the shared code.

You can use `expect` on entities such as functions, classes, or properties. Like a canonical interface, items tagged with `expect` do not include implementation code. That's where `actual` comes in.

In **iOSMain** and **androidMain**, you need to provide the `actual` version of the items specified with `expect` in the common code. The **androidMain** code will be compiled using kotlin-jvm, and the **iOSMain** code will be compiled by Kotlin/Native. Each will be combined with the compiled version of the common code for the respective platforms.

In **shared/src/commonMain/kotlin/common.kt**, add the package and an `expect` for the `platformName()` function:

```
package com.raywenderlich

expect fun platformName(): String
```

You'll see an error saying that there are no `actual` implementations for either JVM, which means Android, or Native, which means iOS.

Next, add a `Greeting` class to the same file in which you use the result of calling `platformName()`:

```
class Greeting {
  fun greeting(): String = "Hello, ${platformName()}"
}
```

Since you don't use `expect` on this class, this is a Kotlin class that is the same for all platforms.

In **shared/src/androidMain/kotlin/android.kt**, add an `actual` version of platformName for Android.

```
package com.raywenderlich

actual fun platformName(): String {
  return "Android"
}
```

In **shared/src/iosMain/kotlin/ios.kt**, add an `actual` version of platformName for iOS.

```
package com.raywenderlich

import platform.UIKit.UIDevice

actual fun platformName(): String {
  return "${UIDevice.currentDevice.systemName()}"
}
```

Notice the `platform` package import of a **UIKit** class. There my be an unresolved reference error here. That's okay for now.

If you click on the **E** in the gutter of the Android Studio editor, you get taken to the corresponding `expect` definition. You see that the error you had before is gone now that you have `actual` versions of `platformName()` for both platforms.

Clicking the **A** in the gutter, you can choose to navigate to any of the `actual` implementations.

Building your projects

There are two small things you need to do before building:

1. Adding an Android manifest
2. Giving Gradle an SDK version for Android

First, right click on **shared/androidMain** and select **New File**. Name this file **AndroidManifest.xml**

Open the file and add these contents:

```
<?xml version="1.0" encoding="utf-8"?>
<manifest xmlns:android="http://schemas.android.com/apk/res/
android"
  package="com.raywenderlich">

</manifest>
```

Then, Add this to the bottom of **shared/build.gradle.kts**:

```
android {
  compileSdkVersion(29)
  sourceSets["main"].manifest.srcFile("src/androidMain/
AndroidManifest.xml")
  defaultConfig {
    minSdkVersion(21)
    targetSdkVersion(29)
  }
}
```

Now you have shared code that you can build.

Open the **Gradle** panel, find the **build** task folder under **shared/Tasks**, then double-click on **build**.

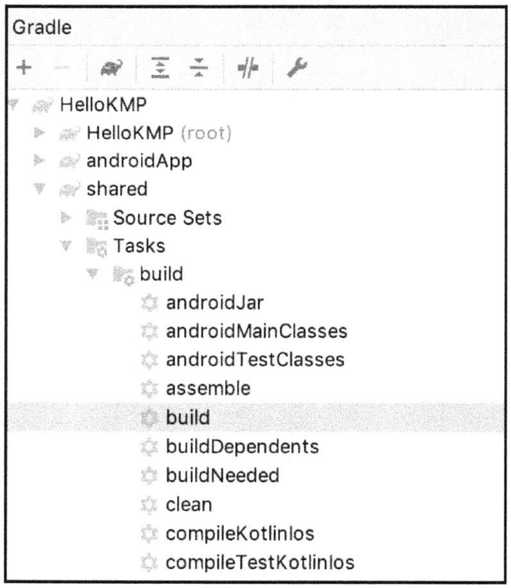

You can then watch the code build in the **Build** panel. You can see Gradle going through a number of build stages and tasks. This will typically take a bit of time to run, especially after a clean of the shared project.

You'll see a **BUILD SUCCESSFUL** message when it's done.

So now you've successfully built the shared project, in which you've defined a `Greeting` class that shows a greeting that's customized for the platform that you're running the app on.

Shared code from Android

Now it's time to use the shared library from the Android app.

In the **androidApp/build.gradle** file, add a packagingOptions call within the `android` block:

```
packagingOptions {
  exclude 'META-INF/*.kotlin_module'
}
```

This addresses a build error that might occur due to duplicated files in the build.

Then add a dependency of the Android project on the shared project to the `dependencies` block.

```
implementation fileTree(dir: 'libs', include: ['*.jar'])
implementation project(':shared')
```

Sync the project Gradle files before you continue.

In **androidApp/src/main/res/layout/activity_main.xml**, add an `id` of `greeting` on the `TextView` that is included in the template android project:

```
android:id="@+id/greeting"
```

Then in **androidApp/src/main/java/com.raywenderlich.hellokmp/MainActivity.kt** in the `onCreate()` function, set the `text` on the `greeting` `TextView` by calling into the shared code and using the `Greeting` class:

```
findViewById<TextView>(R.id.greeting).text =
  Greeting().greeting()
```

You created a `Greeting` object and called it's `greeting()` method.

You should see an import for Greeting pulled in when you use the **option+return** keystroke, along with an import for `TextView`:

```
import android.widget.TextView
import com.raywenderlich.Greeting
```

Build and run the Android app.

There is your greeting that displays "Hello, Android" as determined by the shared code.

The iOS app

Having used the shared project in an Android app, you now turn to using the shared code in an iOS app. But first you need to setup the iOS app project itself.

In a terminal window at the HelloKMP project root, create a directory for the iOS app:

```
mkdir iosApp
```

Then switch to Xcode version 11.3 or later, and choose **File ▸ New ▸ Project**, pick **Single View App**, and click **Next**.

The product name is **HelloKMP**, the organization identifier is com.raywenderlich, and make sure the language is Swift:

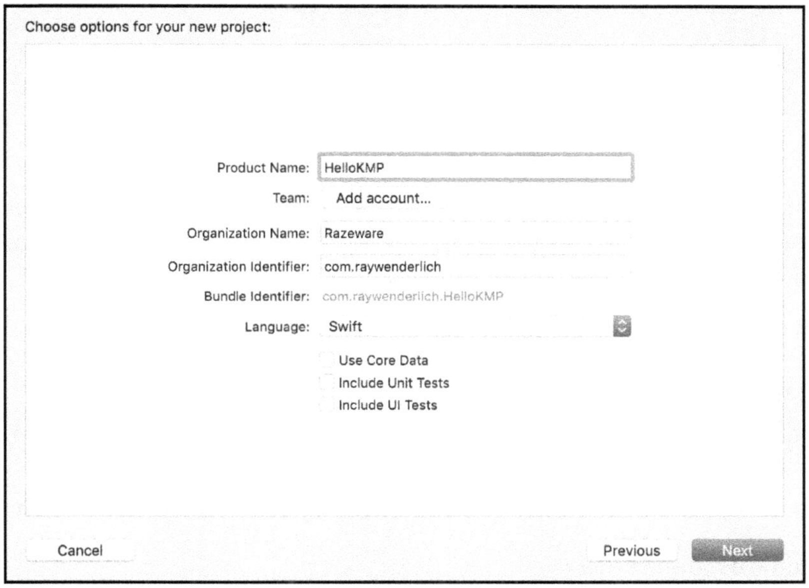

Click **Next**, and place the project in the new **iosApp** folder you just made.

Now build and run the app in the iOS Simulator just to make sure it builds correctly.

Packing the iOS framework

Next, back in Android Studio, you need to add a task to the Gradle build file **shared/build.gradle.kts** for the shared project that will package the framework for Xcode.

Add this to the bottom of the file:

```
val packForXcode by tasks.creating(Sync::class) {
}
```

Inside this block is where you'll build your task.

Start by adding the following:

```
group = "build"
/// selecting the right configuration for the iOS
/// framework depending on the environment
```

```
/// variables set by Xcode build
val mode = System.getenv("CONFIGURATION") ?: "DEBUG"
val sdkName = System.getenv("SDK_NAME") ?: "iphonesimulator"
val targetName = "ios" + if (sdkName.startsWith("iphoneos"))
"Arm64" else "X64"
val framework = kotlin.targets
  .getByName<KotlinNativeTarget>(targetName)
  .binaries
  .getFramework(mode)
inputs.property("mode", mode)
dependsOn(framework.linkTask)
}
```

This first section of the task sets a directory for the framework and determines the correct framework to build based on the selected target in the Xcode project, with a default of **DEBUG**.

Next, add this code to the bottom of the same block:

```
val targetDir = File(buildDir, "xcode-frameworks")
from({ framework.outputDirectory })
into(targetDir)
```

This section copies the file from the **build** directory into the **framework** directory:

Finally, add this to the block:

```
/// generate a helpful ./gradlew wrapper with embedded Java path
doLast {
  val gradlew = File(targetDir, "gradlew")
  gradlew.writeText("#!/bin/bash\n"
        + "export 'JAVA_HOME=$
{System.getProperty("java.home")}'\n"
        + "cd '${rootProject.rootDir}'\n"
        + "./gradlew \$@\n")
  gradlew.setExecutable(true)
}
```

Here, a bash script named **gradlew** is created in the framework directory that Xcode will call to build the shared framework.

The script uses the version of the JDK that is embedded in Android Studio.

At the bottom of the **build.gradle.kts** file, you need to specify that the shared code build task depends on the new `packForXcode` task:

```
tasks.getByName("build").dependsOn(packForXcode)
```

You then need to run a project Gradle sync due to the changes to **build.gradle.kts**

Now you can build the shared code into an iOS framework, using the Gradle panel in Android Studio like you did before.

When the build is done, check that the packaged Xcode framework is in the expected directory.

```
ls -l shared/build/xcode-frameworks
```

You should see the file **shared.framework** in the folder.

Go back to Xcode to finish the iOS app setup. Choose the app target and go to **General** settings.

In the **Embedded Binaries** section, click the plus and then select **Add Other** and **Add Files**. Navigate to and choose the shared framework **shared/build/xcode-frameworks/shared.framework**.

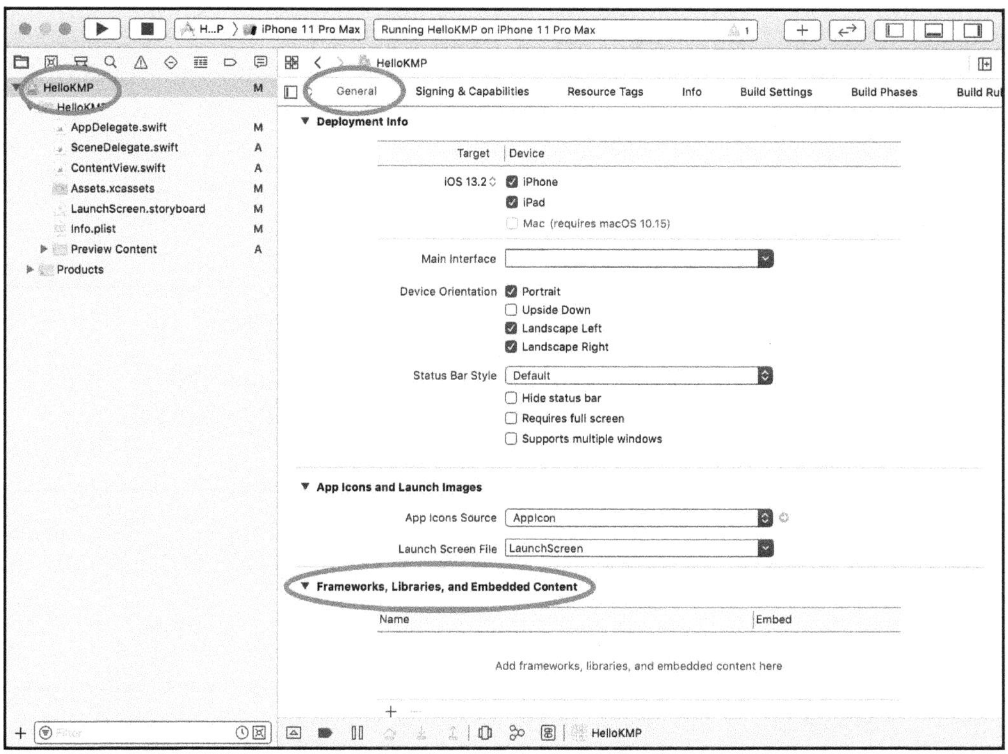

Since Kotlin/Native produces full native binaries, you need to disable the **Bitcode** feature for the project in **Build Settings**. Search on bitcode in the search box and choose **No** for **Enable Bitcode**.

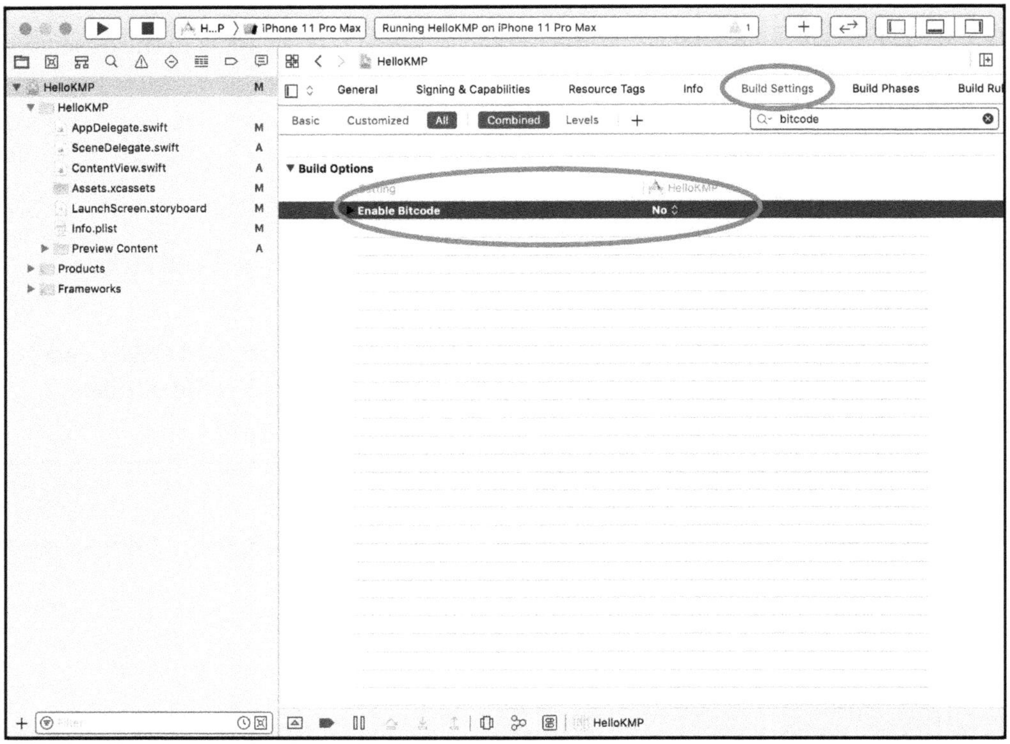

Now you need to update framework search paths for the iOS project.

In **Build Settings**, search for **Framework Search Paths**, and then add the framework directory you setup in the new Gradle task, using **$(SRCROOT)/../../shared/build/xcode-frameworks**.

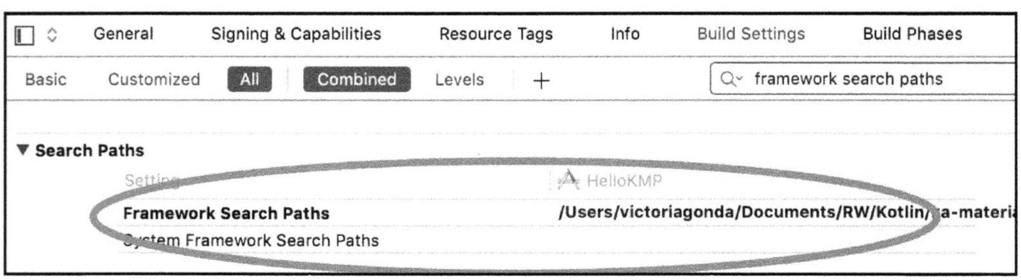

Xcode will then set the absolute path based on the **SRCROOT** value.

The last step you need for setting up the Xcode project is to add a new build phase to have Xcode build the shared code.

Switch to **Build Phases** and add a new **Run Script**.

In the run script, change the directory to the framework directory, and then call the bash script you created in the `packForXcode` task, passing in the Xcode configuration value.

```
cd "$SRCROOT/../../shared/build/xcode-frameworks"
./gradlew :shared:build -PXCODE_CONFIGURATION=${CONFIGURATION}
```

Then move the new run script to the top of the Build Phases, just below Dependencies.

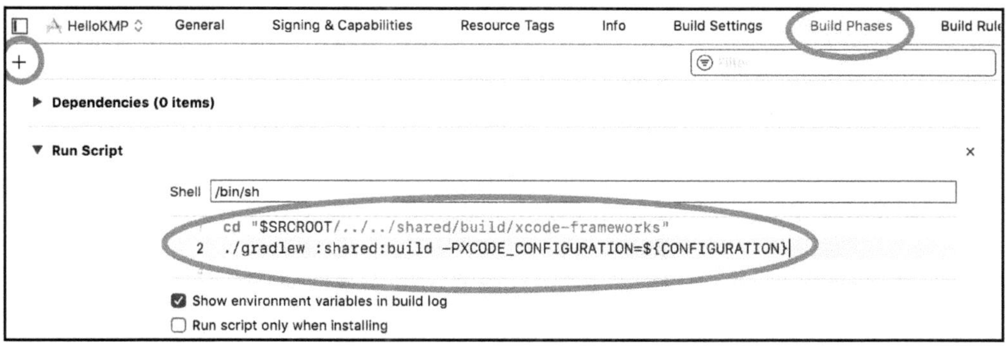

Now build and run the app to make sure there are no build errors due to any of these changes.

So you can run the iOS app from Android Studio, add the following line to **gradle.properties**:

```
xcodeproj=iosApp/HelloKMP
```

Sync Gradle. Then, select the iOS app to run.

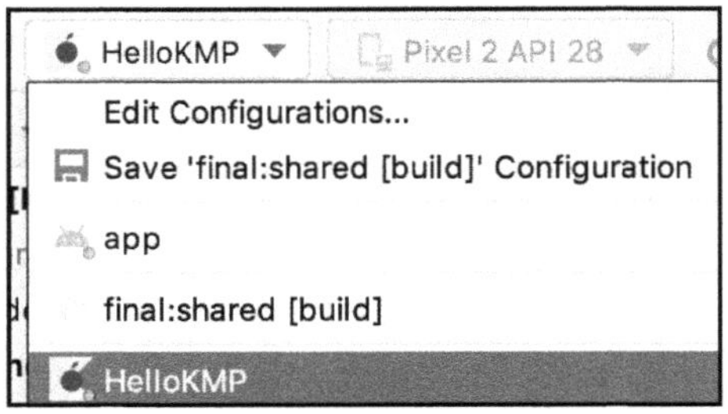

Note: To run this project in Xcode, you need to do additional configuration to inform Xcode how to build using the shared Kotlin code.

Shared code from iOS

With the iOS app project in place and linked up with the shared project, next you'll use the shared code in the iOS version of the HelloKMP app. The iOS app will consist primarily of user interface code, relying on the shared code to do most of the work.

Open **iosApp/HelloKMP/HelloKMP/ContentView.swift** and ddd an import for the **shared** code to the top of **ViewController.swift**:

```
import shared
```

This gives you access to the shared code in the Swift file. It might give you an error in Xcode without the extra Xcode configuration, and that's okay.

In the `ContentView` `body`, update the `Text` to call into the shared code:

```
Text(Greeting().greeting())
```

This simple Swift code is literally identical to the line in Kotlin that was used in the Android app. You create a `Greeting` object and then call its `greeting()` method.

You can now build and run the iOS app to see that everything is working.

When the app comes up in the simulator, there is your greeting that displays the iOS system name as determined in the shared code.

Challenge

You have a real albeit simple Kotlin Multiplatform app for iOS and Android that uses shared code between the two platforms. Your challenge for this chapter is to add the iOS `systemVersion` into the greeting in the iOS app. As a hint, you can use `UIDevice.currentDevice.systemVersion` to obtain the system version.

There are two things to consider when working on this challenge:

1. Where do you need to add this code to show the system version?
2. Do you need to rebuild the shared code before running the iOS app?

With those questions in mind, go ahead and tackle this challenge. You can check your solution in the challenge project for this chapter.

Key points

- **Kotlin Multiplatform** is a new and fast-growing approach to cross-platform app development.
- KMP lets you share Kotlin code between iOS, Android, web, server, and more.
- There are a number of advantages to KMP, including developer familiarity with Kotlin, native performance, native UI code, and the consolidation of your app business logic into a shared module across all platforms.
- You use the **expect** and **actual** keywords to create a common interface within the shared code that relies on concrete implementations on different platforms as needed.

Where to go from here?

You've just scratched the surface of Kotlin Multiplatform development in this chapter. There are a growing number of resources out there on KMP, so be sure to seek them out to see how to build more realistic apps, including doing things like networking, parsing JSON, and storing data locally in your app.

The Kotlin Multiplatform community is just getting started, so there's a great opportunity now to contribute to the KMP ecosystem.

27 Conclusion

Congratulations! You've completed your introduction to programming in Kotlin. The basic and intermediate skills you've honed throughout these chapters will set you up to begin developing apps in this diverse and evolving language.

While Kotlin is newer and not as widely used as some other languages, we hope that this book has shown you all the great uses it can have for organizing and leveraging your code for clean and modern apps.

And, remember, if you want to further your understanding of Android app development after working through *Kotlin Apprentice*, we suggest you read the *Android Apprentice*, available on our online store:

- https://www.raywenderlich.com/books/android-apprentice/

If you have any questions or comments as you work through this book, please stop by our forums at http://forums.raywenderlich.com and look for the particular forum category for this book.

Thank you again for purchasing this book. Your continued support is what makes the tutorials, books, videos, conferences and other things we do at raywenderlich.com possible, and we truly appreciate it!

Wishing you all the best in your continued Kotlin adventures,

– The *Kotlin Apprentice* team

www.ingramcontent.com/pod-product-compliance
Ingram Content Group UK Ltd.
Pitfield, Milton Keynes, MK11 3LW, UK
UKHW051448290926
15471UKWH00008B/1079

9 781950 325375